Data
and
Society

Data and Society

and

Paul Beynon-Davies
Cardiff University, UK

World Scientific

NEW JERSEY · LONDON · SINGAPORE · BEIJING · SHANGHAI · HONG KONG · TAIPEI · CHENNAI · TOKYO

Published by

World Scientific Publishing Co. Pte. Ltd.

5 Toh Tuck Link, Singapore 596224

USA office: 27 Warren Street, Suite 401-402, Hackensack, NJ 07601

UK office: 57 Shelton Street, Covent Garden, London WC2H 9HE

Library of Congress Cataloging-in-Publication Data

Names: Beynon-Davies, Paul, author.

Title: Data and society / Paul Beynon-Davies.

Description: New Jersey : World Scientific, [2022] |
    Includes bibliographical references and index.

Identifiers: LCCN 2021012082 | ISBN 9789811237249 (hardcover) |
    ISBN 9789811237256 (ebook for institutions) |
    ISBN 9789811237263 (ebook for individuals)

Subjects: LCSH: Information theory. | Data structures (Computer science)--Social aspects. |
    Information organization--Social aspects. | Communication--Social aspects. |
    Communication--Data processing. | Collective memory.

Classification: LCC Q360 .B496 2022 | DDC 303.48/33--dc23

LC record available at https://lccn.loc.gov/2021012082

British Library Cataloguing-in-Publication Data

A catalogue record for this book is available from the British Library.

For any available supplementary material, please visit
https://www.worldscientific.com/worldscibooks/10.1142/12287#t=suppl

Desk Editors: Balasubramanian Shanmugam/Lai Ann

Typeset by Stallion Press
Email: enquiries@stallionpress.com

Printed in Singapore

For my mother Enid Yvonne

About the Author

Paul Beynon-Davies is professor emeritus at the Cardiff Business School, Cardiff University. Before taking up an academic post, Professor Beynon-Davies worked for several years in the Informatics industry in the UK, both in the public and private sectors. He has published widely, having 17 books and over 100 peer-reviewed academic papers to his name, many in leading journals.

Contents

List of Figures

List of Tables

Prologue

An institution is a data structure's way of making another data structure.

The Data and Society Mix

Let us begin to set the tone for this book by examining how the relationship between data and society is currently conceived and how we might conceive of it with more clarity. To help us do this, try to consider data and society as two circles drawn within some visualisation, such as a Venn diagram. A Venn diagram is an illustration that uses circles to show the relationships of things, or more precisely sets of things.

So, if you were allotted one circle for the things comprising data and another circle for the things comprising society, how would you draw such circles upon the visualisation? Perhaps you might draw these circles as overlapping, such as that illustrated in Figure P.1.

If you represent the relationship between data and society in this way, you will be in good company. Most literature thinks of the relationship between data and society as such, often implicitly rather than explicitly. Here, data and society are seen as two separate sets of things, but which overlap to form an intersection (the cross-hatched area in Figure P.1). The literature then goes off to unpack the intersection of the two circles and partners the term *data* in this manner with terms descriptive of the domain of society — *ownership*, *control*, *surveillance*, *privacy*, to name but a few. In doing so, the literature rarely considers the nature of data itself, except in some surface way, and as a consequence, regards data as merely

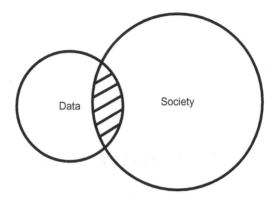

Figure P.1: The intersection of data and society.

additive in terms of terminology. This view of data and society as additive influences the way these topics of significance are approached. Because in taking this viewpoint the literature fails to give a satisfactory account of why the ownership of data is problematic, why data is so significant within systems of control, why you cannot conduct surveillance without data and why protecting the privacy of personal data is so important to the contemporary identity of the individual.

Within this book, we want to promote an alternative viewpoint of the relationship between data and society. Rather than explaining how data fits with or contributes to some burning societal issues, we want to explain how data is *constitutive* of many such issues. The term constitutive is used here in the sense of data having power *to institute, establish or enact* society. So, as a visualisation of this viewpoint, we would draw the Venn diagram something like that illustrated in Figure P.2. Here, data and society do not form an intersection of two circles. Instead, one circle is enclosed by another. Data for us is an enduring and existential subset of society. By this, we mean that data cannot exist without society, but society cannot exist without data.

Alright, you might say, these are large statements — so prove them; provide evidence of their veracity. We will do so within chapters of this book, but first an important point about our approach. Our viewpoint means that you cannot rely upon a surface rendering of how data ices the societal cake. If you are to properly understand the constitutive nature of data, you must start from first principles and examine closely the nature of data itself. You must also focus on the mechanics of data — how data

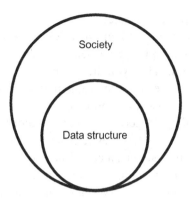

Figure P.2:   Data structures as a subset of society.

is represented and articulated in records or more generally in data structures. This is why we have labelled the subset (the inner circle) as *data structure* rather than *data* in Figure P.2. In this manner, we shall show how much of the contemporary institutional infrastructure of society is built through, not upon, an infrastructure of data structures.

We believe that when you step back and view the landscape of data and society, many of the claims we make about the position of data structures within society become self-evident. So, let us begin by highlighting some of the ways in which the record (the most common-place of data structures) is so central to our personal lives — not only who we are but how we live.

The Centrality of Records

Our contemporary lives can be most readily examined through records because modern life is documented through records. You are born and are issued with a birth certificate. You pass school and university examinations and are issued with certificates of scholarship. You learn to drive and apply for a driver's licence. You purchase a car and apply for a vehicle licence. You undertake gainful employment and get recorded in employment, national insurance, and taxation records. You decide to travel but must prove your citizenship by applying for a passport. You perhaps get married and are issued with a marriage certificate. If you have children, your parental details get recorded on their birth certificates. You unfortunately lose your job and must apply for numerous welfare benefits with different government agencies. Such agencies establish records about you for their purposes. When you retire from work, crucial records held about your public and private pension scheme will determine the income available to you. When you die, your demise is recorded in a death certificate. After your death, numerous records are utilised by your descendants in resolving issues of probate.

However, most of these records are public records that act as traces of the conventional life of a citizen experienced within some nation-state. There will also be numerous instances of private and specialised records held about you. For instance, you might join the military, or you might spend a period in prison or in a psychiatric hospital. In such institutional settings, there will be a whole collection of records opened about you and probably used to do things with you.

The key consequence here is that your life is documented in records, but your life is also lived through records. The verb 'to document' suggests merely the act of representation. However, records are not passive devices that catalogue major events in your personal biography. They are very much active. Records prescribe what you can do in society. This means that the very notion of being able to act as an individual within society is normally done through the records held about you. Hence, to open a financial product such as a bank account, you normally have to provide some record of permanent residence; to take up gainful employment you have to provide evidence of a national insurance record and to travel between certain countries you have to validate your identity through a passport or a visa. If you cannot prove certain institutional facts held about you in and through records, you are often prohibited or proscribed from acting. For example, if you cannot prove you are a citizen of a particular country through a record such as a passport or a national insurance record, then your freedom to do certain things may be heavily limited, such as to work or to obtain certain benefits from the nation-state.

Records are Boring

An allegory is useful here — one which has been told many times in many different quarters. It goes something like this. Two young fish are swimming along when they meet an older fish. The older fish greets them while passing by saying, 'morning, how's the water?' Having swam a little further on, one young fish pauses, turns to the other young fish, and asks, 'what's water?'

In the last section of this prologue, we have tried to introduce the idea that the record is clearly central to modern existence. Indeed, to exist as an identifiable person, we must be recorded. In this sense, the record is something of an existential token which opens certain institutional 'doors' for us but also closes off a range of other 'exits' and 'entrances'.

It is therefore surprising to find that an examination of the nature of records is typically seen as a rather boring endeavour. This may be for several reasons — perhaps because we tend to take three inherent positions in relation to records. First, records are accepted; second, records are considered understood; and third, records are seen as of concern purely to administrators, bureaucrats or technologists. Each of these positions, we shall show, is open to challenge.

We all tend to view records in the main as mundane and as such accept the position of records as unexamined background to our everyday existence. Records are a bit like the young fish's water — they are an inherent and important part of our surround-world. However, because they are mundane and accepted, we all tend to assume that we understand what records are used for, or at least what they should be used for. This may be because we assume records to be of interest only to the archetypal 'record-keepers' — administrators or bureaucrats, librarians and archivists, or more recently, to those persons working within the community of practice which is information and communications technology (ICT).

We want to persuade you, in reading this book, that records are not mundane but interesting and frequently mysterious artefacts. We also want to question the assumption that we all understand truly what records are. Records, as an area of study, turn out to be something that has only been considered in a rather surface way by many disciplines and professions — even by those disciplines which should have 'records management' at the heart of their endeavour. This is surprising in that, as hopefully we have demonstrated in the opening paragraphs, records are such important 'scaffolding' for modern life.

Within this book we want to take the position of the young fish and ask strange questions such as *what are records* and *why do we have records*? To provide such an answer, we seek to develop a framework for better understanding the key purposes that records serve in human societies. We shall demonstrate that records not only have a long history, dating back probably to the dawn of human civilisation, they also make history. People throughout history and across different cultures make records with specific purposes in mind, and such purposes are the very stuff of history itself. We also want to break with the notion that records are a particularly 'Western' construct embedded in the operations of industrialised bureaucracies. The presence of the record across history and across human cultures suggests that they serve a very central place in what it is to be human. Although the record appears in a multitude of forms (and in some very strange forms) across human history and cultures, there are some universals of record-making and use which are apparent across time and space.

Sensemaking and Sensebreaking with Records

We think this book is worth reading if only because there is surprisingly little direct literature examining the nature of the record, particularly the modern electronic record. This is perhaps because the record, particularly the official record, as we have mentioned, is part of the accepted and unexamined background of our various life-worlds. However, it is particularly interesting that the increasing prevalence of our modern technologies used for managing records appears to have lulled us into a sense of greater complacency. Over the last six decades or so, the rise of the digital computer and associated digital communications has not only increased the centrality of the record in institutional life, it has pushed the record even further into the background of our various life-worlds.

There is no doubt that such technologies have made the making and use of records very much easier. We can now manipulate records in nanoseconds, meaning that it is possible to have almost instantaneous access to many millions of records of various forms at the touch of a button and in the blink of an eye. Frequently, we are also not conscious of making many records, as our technologies automatically do this for us. They leave traces of our existence as records, which we may not be aware of. Therefore, we will argue in this book that the rise of digital computing and communications technology has reinforced and bolstered the central place of the record within the 'infrastructure' of modern society. However, such technologies also frequently serve to obscure the place that such infrastructure plays in the life of the very people it affects.

You may think that records are produced for obvious reasons — perhaps, to inform certain persons about what is going on somewhere. However, when you take a close look at records in situ and in use, such certainties become open to doubt. Records are used to fulfil multiple purposes in different institutional settings. Sometimes records are used for purposes for which they were not originally intended.

Certainly, records can be used to inform, but about what? Records can be used as collective memory of what has happened or what is happening, but they can also be used to make things happen in the future. All records in some sense misinform as well as inform, because in the very nature of creating a memory trace of something or someone the maker of the record makes a decision about what is significant to record, and, as a consequence, what is not. Hence, records are not only memory traces, they are deliberate acts of forgetting. Sometimes records are deliberately created to misinform in the sense they may be designed either explicitly or implicitly to portray a particular worldview, and such a worldview may be open to question by various groups and individuals in society. This means that records in many settings inherently carry with them the 'politics' of their creation. Hence, records and record-making should not always be seen to be inevitably beneficial because they are used frankly for some very evil purposes. Many records are also not always useful in the sense that the making of such records serves to disable performance as well as support performance.

Our Mission

Although there is little written about the nature of the record itself, there is fortunately quite a lot of substantive literature of use from various areas that can help us understand this nature. In part, this book is an attempt to bring together this diverse literature and present it in a more unified whole.

This book's primary aim is to expand conventional notions of what the nature of the record (or more broadly that of the data structure) constitutes. We want to broaden the focus on the record and examine its place across cultures and societies. In doing so, we hope to better understand why we as humans make records. In doing this, we can also better understand some of the unintended consequences of the use of records, which particularly plague us in the modern world.

We have tried hard not to make this a typical dry, academic tome. One device we hope you find useful is the close examination of the use of records in many different situations. These cases are not only taken from the historical world and from other cultures, they are also taken from various aspects of the modern experience of the record. The cases of modern records management are particularly useful to highlight the dangers as well as the potentiality inherent in our use of the record.

Records are, of course, not typically used in isolation. Records are frequently aggregated. The aggregate then becomes a record in itself and is used in various ways to inform action in institutions and society at large. Traditionally, the aggregation of records has been the realm of statistics. In its more recent guise, aggregation is key to the idea of big data, the associated area of data analytics and the broader area of data science. We examine some of the ways in which some of these technologically sophisticated ways of manipulating data exacerbate some of the issues we raise in relation to the record and its place in society.

A Short Exercise in Sensebreaking

Before we look at the contents of this book, let us end the prologue with a short exercise in sensebreaking. Sensebreaking is a standard anthropological technique that is particularly useful for thinking about the accepted or conventional in different ways. Now try a short exercise in sensebreaking to get a feel for what we are attempting in this work. Deoxyribonucleic acid (DNA) is a nucleic acid that is normally seen as the motor of organisation amongst all known living organisms. Soon after it was discovered, DNA was referred to as a 'code'. In other words, the molecular structure of this acid is generally seen as containing instructions needed to construct other components of cells, such as proteins and RNA molecules.

As a code, DNA is by implication seen as acting as a biological record. In this sense, modern science has no problem in thinking of *a person as DNA's way of making more DNA*. Now substitute institution for person in the underlined phrase within this last sentence and data structure (or record) for DNA. You should get something like: *An institution is a data structure's way of making another data structure.* By the end of reading this book, we shall convince you the reader that this curious statement is not too far from the truth.

A Quick Overview of the Book

In this final section, we provide a quick overview of each substantive chapter within the book. The 15 chapters are designed to be read in sequence. The early chapters build a theory of data structures from the ground up. Later chapters apply such theory in explaining and sometimes deconstructing core problematic themes in the relationship between data and society such as power, control, commerce, and surveillance. Having said this, we have deliberately repeated and reemphasised many aspects of the core theory constructed within this book throughout each chapter, so we would hope that each can be read as an independent essay on the ever-tightening relationship between data and society.

Chapter 1: Making Marks — The Materiality of the Record

We begin at the beginning and examine the human urge to externalise things through representation. To set this in its proper context, we examine the earliest of such marks — a common set of painted markings on cave walls with a worldwide distribution and dating to the Upper Palaeolithic (35,000–10,000 BCE) period. We then examine the nature of representation as the externalisation of things through signs — turning substance into form and using such form to signify something. We begin to explain externalisation in terms of a model of information situations. Such a model not only forms the proper context for data structures — it helps us look at data structures from three distinct but interdependent perspectives.

The second half of the opening chapter examines the crucial difference between persistent and non-persistent data and the advantages persistent data has for representation of collective memory — representing a range of important things that happen and do not unhappen — bringing the past into the future. We use the case of Sumerian clay tokens dating to the period (10,000–8,000 BCE) as one of the earliest examples of the use of data to account for things through collective memory. This case is particularly interesting as a demonstration that records come before what we currently think of as writing and indeed influenced the development of writing systems.

Chapter 2: Data Structures

There is typically a lack of clarity when people use the word *record*. Therefore, this chapter considers the more precise concept of a *data structure*, which is typically seen as a form for organising data. This concept is clearly central to the interests of the information disciplines and much of the infrastructure of information and communication technology is clearly taken up with the mechanics of data structures, particularly as it pertains to applications within business and government. As such, we shall expand on this sense of the term data structure and use it to explore the various forms of what people call records. Data structures are made up of data elements, which in turn are made up of data-items. Data structures can be created in almost any substance and are not restricted to the use of graphical characters. Hence, to help make the idea of a data structure strange we examine the important data structure of the *khipu* used amongst the Inka. *Khipu* were created as assemblages of strings or cords formed from the substance of camelid wool. We consider the structure of data represented in *khipu* but also four major acts that can be performed with any data structure.

Chapter 3: Identifying Things — The Informativity of the Record

Having established the nature of records as data structures, we begin to explore the multitude of ways in which records are used within institutional life. In Chapter 3, we examine how records are important in communicating critical notions of personal identity between individuals and institutions. We show how personal identity in the modern world is very much involved with the use of records for authentication of persons, for identification of persons and for enrolment of such persons in various systems of organisation. We show that this association between records and identity has a long history. The British Raj was one of the earliest innovators in the attempt to link personal identification with the measurement of man, otherwise known as anthropometry. This idea was much used in early anthropology in support of the controversial attempt to develop a typology of human races. Alphonse Bertillon was the first to use this idea as part of his solution to the practical problem of identifying repeat criminal offenders in France. In his anthropometric method, 11 different measurements of the body were taken by rigorously trained clerks with specially designed instruments such as callipers, gauges and rulers. These measurements were then recorded on a specially designed card, which became known as a Bertillon card. This approach is very much the precursor to modern biometric systems, which use machines to record data such as fingerprint and iris scans and the reuse of this data in processes of authentication, identification and enrolment.

Chapter 4: Making Lists — The Performativity of the Record

The list is one of the simplest and most common of data structures. In this chapter, we deconstruct the list and show how lists are performative in the sense that the presence of a list-item upon a list determines what happens to people and things. We use the case of the Nazis' use of list-making technologies to run the holocaust as a key malignant example of the use of data structures but also use our analysis to cast light on the important processes of blacklisting, whitelisting, shortlisting and watchlisting increasingly evident in modern society. We then take the enterprise further and show how data structures, such as the list, are crucial 'scaffolding' for the contemporary social order and show how lists and identifiers afford institutional action.

Chapter 5: Coordination Problems

The domain of coordination forms one of the three interconnected domains making up our theory of information situations. Coordination is frequently achieved through the performativity of data structures — the ability of data structures to prescribe and proscribe action. Within this chapter, we examine the issue of coordination in more detail and in doing so use what the philosopher David Lewis refers to as coordination problems. A coordination problem occurs when two or more actors have a purpose or goal in common which must be achieved through joint action. Coordination problems, as we shall see, are resolved through conventions of action, particularly conventions which couple articulation of data structures with certain communicative conventions, which in turn are associated with conventions of activity. To help ground the notion of systems of coordination, we consider a range of examples from manufacturing, software production and healthcare. These examples not only show how data structures are critical to scaffolding coordinated institutional activity, but also illustrate how data structures can be better designed to achieve more effective coordination.

Chapter 6: The 'Life' of the Record

It is strange to think that records have lives, but they do — they are created once, amended many times, retrieved sometimes and eventually deleted or archived. Within this chapter, we make the point that, given that records have a life history, it is important to understand the context in which records are articulated and for this we need the concept of an institutional fact. Such institutional facts are critical to scaffolding institutional action, and as a result, data structures, and more precisely the data contained within them, have been at the centre of numerous debates concerning their proper articulation. This is particularly true of data held about the person in such data structures. It has become accepted that because these data structures identify and describe the person, an individual's right to privacy should be extended to the data structures representing him or her. Data privacy demands that data held about the person should be articulated only in defined ways and that the sharing of such data with third parties should be strictly controlled. Data privacy is normally ensured through data protection legislation.

Chapter 7: Instituting Place, Product, Time and Digital Presence

Data structures do not just represent some thing; the act of making a data structure frequently brings the thing into existence for an institution. Hence, a land parcel, and more precisely the relation of ownership between the land parcel and specific individuals, only exists once the place and relation of ownership are registered in something like a land register. Registers are effectively lists of things frequently managed at national and sometimes international level. Hence, most nation-states register not only places, but also births, deaths, marriages and many other things. Some registers record not only things, but also when such things occurred. Hence the notion of time is instituted in records. The notion of registration is of course not just a matter of creating a record of something — the act of registration is effectively a declaration of something — a communication that something is brought into existence. However, registers are not just important parts of the data infrastructure of nation-states — they are also increasingly important to global digital infrastructure. Therefore, we also look at domain name registries and show how the registration of digital presence is critical to scaffolding digital commerce.

Chapter 8: Building Ontology

We established in earlier chapters that data structures are structures of signs. Semiosis — sign-activity — is a continuous process in which actors engage with the world. Signs, of course, are not isolated entities, they exist in a complex lattice consisting of other related signs. The way in which a certain sign leads certain actors to accomplish information is down to its relationships with other signs within this lattice structure. This notion of a sign lattice helps provide a way of thinking about the notion of ontology — the things held to exist within some institutional domain. In this chapter, we consider how such a lattice might be constructed from base principles established in previous chapters. This gives us a way of better understanding the ways in which institutional ontology is constructed from data structures. It also allows us to introduce the important topic of metadata — data about data. Metadata, as we shall see, is critical to the way in which the contemporary data infrastructure within society is formed and utilised.

Chapter 9: The Power of Records

Soon after the Norman Conquest in 1066, William I sought to consolidate his power by conducting a survey of his new kingdom. This 'Great Description of England' was published in a book, which the common people referred to as the Domesday (pronounced Doomsday) book, because Domesday referred to the day of judgement. This book essentially consisted of a series of data structures that served to document the rights and responsibilities associated with landowners. And as such, it served to consolidate William's power and legalise changes made to the kingdom by Norman possession. Cases such as this reveal that records are not only formative, informative and performative, they also have deontic powers. By this it is meant that records are important to power and its exercise. Records as institutional facts are used to scaffold the rights and responsibilities associated with actors taking action. Given the central importance of data structures to the scaffolding of institutional order, it is important that, at the metadata level, positive and negative powers are assigned to actors in relation to the articulation of data structures. This defines the issue of data control and explains why it has become of increasing concern to institutions. Data control, as we shall see, is a practical response to the need to create and maintain an architecture of deontology in relation to the life of data structures.

Chapter 10: Scaffolding Commerce

In this chapter, we consider the critical role that data structures play in scaffolding finance and trade. Many fundamental economic concepts such as ownership, purchasing, credit and debt are facilitated through data structures such as orders, invoices, payments and contracts. We start by considering the nature of money as a status function facilitated through data structures. This leads us to examine the crucial notion of a ledger — a data structure which underlies the whole notion of accounting and finance. We also consider the role that ledgers play as a registry of transactions. Such a transaction registry is one of the most important applications of a recent technology known as the blockchain, which we demystify in terms of the theory established in previous chapters. We close with an examination of the sharing of data structures which underlies much economic activity in areas such as the supply chain. The sharing of data structures must be based on the proper linkage of articulation, communication and coordination. When the coupling between such actions breakdown, then economic activity can be compromised.

Chapter 11: Data-Driven Actors

The fundamental point we make throughout the book is that data structures are crucial for scaffolding instrumental communication and in turn such communication scaffolds coordinated activity. However, there is something missing or something we have taken for granted within this account. What we have missed out here is the notion of a decision and the act of decision-making. Decisions provide the important linkage between communication and coordination. Pretty much everything seems to be data-driven in modern society. This particularly applies to machine actors — artificial actors that take decisions and undertake activity based on data fed to them. We focus on software actors within this chapter and consider two main types of actors — algorithmic and heuristic actors. We look at the developing field of machine learning to understand some of the potentialities but also some of the problems of such data-driven machine actors.

Chapter 12: The Mechanics of Echo Chambers

The modern phenomenon of social media is reliant upon the scaffolding of data structures, just like other institutional domains. Just like many other aspects of ICT, social media is a technology for creating information situations. However, social media has come under the spotlight for both good and bad reasons. It has been seen as a catalyst for coordinating political protest but also as a vehicle for dissemination of extremist views. Some have even claimed that social media is undermining the very notion of civil society because of the way in which this technology facilitates misinformation, disinformation and malinformation. Certain characteristics of social networks, such as the network effect, strong and weak links and social capital make social media particularly attractive to business, as a prime medium for electronic marketing, particularly viral marketing. However, social media is also impacting upon many other institutional domains and even is affecting the very viability of civil society.

Chapter 13: The Modern Panopticon — Data and Surveillance

Surveillance is typically defined as the close observation of a person or group, usually because that person or group is under suspicion of something. This is the classic rationale for the agencies of the nation-state to conduct surveillance on persons or groups within society who are suspected of engaging in deviant activity. Because of its role as scaffolder of institutional action, the data structure or the metadata which describes it takes centre stage within attempts to build a surveillance society. However, surveillance plays a much more mundane and accepted role within our interactions with digital companies. Some even believe that data has become the new oil within capitalist economies. Others warn of the dangers inherent in the data surveillance infrastructure that digital giants have built.

Chapter 14: Counting Heads

Our aim in this chapter is merely to establish the necessary truth that the analysis of data, particularly data that has been aggregated, must be based upon a firm understanding of the ways in which data structures are made. We want to make the point, recognised by any good statistician, that an aggregate measure is only as good as the data it is built upon and indeed that it is impossible to interpret an aggregate measure properly without understanding the making of data structures that scaffold this analysis.

We use two cases to provide evidence of this important point — one historical and one contemporary. The historical case examines a certain study made by one of the founding fathers of Sociology, Emile Durkheim, and which he intended to be used to demonstrate how Sociology should focus upon the study of what he referred to as social facts. The contemporary case relates to the ways in which statistics were used during the pandemic by governments to take policy action. The case serves to provide further evidence of the critical role that the design of data structures and the associated processes of making such data structures plays within the contemporary institutional order.

Chapter 15: A Social Ontology of Big Data

In the last chapter of the book, we utilise our theoretical framework to provide a critique of not only big data, but also the ways in which an emerging science of data is framed. Big data is big news — within the popular press but also within academia and particularly within disciplines not only such as Computer Science and Information Systems but also Business and Management. We undertake a feature analysis of big data and show that many of these features rely upon social ontology. This in turn enables us to a critique of some of the widely held assumptions of big data and through this to call for a more nuanced conception of data to be utilised within the emerging science of data.

Chapter 1

Making Marks

Introduction

There is continuous debate about what makes us as a species (*Homo Sapiens*) different from the rest of the animal kingdom. For many years, answers to this question were posed in terms of our ability to make and use tools. In recent times, ethology (the study of animal behaviour) has shown that many other species, such as chimpanzees and even certain species of birds, make and use tools, albeit rather primitive ones. Even more recently, there has been interest in thinking of our species as *Homo Signum* (man: the maker of signs) and more particularly in making signs that persist through time. As a species we seem particularly special in making and using a certain class of tool — marks that attempt to externalise aspects of our inner life and commune through this external object with other humans. Many such marks last way beyond the act of making — sometimes by many thousands of years.

So, we begin our exploration of data and society at the beginning and examine the human urge to externalise things through representation. To set this in its proper context we consider the earliest known of such marks — a common set of paintings found upon cave walls with a worldwide distribution and dating to the Upper Palaeolithic (35,000–10,000 BCE) period. We then examine the nature of representation as the externalisation of things through structures, turning substance into form and using such form to signify something to others. This leads us to distinguish between persistent and non-persistent structures and the advantages

1

persistent form has for the representation of collective memory. Collective memory involves a group of actors externalising through structures a range of important things that happen and do not unhappen. Collective memory is important to social organisation by bringing the past into the future. We use the case of Sumerian clay tokens dating to the period (10,000–8,000 BCE) as one of the earliest examples of the use of form to account for things through collective memory. This case is particularly interesting as a demonstration that records come before what we currently think of as writing and indeed influenced the development of some of the earliest writing systems.

Neolithic Data

To start our investigation of the record and its importance to society we need to go back a long way in human history, to the earliest examples of humans making marks with the deliberate intent of *making a mark* — communicating something. Alexander Marshack (2003) suggests that scratches on antler horn from the Upper Palaeolithic (35,000–10,000 BCE) period may constitute some of the earliest use of a tally, related perhaps to calendar events such as the gestation period of a horse or the phases of the moon. Genevieve Von Pettinger (Ravilious, 2010) has identified 26 signs painted on cave walls with a worldwide distribution and dating to the same Upper Palaeolithic period. Figure 1.1 illustrates these signs and plots them in terms of their frequency of occurrence in various cave settings from the top left to the bottom right of the figure.

The cave signs are in at least one sense familiar to modern man — they all consist of graphical symbols. However, the making of marks is not limited to graphical representation. For example, small clay tokens of multiple shapes and frequently marked in various ways have been found in a number of sites in the Near East. Dating from the period between 8,000–3,000 BCE. The archaeologist Denise Schmandt-Besserat (1992) believes that such tokens represent the earliest evidence for explicit and persistent symbols being used to *account* for things.

Sumer, one of the earliest known civilisations, was located in southern Mesopotamia — meaning 'the land between the two rivers' in Greek. This is an area geographically located between the Tigris and Euphrates rivers, largely corresponding to modern Iraq, north-eastern Syria, south-eastern Turkey, and the Khūzestān Province of south-western Iran.

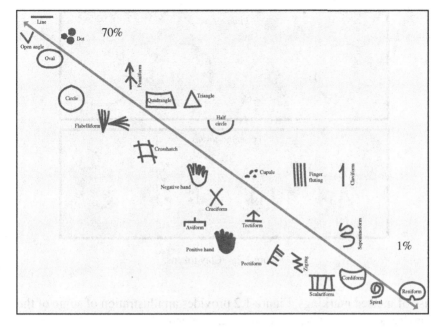

Figure 1.1:   Cave markings.

The civilisation lasted from the late sixth millennium BCE through to the rise of Babylon in the early second millennium BCE.

The cities of Sumer were not the first human cities. However, they were the first urban conurbations to practice intensive, year-round agriculture. It has been proposed that this agrarian revolution created a surplus of foodstuffs which could be stored for later consumption (Rudgley, 1999). This allowed the population to settle in one place instead of migrating with the movement of crops and herds. Intensive agriculture also allowed for a much greater population density. This, in turn, promoted developments such as forms of hierarchical social organisation, an associated division of labour and an invention close to the heart of this book — that of record-keeping.

When this token system came about, circa 8,000 BCE, the first tokens consisted mainly of abstract shapes formed in clay such as cones, spheres, tetrahedrons, disks and cylinders. In about 4,400 BCE, what Schmandt-Besserat refers to as complex tokens started appearing in the early cities of Sumer. These tokens consisted of new more complex shapes and the

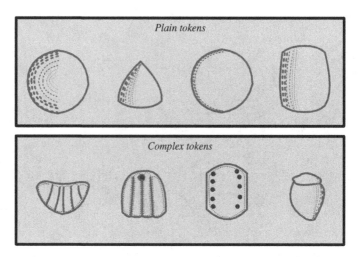

Figure 1.2:   Clay tokens.

use of incised markings. Figure 1.2 provides an illustration of some of the hundreds of distinct types of tokens discovered.

These examples are not introduced for esoteric reasons. We want to argue that cave markings, clay tokens and even modern electronic records have many features in common, centred around the externalisation and representation of things.

The Externalisation of Things

The notion that humans discovered early in our history the need to *externalise* aspects of our inner environment into the external environment around us is a popular explanation of artefacts such as cave markings and clay tokens. The term *representation* is also much used in relation to the activity of making marks performed by humans. However, neither of these terms are particularly clear in the literature. So, to provide such clarity, we need a model which will help us understand what is going on when humans attempt to externalise something. The illustration in Figure 1.3 is an attempt to visualise such a model, developed from a range of the authors' work, and which we shall unwrap in detail, bit by bit, within subsequent chapters of this book. Here, we provide a brief overview of its components and will consider this model in largely abstract terms. Then we shall return to the case of clay tokens and see if our model works as an explanation of these artefacts as a form of externalisation.

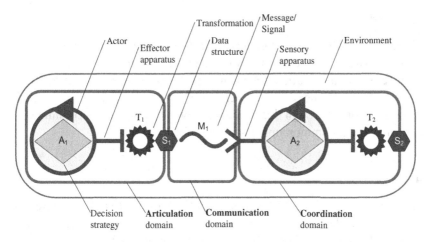

Figure 1.3:   A model of information situations.

Figure 1.3 is a model of what we refer to as *information situations* — situations in which information is accomplished. We contend that such situations provide the proper context for understanding externalisation or representation and that these situations always consist of actors, structures, messages and actions, all taking place within some environment. Let us consider these component elements in more detail:

Actors

We use the term actor for anything that can act. Actors transform their environment in some way and include not only humans but also other animals, machines and certain classes of artefact.

Structures

Structures are things within the environment of actors which undergo a certain form of transformation, which we refer to as articulation. A structure is brought into existence by particular actors by making differences within some substance evident in the environment. Within this book we focus upon structures explicitly produced and used to communicate things between two or more actors. We refer to this type of structure as a data structure. All records, as we shall see, are data structures, as are lists and registers.

Messages

Through the articulation of data structures, messages can be conveyed as signals between one actor and another. This signalling of messages is the essence of communication. One actor creates or effects some articulation of a structure and one or more other actors sense or read the changes made to the structure. Through this process the two or more actors commune — they arrive at a common understanding of something.

Actions

Three types of interrelated or coupled action are illustrated in Figure 1.3. There is first the act that involves articulation of some structure. Then there is the act of communing through this structure between one actor and another — of collectively agreeing as to what structures stand for or count as — this is the essence of communication. Finally, there is usually a responsive action on the part of the receiving or sensing actor, which is normally to articulate some further structure within the environment. This domain of action we refer to as coordination because most of the structures that we focus upon within this book are transformed with the intent of coordinating joint activity.

We assume here that actors are embodied (Varela *et al.*, 1993, Mingers, 2001) meaning that an actors' agency (i.e. its capacity to act) involves interaction with its external environment, and that such interaction relies upon two critical forms of apparatus making up the body of the actor: a sensory apparatus and an effector apparatus. A sensory apparatus consists of a series of sensors that continually monitor differences in the state of the external environment of the actor. An effector apparatus consists of a series of effectors that allow the actor to perform instrumental action in relation to this external environment — to manipulate structures within the external environment by making differences to such structures and through so doing to change the state of the external environment.

Between the sensory and effector apparatus of some actor lies an internal environment, which we have referred to in previous work (Beynon-Davies, 2011a) as the actor's *psyche*. Daniel Dennett (1996) denotes this internal environment with the term 'mind', but we want to avoid any unnecessary and confusing meanings associated with this commonly used term. According to Dennet and others with an evolutionary bent, psyche is considered an internal environment that emerged and developed in order to make interaction with the world more successful for organisms such as *Homo Sapiens*. This internal environment is in a state of constant flux and is primarily involved in controlling the actor's actions. Psyche, or the operation concerned with an actor's internal environment, can be contrasted with *techne*, concerned with activities in which an actor transforms structures within the external environment.

To suggest this interaction between psyche and techne within Figure 1.3, actors (A_1 and A_2) are represented as cyclical entities. By this, we are attempting to indicate that an actor is continually reproducing its internal environment in continuous interaction with its external environment. The actor is continuously evaluating the results of its completed actions upon the external environment and feeding back such evaluations to help continuously form its internal environment. Through such continual reconstruction as well as improvisation, the actor learns or acquires certain conventions which implement *decision strategies*. Such decision strategies enable the actor to make effective choices between alternative courses of future action within certain environments.

So, to summarise, consider the minimal situation in which an actor A_1 articulates some physical structure S_1 using his/her effector apparatus. This corresponds to a domain of action we refer to as the articulation domain. The articulation T_1 of structure S_1 is sensed by the sensory apparatus of some other actor A_2. The sensed physical state of structure S_1 serves to communicate, through acquired conventions, some message M_1 to actor A_2. These actions take place in what we refer to as the communication domain. Finally, the message M_1 acts as a stimulus to the transformation T_2 of some structure S_2 within some coordination domain. This coordination may lead to further articulation of S_1 in the articulation domain, and so on. This process by which actors turn psyche into techne is what we believe is externalisation at heart.

Let us take this model of information situations and start unpacking examples in terms of it. Take the example of Sumerian clay tokens, described earlier in this chapter. Figure 1.4 illustrates one likely information situation relevant to this historical domain. Clay tokens are structures formed in clay by human actors interacting within the first cities on Earth over 10,000 years ago. They are articulated to form certain shapes with the intention of informing other actors of certain things. The sensory apparatus of another actor perceives the shape of the token and knows through conventions he or she has acquired that this shape communicates one amphora — a clay jar used to typically store oil or wine. The structure

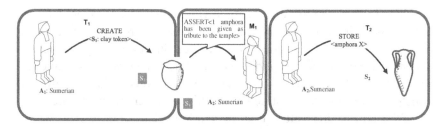

Figure 1.4:   An information situation in early Sumer.

probably also conveys other things as a message. Perhaps that this container is given as tribute to the temple complex. This message is likely to stimulate action on the part of the receiving actor, perhaps causing him to store the signified amphora in the warehouses of the temple complex.

In the next few sections, we shall unpack some of the foundation of this model in greater detail. We shall then build upon this foundation in further chapters and demonstrate how this situated model helps explain the place of data structures in many varied institutional settings.

Making Differences Through Structures

Gregory Bateson (1972) in his *Steps to Ecology of Mind* defines information tantalisingly as 'any difference that makes a difference'. Our model of the information situation exploits this idea by placing at the centre of externalisation a pattern of physical differences articulated by some actor. Such physical differences made as some structure can then be used to make further patterns of physical differences within the psyche of some other actor.

A physical environment without evidence of difference conveys nothing. In other words, if the environment within which an organism exists is entirely uniform in nature then it will have no effects upon such organisms. Fortunately, differences are endlessly transmitted around the physical environment. Differences in the surface of an object become differences in the wavelengths of light. Differences in light signals become differences in stimulation on the sensory cells making up the eye of some organism such as a prairie dog or a Sumerian priest. These differences stimulate in turn differences in patterns of activity in the nervous system of the organism, which in turn stimulate differences in bodily movement such as posture and locomotion.

Whichever way you look at it, the accomplishment of information (informing) is built from base acts of discrimination or distinction by particular actors. The essence of discrimination or difference is being able to 'draw' a boundary around some thing: some aspect of the physical environment. In doing so an actor distinguishes that which is inside the boundary and hence part of the thing, such as 'it', from that which is outside the boundary and not part of the thing, such as 'me'.

George Spencer-Brown (1969) symbolises this as O, where the circle represents the boundary and the act of 'drawing' the boundary amounts to the base act of discrimination, which, it is further argued, may be the base operation of the process of perception/cognition. This is similar to Rosch's (1973) base act of categorisation: distinguishing something from something else. It is also interesting that the circle appears to be one of the most common symbols painted on cave walls by our remote ancestors (Ravilious, 2010) (Figure 1.1).

Spencer-Brown (1969) proposes in his *Laws of Form* that all types of experience involve the process of severing a formless space by drawing a distinction in it and then arranging indications or tokens of that distinction. First then we have a formless space — an original undifferentiated wholeness. Then we draw a distinction within this space, causing it to be severed or taken apart, such as distinguishing *me* from *not-me*. Then we represent one of the parts, the distinguished space, by a token, such as a personal name.

The Modulation of Matter or Energy

The making of some difference implies also making a similarity. Difference and discrimination is hence critical to the concept of *modulation*, which we adapt from that used in signal engineering. Modulation is the process by which variety (Ashby, 1956) is introduced into a signal: a measure of the number of possible states or differences a signal can take. If we are unable to modulate the pattern of a signal, then nothing can be communicated between the sender and receiver. Once we can vary the signal then it becomes possible to code certain messages using coherent differences in the signal. Coding is thus the translation of a signal from one medium into the same pattern expressed differently in some other medium.

Consider the example of a honeybee that has returned from a foraging trip to the hive. Bees carry with them a pouch of material from the hive, which they release as they re-enter. The odour emanating from this pouch indicates to guarding bees at the entrance that they are part of the hive and provides the foraging bee with safe entry. In this example, the foraging bee is the sender, and the guarding bee is the receiver of the signal. The message is coded as a signal in terms of a pattern of pheromones or odours and transmitted through the air by diffusion. The distinct patterning of pheromones constitutes modulation in this medium.

The Patterning of Structures

Differences and similarities are thus core elements of patterns. We recognise or identify a pattern when we (as actors) observe a consistent difference repeating or recurring across situations. Alternatively, we might recognise a pattern as a similar set of differences that replicate over time. Data structures therefore must be patterned objects created in some substance through the articulation of differences.

When a forager honeybee returns to the hive, her odour signals her identity as a member of the hive. Hence, at the level of structures, we might say that the bee odour is 'written' by the forager bee on a particular medium and 'read' by attending bees along this medium. The odour is clearly a pattern of pheromones that can be used consistently and coherently across situations in which two bees meet to authenticate each other as fellow hive members. We shall say more about data structures as means for authentication of actors in Chapter 3.

The warning calls of the prairie dog is another relevant example from ethology. Such warning calls can be considered as consistent patterns of sound produced by the vocal organs of this animal. As a pattern, each prairie dog call consists of between 2–25 separate and individual barks. Such calls are also repeated within larger units known as bouts. Each call can last for as long as 30 minutes and can be heard over a distance of one mile; the intensity of the signal increasing as danger moves closer and only ending when danger has passed (Beynon-Davies, 2011b).

In the case of clay tokens, differences were signalled mainly through the modulation of shape of the such tokens. The 'form' of a given clay token clearly signalled a distinctive pattern for actors in ancient Sumeria. Over the millennia, the variety of this sign-system increased with a greater range of modulated forms. Sometimes, for instance, markings or incisions were used to extend the range of patterns possible within the medium of clay.

Natural, Embodied and Persistent Structures

The making of marks clearly refers to the externalisation of some 'things' through the articulation of some medium. However, what is a medium? First, it is some aspect of matter or energy used for communication. Second, such matter or energy must have properties that facilitate the coherent coding of messages through modulation. Third, both the 'writing' and 'reading' of particular messages rely upon particular sensory modalities available to particular actors (senders and receivers of such messages). It relies upon the sensory and effector apparatus of such actors.

Therefore, the notion of a data structure in Figure 1.1 cannot be divorced from the notion of an actor perceiving (sensing) and acting (effecting) upon physical patterns. Following Sebeok (1976), we can classify structures in terms of the type of matter or energy used to signal something. Theoretically, any form of matter, whether it be solid, gas or liquid, can be used as a signalling medium. Likewise, any form of chemical or physical energy can be used to provide a signal for communication.

A signal therefore consists of the patterned modulation of energy or matter along some channel or medium. For instance, human speech travels as a signal consisting of a pattern of sound waves (acoustic energy through air), while facial expressions rely upon the reflectance and transmission of light (optical, reflected, physical energy). Matter in its various guises as gases, liquids or solids can also be used to build signalling structures. Hence, honeybees can communicate through the transmission of particular odours (gases diffusing through air) and through vibrating honeycomb within the hive (manipulation of a solid). Humans can use complex assemblages of knotted strings (solids) formed from the natural material of camelid (Llama or Alpaca) wool (we shall discuss this case in Chapter 2) or shapes formed in clay to represent things.

Coding refers to the process by which a message is represented in some structure (such as a signal of energy) through some pattern. For instance, a pattern made by one of the distinct vocalisations of a prairie dog is used when a coyote approaches. Two dominant frequencies are evident in the pattern, which is divided into 45 segments of short barks of about one-tenth of a second in duration. Hence, prairie dogs learn to reform consistently vocal patterns which code certain messages.

Next and for our purposes, it is important to distinguish between three distinct types of structures in terms of the source of signalling: natural, embodied and disembodied or persistent structures.

Natural structures

Structures produced from the natural environment signal natural signs. Natural signs signify what Searle (1995) refers to as brute facts — features of the physical, chemical and biological world. Hence, structures in the external environment of some actor are continuously signalling their properties and can be picked up by sensors within the sensory apparatus of such an actor. A prairie dog on alert will sense the movement of a predator such as a coyote within distance of sight of a colony. A honeybee will sense the distinct colours of flowers in its range.

Embodied structures

Changes enacted by the actor using its effector apparatus will signal to other actors and hence also act as structures. This is what we mean by embodied structures in the sense that the structure is not present without transformations exercised by actors. Such structures are clearly reliant on some form of immediate bodily action on the part of the actor.

Hence, a honeybee might move its body in various ways within distinct forms of 'dance' or a human might make particular facial expressions. Darwin (1998) in *The Expression of the Emotions in Man and Animals* detailed a number of propositions relating to human facial expression. First, he believed that such structures display evidence of the fact that *Homo Sapiens* as a species experience a common range of mental states, which we refer to as emotions. Second, such emotions are expressed by a common and shared range of facial expressions. Third, humans share a range of such emotions and the facial expressions associated with them with the higher apes. Fourth, the evidence of the universality of emotive expression in humans and their appearance in closely related species demonstrates the evolution of this range of behaviours in man. Work by Ekman and Friesen (1971) and others have largely supported these propositions. Figure 1.5 illustrates the six most common forms of emotive facial expression found in man.

Persistent structures

Finally, actors may produce artefacts that are given independent existence beyond the body of the actor. Such artefacts can hence persist beyond any one communication and can signal to multiple actors sometimes remote in

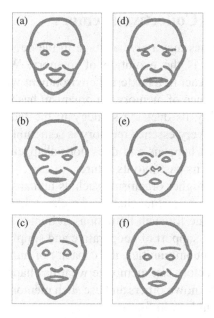

Figure 1.5:   Human facial expressions.

time and space. These artefacts amount to some physical transformation of the environment or umwelt (Uexküll, 1957) of particular actors, typically using tools for such transformation. Such artefacts thus form an important part of techne. This is what we mean by disembodied or persistent structures.

Clay tokens are one of the first examples we have of persistent structures evidently used for the basis of information accomplishment. Such artefacts then achieved an independent existence of the actors creating them and could persist in the sense that they could be transported through time and space by other actors.

These distinctions are potentially useful in defining techne or technology. Anything produced solely and directly by the body is not techne but may be artefactual. Human speech is an artefact, a creation, reliant on the innovation of human spoken language. However, speech requires the body for its production, and solely the body. Writing or written language is however techne. To produce writing, one typically uses the body, but one augments this use through tools, whether such tools be clay and stylus, threads of llama or alpaca wool or keyboard and computer screen. The data structure in this case becomes disembodied (Derrida, 1971) and takes on a life of its own independent of the actor that created it.

Individual and Collective Memory

Dennett (1996) argues that a crucial stage in the development of psyche amongst organisms is the evolution of memory. Without memory an organism can only react to its external environment with a fixed decision strategy. In the absence of memory, an organism has no capacity to learn and hence to modify its decision strategy in the face of changes to its environment. At its very essence memory is something within the psyche of the organism that happens and does not unhappen. Through memory the organism brings its past into its future.

However, even higher organisms such as humans display limitations of memory. The rise of techne such as the clay token can be seen as an attempt to compensate for such limitations in human psyche, particularly human cognition. In support of cooperative and simple activities between individuals in small communities, the capacity of human memory is sufficient. Individual actors can memorise what has happened in relation to their activities with known others and use such memory to make decisions as to how they should act in future.

However, as communities grow in size, the complexity of activities also increase. In particular, activities of economic exchange typically take place between strangers and generally are reliant typically on some division of labour. In such circumstances, humans invented the externalisation of memory in records. Records compensate for the limitations of individual human memory and extend it into social or collective memory. Records of economic transactions, for instance, institutionalise memory of past economic exchanges and the obligations placed upon individuals engaged in such exchange. Accurate record-keeping is also critical in establishing and sustaining trust between strangers engaging in economic exchange and for supporting social relationships such as ownership and debt.

Michael Hobart and Zachary Schiffman (1998) offer a useful historical perspective on the long-term nature of data structures. Although both writing and speech constitute communication and therefore enable the accomplishment of information, they limit their definition of the First Information Age to the invention of writing. In their eyes, writing is seen as the first information technology. However, Schmandt-Besserat and others would argue that writing is actually not the first information technology. Marcia and Robert Ascher (1997), for instance, emphasise that writing is actually not a necessary condition for civilisation. Instead, some medium for record-keeping is required, such as the case of clay tokens and the case of the Inka *khipu* which we consider in Chapter 2.

Sumerian Clay Tokens

Let us return to the case of Sumerian clay tokens and apply our model of externalisation and representation more completely to them.

Clay tokens are clearly data structures. Such tokens are instances of the externalisation of things in the substance of clay. Actors deliberately had to take a lump of clay and form a certain structure with it. The structures were created with the direct intention of informing other actors. The clay tokens are not natural structures or embodied structures but persistent structures. After their articulation, the tokens were baked, making them persistent and available to be found thousands of years later. In about 3,250 BCE, tokens started to be enclosed in hollow clay balls which Schmandt-Besserat refers to as *clay envelopes*. After the envelope was completed, it was baked, making the record persistent or difficult to alter.

The medium for modulation in this case was clearly clay. The clay was modulated in two distinct ways: through shape and incision. Schmandt-Besserat (1996) identifies 16 main types of tokens based primarily upon shape (Figure 1.6). These include cones, spheres, discs, cylinders, tetrahedrons, ovoids, rectangles, triangles, biconoids, paraboloids, bent coils and ovals/rhomboids. She also identifies a number of subtypes based upon variations in sizes and markings. For example, cones, spheres, disks and tetrahedrons are typically represented in two sizes — 'small' and 'large'. Many shapes also have incised markings consisting of lines, notches, punches and pinched appendices.

Schmandt-Besserat (1992) argues that tokens were a conceptual leap, constituting a new means of encoding data. She believes that such tokens represent the earliest evidence for accounting and record-keeping in that these tokens are some of the earliest examples of data structures used to record economic information. Specifically, clay tokens were used to code two distinct concepts. First, they served as counters and as such represented quantities of things. Second, they served to stand for some economic good or commodity. Hence, a given token signified both a type of commodity and the quantity of this commodity.

Certain clay tokens were meant to look like what they represented, such as in the case of the token which stood for an amphora of wine.

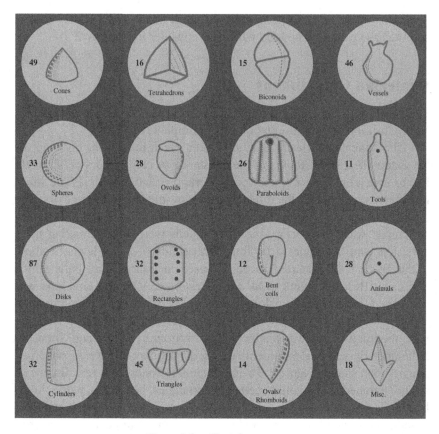

Figure 1.6:   The token system.

However, most clay tokens were patterns in which there is no obvious association between the shape and what it represented. Hence, there is no obvious association between a cylindrical clay token and a domesticated animal. As such, the majority of token types consisted of conventional patterns (Lewis, 2002): structures to which a conventional meaning was clearly assigned by groups of actors.

The clustering of tokens at various archaeological sites suggests that a given token typically signified a small quantity of a given commodity. Tokens are frequently found in clusters varying in size from 2 to about 100. This suggests that there appears to have been a one-to-one correspondence between a given token and one unit of the commodity signified. Hence, one jar of oil could be represented by one ovoid, six jars of oil by six ovoids and so on. There were apparently only a few tokens that stood for a collection of items. For example, the lentoid disk probably signified a flock of perhaps 10 animals. This meant that the token system did not allow the user to express numbers abstractly. In other words, there was no token for the concepts of one, two and three independently of the commodity counted.

The essential purpose of tokens was to keep records of things: an accounting. The shape of the token signified the thing about which the record was made. Hence, a conical type of token probably stood for a small measure of grain, while a spherical token stood for a larger measure of grain. In contrast, a cylinder token probably stood for a domesticated animal, a tetrahedron token for a unit of labour and an ovoid token for a jar of oil.

We clearly have no direct access to the institutions within which clay tokens were used and to the purpose to which such tokens were put. However, the evidence for as them constituting one of the earliest forms of accounting within one of the first human societies is three-fold. First, the creation of the token system coincided with a new settlement pattern characterised by larger communities. In other words, the rise of the first tokens coincides with the advent of a hierarchical or rank society and the emergence of a new type of leadership overseeing community resources. Second, the tokens recovered in the tombs of prestigious individuals suggest that, from the Neolithic to the Bronze Age (6,000–3,500 BCE), the use of clay tokens served as an instrument of power for an elite controlling access to commodities. Third, in all the major ancient Near Eastern cities such as Uruk and Susa, complex tokens occur in archaeological levels in which seals featuring the ruler have been discovered. They also occur in public buildings built according to an identical plan and decorated with typical mosaics and containing grain measures. In other words, the administrative centres that yield complex tokens were the seats of a large bureaucracy, housed in similar buildings, using the same administrative devices (complex tokens, seals and grain measures) and, most importantly, were headed by the same powerful ruler. The complex tokens can be considered, therefore, as being an essential element of an emerging temple bureaucracy used by Sumerian rulers to govern and control the distribution of commodities in the first city-states.

Since tokens of different kinds and in different quantities could be stored together, it has been proposed that they were used as one of the earliest forms of accounting record. Such records precluded the need for any individual to memorise accounts. They could be referred to and understood at any future time by someone who knew what the token represented. The token-system was also open-ended in that an accounting of new types of commodities merely required the addition of a new type of token to the token-system, consisting of a new shape or an existing shape with new or distinctive markings (Rudgley, 1999).

Another advantage of the system was that people speaking different languages found it easy to adopt this system based on physical artefacts. The evidence of extremely wide distribution of such tokens throughout the Near East in Neolithic times seems to support this inference. Also, because of the one-to-one correspondence between the token and the commodity represented, it was relatively easy to apply operations such as addition or subtraction within the system. However, when the numbers of things to be counted was large, such operations would have been time-consuming and tedious.

Evidence from archaeological investigation suggests that the use of tokens for keeping accounts followed an annual cycle of activity associated with agriculture (Mattesich, 1989). Tokens appear to have been discarded after the harvest and threshing, when the crops would be stored. This suggests that transactions were made in the course of the year to be completed at the time of the harvest. If this was so, the usual length of keeping accounts in archives was less than a year.

It is therefore likely that the clay tokens could have fulfilled a number of distinct purposes within these early societies. According to Schmandt-Besserat (1992), 'Tokens and clay tablets functioned as an extension of the human brain to collect, manipulate, store and retrieve data. In turn, processing an increasing volume of data with more complex tokens brought people to think with greater abstraction'. The creation of a clay token might have been used to make commitments such as that a given actor promised to hand over one unit of cloth as tribute to the temple. It might also have been used to declare that the signified tribute had been paid to the temple. Finally, it is likely to have been used to assert that a given quantity of a particular commodity was held in the temple stores. We consider in more detail the distinct purposes to which data is put in Chapter 4.

The Rise and Rise of Data

Thus, data are differences made in some substance with the intention to inform — to make differences in the psyche of some other actor or actors.

As we have mentioned, the essence of making a difference is being able to 'draw' a boundary around something and in so doing distinguishing that which is inside the boundary and hence part of the thing from that which is outside the boundary and not part of the thing. A basic difference between something and something else is typically coded as a binary digit, a 0 or a 1. This explains why the most basic unit of discrimination and hence the most basic way of coding data is in terms of binary digits, otherwise known as *bits*. It can be shown that all other forms of coding can be collapsed into this basic form of coding in bits. That is why bits are the most fundamental way in which symbols are formed as data.

We have become a global society of record-keepers and hence our capacity to store data is increasingly important to our ways of organising. Not surprisingly, the amount of data created and stored in data structures of various forms by both organisations and individuals is growing astronomically. This storage capacity of data is not typically measured in bits but in bytes. A byte stands for by-eight and consists of a collection of eight bits. A kilobyte amounts to 10^3 bytes (10 with 3 zeros following it), a megabyte 10^6 bytes, a gigabyte 10^9 bytes, a terabyte 10^{12} bytes, a petabyte 10^{15} bytes, an exabyte 10^{18} bytes and a zetabyte 10^{21} bytes. We are generating more data now than at any time in human history. It is claimed that between 10,000 BCE and 2003 CE we as a species created five exabytes of data, which is equivalent to the estimated amount of data in all the physical books held in the US Library of Congress — the largest physical library in the world. We now are estimated to create five exabytes of data every two days!

This rise in the volume of data stored is typically used to characterise the rise of the digital society or what is sometimes confusingly called the information society. However, the volume of contemporary data only tells a limited part of the story. Critical questions are often left unexamined such as:

- What are the potential forms that data structures can take?
- What is the purpose of making such marks in various media?
- Why do we accumulate such mountains of data structures in the modern world?
- Who or what articulates such data structures?
- What do we do with data once it has achieved its purpose? How much of this data is kept and how much discarded?

The main purpose of this book is to examine critically many of the issues raised by such questions.

Conclusion

Within this chapter, we introduced a model of information situations which helps explain why we as a species choose to externalise things through data structures. At the heart of externalisation is some structure formed by some actor as a pattern of physical differences that can be used to make further patterns of physical differences within the psyche of some other actor. We shall return to aspects of our model of information situations many times in further chapters as it is central to understanding how formed structures can count as or stand for other things. As we shall see, this process of counting as or standing for is fundamental to understanding the relationship between data and society.

Within our model, actors articulate physical structures using their effector apparatus. This corresponds to a domain of action we refer to as the articulation domain. The articulation of structures is sensed by the sensory apparatus of some other actors. The sensed physical state of structures serves to communicate, through acquired conventions, some message to actors. These actions take place in what we refer to as the communication domain. Finally, the messages act as a stimulus to the transformation of some structures within some coordination domain. This coordination may lead to further articulation of structures in the articulation domain, and so on.

Our case from pre-history, the Sumerian clay token, is a classic example of a data structure. As a structure, it has a physical form consisting of a shape formed in clay. The physical makeup of the tokens themselves and the ways in which the features of each token allowed the user to distinguish between one type of token and another constituted the articulation of such structures. We clearly do not have direct access to the human community that used this particular data structure and therefore the coding or meaning of tokens is subject to much interpretation. There is clearly however sufficient evidence from the archaeological record to suggest the use of tokens to communicate quantities of specific commodities. Such tokens appear therefore to have been used to externalise and represent the accumulation of agricultural and manufactured products by a community and to account for this collective wealth for the purposes of economic redistribution.

In Chapter 2, we focus in much more detail on the first domain within our model of information situations — that of articulation. We consider what actually the structure in the term data structure means and highlight the need to think rather differently about what data structures do. Conventionally, data structures are seen merely to correspond to aspects of a separate institutional reality. We shall convince you that this conception is misconceived. Data structures are not mirrors of the world. Data structures are not separate but entangled within the very institutions of our societies.

References

Ascher, M. and Ascher R. (1997). *Mathematics of the Inkas: Code of the Quipu* (New York: Dover Publications).

Ashby, W. R. (1956). *An Introduction to Cybernetics* (London: Chapman Hall).

Bateson, G. (1972). *Steps to an Ecology of Mind* (New York: Ballantine Books).

Beynon-Davies, P. (2011a). Significance: Exploring the Nature of Information, Systems and Technology (Houndmills, Basingstoke: Palgrave).

Beynon-Davies, P. (2011b). "Information on the Prairie: Signs, Systems and Prairie Dogs." *International Journal of Information Management*, **31**(3): 307–316.

Darwin, C. (1998). *The Expression of Emotions in Man and Animals* (Oxford: Oxford University Press), 3rd edition.

Dennett, D. C. (1996). *Kinds of Minds: Towards an Understanding of Consciousness* (London: Weidenfield and Nicholson).

Derrida, J. (1971). "Signature, Event, Context." A communication to the Congres Internationale des Societes de Philosophie de Langue Francaise, Montreal, Canada.

Ekman, P. and W. V. Friesen (1971). "Constants Across Cultures in the Face and Emotion." *Journal of Personality and Social Psychology*, **17**(2): 124–129.

Hobart, M. E. and Z. S. Schiffman (1998). *Information Ages: Literacy, Numeracy and the Computer Revolution* (London: John Hopkins University Press).

Lewis, D. (2002). *Convention: A Philosophical Study* (Oxford: Blackwell).

Marshack, A. (2003). *The Art and Symbols of Ice Age Man. Communication in History: Technology, Culture and Society* (Boston: Pearson Education).

Mattesich, R. (1989). "Accounting and the Input-Output Principle in the Prehistoric and Ancient World." *ABACUS*, **25**(2): 74–84.

Mingers, J. (2001). "Embodying Information Systems: The Contribution of Phenomenology." *Information and Organization*, **11**(2): 103–127.

Ravilious, K. (2010). "The Writing on the Cave Wall." *New Scientist*, **2748**: 12–14.

Rosch, E. H. (1973). "Natural Categories." *Cognitive Psychology*, **4**(3): 328–350.

Rudgley, R. (1999). *The Lost Civilisations of the Stone Age* (New York: Simon and Schuster).

Schmandt-Besserat, D. (1992). *Before Writing* (Austin, TX: The University of Texas Press).

Schmandt-Besserat, D. (1996). *How Writing Came About* (Austin, TX: The University of Texas Press).

Searle, J. R. (1995). *The Construction of Social Reality* (London: Penguin).

Sebeok, T. A. (1976). *Contributions to the Doctrine of Signs* (Bloomington, IN: Indiana University Press).

Spencer-Brown, G. (1969). *Laws of Form* (London: Allen and Unwin).

Uexküll, J. (1957). *A Stroll Through the Worlds of Animals and Men: A Picture Book of Invisible Worlds. Instinctive Behavior: The Development of a Modern Concept*, C. H. Schiller (ed.) (New York: International Universities Press).

Varela, F. J., E. Thompson and E. Rosch (1993). *The Embodied Mind: Cognitive Science and Human Experience* (Cambridge, MA: MIT Press).

Chapter 2

Data Structures

Introduction

James Beniger (1986) has convincingly argued that the invention of technologies such as the clay tokens considered in Chapter 1 are implicitly linked to a society's ability to control the actions of its members. In these terms, it is no accident that the invention of persistent data structures, such as the clay tokens considered in the last chapter, arose at the same time as the movement of the human population into the first cities supported by early agriculture. The first truly persistent data structures were likely invented as a means of recording and hence controlling the movements of things (such as wine, grain and livestock) important to these early societies.

Within this chapter, we focus upon what we referred to as the articulation domain within our model of information situations introduced in Chapter 1 (see Figure 2.1). It would be tempting to just use the noun *record* throughout this book to denote the primary thing we are interested in considering and explaining. However, there is typically a lack of clarity when people use the word *record,* certainly in the context of modern usage. The word can be used to refer not only to an artefact (*this record was played at our wedding...*), but also to the act of recording (*we made a record of the wedding...*). It can be used to stand for the recording of many different things (*sounds, images, events ...*) and on many different media (*photographs, video, a database...*). It can also be used to refer to stored facts about a person (*a parking offence...*) or some happening (*a stock movement*) as well as the best thing ever done by somebody

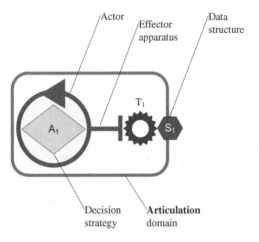

Figure 2.1:   The domain of articulation.

(*the highest a person has jumped in the high jump...*). It can even be used to indicate the official revelation of something by somebody (*she went on record...*).

Therefore, we will not entirely abandon the term record within this book, but we will consider the important, more precise and more encompassing concept of a data structure, which is a form for organising data. This concept is clearly central to the interests of the information disciplines (Information Science, Information Management, Information Systems, Computer Science). Much of the infrastructure of information and communication technology, for instance, is clearly taken up with the mechanics of data structures — storing, retrieving and manipulating data structures. As such, we shall expand on this sense of the term data structure and use it to explore the various forms that structures such as lists, registers and indeed records may take. As structures, data structures are made up of data elements, which in turn are made up of data items, and such structures can be created in almost any of the substances considered in Chapter 1. Hence, to help make the idea of a data structure strange — to sense break with contemporary notions of data and records — we examine two strange cases. The first of which are the predator-calls of the Gunnison prairie dog, which we alluded to briefly in Chapter 1. Examining these calls, as embodied signals, provides us with a straightforward example with which to demonstrate the role that data structures play within information situations. It also serves to demonstrate that data structures are not unique to the human species. The second case examines the important artefact of the *khipu* used amongst the Inka in South America. *Khipu* were created as assemblages of strings or cords formed from the substance of cotton or camelid wool. We consider the structure of data represented in *khipu* and why this data structure was so important to the Inka.

Data Structures

Within Chapter 1, we introduced a model of information situations. Central to this model was the idea of actors articulating structures with the intention of informing other actors of something. We referred to such structures as data structures but without really delving very deeply into their nature. In this chapter, we spend more time in explaining the properties of this critical artefact, how it is articulated and what such articulation contributes to information situations.

First, let us summarise what we have learned so far in Chapter 1. Data are differences made in some substance, typically by some actor articulating some structure. Certain differences made in a substance can be used to code signals/messages through modulation. Theoretically, any form of matter, whether it be solid, gas or liquid, can be used to form data. Likewise, any form of chemical or physical energy can be used to provide a signal for communication. The medium or substance in which differences are made has an important bearing on the way in which data structures are both formed and used. Embodied data such as human speech or human facial expressions are fleeting — they disappear shortly after differences have been made in the body of the individual. This helps explain how data structures as signals differ from data structures as records. Data structures can be formed in non-persistent substances such as airwaves but in such circumstances can only be used as transient messages. Forming data with a persistent substance such as clay (Chapter 1) has the important advantage of being able to act as collective rather than individual memory of something. Persistent structures can be accessed by many different actors across different times and situated in many varied locations.

A data structure is a term that is used broadly to refer to some systematic form for organising data (Tsitchizris and Lochovsky, 1982).

The concept of the data structure itself is treated within much of the research and practice of the information disciplines largely as a technological artefact, helping to support but somewhat isolated from considerations of institutional order. As such, this view of the data structure comprises an important part of the accepted and relatively unexplored background to the conduct of investigation and explanation in these disciplines. In turn, this relatively unchallenged worldview of the data structure influences the way in which 'design' is both contemplated and conducted in relation to such artefacts.

Although data structures are not really thought about much, by academics, professionals or indeed the general public, the data formed in such structures are critically important both to organisations and to individuals, in the sense that much organisational and individual action is reliant upon data structures. As we hinted at in the Prologue, what we shall refer to in later chapters as institutional facts about you are enacted through data structures. Such institutional facts as citizenship, education, employment, marriage, parenthood, healthcare, welfare and inheritance, to cite just a few examples, all rely upon the enactment of different data structures.

Therefore, persistent data structures come in a vast variety of different forms and may be used for a multitude of different purposes. Data structures may be paper forms, letters, documents and memos. They may be electronic tables in a database or electronic documents held on some data server or even emails, texts and social media messages. However, all data structures have a common core of features. Any data structure can be seen to consist of a set of data elements, which in turn are formed of data items. For instance, in a physical filing cabinet, a drawer of the cabinet might form the data structure while a hanging section placed in the drawer might be the data element and an individual paper form placed in a section might be the data item. In an electronic database, a table would be the data structure while a row of the table would be a data element and an individual attribute of a row would comprise a data item.

However, data structures do not need to come in these forms familiar to individuals in modern industrialised societies. As we have seen in Chapter 1, tokens formed in clay and used by the ancient Sumerians can be considered data items enclosed in larger structures of clay envelopes. In this chapter, we consider another strange case of a data structure — that of the Inka *khipu* (Beynon-Davies, 2007).

The Inka

The Inkas were a sophisticated society that existed in the high Andes of South America (D'Altroy, 2002) for a comparatively short time (c. 1200–1572 AD). This civilisation was remarkable in that it operated effectively without the benefits of a 'written' language or any mode of transportation based on the wheel. To understand the significance of the artefact of the *khipu,* we first need to understand something of the culture in which it was articulated.

The Inka created their empire, which they referred to as *Tawantinsuyu* (meaning 'the four parts together') through conquest. This conquered territory stretched across modern-day Peru and Ecuador, reaching the coast of modern-day Peru as well as extending into modern Colombia, Bolivia, Argentina and Chile. The four parts referred to were based in the Inkas' conception of the way in which their world was divided. The political and cosmic centre of the empire was the city of *Cusco.* Radiating from this centre were the lands and peoples associated with the four parts: *Chinchaysuyu, Antisuyu, Kollasuyu* and *Cuntisuyu.* Chinchaysuyu encompassed the lands and peoples of the Peruvian coast, the adjacent highlands and the northern Andes. Antisuyu included the warm forests that lay to the north and north-east of Cusco. Kollasuyu formed the largest part of the empire and ran from Peru's central highlands through the Altiplano area to central Chile and Argentina. Cuntisuyu was the smallest part and included the stretch of land that ran south-west from Cusco to the Pacific Ocean.

The Inkas were a highly ordered society. At the top of the society was the *Sapa Inka* or 'emperor' who ruled by divine right as the son of the sun. Worshipped as a living god, the *Sapa Inka*'s official wife was his full-blooded sister. The *Sapa Inka* also maintained a harem of concubines whose offspring held positions of power and influence in the Inka Empire. This hereditary aristocracy formed the upper class of Inka nobility, and was occasionally supplemented by Inkas assigned this rank through merit or exceptional service. Below the ruling class were the *curacas,* who formed the lower echelons of Inka nobility. These individuals generally filled the administrative offices of government and supervised the large 'bureaucracy' of the empire.

Officials called the *cacique* were placed at the head of agricultural communities made up of a group of individuals and families known as *ayllu*. Land was redistributed by the state amongst the *ayllu* every year according to the number of active people. *Ayllu* also had rights to water and herds. The land at the disposal of each *ayllu* was divided into three unequal parts: the largest of which was given to the community to farm. The other two land parts were consecrated to the cult of the sun and to the state. Communities also paid a tribute of textiles to the state and a periodic tax of labour. This labour tax, consisting of up to three months labour per calendar year for each active individual, was used for collective works such as building roads, monuments and irrigation canals.

The activity of the Inka Empire relied on a number of critical elements: a large and efficient transport network, data specialists (the *chaskis* and the *khipucamayuq*) and a data structure (*khipu*).

The Inka transport network consisted of thousands of kilometres of purpose-built roads and rope bridges which straddled Tawantinsuyu. Most of the roads were stone-lined and in places extremely narrow, allowing only foot travel and transport of goods using llamas. However, the roads could not be used by everyone. Only those on official business, the *chaskis* and the emperor and his armies were permitted to use the transport network.

The *chaskis* were highly trained runners employed purely in delivering messages throughout the Empire. A long series of small shelters stocked with food and water and known as *tambos* were arranged along the transport network. Individual *chaski* would transport messages by running between two such posts, and then pass them on to the next runner. A relay of *chaski* could transport a message in this manner up to 250 km in one day and it is claimed that a message could be delivered from Cusco to Quito, a distance of over 1,500 km, within a week.

The Inka 'bureaucracy' sent and received many messages daily in support of the activity of the empire. Typically, such messages contained details of resources such as items required or available in store houses, taxes owed or collected, census data and the output of mines or the composition of particular workforces. Messages had to be clear, compact and portable. For this purpose, a form of artefact known as the *khipu* was used, consisting of an assemblage of coloured, knotted cotton or camelid (llama or alpaca wool) cords.

Khipu

In the language of the Inka the word *khipu* means *to knot* and hence specialist personnel known as the *khipucamayuq* (the keeper of the *khipu*) were responsible for encoding and decoding messages represented in *khipu*. To articulate a *khipu*, the assemblage was placed on a large wooden rack by a *khipucamayuq*. Encoding or 'writing' a *khipu* involved tying together a complex network of cords of different materials and colours and tying into them a series of different forms of knot. Decoding or 'reading' a *khipu* involved a *khipucamayaq* both in visual inspection and running his fingers rapidly over the knots, rather like a Braille reader.

Several hundred examples of *khipu* survive and typically vary from having a few cords to, in the largest case, being over 3 metres long and having over 2,000 cords (Urton, 2003). Andean scholars believe that there is sufficient evidence to suggest that *khipu* were persistent data structures. This inference is based upon the historical record, which suggests that *khipu* were rolled up and transported by chains of specialist runners over long distances. The creator and 'sender' of the *khipu* must therefore have been different from the reader or 'receiver' of *khipu*. This implies some form of encoding of data in such artefacts using what we shall refer to in Chapter 8 as a mutually understood ontology: a shared set of representations of the world amongst a population of actors.

This interpretation suggests that *khipu* were used by the Inka as a structure in which data was recorded by tracing figures in space with pieces of cord. At the level of data, *khipu* can be considered purely as physical artefacts and analysed solely in terms of their methods of construction. A number of dimensions of difference (Chapter 1) have been identified within *khipu* for encoding the variety demanded of the construction of messages with a significant meaningful content. William Conklin (2002) and Gary Urton (2003) suggest that these elements were used by a *khipucamayuq* in a sequence of decision-making related closely to the natural order of construction of *khipu*. First, the maker of *khipu* would consider the construction of cords. Then he would consider the placement of cords upon other cords. This would be followed by choices concerning the construction of knots as well as the placement of knots upon cords.

We shall not consider all these dimensions of difference here, as the author has covered these elsewhere (Beynon-Davies, 2007). Instead, to demonstrate the different ways in which *khipu* could be constructed we shall focus on just three dimensions of difference in this chapter — the construction of cords, the positioning of cords and the types of knots articulated.

The construction of cords within *khipu* varies in terms of the type of material used, the spin and ply of threads/cords, the colour of threads and the overall colour of cords. Normally a single *khipu* cord was produced from fibres of camelid (alpaca or llama) wool. Sometimes cotton was used and when used was usually dyed. Cotton or camelid fibres were spun using a drop spindle to produce a thread and such threads could be spun in either of two ways. A clockwise or rightward spinning motion produces an 'S' thread — this is so-called because the fibres in the thread run obliquely from upper left to lower right. An anti-clockwise or leftward spinning motion produces a 'Z' thread — so-called because the fibres run obliquely from upper right to lower left. Many cords in *khipu* are left with their natural cotton or camelid hues. Some cords, particularly those of cotton, are dyed a particular colour. Hence, a *khipu* thread has a particular colour. Maria and Robert Ascher (1997) identify different shades of red, reddish orange, reddish brown, brown, greyish brown, yellowish brown, yellow, olive green, greyish green, greenish blue, blue and black. Finally, the relative placement of cords on the main cord of a *khipu* is likely to be a significant difference. The positioning of cords and, as a consequence, the spaces between cords was probably used to indicate the presence or absence of key elements of a message. For instance, pendant cords

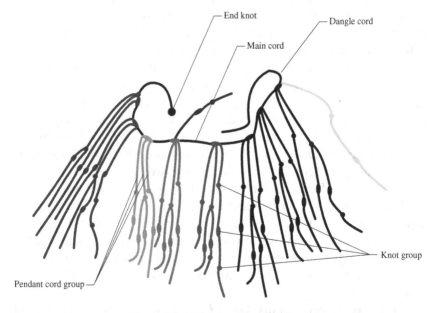

Figure 2.2:   The structure of a *khipu*.

frequently are organised into groups of cords followed by a distinct space on the main cord.

Most scholars agree that the knot is the fundamental difference made within a *khipu*, and they come in different types and can be placed in different positions upon a pendant cord. Three main types of knots are tied on pendant cords: a single knot, a loop knot with multiple turns and a figure of eight knot. Knots are also placed at different positions. For example, a figure of eight knot always appears on the bottom of a pendant cord.

The structure of a typical *khipu* is illustrated in Figure 2.2. The central spine of a *khipu* constituted the main cord, which is typically terminated with an end knot. Along the main cord a series of pendant cords are tied, usually in clusters of a number of cords followed by a space upon the main cord. To each pendant cord, a series of knots of different types are tied forming a knot group.

Articulation of Data Structures

A *khipu* was clearly an important data structure for the Inka. As we shall see, the group or cluster of pendant cords placed close together along the main cord constituted a data element. Finally, a related collection of knots upon a pendant cord constituted a data item.

The substance in which the differences were made is wool fibre, which is twisted and knotted in various ways. The key question then becomes, how many distinct differences can be made in a *khipu*. This expresses an idea of the complexity or variety of this data structure. In previous work (Beynon-Davies, 2011a) we have estimated that a given knot (a data item) upon a *khipu* could be created in 38,40 different ways. Given that a *khipu* can be made up of thousands of distinct knots, then the variety of the entire data structure is exponentially large. The variety of a data structure gives a clue as to the amount of messages that can be coded and communicated using a particular data structure.

Persistent data structures such as a *khipu* have the key advantage that external objects can be manipulated by multiple actors, at different places and at different times. Such persistent structures, as we have seen in Chapter 1, achieve usefulness as systems of record-keeping. There are thus particular advantages to the use of persistent data structures within communication. First, the number of actors involved in communication is no longer limited to those immediately present within the communication situation. As a consequence, a persistent data structure turns one-to-one or one-to-many communication into many-to-many communication. Second, the senders of a communication can be physically dislocated in time and space from the receivers of a communication. This extends the innate cognitive capacity for memory within the organism, but it also has the potential for turning individual memory into collective or social memory. This can be summed up by saying that within a system of persistent data, structures can not only be written and read from, they can also be updated and deleted (see Chapter 6).

The domain of articulation, evident within our model of information situations, can be defined in terms of four basic acts of transformation performed on data structures. These four base acts of articulation form the means from which all forms of data manipulation can theoretically be built. We refer to these actions as create, read, update and delete. Create or 'write' actions involve encoding new data in a data structure. Update actions involve recoding existing data within a data structure. Delete actions involve removing some existing data structure or part of from existence. Retrieval or 'read' actions involve decoding data from an existing data structure.

Clearly, *khipu* were articulated within important data systems for the Inka. Each administrative unit had one or more *khipucamyuq*. A *khipucamyuq* might create a pendant cord with its associated knot group and tie this cord to the main cord. Another *khipucamyuq* would read the *khipu* in a different place at a different time. In contrast, an update act might involve changing the configuration of a particular knot group upon the pendant cord.

After construction, a *khipu* would then be rolled up as a package and transported and delivered to a destination sometimes over thousands of miles distant by groups of *chaski* acting as a relay between *tambos*. At its destination the *khipu* was unravelled and decoded by another *khipucamyuq*. Sometimes, such *khipu* were then stored as records of things important to know about in the Inka empire. Many examples of *khipu* have been excavated at storehouses situated all over the empire.

Figure 2.3 illustrates one information situation in which a *khipu* is created by a *khipucamayuq*, perhaps situated in the capital of the empire. This *khipu* is unravelled after transportation by another *khipucamayuq*, situated in a remote administrative unit located on the Pacific coast. The *khipu* is decoded and the message interpreted. In this case, part of the data

Figure 2.3:   An information situation amongst the Inka.

structure, perhaps a single group of pendant cords, is used to order members of an identifiable *ayllu* to perform a labour tax, consisting perhaps of repairing a number of the rope bridges across the high Andes. This message acts as a trigger or directive (see Chapter 4) to this activity.

Persistent and Non-persistent Data Structures

In Chapter 1, we defined the difference between persistent and non-persistent data structures largely in terms of the substance in which the data structure is formed. However, this difference in form triggers a number of consequential differences in the ways in which such structures can be used within information situations. Take the difference between the spoken word and a *khipu*. This non-persistent and persistent data structure varies in terms of senders and receivers, materiality, articulation, actors, disposal, time and space and agency.

Sender and receivers

Firstly, there is the fairly obvious point that whereas it makes sense to talk of a speaker and hearer or more broadly a sender and receiver in terms of acts of speech, it makes more sense to refer to the writer and reader of a data structure or more broadly perhaps a creator and user. Both an act of speech and an act of creating a data structure such as a *khipu* are likely to be embodied acts (Mingers, 2001), meaning that an actor uses one or more parts of his or her effector apparatus (Chapter 1) in making the spoken sentence or the data structure. In the case of the spoken sentence, the actor primarily uses her larynx to manipulate sound. In the case of the data structure such as a *khipu*, however, the actor creates or forms an artefact using their hands from some persistent material such as cotton or camelid wool. The material form persists beyond the act of its creation — it is truly externalised (see Chapter 1).

Materiality

This difference in labelling of actors is related to a difference in the material from which data structures are formed, as compared to the material of speech. Speech is clearly composed of sound waves which degrade in air. This means that the life of an act of speech is a short one and inherently bound to a specific performance of situated action between two or more actors — all of whom are co-present. A data structure in comparison is typically designed to persist beyond the act of creating this artefact. This inherently means that a data structure, as an instance of persistent communication, has a 'life' over and above the actors who produce and consume it (Derrida, 1971).

Articulation

In an earlier section, we mentioned that a data structure can be articulated in four major ways: created, updated, read and deleted. A message created as speech can only be read. However, a persistent data structure can also be updated and deleted. Hence, an Inka speaking in *quechua* (the language of the Inkas) can create a message as spoken words and a hearer of such a message can be informed by it. Once the message is spoken nothing more can be done to it. In contrast, a *khipu* can not only be initially created; it can be potentially changed (updated) many times. For instance, pendant cords can be added to an existing *khipu,* perhaps by a different *khipucamayuq.*

Forgetting

In the case of an act of speech, it makes sense only to think of one actor sending or 'creating' a series of sound waves and another actor (or a limited number of co-present actors) receiving or 'reading' such vibrations in air. In the case of the life of a data structure it is likewise initially created once by a certain actor. But with a persistent data structure, the artefact must be deliberately disposed of or deleted once by one actor. In the sense of data structures acting as collective memory, there must be a deliberate act of 'forgetting' as well as 'remembering' in the case of persistent data structures. Hence, it is likely that *khipu* would be disposed of or 'archived' once the messages they conveyed had been passed onto appropriate actors.

Actors

Speech can be created by an actor and potentially read by a number of actors, provided they are co-present with the creating actor. In contrast, within the 'life' of a persistent data structure, it may be read and possibly updated a number of times and these acts may be undertaken by a multitude of different actors. Hence, a *khipu* might be read and possible updated by many *khipucamayuq*. In this sense, any one data structure in terms of its life history is perhaps better considered an institutional 'conversation' or 'dialogue' between some defined collection of actors.

Time and space

As we have seen, the whole point of creating persistent data structures, such as *khipu,* is to enable communication across time and space between multiple actors. As Wheeler (1969a) states, 'unlike direct forms of communication, the written record has the capacity for facelessness that is missing from interpersonal communication ... just as the record may be separated from the person to whom it refers, so it may be separated from those who provided the information in the first place'.

The pendant cords of a *khipu,* for instance, as 'utterance' persist beyond their act of production (Derrida, 1971). The very persistence of the *khipu* enables it to fulfil a purpose subtly different from speech: that of referring to or predicating things across time and space to multiple actors. This means that the creator of a data structure is likely to be remote from the consumer of this data structure — where the term remote implies some temporal distance as well as probably some spatial distance. In the case of the Inka a *khipu* would communicate something to a *khipucamayuq* a thousand kilometres across space and some days after the creation of this data structure. The communication is also likely to travel between one actor and many other remote actors situated in many different locations across the high Andes.

Agency

The properties of a persistent data structure listed above lead us to break with the framing of the data structure employed in much literature — that only humans act in relation to data structures. In other words, humans have agency, but data structures do not. Following Cooren (2004) and others, we feel it important to think of data structures as having a limited form of agency — as being performative as well as informative. We shall explain what we mean by the performative nature of data structures in Chapter 4.

Signalling Games

In Chapter 1, we introduced our model of information situations. Within the current chapter, we have hinted that data structures are used to code things of interest to a community of actors. The way in which a structure is articulated by an actor forms a message which is used in the accomplishment of information by other actors. To articulate a structure, an actor must use a collectively agreed form of coding. How does such coding come about and how does it become collectively agreed? The important point is that we do not need to think of coding as arising through conscious 'design'. Coding, and the conventions of communication which arise from it, can emerge through spontaneous patterns of interaction performed by a community of actors in relation to states of a particular environment.

We can demonstrate this by conducting a thought experiment with our model of information situations. Thought experiments are of course considered a valid form of doing and presenting 'research' in disciplines such as philosophy (Cohen, 2005). However, such abstract 'experiments' are also well-utilised in the natural sciences, in areas such as theoretical physics and theoretical biology. For instance, Einstein formulated many of his theoretical insights by conducting thought experiments of various kinds. One famous experiment involved him in thinking about what would happen if someone was travelling in an elevator accelerating toward the speed of light. This enabled him to formulate some classic features of his theory of relativity. In contrast, Axelrod (2006) has used the thought experiment of a prisoner's dilemma game to argue for the evolution of cooperation as an effective survival strategy amongst species.

So, let us conduct such a thought experiment and consider our model of information situations as a sender–receiver game (Skyrms, 2010) in which we have two actors (A_1 and A_2), two states of the environment (E_1 and E_2) and two acts or transformations that can be taken in response to these states (T_1 and T_2). One actor (A_1) observes the states in the environment and decides to send one of two possible messages (M_1 or M_2) by articulating structures (S_1 and S_2) to the other actor (A_2) who is the receiver of the message. The receiving actor (A_2) cannot directly observe the state of the environment sensed by actor A_1 but can choose to perform one of two acts (T_1 or T_2) in response to the message it receives.

Figure 2.4 visualises the major elements of this thought experiment. The entire range of possible patterns of order corresponding to this thought experiment is laid out as a sequence in Figure 2.4. In terms of our deliberately constrained thought experiment, eight distinct information situations are possible, linking states to structures, messages and transactions. However, only some of these situations will emerge as conventions of communication between the actors involved.

Let us assume that the actor A_2 having acted in each case, both A_1 and A_2 receive some 'payoff'. Consider the simple situation where there is exactly one 'correct' act for each state of the environment. Both actors receive a positive payoff if the correct action is chosen following transmission and receipt of some message — otherwise they receive a negative payoff.

It can be expected in this 'game' that the actors will eventually settle upon some system of equilibrium where particular messages are always associated with particular states of the world and actions taken. This will occur because the association between particular messages, structures and actions will be reinforced by positive payoff.

In such cases, the association amounts to the establishment of a convention (Lewis, 2002) (which we shall examine is some detail in Chapter 5). This will mean that two of the eight possible information situations will become, through the pressure of such payoff, the conventions adopted amongst this community of actors. For instance, a convention might become established in this manner between the state of the world E_1, the structure S_2, the message M_2 and the transformation T_1. In other words, whenever one actor observes S_1, it articulates the structure S_2 which signals message M_2 and all receiving actors of this message effect transformation T_1. This is labelled information situation 3 in Figure 2.4. Likewise, a further convention might become established between the state of the world E_2, the structure S_1, the message M_1 and the transformation T_2. This is labelled information situation 6 in Figure 2.4.

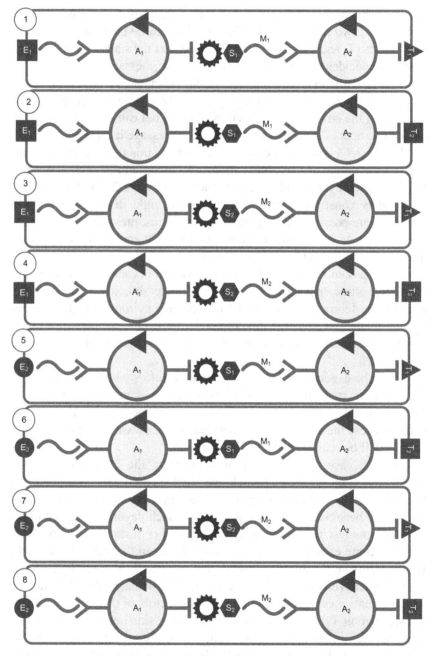

Figure 2.4:   A thought experiment with our model of information situations.

The thought experiment of the sender–receiver game described here has been proposed as a useful meta-model for theorising about the evolution of information situations amongst many social animals, including humans (Skyrms, 2010). Consider the case of the prairie dog (Slobodchikoff *et al.*, 2009) which are formally classified as rodents within the squirrel family, *Sciuridae*. There are five species of prairie dog: black-tailed, Gunnison, white-tailed, Utah and Mexican. Gunnison prairie dogs are the most studied and live in the 'four corners' area of the South-western United States — a boundary area between the states of Arizona, Colorado, New Mexico and Utah. Prairie dog colonies are made up of a number of distinct groups that defend territories. These groups, sometimes referred to as clans or coteries, occupy an area consisting of one or more burrow openings, an underground burrow system and the food resources growing within the territory. Territorial boundaries are defended by all members of the territorial group, which can vary in size from one individual to several males and females.

As far as their sensory apparatus is concerned, prairie dogs have good sight and hearing. They have dichromatic colour vision, meaning that they see well in the blue and yellow parts of the visual spectrum, but not well in the red range. They can also hear sounds in much the same auditory range as humans. Prairie dogs use a number of different parts of their effector and sensory apparatus to communicate. They communicate through sounds such as alarm calls and through visual signals such as wagging of their tails and standing upright in an alert posture; they also seem to communicate through the use of olfactory and odour cues given off by glands situated both in their anus and in their faces.

Alarm calls are by far the most well-studied forms of prairie dog communication, particularly amongst Gunnison prairie dogs (Slobodchikoff *et al.*, 2009). The alarm calls comprise loud and often repetitive vocalisations that sound similar to certain forms of bird call. Such calls are given by one or more prairie dogs within a colony when a predator is detected. A particular type of call produces a distinct escape response on the part of other prairie dogs on hearing the call. All five species of prairie dog produce such calls, but the acoustic structure of these calls varies between species.

In close studies of the behaviour of Gunnison prairie dogs, a number of clear patterns of order are evident, which may be expressed as a series of information situations in which the structures (S) produced are predator-calls and the transformations produced are flight responses (T). Some known information situations are expressed below:

- IF the predator-call produced by prairie dog A_1 is S_1 THEN M_1 is 'human' and A_2 runs and dives into burrow and performs a colony dive. In fact, all animals sensing S_1 within a colony dive into their burrows.
- IF the predator-call produced by prairie dog A_1 is S_2 THEN M1 is 'hawk' and A_2 runs to burrow and performs a limited dive. This means that only those dogs within the flight path of this bird of prey dive into their burrows.
- IF the predator-call produced by prairie dog A_1 is S_3 is 'coyote' THEN A_2 runs to burrow and stands at alert.
- IF the predator-call produced by prairie dog A_1 is S_4 THEN A_2 stands at alert at its current position.

From the point of view of evolutionary biology, each of these decision strategies makes sense or has a payoff in terms of the likely intentions of the predator denoted by a particular call. Predatory humans with rifles frequently walk around the edges of prairie dog colonies and can shoot any prairie dog from several hundred metres away. An appropriate act to make in response to the presence of such a predator is for the entire colony to run to the nearest burrow and dive inside. In contrast, red-tailed hawks stoop with great speed to capture prey. However, once committed to a dive they cannot capture prairie dogs outside of the immediate trajectory of their dive. Hence, an appropriate survival strategy is for only individuals within the flight path of the hawk to run to the nearest burrow and to dive in.

It is noteworthy that the relationship between states of the world, structures, messages and actions appears to be inherited in cases such as that of the warning calls of prairie dogs. Hence, a prairie dog can emit a call for 'hawk' even when it has never previously seen a hawk. These signalling patterns have evolved amongst particular species as a survival strategy. The payoff of survival has served to select a particular system of equilibrium within this signalling game.

Such inherited patterns are typically contrasted with that of arbitrary conventions of signalling familiar within the human sphere. Millikan (1984) argues that a pattern such as an information situation is only conventional if it is reproduced purely by weight of precedent and only if it is unlikely to emerge or re-emerge in the absence of such precedent. Conventional patterns are thus arbitrary patterns for which other patterns might well be substituted except for historical accident. Within signalling games conducted in the human sphere, most, but not all, patterns are conventional in the sense outlined by Millikan. Signalling games amongst the species *Homo Sapiens* are mostly (but not always) a collective accomplishment reliant upon conventions of information situations.

Coding Things

So, what signalling games were played with the *khipu* amongst the Inka? What conventions of association between particular configurations of knots and cords, messages and actions existed amongst this now-extinct society?

The way in which data was encoded in *khipu* is still very much a matter of debate and investigation. Leland Locke in the 1920s established that 100 or so of the remaining *khipu* were used to store the results of record-keeping possibly in support of Inka imperial administration (Mann, 2005). Urton has shown how *khipu* acted as a complex accounting system which enabled census and tribute data collected in the empire to be synthesised, manipulated and transferred between different accounting levels within this administration (Urton and Brezine, 2005).

Evidence suggests that knot groups tied on pendant cords within certain *khipu* represent numbers to the base 10 (decimal). Particular knot types such as single, figure of eight and long knots and their positioning upon pendant cords signify distinct numbers. The closer the knot to the top of a cord, the higher the number. At the very top, a single knot represented multiples of 10,000, then 1,000, then 100, then 10 (Figure 2.5).

The Aschers (1997) agree with Locke that knots tied to pendant, subsidiary or tertiary cords could be used to code numerals or magnitudes of things. However, they also propose that numbers could be used as identifiers for things such as administrative units and products. In this sense, they propose the use of knot groups as a more extensive form of coding. In this perspective, a given knot group on a *khipu* can be considered as similar in nature to a modern bar code, with individual knots substituting for the bars of the code.

To illustrate the way in which this might be coded in a *khipu*, consider the data structure in Figure 2.5 as a record of the tribute supplied to the Inka state in a particular year by a particular provincial area of the Empire.

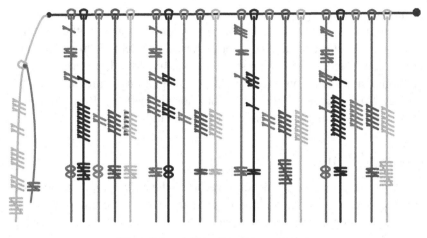

Figure 2.5:   A *khipu* thought experiment.

Within this *khipu,* the dangle cord and its subsidiary cord identify the particular tributary unit to which the records apply. The main body of this *khipu* is made up of four groups of five pendant cords each, in which a common pattern of knots is tied to these groups of pendant cords. Each cord in a pendant group would have a certain colour. The first pendant cord in a group identifies a particular tributary unit of 100 people. The second pendant indicates the amount of maize supplied to the Inka state by the tributary unit. The third pendant represents the number of llamas supplied as tribute. The fourth pendant records the labour tax paid. The final and fifth cord in the group records the number of units of cocoa supplied to the state. Hence, the leftmost pendant group begins with a cord identifying the tributary unit = 13,201. This is followed by a pendant group recording specific elements of tribute: 185 units of maize, 21 llamas, 54 units of labour and 64 units of cocoa.

Data Structures and the Inka State

As we began this chapter, there is evidence to suggest that the evolution of data structures in human cultures appears inherently associated with the rise of the state and its need to control the flow of goods and services in relation to its populace (Beniger, 1986). The Inkas faced the challenge of administering a populace which outnumbered them by about a hundred to one (D'Altroy, 2002). Tawantinsuyu was divided into 80 provinces and was administrated by a provincial administration consisting of an umbrella of Inka officials supervising a hierarchy of ethnic lords appointed to state service.

As indicated above, various elements of tribute were collected from the provinces by the Inka state. The wealth of Inka society was based primarily upon agriculture and the herding of livestock. Mining, metalwork and textile weaving were also significant activities for the various ethnic groups subject to Inka control. Goods and artefacts produced from such systems of activity were stored in vast storehouses distributed throughout various provincial areas. However, the main element of tribute paid to the Inka state was a labour tax in which each 'taxpayer' had to work a specified number of days each year on state projects such as road construction.

Most taxpayers were appointed to tributary units of 10 to 10,000 households. At the lowest level, tributaries were grouped into five accounting units of 10 members each. One person from each of these groups of 10 would serve as a *Chuka Kamayoq* or 'organiser of 10'. Five groupings of 10, making a group of 50 tribute payers, would be placed under the authority of a *Pichqa-Chunka-Kuraca* or 'lord of the 50'. Two groups of 50 would be combined into a unit of 100 tributaries led by a *Pachaka Kuraca* or 'lord of 100'.

This hierarchical system of tributary units would continue up to the head of one of the 80 provinces of the empire known as a *T'oqrikoq*. These provincial lords were normally ethnic Inka and had overall responsibility for administering the population and lands of the province, as well as ensuring that the roads and bridges were in good working order. Provincial lords were in turn placed under the control of an appropriate lord of the four quarters, called *Apu,* which served directly the Inka emperor based in Cusco (Urton and Brezine, 2005).

Therefore, a number of activity systems of the Inka Empire such as tax collection, the administration of workforces in the building of collective works and the distribution of goods within the Empire relied on an effective system of communication. There is clear evidence of the use of *khipu* for the keeping of records within wider communication systems. Using the data recorded in *khipu,* 'accountants' in the Inka empire assessed levels of tribute due, recorded tribute paid and assigned aspects of performance to tributary units.

At the provincial level, the Inka also took censuses to keep track of the population. Census data included records of births, deaths, marriages, and other changes of a person's status. Individuals of each sex were assigned to one of ten categories corresponding not with their chronological age but to their stage in life and ability to perform useful work. Separate *khipu* were apparently kept for this purpose by each province.

Lower down the administrative hierarchy, Urton (2005) proposes two major communication flows reliant on the use of *khipu:* communication flow concerning tribute flowed up the administrative hierarchy and decisions detailing appropriate performance flowed down through the administrative hierarchy. He further claims that data would be partitioned based on the administrative units described above. Hence, local accountants would pass data as to completed tasks upward through the hierarchy. Data at each administrative level would represent the summation of accounts from the level immediately below. This data would eventually be used by imperial accountants based in the Inka capital of Cusco.

There is also evidence of data verification within Inka administrative systems. The governor of each province was required to keep a copy of *khipu* accounts so that 'no deception could be practiced by either the Indian tribute payers or the official collectors' (Urton and Brezine, 2005). Not surprisingly, historical accounts claim that even the smallest of Inka villages had as many as four *khipucamayuq,* and that the records kept by each *khipucamayuq* within a village were cross-checked.

We began this chapter by considering Beniger's (1986) thesis that the invention of information technologies are implicitly linked to a society's ability to control the actions of its members. This appears to have some synergy with Max Weber's (1946) attempt to explain the rise of rationalisation in Western societies and its exemplification in bureaucracy. Bureaucracy for Weber is a type of organisation based upon precisely defined offices underpinned by rules of procedure. Such operative practices, as we shall see, are enhanced through the scaffolding of data structures. Weber's theorisation offers a way of explaining the explosion of data structures evident in the rise of the modern nation-state.

Reversing the Ontological Status of Data Structures

Before we conclude this chapter, we want to establish the key principle that we should never take data structures for granted. Ontology, as we shall see (in Chapter 8), is a theory of reality, being or what things are seen to exist. Within this book we want to reverse the conventional ontology associated with data structures (Baskerville *et al.*, 2019). In other words, we want to question the conventional ways of thinking about why data structures exist or be.

Conventionally, and as conceived in the dominant literature, a data structure is viewed purely as a technological artefact. In this view, data structures, their elements or their items are taken to represent propositions about things in some institutional reality. The institutional reality is also assumed to be observer-independent, meaning that it is the same for all actors. Hence, in a manufacturing setting, a picking-item, which relates a given identifier for a shipping item with a given identifier for a truck, serves as a proposition about these things to workers within the institutional reality of a supply chain.

Within formal logic data elements or data items as propositions may take only one of two values, namely, true, or false. We either assert the truth of a given proposition by writing a data element or data item to the data structure or we retract a given proposition by deleting the corresponding data element or data item from the data structure. This implies that the state of a data structure at any given time consists of true statements about the real-world domain it represents — in this case the loading of shipping onto transportation. This so-called *correspondence view* of truth implies that there is a necessary separation between institutional reality and data structures. It also implies that a data-item as an externalisation or representation is taken to correspond to some real-world thing, or more likely a set of things important to actors within some institutional reality.

We shall argue that we need to reverse this conventional ontology associated with data structures. Data structures are not separate from institutional reality; they are very much entangled within it. In fact, data structures are constitutive of such realities in the sense that they 'scaffold' action and interaction between actors working within and between institutions. Data structures, as we shall see, are not only forms of structure, they serve to inform institutional actors and often prescribe or proscribe action on the part of such actors. Data structures are important to instituting of facts about things and through this process are critical to the production and reproduction of institutional order.

As we shall see, this ontological shift causes us to reframe many notions associated with data but named often with rather unsatisfactory terms. These notions include data collection, data privacy, data protection (see Chapter 6), data security, data governance and data control (see Chapter 9). Take just the first of these — that of data collection (we shall examine other terms in later chapters). The term *data collection* tends to suggest that data is in some sense out there waiting to be collected by somebody. This is a reflection of the conventional view of the data structure in which data corresponds to objective things in some external and independent reality. However, the use of this term tends to mask the important fact that a data structure always has to be created by somebody, normally with the intention of informing some other actor or actors. Hence, in the process of creation, some actor (even a machine actor) must make decisions about both what to represent and how this representation should communicate. So, data is never out there waiting. Data is contingent and only comes into existence through information situations.

Conclusion

All data structures can be described at a high level of abstraction in terms of a hierarchy of data items, data elements and data structures. A data item is the lowest level of data organisation. A data element is a logical collection of data items and a data structure is a logical collection of data elements. Both persistent and non-persistent data structures can be analysed in such manner. However, we have focussed upon persistent data structures because of the advantages such structures have for institutions.

There are particular advantages to the use of persistent data structures within communication. Persistent data structures such as a *khipu* have the key advantage that external objects can be manipulated by multiple actors, at different places and at different times. This turns individual memory into collective or social memory.

The use of physical structures as forms of data representation seems characteristic of many human cultures. A system of persistent data structures is an example of techne or craft. Such a system consists of crafting external representations of things which could stand independently of the body, detaching such representations not only from immediate situated experience but also from the immediate communication of such experience. There is evidence to support the idea that this first intellectual leap was taken because of the importance of recording things to coordinated activity. Hence, within this conception, even though *khipu* would not traditionally be considered a form of 'writing', there is substantial evidence to suggest the use of this artefact as a form of record or data system.

Over the last two chapters we have focussed mainly on the use of data structures for an accounting of things. In Chapter 3, we look at the relationship between data structures and personal identity. In other words, data structures, particularly within contemporary society, are critical to answering the question of *who you think you are;* or more precisely *who an institution thinks you are.*

References

Ascher, M. and R. Ascher (1997). *Mathematics of the Incas: Code of the Quipu* (New York: Dover Publications).

Axelrod, R. (2006). *The Evolution of Cooperation* (New York: Perseus Publishing), Revised edition.

Baskerville, R. L., M. D. Myers and Y. Youngjin (2019). "Digital First: The Ontological Reversal and New Challenges for IS Research." *Management Information Systems Quarterly,* **44**(2): 509–523.

Beniger, J. R. (1986). *The Control Revolution: Technological and Economic Origins of the Information Society* (Cambridge, MA: Harvard University Press).

Beynon-Davies, P. (2007). "Informatics and the Inka." *International Journal of Information Management,* **27**(5): 306–318.

Beynon-Davies, P. (2011a). *Significance: Exploring the Nature of Information, Systems and Technology* (Houndmills, Basingstoke: Palgrave).

Beynon-Davies, P. (2011b). "Information on the Prairie: Signs, Systems and Prairie Dogs." *International Journal of Information Management,* **31**(3): 307–316.

Cohen, M. (2005). *Wittgenstein's Beetle and Other Classic Thought Experiments* (Oxford: UK, Blackwell).

Conklin, W. J. (2002). A Khipu Information String Theory. In *Narrative Threads: Accounting and Recounting in Andean Khipu.* J. Quilter and G. Urton (eds.) (Austin, TX: University of Texas Press), pp. 53–86.

Cooren, F. (2004). "Textual Agency: How Texts Do Things in Organisational Settings." *Organization,* **11**(3): 373–393.

D'Altroy, T. N. (2002). *The Inkas* (Oxford: Basil Blackwell).

Derrida, J. (1971). "Signature, Event, Context." A communication to the Congres Internationale des Societes de Philosophie de Langue Francaise. Montreal, Canada.

Lewis, D. (2002). *Convention: A Philosophical Study* (Oxford: Blackwell).

Mann, C. M. (2005). "Unravelling Khipu's Secrets: Researchers Move Towards Understanding the Communicative Power of the Inka's Enigmatic Knotted Strings which Wove An Empire Together." *Science,* **309**(5737): 1008–1010.

Millikan, R. G. (1984). *Language, Thought and Other Biological Categories: New Foundations for Realism* (Cambridge, MA: MIT Press).

Mingers, J. (2001). "Embodying Information Systems: The Contribution of Phenomenology." *Information and Organization*, 11(2): 103–127.

Skyrms, B. (2010). *Signals: Evolution, Learning and Information* (Oxford: Oxford University Press).

Slobodchikoff, C. N., B. S. Perla and J. L. Verdolin (2009). *Prairie Dogs: Communication and Community in Animal Society* (Cambridge, MA: Harvard University Press).

Tsitchizris, D. C. and F. H. Lochovsky (1982). *Data Models* (Englewood-Cliffs: Prentice-Hall).

Urton, G. (2003). *Signs of the Inka Khipu: Binary Coding in the Andean Knotted-String Records* (Austin, TX: University of Texas Press).

Urton, G. and C. J. Brezine (2005). "Khipu Accounting in Ancient Peru." *Science*, 309(5737): 1065–1068.

Weber, M. (1946). *Essays in Sociology* (Oxford: Oxford University Press).

Wheeler, S. (ed.) (1969a). *On Record: Files and Dossiers in American Life* (New York: Russell Sage Foundation).

Wheeler, S. (1969b). Problems and Issues in Record-Keeping. In *On Record: Files and Dossiers in American Life,* Wheeler, S. (ed.) (New York: Russell Sage Foundation), pp. 3–24.

Chapter 3

Identifying Things: The Informativity of the Record

Introduction

In the classic thriller *The Day of the Jackal* (Forsyth, 2011), the assassin visits a London cemetery and writes down details from a gravestone of a person who died in childbirth. He uses these details to apply to the national registry of births for a birth certificate for this person. This birth certificate is then used to apply for a passport from the national passport's agency. Finally, this passport is used both to gain entry to France and to enrol in various services within the country such as hiring a car. But this breakdown in institutional order is not complete fiction nor is it something set in the past. In 2013, for instance, a report was published indicating that the identities of 42 dead children were used by undercover London metropolitan police officers. The process by which these identities were acquired had many similarities to that described in the novel by Frederick Forsyth.

Within this chapter, we focus upon the communication domain within our model of information situations (see Figure 3.1). Having established the nature of records as data structures (in Chapter 2), we need now to demonstrate more clearly how data structures inform actors — what we might refer to as the *informativity* of the record. A sign is something which stands for some other thing. It is through accomplishing the stands for relation that information can be said to have occurred in the psyche of some actor. As we shall see, this notion of a sign is similar in nature to John Searle's concept of a status function. Through this latter concept, we

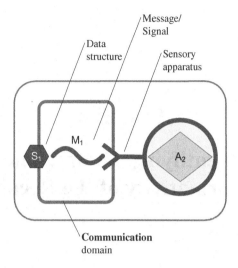

Figure 3.1:   The communication domain.

have a way of exploring the multifarious ways in which records are used within institutional life. Indeed, we begin the journey of establishing how records *scaffold* the very notion of an institution.

We begin our exploration with an examination of how records are important to communicating critical notions of personal identity between individuals and institutions. We shall show how personal identity in the modern world is very much involved with the use of records for authentication of persons, for identification of persons and for enrolment of such persons in various areas of institutional activity.

 Modern India is involved in the attempt to assign a unique identifier with an associated record to each one of its estimated 1.2 billion citizens and intends to use such records as the primary means for citizens to access not only public services, but also private services such as banking. This association between records and personal identity has a long history. The British Raj was one of the earliest innovators in the attempt to link personal identification with the measurement of man, otherwise known as anthropometry. This idea was much used in early anthropology in support of the controversial attempt to develop a typology of human races. Alphonse Bertillon was the first to use this idea as part of his solution to the practical problem of identifying repeat criminal offenders in France. In his anthropometric method, 11 different measurements of the body were taken by rigorously trained clerks with specially designed instruments such as callipers, gauges and rulers. These measurements were then recorded on a specially designed card, which became known as a Bertillon card. This approach is very much the precursor to modern biometric systems that use machines to record data such as fingerprint and iris scans and the reuse of this data in processes of authentication, identification and enrolment.

The Notion of a Sign

Within our model of information situations first introduced in Chapter 1, structures are used to communicate things between two or more actors. A data structure is articulated by one actor. This data structure is then sensed by one or more other actors and serves to communicate through conventions of coding some message to such actors. This message may act as stimulus to further action by these sensing actors.

The component elements of this model can be transposed quite easily onto Charles Sanders Peirce's concept of a sign. Bertrand Russell (1959) viewed Charles Sanders Peirce as one of the most important philosophers of the later 19th and early 20th centuries. 'Beyond doubt [...] he was one of the most original minds of the later nineteenth century, and certainly the greatest American thinker ever' (Russell, 1959, p. 276). His vast amount of work makes contributions to areas as diverse as mathematics, logic, physics, computer science, ethics, linguistics, psychology and the philosophy of science, to name but a few. However, it is for his contributions to semiotics — the doctrine of signs — that Peirce is most well known.

For Peirce, a sign is some thing (A) that stands for some other thing (B) to someone (C). This makes a sign a triadic (three-fold) relation. consisting of the representamen (A), the object (B) and the interpretant (C). The representamen (A) is the signifier, sign-vehicle or representation. The object (B) is the signified or referent; that which is represented. The interpretant (C) is the concept or meaning of the symbol formed through some process of interpretation or information by some actor.

In our terms, a data structure, or more realistically a data-item, is the representamen. What it represents or codes is the signified or referent object. What concept is communicated by the representamen or what it means to some actor is the interpretant. Hence, the physical and sensed properties of a particular roundish clay token incised with a cross

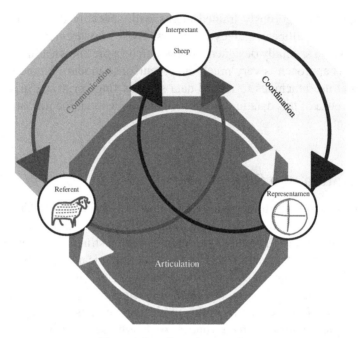

Figure 3.2:   Clay tokens as signs.

constitutes the representamen (see Chapter 1). The object, referent or the signified refers to what this physical structure stands for — in this case, some instance of a domesticated animal (see Figure 3.2). The interpretant refers to what a token of this form is interpreted as meaning (thought to mean) by one or more actors within this setting.

Take another example from the two historical cases we have already considered in Chapters 1 and 2. In the case of the Inka *khipu*, a pendant cord (representamen) placed upon a *khipu* might represent to a *khipuca-mayuq* (interpretamen) a nominated number of workers from an adminis-trative unit assigned to labour for the state (object/referent) (Figure 3.3).

However, there is a tendency to think of the triadic nature of signs as static and immutable things. This is not the case because signs constitute action-events. Indeed, we would argue that signs are accomplished in the coupling of actions of articulation, communication and coordination. This is why we have placed these three types of action as backdrop to the three elements of a sign in Figure 3.2.

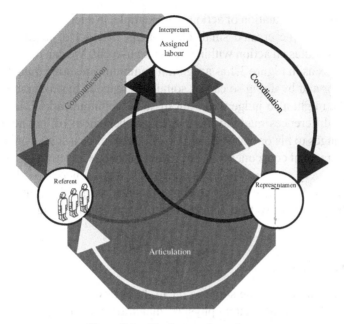

Figure 3.3:   Pendant cords as signs.

For Peirce, the sign is is not in the thing itself (such as the clay token) or the thing it is meant to refer to (such as a domesticated animal), nor is it in the conception or thought of the thing (such as a unit of tribute). A sign, such as this, is an activity in which a sign-event is accomplished by a particular actor in thought (Hoopes, 1991). But all sign-events are teleological events, they have purposes or consequences. All sign-events are related to the expectations, conventions or habits of the actor accomplishing the sign-event. For instance, a Sumerian temple worker sees a clay token of this form as a sign of tribute having been made because he knows or expects that the articulation of such a token has been undertaken by some other actor with the intended purpose of recording the transfer of livestock to the temple storehouse.

So how do we know whether the transformation of some substance constitutes a sign? For Peirce, we apply the pragmatic test of whether the making of such difference to the substance, makes a further difference in turn to some actor (Bateson, 1972). In other words, we must judge any potential sign in terms of its consequences, whether it has any practical bearing on some situation of action. For example, in ancient Sumeria, as we have seen, people created small clay tokens. The act of making such a token constitutes an action within a wider sign-event. We can only judge an incised disk as in Figure 3.1 as a sign if it communicates something to some other actor and by doing so causes some difference to the cognition of this actor. We might also judge the result of such 'communication', in turn, in terms of differences made to the consequent behaviour of that actor, perhaps changes to his or her work activity. So, for Peirce a sign is only a sign if it has practical consequences — if it causes change to action. As we shall see, this is very similar to Searle's notion of a status function — the notion that to form the social world we conventionally assign a certain status to some things which we take collectively to count as something else.

The Identifier

We might summarise the story so far in the following way: signs matter. Signs are built from matter (physical material), but matter both to individuals and to institutions. In the contemporary world, we have built sophisticated technologies to help us with this matter. However, such technologies frequently mask for us the key matter of importance.

Within the rest of this chapter, I shall deliberately consider an apparently mundane artefact that should matter to anyone interested in the linkages between data and institutional order — that of the *identifier*. Identifiers are data-items commonly found within the data elements of data structures. My wish is that we take these artefacts more seriously because I think they play a critical role within the reproduction of institutional order. I also want to show that the difference in conception engendered by this perspective has practical consequences.

An identifier, as already stated, is an example of a sign, which typically would form a data-item within a data element within a larger data structure. Data-items within data elements typically do one of two things. They refer to something, in which case they are identifiers for something. Or they describe something, in which case they are *properties* or *attributes* of something. We use the term *thing* here in an entirely neutral way to stand for anything that can be referred to or described. It may be a physical thing such a person or place or product (see Chapter 7). It may also be something which has a purely institutional status such as a contract or a sale or a payment (see Chapter 10). In the current chapter, we shall focus upon the use of identifiers for referring to persons — so-called personal identifiers — because of the important role such identifiers play within modern societies and their institutions. In Chapter 7, we shall consider the importance of identifiers of place, product, time and digital presence.

An identifier is anything which can be taken to *refer* to some other thing across time and space to multiple actors. Referring is a critical function within communication which allows a sender to specify one and only one thing to which a message applies, while also providing the means for a receiver to identify the thing from the message. Identifiers are particularly useful within acts of communication because they can refer to some instance of a thing without actually the need to describe it. They can also refer to this instance across many different information situations. For instance, personal names such as 'John Smith' are typical identifiers while a definite description of this person might consist of the phrase 'the man with red hair and a pronounced limp'.

Consider a data-item important to many institutional settings — the passport number as a personal identifier. Each country in the world is able to create its own *form* for such an identifier. To take just one example, within the UK, a passport number currently consists of nine digits. So key facts important to the institutional governance of the UK are established in the form:

[<Passport no.> REFERS TO <Person>]

For instance:

[109999555 REFERS TO John Smith]

Note, we cannot actually represent or record as a fact the relationship between a physical thing and a sign directly. We actually have to use other signs as proxies. The fact we have just listed above actually relates two identifiers. One is a 'natural' identifier and consists of a personal name; one is a 'surrogate' identifier, created by a particular institution (in this case the UK Passport Office on behalf of HM Government) to uniquely refer to a certain person. Both natural and surrogate identifiers can refer to some thing, but surrogate identifiers enforce the uniqueness of reference across information situations. Hence, the surrogate identifier *109999555* will always refer to one and only one British citizen. The natural identifier *John Smith is* sufficient to refer to this person in many contexts. However, in certain situations the referring function will break down, potentially because there is likely to be more than one person named *John Smith* in the UK.

Status Functions, Signs and Institutional Facts

An identifier is a type of what John Searle calls a status function; Charles Sanders Pierce calls a sign. For Searle, status functions are produced through constitutive rules of the form:

[X (some thing) counts as Y (some other thing) in C (some context)]

Pierce (1931), as we have seen, would say something similar but add actors, such as:

[X stands for Y to Z in C]

where Z is some actor or actors.

As we have seen, an identifier forms the X term within a constitutive rule when it serves the function of referring to some unique instance of some thing. So, the term 109999555 is an identifier if it counts as a specific person in some institutional context such as the domain of British citizenship.

But identifiers do not describe. For this, constitutive rules need to work within a process which Pierce refers to as infinite semiosis. This is the process by which one sign/status function counts as or stands for another sign/status function, which in turn counts as or stands for another sign/status function, and so on … In other words:

[A counts as or stands for B; B counts as or stands for C; C counts as or stands for D…]

The process of infinite semiosis is particularly evident in the way in which actors use signs or status functions to abstract. The idea of classification or instantiation is a key example of abstraction [Chapter 8]. As a constitutive rule, classification can be expressed as:

[X ISA Y in C]

The relation ISA (Brachman, 1983) here may be taken as a special type of counts as or stands for relation. The terms X, Y and C in this rule are placeholders, meaning that they refer to some as yet unspecified value. Within this rule X is normally a placeholder for some identifier, while Y is a class or category to which the thing identified by X applies. C denotes the institutional context in which this particular classification rule holds.

Constitutive rules are important because they serve to generate what John Searle calls institutional facts. Hence, an example of an institutional fact generated by the instantiation rule would be:

[109999555 ISA British citizen in the context of international travel]

Here, the terms within the rule are given values or instances. X is given the value <109999555>, Y the value <British citizen> and C the value <International travel>.

Institutional facts such as this not only serve to identify these particular things to the institution concerned, they bring these things into existence for the institution. Hence, such facts serve to help define the so-called ontology of the institution — its notion of what reality is (see Chapter 8). Institutional facts such as what counts as a British citizen clearly do not work in isolation. They typically work within wider data structures such as lists, which we discuss in Chapter 4. The very act of creating or making an item within an institutional list declares that something exists.

A passport as an identity token does not just, of course, contain details of the passport identifier, which refers to a particular person. The passport number as the main identifier is not the only sign or status function used on a passport. Hence, when a particular passport as a data structure is issued it serves to declare a whole series of institutional facts about the person, such as:

[109999555 GIVEN NAME Joe]
[109999555 SURNAME Bloggs]
[109999555 DATE OF BIRTH 15/03/1957]
[109999555 SEX male]
[109999555 NATIONALITY British]

The relations between status functions here are all matters of attribution or designation (see Chapter 8). In other words, they all attribute particular values to an identified person. Hence, through a process of infinite semiosis we start to form what we shall call a necessary scaffold for that part of the institutional reality which is defined by the context in which these facts are utilised, whether this is within international travel or financial transactions or acts of leisure.

What is an Institution?

For Searle (2005), an institution is simply a system of constitutive rules through which institutional facts are produced: '*an institution is any system of constitutive rules... Once an institution becomes established it then provides a structure within which we can create institutional facts*'.

Consider a simple domain consisting of a number of interrelated patterns of action involved with managing the flow of production material through production units within a large manufacturing plant. Two key things of interest are important to this domain. The first thing is the stillage — a standardised container used to store and transport production material. The second thing is the production location. The manufacturing plant concerned is divided into a number of different production units with a number of different production locations within each unit. Stillages are placed within such designated production locations and move between production locations as the material they contain gets transformed within manufacture.

Two identifiers are particularly significant within this institutional domain to refer to such things of interest — that of a stillage code and a production location code. Constitutive rules implement identification here through the *refers to* relation, such as:

[26441 REFERS TO Stillage]
[PL0102 REFERS TO Production location]

Such structures amount to a series of institutional facts about things deemed to exist in this domain. However, these identifiers are used in the construction of larger structures of list, which we consider in more detail in Chapter 4. Consider one such list — the 'stock location' list:

[26641 LOCATED AT PL0102]
[26643 LOCATED AT PL0102]
[24536 LOCATED AT PL0102]

...

This stock location list consists of a series of further institutional facts built upon a bedrock of previously established institutional facts — identifiers of stillages and locations. These institutional facts assert further aspects about the reality of this institution, namely that, given stillages are currently placed and can be found at given locations around the manufacturing plant. However, what at first sight looks like the same structures may be used by different actors in different ways. So, forklift truck drivers around the plant may be given lists which look very similar in form to that above in that it relates a given stillage with a given location through identifiers. However, the institutional facts here will be different because of a difference in context. The forklift truck driver is informed not only as to where a given stillage currently is but where it should be moved to. This stock movement list might take the following form:

[26641 MOVE TO PL0202]
[26643 MOVE TO PL0202]
[24536 MOVE TO PL0202]
...

This iterative process of sign application, where one institutional fact is used in the formation of a further institutional fact, and so on, is the basis by which institutions are constituted. Such institutional facts, as we shall see in Chapter 4, serve to scaffold institutional action — they get things done. And the activity of doing things is likely to generate further institutional facts. In the current case, the institutional facts serve to coordinate stock movement activity, which is likely to lead to a further modification of facts within the stock location list.

One crucially important identifier for the constitution of institutions through institutional facts is the personal identifier — data which refers to the person. Because of its centrality within the modern institution, we spend the rest of the chapter considering this.

Personal Identity

In the Book of Revelations from the Bible, one of the prophecies states: 'And he causeth all, both small and great, rich and poor, free and bond, to receive a mark in their right hand'. A classic example here of the centrality of records to modern existence is the importance of personal identifiers in modern life — 'marks' of personal identity.

The government of modern India has now assigned a unique code number to each of its estimated 1.2 billion citizens (*The Economist*, 2010). Such 'universal identity numbers' (UIDs) by their very nature are meant to act as identifiers for persons in many forms of contemporary activity on the subcontinent, such as in interactions with government and the private sector. Use of such identifiers is also predicated upon a number of positive effects such as instrumental ways of improving government services and reducing corruption. For instance, two-thirds of the subsidised grain that the government allocates to the poor in India is either stolen or adulterated by middle men. High levels of voter fraud also exist, and registration for government work programmes is difficult for the poor because of its time-consuming nature. UIDs are meant as tools in the alleviation of such issues. They are considered important in a country where many people lack documentation or even surnames. Hence, it is intended that these identifiers will eventually be linked to biometrics such as iris scans and fingerprints to make the process of identification easier and faster in situations such as voter registration (*The Economist*, 2011). More of biometrics later.

In contrast, during the period 2002–2010 the UK government of the time attempted to relate the rights and entitlements of citizenship with a standard identifier for all British citizens and its representation in a national identity smartcard. The scheme to introduce this identity token for all UK citizens was finally abandoned in December 2010 (Beynon-Davies, 2011). On the one hand, the attempt to introduce such an identity token brought into focus the critical role that personal identity and its management plays as supporting infrastructure in areas such as digital government and digital business. On the other, the introduction of a national identifier and associated token raised major challenges to data protection, data privacy and public trust in the information governance of this nation-state. Indeed, such difficulties constituted a major part of the rationale for the abandonment of the project.

As these two cases demonstrate, personal identity is a significant and problematic area for modern individuals, organisations and the societies within which they work. However, the problematic nature of personal identity is not a new phenomenon. We shall argue that personal identity has been of enduring concern for many hundreds if not thousands of years and is probably inherently associated with the ways in which humans build significance through data structures. Within modern life, as the case of the Indian UID demonstrates, many aspects of personal identity are made digital, are stored in and utilised by machines. This is so significant for societal action that the so-called management of personal identity is a burgeoning area of practical application within information technology. However, as the case of the UK national identity card demonstrates, the instantiation of personal identity as a technical phenomenon raises major concerns for notions of the information society and information polity.

Criminal Identification in the British Raj

Modern India's attempt to assign a unique code number to each of its estimated 1.2 billion citizens actually has a long pedigree. The British Raj was one of the earliest innovators in the attempt to link personal identification with the measurement of man; otherwise known as anthropometry (Cole, 2001). This idea was much used in early anthropology in support of the controversial attempt to develop a typology of human races. At this time, anthropometry involved measurements of bodily features such as the shape of the cranium and length of the lower arm.

As mentioned in the introduction, Bertillon innovated a solution to the problem of identifying repeat criminal offenders in France. In his method, eleven different measurements of the body were taken and recorded as a data structure known as a Bertillon card. A physical description of the person was also included on the card, formed in terms of a precise morphological vocabulary which defined key features of the individual. The card also usually contained two photographs of the individual — one full face and one in profile. Finally, a description of the shape and position of any peculiar marks was also included in the record of the individual.

Bertillon was well aware that measuring individuals and recording such measurement on his cards was only a partial solution to criminal identification. He also developed a classification scheme for such cards based solely on anthropometric measurements. Cards were first classified by sex, then by head length ('small', 'medium', 'large'), then head breadth and so on. This scheme allowed for quick retrieval of his cards based upon key, measurable facets of an individual. Hence, Bertillon placed more faith in the structured record than in the new technology of the photograph, which he felt provided a much more imprecise method of personal identification.

Suppose a new suspected criminal came to the attention of the police authorities and was measured in this way. His card was taken into the card archive and the anthropometric classification was used to obtain a match with existing cards. Assuming a tentative match was made, then the Bertillon operator would confirm the match in terms of the physical description and the distinctive marks. Assuming a match, such a record would prove that the individual had offended previously.

The idea for the Bertillon system was first proposed in 1879 but rejected by the French authorities. Bertillon had to wait until 1883 for his system to be tested and to be proven able to identify repeat criminals. Following the rapid deployment of the system throughout the French justice system, Bertillon's manual for his 'method' was translated into several languages and spread rapidly throughout the police departments of the Globe. The Bertillon method was instituted in the US in 1887, in Argentina in 1891 and in Great Britain in 1894.

Interestingly, the Bertillon system made no use of a biometric identifier we now regard as commonplace: the fingerprint. People have been leaving their fingerprints around for millennia (Cole, 2001). Fingerprints appear on cave paintings and ancient pottery throughout Europe, Asia and North America and they may have been used as a means to denote identity and authority in terms of such artefacts. We know that fingerprints embossed within clay seals were used to 'sign' documents in ancient China and this practice spread to Japan, Tibet and India. However, it was only in the late 17th century that Europeans began to describe the idea of the fingerprint. Its use as an identifier within processes of formal identification was not considered in the West until the 19th century.

The first use of fingerprints as forms of identification actually occurred not in Britain but in India during the time of British rule in the subcontinent — the so-called 'Raj'. This was in response to the problems of administering a large native population with a small corps of civil servants. The agents of the East India Company and later the British Foreign Service were overwhelmed with a population composed of a vast variety of ethnic groups and languages. William Herschel, an administrator in the Civil Service of the Raj, is normally credited with taking the first fingerprint — in fact, it was a handprint — and using this as proof of identity.

The story goes that he was driven to this idea in his attempt to prevent the fraudulent claiming of pensions. Colonial officials believed that many persons with obvious signs of 'vitality' were claiming pensions by impersonating deceased relatives. Administrators were expected to make identifications based on signs of identification noted in a pension roll. These included written descriptions of such things as hair colour, eye colour and complexion. Because of the ambiguity associated with such descriptions a pension could in practice be collected by almost anybody presenting him or herself to a pensions inspector.

Herschel had first used the idea in 1858 of a handprint on a deed to identify a road contractor and prevent him from repudiating the contract at some later date. It was several years later that he took repeated impressions of his own fingerprints over a period of time and confirmed to himself that they had not changed. In 1877 he proposed in a letter to the Inspector of Jails and the Registrar-General of India that fingerprints should be used for the identification of criminals across India. However, these key colonial administrators were not impressed, and Herschel's idea remained untested.

Parallel to this, in the late 1880s, colonial administrators in India began discussing the introduction of a criminal identification system for the subcontinent. The Bertillon system of anthropometry gradually began being adopted across India for this purpose. However, administrators began to question both the efficacy and the efficiency of this system of identification for repeat offenders.

They questioned whether Bertillon's morphological vocabulary designed for recording features of Europeans was applicable to the variety of races found in the subcontinent. They therefore modified aspects of the system and dropped certain features such as eye colour because they claimed that there was little variation in this feature among the Indian races. They also questioned the inconsistency in the application of the system by dispersed administrators across the vast distances of the Raj. They were therefore looking for a method of identification that reduced inherent problems of interpretation they saw as embedded within the Bertillon method. In essence they were looking for the development of automatic instruments of measurement that did not demand the intervention of a trained administrator to capture identifiers. Fingerprints seemed ideally suited for this purpose. However, as Bertillon himself found, it was no good collecting fingerprints of persons unless you had an associated way of creating a record of fingerprints that could be classified and indexed such that it could be retrieved easily and efficiently at some later date.

Step in Francis Galton, a contemporary and friend of Charles Darwin, who took up the challenge. His original objective was, however, not criminal identification. Instead, he looked to fingerprinting as a possible mechanism to record objectively signs of heredity. Nevertheless, although he invested considerable time and effort to the challenge, he failed on both fronts: failing to develop a satisfactory classification scheme for finger-prints and, as a consequence, failing to prove that fingerprints were signs which could be used to prove the relationship between parent and off-spring. However, Galton did achieve some success. Galton's system for collecting fingerprints is still very much used today (although the technol-ogy for doing so has changed). Four fingers of the right hand are placed onto an inked plate, then onto a defined part of the record card. This is repeated with the four fingers of the left hand. Then rolled prints of each figure are taken and recorded on labelled elements of the record card.

It was left to a colonial police official, Edward Henry, and his associ-ates to devise a workable fingerprint classification scheme based upon features of fingerprint patterns such as 'loops', 'whorls' and 'ridges'. Around 1895 this system was introduced into the police department in Bengal. After an evaluation which proved the effectiveness of the scheme, the Henry system spread to other provinces of India. In 1897, fingerprint records were first used in support of a criminal prosecution. In 1899 the colonial legislature passed the Indian Evidence Act, which endorsed the use of fingerprints in criminal investigation and as a valid form of evi-dence in the courts of justice. This led to the establishment of a criminal identification system (as illustrated in Figure 3.4) which has many fea-tures in common with the personal identity management systems of the modern age.

Personal Identifiers

So, what does this case of Bertillon cards, fingerprints and the British Raj tell us about the nature of personal identity and its linkage to data struc-tures? Personal identity is critical to the notion of data systems in contem-porary society, because of the way in which identity increasingly becomes reified in personal records. Developments, such as those described, founded the infrastructure upon which modern personal identity manage-ment takes place.

Consider gender as a key aspect of personal identity. I communicate my gender in a number of ways. Clothing masks many aspects of my anatomy so my gender may not be immediately obvious to a distant observer. Hence, how I choose to behave or 'perform' will be a significant

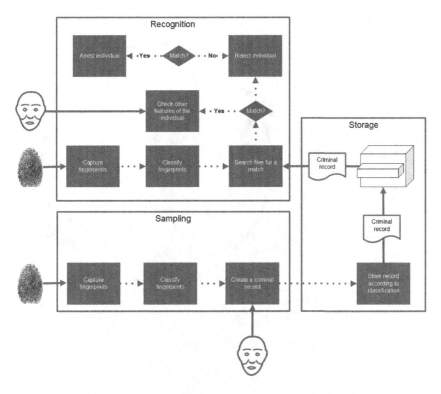

Figure 3.4:   The criminal identification system of the British Raj.

way in which my gender is communicated. For instance, dress code is frequently used to signify gender. Within face-to-face communication, such visual cues may be sufficient to signify this aspect of my identity. If such performance proves insufficient, a communicative act such as the statement — 'I am a man' — can be used to signify my gender. However, such signification breaks down when communication is remote in time and space. For such remote communication, my gender is likely to be recorded in persistent forms of signification as records and tokens such as birth certificates, passports and identity cards. A 'reading' of such records within remote communication is necessary to signify appropriate gender.

So why is personal identity so important within contemporary human action? We propose that the signification of identity is important to coordinated action because of the way it conflates three critical and entangled processes of specialised signification or semiosis essential to institutional activity: authentication, identification and enrolment (Beynon-Davies,

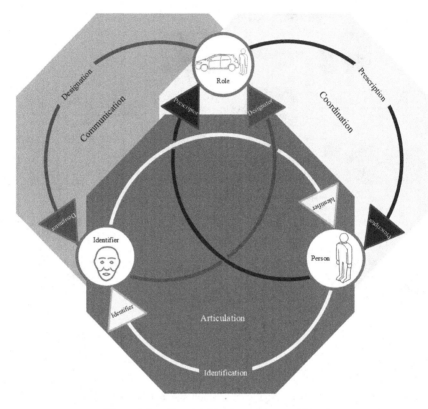

Figure 3.5:   The signification of personal identity.

2007) (Figure 3.5). These processes communicate three different things about the identity of the individual. In other words, personal identity is normally accomplished within three interdependent signification processes which rely on the scaffolding of the three types of action proposed in our earlier model of information situations (in Chapter 1) — that of articulation, communication and coordination.

Authentication involves answering the question: *Am I who I claim to be*? Authentication is signalled by identifiers: data-items which refer to things. Within face-to-face interaction, standard or 'natural' identifiers are used for the communication of identity. The contemporary problematic nature of remote communication in support of remote interaction demands the use of surrogate identifiers (Clarke, 1994). Identification in the large involves answering the question — *Who am I*? — and is typically signalled by attributes or properties of things, including a history of events within which the individual has participated. These types of signs are sometimes referred to as designators and the application of their use as designation. Enrolment is a term we adapt from actor-network theory (Latour, 2005). Enrolment in the large involves answering the question, in relation to a particular system of activity, *how am I expected to perform and how will others perform towards me?* Enrolment is largely signalled by the intentions associated with acts of communication. These signs are sometimes referred to as prescriptors and effectively define the package of behaviours expected of the individual — the role a person is expected to play within a particular institutional setting.

The whole point of unpacking the issue of personal identity in this manner is to help explain why and how identity is critical to enrolment in the activity systems of contemporary societies. The possession of appropriate identity privileges individuals with rights, responsibilities and activities in a particular activity system. For instance, a validated identity such as that of a taxpayer will enrol the individual in a whole range of rights, responsibilities and expected actions in the activity systems associated with fiscal matters. It will also entitle the individual to access services provided by the tax authorities of a particular nation-state. As another example, consider the activity system of driving an automobile in the European Union (see Chapter 9). To become enrolled in this activity system, the individual must acquire a critical form of institutional identity. She must first pass a driving test and, if successful, receive a driving licence on which is recorded a driver identifier.

However, as we have seen, identity may not only enrol persons, it may also prohibit such enrolment for particular activity systems. Hence, within the British Raj, authenticated identity not only served to enrol a person within the pension system, it also served as an attempt to prohibit unauthenticated persons from access to such pensions. Likewise, most driving licences within the European Union are issued for a limited class of vehicles, meaning that drivers are prohibited from driving outside the classes designated upon their driving licence.

The relationship between personal identity and signs described above makes clear that identity is a process of information (Boland, 1987) and therefore a critical part of many information systems within society. Within acts of communication (Chapter 4), identity is signified by identifiers. Identifiers serve to signify a particular person; they also relate the person to a set of designators making up the identity of the individual. In turn, a personal identity is likely to signify a set of prescriptors determining constraints on the behaviour of some person (Chapter 9).

In a semiotic sense, personal identifiers can hence be seen as symbols relating to the referents of the multiple identities that individuals may experience in the information society. Hence, the issue of personal identification is distinct from and reliant upon the precursor process of authentication as described above. In turn, identification is a necessary pre-condition for enrolment in many activities in contemporary life.

This helps explain why identifiers are ubiquitous in the information society. The identifier is a symbol or set of symbols that can be used to authenticate a thing such as a product, a place or in our case a person. Authentication in terms of personal identity involves validating the association between the identifier and the person. For example, possession of a valid passport is taken as an authentication token in travel situations between countries. However, it is also used as a form of strong authentication in many other personal transactions in modern life. Fingerprints, as we have seen, were developed as a means of adding a strong identifier to criminal records within the British Raj.

Identification is the process of using an identifier to connect to a stream of data (designators) constituting a person's identity. Personal identifiers are hence used to assign identities to individuals — e.g. legitimating somebody as a legal resident, credit-worthy customer or taxpayer or classifying somebody as a criminal. In earlier societies, identification though a limited range of natural identifiers was probably sufficient in support of the activities of individuals. With the rise of the state and the complex activities needed to support such forms of human organisation, as well as an increase in levels of remote communication, we would expect to see an increase in the number and forms of identifier used, perhaps to a stage in which a different identifier is required for each activity system within which the individuals participates. The attempt to build 'systems' to resolve problems of personal identity forms part of the reaction to this control crisis for such societies.

The Web of Personal Identity

Therefore, one of the key sources of problematisation in modern society is the complexity of the 'syntax' of identity. The syntax of identity is concerned not only with the complex web of possible identifiers, but also with the complex relations between identifiers and designators (attributes and transactions). Individuals within Information Societies utilise a complex web of identity for existence and action. Hence, a given individual is likely to be identified in a host of different ways by a wide variety of identifiers: credit card numbers, debit card numbers, driving licence numbers, passport numbers, library card numbers, national identity card numbers and so on. We must also distinguish between an identifier and its representation as a physical token. Hence, for instance, it is important to distinguish between a driving licence number and the physical token of a driving licence or a passport number and the physical token of a passport.

Each identifier can be used to determine an aggregation of other signs associated with a person and stored typically as two types of data-items within data structures: attributes and transactions. Attributes designate relatively persistent properties assigned to the individual. For instance, knowing a person through some identifier may allow one to determine the person's age, gender, home address, home telephone number and so on. The process of identification hence involves associating an identifier with an aggregation of data attributes held about the individual in institutional data systems (see below). Such data systems may store not only personal attributes (age, gender, ethnicity), but also possessions (phone, home) and behaviour (language, sexuality). Data systems are also likely to record events in which the individual has participated (e.g. purchases, enquiries, registrations, payments). Such events are enacted as transactions (patterns of acts of articulation) (see Chapter 10) within data systems. This is really a reflection of the increasing complexity of activity experienced during industrialisation and subsequently into the modern world, which has led to a control crisis in the management of personal identity.

So, to summarise, to perform their roles in numerous situations, people have to enrol within numerous activity systems. To do this, they normally have to apply to become a validated identity to such activity systems. This typically involves creating some data structure such as an application 'form'. In doing so, the actor engages in what we shall refer to in Chapter 4 as a communicative act, which expresses a wish to engage in the behaviours of the activity system, such as accessing services. Organisations will typically validate details recorded about the individual by reading personal data structures held on other data systems. Such data sources will either assert or reject the validity of a person's identity. Decisions will be made on the basis of the validity of a person's identity as to whether or not to enrol the person into a particular activity system. Assuming so, a personal data structure with an associated personal identifier may be created to represent such enrolment in the activity system. This commits the organisation to providing participation and declares such entitlement to the individual.

The identifier supplied to the person will then normally be required in all future interactions between the person and the activity system. The person will need to provide the identifier in any interaction as an assertion of her rights to entry, which will be read by systems of the organisation. This will serve not only to authenticate the individual to the system but also to pull down other designative attributes of the individual held in her personal record. Once identification is achieved, the person is able to utilise the services provided by the activity system. Accessing such services may cause changes to be made to data structures held about the individual, such as the storage of further transactional data.

Forms of Personal Identifier

As indicated in the previous section, personal identity is signalled through various symbols. A number of forms of identifier are available for authenticating a person and associating further data with such a person. These forms include appearance, social behaviour, names, codes, knowledge, tokens, biodynamics and natural physiography (Clarke, 1987).

Within face-to-face communication, facets within the sensory modalities of sight and hearing are normally used to code identifiers as symbols. Hence, appearance, names, social behaviour and aspects of knowledge are typically regarded as 'natural' identifiers. Appearance concerns how a person looks, including features such as gender, skin colour, hair colour, colour of eyes, facial hair or distinguishable markings such as a birthmark. Names concern what the person is called by other people, including forename(s), surname, maiden names, nicknames and also-known-as names. Social behaviour concerns how the person interacts with others, including style of speech and accent. What a person knows in relation to some activity system might also be used as an identifier.

As we have mentioned previously, such natural identifiers are deficient in producing the characteristic of uniqueness demanded by organisations and their data systems. For this reason, surrogate identifiers, such as fingerprints from the Raj case, were invented as mechanisms for use in remote identity management. Surrogate identifiers constitute additional features such as codes and tokens as well as technologies that 'measure' and record aspects of the individual such as biodynamics and aspects of physiography used to uniquely identify individuals. Codes are what the person is referred to within a particular activity system such as a series of numbers or letters which can be human-readable, machine-readable or both. Tokens constitute what the person has in his or her possession, such as a birth or marriage certificate, passport, drivers' licence and credit card. Biodynamics are what the person does, such as the way in which someone's signature is written, statistically analysed voice characteristics, keystroke dynamics in relation to login-id and password. Natural Physiography amounts to what the person is in terms of features such as skull measurements, teeth and skeletal injuries, thumbprint, fingerprint sets and handprints, retinal scans, earlobe capillary patterns, hand geometry and DNA patterns. If such characteristics are readable by machine, then they are referred to as biometric identifiers.

From the database design literature, we can glean a number of characteristics of good surrogate identifiers used by a data system in support of a given activity system. First, every relevant person for the activity system in question should have an identifier (universality of coverage). Second, each relevant person should have only one identifier and no two people should have the same identifier (uniqueness). Third, the identifier should not change, nor be changeable, without authority (permanence). This implies that the identifier should be non-mnemonic since if any meaningful association is built into an identifier, such an association may change over time. Fourth, the identifier should be available for use at all times within the activity system (indispensability). Fifth, no other form of identification should be necessary or used for the activity system in question (exclusivity).

Biometrics

As we have seen from our examination of the historical record, biometric identifiers such as fingerprints became important because of the way in which they satisfy many of the properties of a good institutional identifier for persons. A biometric is typically defined as a measurable physiological and/or behavioural trait that can be captured and subsequently compared with another instance at the time of verification. Therefore, this definition conflates the issues of natural physiography with that of biodynamics. Biometrics includes fingerprints, iris scans, retina scans, hand geometry, face recognition, voice recognition, signature recognition and keystroke patterns. Biometric identifiers are therefore somewhat ambivalent in terms of the distinction between natural and surrogate identifiers. On the one hand, they can be seen as natural identifiers in the sense that they are based upon the physical characteristics of the person. On the other hand, they can be seen as surrogate identifiers in the sense that they rely upon the creation of electronic profiles captured and processed by technologies.

A biometric is typically defined as a measurable physiological and/or behavioural trait that can be captured and subsequently compared with another instance at the time of. The key to the power of biometrics as an identity technology is the amount of randomness and complexity that the biometric contains. In terms of three forms of biometric identification, iris scanning offers the strongest form of authentication, followed by fingerprints and facial recognition. This is because different degrees of freedom (independent dimensions of variation) are associated with different aspects of physiography. Irises have about 249 degrees-of-freedom, fingerprints have approximately 35 degrees-of-freedom whereas faces have only about 20 degrees-of-freedom.

A biometric can be used in both processes of authentication and identification. In such processes biometric technology is typically employed in a number of distinct phases. In sampling, a device is used to capture a number of samples of the biometric for an individual. An 'average' of the measurements taken is then used to produce a digital template or profile for the individual. In a storage phase, this digital template is typically encrypted and stored either on some local token such as a smartcard or held remotely in a database system. In a recognition phase, a biometric reader is then typically attached to an access device associated with some remote delivery channel. To use the device to access the channel, a match must be made between the measurements produced by the reader and the previously stored template. This is at its core a process of authentication. When such biometric data is also used to match with other identifier and attribute data held on the individual, it impinges on the process of identification.

Biometrics, particularly used in combination, are normally seen to be a secure and convenient method of building identifiers that satisfy many of the characteristics of good identification systems such as uniqueness. However, biometric systems are not foolproof since they can make two major types of errors amongst others. False matches or false positives involve inferring that biometric measurements taken from two or more different persons are associated with one person. False rejections or false negatives involve inferring that biometric measurements taken from the same person are associated with two or more different persons.

Conclusion

Wheeler (1969a) states that 'An important function of the record is to 'act as a social control ... the existence of a record itself serves as a social constraint: persons are generally motivated to develop a 'good' and not a 'bad' one ... a powerful form of social control may be wielded by those who have it within their discretion to make an event 'a matter of record.' This is particularly true of the criminal record. Such records not only serve as a memory of activity regarded as deviant by society, they serve to declare the person identified and described as a criminal and in doing so are important to mechanisms of social control within society.

Within the case of the British Raj considered in this chapter, data structures constitute the substance or representation of signs used within this enacted environment and includes not only the paper and written English which comprised the criminal record, but also records of anthropometry such as fingerprints. Such data structures were used for the communication of identity, particularly the use of a fingerprint as a form of strong identifier for individuals and its association with other designators held about the person. These signs were used in coordinated action such as the use of criminal records for the identification of repeat criminals and the subsequent enrolment of such individuals in the criminal justice system of the British Raj.

The patterning of order amongst actors in situations such as that described in this case is enacted through three interrelated forms of action familiar from our model of information situations (see Chapter 1). Acts of articulation involve the forming of data in some substance. The classic example here is the creation of a criminal record. Acts of communication involving message-making and interpretation. In terms of the case considered, such acts include decisions as to the categorisation (Rosch, 1973) of the identity of particular individuals as criminals and the communication of this identity to other actors within the criminal justice system. Acts of communication support the performance of coordinated action amongst a group of actors. The identification of repeat criminals was critical to the 'performance' of criminal justice during the British Raj, supporting the arrest, trial and incarceration of individuals.

We have established in this and previous chapters that data structures are informative in the sense that they serve to identify and describe things of interest to institutions, such as persons. In Chapter 4, we demonstrate how data structures are also performative — they serve to get things done. To do this we show how identifiers play a key part in a common but very important data structure — that of the list.

References

Bateson, G. (1972). *Steps to an Ecology of Mind* (New York: Ballantine Books).

Beynon-Davies, P. (2007). 'Personal Identity Management and Electronic Government: The Case of the National Identity Card in the UK.' *Journal of Enterprise Information Management*, **20**(3): 244–270.

Beynon-Davies, P. (2011). 'The UK National Identity Card.' *Journal of Information Technology (Teaching Cases)*, **1**(1): 12–21.

Boland, R. J. (1987). The Information of Information Systems. In *Critical Issues in Information Systems Research*, R. J. Boland and R. A. Hirschheim (eds.) (New York: John Wiley), pp. 21–40.

Brachman, R. J. (1983). 'What ISA is and is'nt: An Analysis of Taxonomic Links in Semantic Networks.' *Computer*, **16**(10): 30–36.

Clarke, R. (1987). 'Just Another Piece of Plastic In Your Wallet: The 'Australian Card' Scheme.' *Computers and Society*, **18**(1): 7–21.

Clarke, R. (1994). 'Human Identification in Information Systems: Management Challenges and Public Policy Issues.' *Information Technology and People*, **7**(4): 6–37.

Cole, S. A. (2001). *Suspect Identities: A History of Fingerprinting and Criminal Identification* (Cambridge, MA: Harvard University Press).

Latour, B. (2005). *Reassembling the Social: An Introduction to Actor-Network-Theory* (Oxford: Oxford University Press).

The Economist (2010). 'All too Much.' 394: 5.

The Economist (2011). 'Costing the Count.' 399: 81.

Forsyth, F. (2011). *The Day of the Jackal* (London: Arrow).

Hoopes, J. (ed.) (1991). *Peirce on Signs: Writings on Semiotic by Charles Sanders Peirce* (London: University of North Carolina Press).

Peirce, C. S. (1931). *Collected Papers* (Cambridge, MA: Harvard University Press).

Russell, B. (1959). *Wisdom of the West: A Historical Survey of Western Philosophy in its Social and Political Setting* (Oxford: Bloomsbury).

Rosch, E. H. (1973). 'Natural Categories.' *Cognitive Psychology*, **4**(3): 328–350.

Searle, J. R. (2005). 'What is an Institution?' *Journal of Institutional Economics*, **1**(1): 1–22.

Wheeler, S. (ed.) (1969a). *On Record: Files and Dossiers in American Life* (New York: Russell Sage Foundation).

Wheeler, S. (1969b). Problems and issues in record-keeping. In *On Record: Files and Dossiers in American Life*, S. Wheeler (ed.) (New York: Russell Sage Foundation), pp. 3–24.

Chapter 4

Making Lists: The Performativity of the Record

Introduction

You, the reader will have probably heard of a series of data structures made famous by the film *Schindler's List,* based upon the original book *Schindler's Ark* by Thomas Keneally (1983). The director Steven Spielberg implicitly signals in his title for the film that actor held to be important as the creator of these data structures, Oskar Schindler. In fact, Schindler, the key character in the film, appears to have had little to do with the actual production of nine such lists which were used to assign Jews from the Warsaw ghetto to work in his factory. Thomas Keneally, in contrast, in the title of his book, focuses upon the performative outcome of the data structure. The analogy is made here between Noah saving endangered animals from the flood through the building of his ark and Schindler saving endangered individuals through the update of certain data structures with certain data elements. The crucial point is, of course, that these lists were *performative* in the sense that, if a person was identified on a particular list, their work in Schindler's factory enabled them to escape the death camps.

This chapter focusses upon what we referred to as the coordination domain within our model of information situations (Figure 4.1). Within previous chapters we have established that data structures are forms of structure (see Chapter 2) created by certain actors which serve to inform (see Chapter 3) other actors. In the current chapter, we describe how data

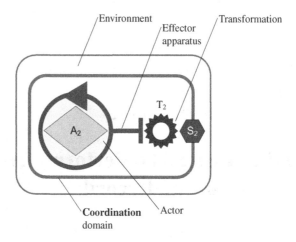

Figure 4.1:   The domain of coordination.

structures also perform — they get things done. To help us establish the way in which data structures are performative, we focus upon one type of data structure used in almost all institutional settings — that of the list.

The list is one of the simplest, most utilised but typically underestimated of data structures. We first consider what the list is as a data structure — how it is a structure and what it is typically used to inform actors of. We then deconstruct the notion of a list and show how lists are performative in the sense that the presence of a list-item upon a list determines what happens to people and things. We use a number of examples of list-making to do this, including the case of the Nazis' malignant use of list-making technologies to operate the Holocaust — the mass extermination of the Jews in the Greater Germanic Reich. However, such examples of list-making are not a thing of the past. We use our analysis to cast light upon important processes of shortlisting, blacklisting, whitelisting and watchlisting in modern society.

We then take the enterprise further and show how data structures such as the list are crucial 'scaffolding' for the contemporary social order. To do this, we need to explain the role that data structures play as communicative acts. Data structures can be used to assert, direct, commit, declare or express something and, through communication of such intentions, afford institutional action. This leads to the inevitable conclusion that all persistent data structures, such as lists, have agency — they act in limited but important ways to help construct and reconstruct institutional order.

We end the chapter with a look at who owns data, particularly data held about persons. This has proven important in that personal data is frequently now used in ways in which the data subject (the person to which the data refers or describes) may be unhappy with. Some have argued that a data subject should have the right to request the act of forgetting something from the collective memory held about them by certain institutions. This helps unpack the notion of a *data right* which underlies several issues which we explore in further chapters.

An Infinity of Lists

Goody (1977) provides a review of a number of uses made of lists by ancient cultures. He sees the list as a particularly important artefact because of its central role within the 'domestication of the savage mind'. This refers to the transition between ways of thinking characteristic of primitive societies to those ways of thinking characteristic of societies in the modern age. In a similar vein, Eco (2009) believes that societies make lists as part of their attempt to impose order or control on the world. He argues as such, that society is reflected in an infinity of lists. This idea has some pedigree. Schmandt-Besserat (1978), as we have seen Chapter 1, has proposed that clay tokens dating back to 8,000 BCE are some of the earliest examples of lists of commodities used amongst the first city-states. Ezzamel (2009) has argued that the construction and dissemination of lists were performative rituals critical to the maintenance of the ideological order of ancient Egypt. As described in Chapter 2, Urton (2003) has argued for the place of assemblages of knotted strings, known as *khipu*, as unique artefacts for the making of lists amongst the Inka. Rosenberg and Grafton (2010) consider the history of the timeline, a particularly interesting type of list.

More recently, Lyon (1994) has pointed to the dangers of what he refers to as social sorting — the way in which contemporary institutions make life-critical decisions about individuals on the basis of inclusion or exclusion of personal identifiers on particular lists. He argues that such lists are explicitly devices which serve to sort those persons regarded as 'eligible members' of a particular institutional area and to exclude others, regarded as in some way 'undesirable' (Lyon, 2004). Gawande (2010) takes a more positive outlook on the list, arguing for the importance of checklists as key aids in the control or coordination of behaviour in critical areas of contemporary life such as engineering and surgery.

Within this chapter, we want to argue that lists not only have history, but also they make history. Lists are also debated and discussed not only in the academic media, but also in the entertainment media. For instance, there are a number of infamous lists described in Black's (2002) study of the malignant institutional order which constituted the 'holocaust'. He particularly focusses on the way in which this order relied upon the various ways in which the Nazis used electronic tabulators to produce and manipulate lists of persons to be transported to the death camps. In another list made famous by the film directed by Steven Spielberg, nine important lists were used to assign Jews from the Warsaw ghetto to work in the factories of Oskar Schindler (Keneally, 1982). These lists enabled a small and select group to escape the death camps.

Usher (2014) cogently and eloquently lists some of the key functions that lists play in human society. Many of these functions associated with the list as a data structure will be considered in this chapter.

'1. Life is chaotic — often unbearably so. The ability to divide some of that chaos into lists, to make the onslaught manageable, can bring much-needed relief.
2. Human beings are fearful of the unknown and as such have a real need to label and group things, to assign them to comfortable lists.
3. Lists can make us more productive and eradicate procrastination. Nothing on earth, resignation aside, cuts through the thick fog of a daunting workload as effectively as a to-do list.
4. Everyone is a critic. Ranking things — best to worst, biggest to smallest, fastest to slowest — can be strangely addictive, no doubt because it makes us feel knowledgeable.
5. Time is precious. Distilling huge swathes of monotonous information into easily digestible lists ensures that we have more time to enjoy ourselves and make lists.'

The Idea of Lists

Within Chapter 2, we defined a data structure as a particular way of organising data. In this sense, a data structure is clearly an abstraction — a set of principles for both storing and accessing data. In certain literature, this abstraction is sometimes referred to as an abstract data type. However, data structures such as lists are clearly instantiated (Chapter 7) — given form. In this sense, a specific instance of a list, such as a product list, passenger list or picking list is also a data structure (Kent, 2012). In the concrete, a data structure is used to represent things and through such representation to help constitute institutional order. Within the discussion that follows, we shall utilise the term data structure both to refer to an abstraction and to an instantiation, and we shall try to be clear within the body of the argument when the particular sense of the term applies (Beynon-Davies, 2015).

At its most basic, a list corresponds to a set of elements: an assembly of distinct 'things', considered as a thing in its own right. Most lists used for modern institutional purposes are actually built upon the abstract data type of the ordered set known as a *sequence* or a *tuple*, implying that both the elements of the list and the position of the elements in a list are significant — hence the tuple <1,2,3,4> is different from the tuple <2,4,3,1>.

We mentioned in Chapter 2 that, treated purely as artefact, a data structure can be considered a set of data elements, which in turn consist of a set of data items (Tsitchizris and Lochovsky, 1982). In the discussion which follows, we shall treat the list as a data structure consisting of a set of list-items. Each of these elements will take a similar form which we shall model upon a binary relation (Frost, 1982). A binary relation can be considered a triple of data items, in which the first data item is termed the subject, the second the relation and the third an object. Subjects, relations and objects are unrestricted within the original theory of binary relations (Frost, 1982). However, to start from first principles, we shall use an even simpler representation in which the subject and object of such relations will be restricted to the use of identifiers as discussed in Chapter 3, and the relation itself will be specified as an infix predicate — i.e. a predicate that comes between the subject identifier and the object identifier.

Binary relations are useful because it can be shown that many other forms of data structure can be constructed from these simple, atomic forms (Frost, 1982). For instance, a related set of binary relations can be used to form a tuple. Tuples are an inherent and important construct within Codd's (1970) theory of a relational database. A relation within a relational database is formed from a set of tuples. This particular data structure, of course, underlies the data management systems used within mainstream digital computing systems.

However, there is another reason we choose to focus on the list and identifier. We deliberately utilise the idea of the list and the associated construct of an identifier to help ground the notion of a data structure because, as is evident from the previous section, such artefacts are ubiquitous and as such are typically treated as mundane and accepted. Within the current chapter, we shall use these artefacts as sensebreaking devices — to attempt to break through entrenched and limiting conceptions embedded within the worldview of many disciplines — even the information disciplines. We shall also deliberately use the term list rather than file, table (relation) or record because the term list has some useful connotations in everyday English usage. People inherently connote the creation of lists with doing things. They create shopping lists, picking lists, to-do lists, admissions lists and checklists. But we would argue that files, tables and records, as other forms of data structure, are constitutive of and help constitute institutional order, in much the same way as described for the list and the identifier in this study.

So, lists for us are sets of binary relations. Also, binary relations, at least within the context of this study, consist of a coupling of two identifiers with an infix predicate. Let us look at some examples.

Lists Matter

So, let us consider lists and why they matter. As we have seen in Chapter 3, lists as data structures are collections of signs, or more particularly of identifiers. Suppose we build a list of the following form:

> *[109999555 REFERS TO John Smith]*
> *[105599544 REFERS TO Anwar Prakash]*
> *[103399565 REFERS TO Zu Cheng]*
> ....

This list consists of a series of binary relations. The first data item in each list-item is the subject and, in this case, constitutes a UK passport number, as discussed in Chapter 3. The last data item is a natural identifier for a person — a personal name. Both data items are related or predicated through the REFERS TO relation. This predicate effectively implements what we called identification in Chapter 3. It associates a given surrogate identifier with some natural identifier for the person.

This list can be used in a number of different ways by different institutional actors across different government agencies. Take two instances.

A member of the UK Passports Office can use this list to *declare* British Citizens. In doing so, such actors are inherently using the identifiers in this list to instantiate a class (see Chapter 7), in the following manner:

[109999555 ISA British citizen]
[105599544 ISA British citizen]
[103399565 ISA British citizen]
...

The relation ISA in these list-items serves to classify a particular identified person as a British citizen. Passports and passport identifiers were originally designed to enable the declaration of citizenship and as such to enrol persons into the institutional domain of international travel. However, such tokens and identifiers are now used in many other situations relating not only to government and its agencies, but also in interaction with private sector institutions.

For instance, a member of the UK Borders Agency can use a list-item from the list above to authenticate a person. In other words, a fact from this list *asserts* that the individual is who they say they are. However, passports and passport numbers are used as a form of personal identification in many other settings. For instance, many financial institutions demand the strong authentication provided by a passport when opening a financial product such as a bank account. Passports are frequently used by young people to prove their age. The usefulness of this token and associated identifier is particularly evident in that some 71% of the UK resident population hold a passport, according to the 2011 census. More of censuses later.

Passport numbers are, of course, not the only identifiers important to scaffolding the institution of governance. Other personal identifiers are used in other institutional settings and provide access to the activity systems of these institutions for individuals. For example, the NHSNo is used within the institutional context of the UK National Health Service while a national insurance number (NINo) is used within the institutional context associated with legal employment by UK institutions.

Listing Quality

Let us build a more substantial case to examine why lists matter. Let us demonstrate how identifiers and lists matter to individuals and organisations within the contemporary institutional order of academia using two related contemporary examples.

Within the academic world, traditionally a journal article is identified by a composite of its attributes such as journal name, author(s), date of publication, article title, volume number, issue number and page numbers. This particular combination of data items is often cumbersome to use in searches for articles and is frequently error-prone, typically because of incorrect representation of such details within references. This particular approach to identification of articles is also becoming obsolete as many online-only journals have moved away from the practice of publishing in delineated volumes and issues.

For such reasons an approach to uniquely identifying publications or their parts through a digital object identifier (DOI) has been developed internationally. A DOI is a character string used to uniquely identify a digital object, such as an electronic document. The DOI system is implemented through a federation of registration agencies coordinated by the International DOI Foundation (more about registers and registries in Chapter 7). Organisations such as journal publishers pay to become registrants within the DOI system, which enables them to assign DOIs for their electronic documents (DOI, 2014).

A DOI is divided into a prefix and a suffix, separated by a slash. The prefix identifies the organisation registering the identifier known as the registrant, while the suffix is chosen by the registrant to uniquely identify a specific digital object. For example, within the DOI 10.1000/182, the prefix is 10.1000 and the suffix is 182. In terms of the prefix, 10 refers to the particular DOI registry, while 1000 identifies the particular registrant; in this case the International DOI Foundation itself. The suffix 182 identifies a single digital object — the latest version of the *DOI Handbook* (DOI, 2014).

One key advantage of a DOI is that it can be used to identify a complete journal, an individual article in the journal or a single figure in the particular article. Another key advantage is that within the DOI system a clear separation is made between an identifier for a particular object and its so-called metadata (see Chapter 8), such as the location where the object can be accessed. This means that while the DOI for a document remains 'persistent' for its lifetime, its metadata, such as its location, may change a number of times. DOIs plus their associated metadata are deposited by a registrant in the international DOI registry. The metadata, such as the document's location are updated, whenever this changes.

Now consider lists and why they matter to the institutional order of academia. Within business schools in the UK, academics are encouraged by their deans to treat one particular list with respect. This is the ABS (Association of Business Schools) list of journals and their rankings. This particular list has driven the activity of academics within business schools in the UK for many years.

To understand why lists matter so much here, we need to describe something of the context of this institutional order. Each year funding bodies in the UK allocate billions of pounds sterling of research funding to higher education institutions. As major input into decisions as to where to best allocate such funding, the British government, through its funding agencies, has required all UK higher education institutions to engage in a regular audit of the quality of their research. This audit (known in the past as the research assessment exercise or RAE) has been conducted in approximately a four- to five-year cycle, starting in 1986 (1986, 1992, 1996, 2001, 2007) (Barker, 2007). The latest audit (now known as the Research Evaluation Framework (REF) was conducted in 2013, and one is due at the time of writing.

To help manage the process, a number of performance indicators are requested within each submission and form the basis on which the quality of research is assessed by panels. The key such performance indicator is a listing of the four best quality publications for each academic submitted by a university under a particular unit of assessment. As such, this publication list of DOIs in association with a list of rankings of business journals becomes a key facet serving to define a 'research-active' member of some university department.

In the past, many panel members claim that they assess the quality of a particular submission by either reading each and every paper submitted or reading a majority sample from those submitted (Cooper and Otley, 1998). Many others believe that panel members either formally or informally use lists of journal rankings to establish a convenient proxy for the 'quality' of journal papers. Within the Business and Management unit of assessment, for instance, there is much discussion of the use of one particular rankings list: that published on a regular basis by the ABS.

Therefore, the outcomes of lists and list-making often have important consequences for both institutions and institutional actors. For instance, REF panel members make decisions as to ranking of particular university departments in the UK and, as a consequence, implicitly rank the quality of research of individual academics. On the basis of a list of the rankings assigned to university departments, the UK government, through its funding agencies, decide how much to award each university in terms of research funding. For low-rated departments, this means that they will receive no monies for research and will have to rely on money provided for teaching. For high-rated departments, monies can contribute many tens of thousands of pounds sterling per research-active academic. The proportion of money assigned for both teaching and research to universities is a key determinant of the amount of infrastructure support provided to academics for the conduct of research. For instance, higher-rated university departments are generally more able to provide lower teaching quotas to staff and to support activities such as conference attendance.

Listing the Holocaust

We opened this chapter by mentioning the series of lists made famous following the film by Steven Spielberg, *Schindler's List*, based upon the original non-fiction book *Schindler's Ark* by Thomas Keneally. The crucial point about these lists of course is that the lists were performative in the sense that if a person was identified on a particular list, their work in this factory enabled them to escape the death camps. So, lists have history in the sense that they document happenings, but they also make history in the sense of changing and even saving people's lives.

One of the most important of lists is of course a census. The notion of a census as an accounting of people or things seems to be pretty much universal across human cultures in which states have formed. Indeed, as we have seen in Chapter 1, there seems some suggestion that a listing of things is inherently associated with the rise of the state in the sense that human innovations such as cities, the rise of agriculture and the keeping of records seemed to have emerged in tandem. Censuses, of course, in their basic form are classic examples of a listing of persons.

Hence, there is evidence of the collection of census data in the system of clay tokens studied by Schmandt-Besserat and dating between 8,000 and 3,000 BCE (Beynon-Davies, 2009) (see Chapter 1). However, the first documented census was undertaken by the Babylonians over 5,000 years ago. Records suggest that such a census was undertaken every six or seven years and counted the number of people and livestock, as well as quantities of butter, honey, milk, wool and vegetables.

In Chapter 2, we have seen how among the Inka in the high Andes assemblages of knotted string were significant artefacts

(Beynon-Davies, 2007). At the provincial level, the Inka used *khipu* within annual censuses of the population. Census data included records of births, deaths, marriages and other changes of a person's status. Individuals of each sex were assigned to one of ten categories corresponding not with their chronological age but to their stage in life and ability to perform useful work. Separate *khipu* were apparently kept for this purpose by each province within the Inka empire.

In all these examples, lists as data structures are performative — they are used to get things done. Now consider a much more malignant example of the performativity of lists. Black (2002), documents the way in which tabulating machinery based on an original design by Herman Hollerith were used by the Nazis to compile efficiently and effectively two censuses of the German population in 1933 and 1939. These censuses, which effectively could not have taken place without the use of Hollerith technology, allowed the Nazi regime to produce a listing of Jews and other nominated groups in the population. The express purpose of such lists, of course, was to identify those persons for eventual transmission to the death camps. Tabulating machines were even used in the death camps themselves to produce a listing of the throughput through the gas chambers and ovens and from this to calculate the efficiency of the extermination effort.

Scaffolding the Institutional Order

Thus lists and identifiers clearly matter both to individuals (such as academics) and to institutions (such as UK universities). The very presence of such artefacts directs the actions of numerous different actors acting within the space or frame of numerous different institutions. However, how do these artefacts work? How is it possible to theorise about the significance of lists and identifiers to institutional action?

We start by establishing that lists, just like identifiers considered in the last chapter are both examples of what Searle calls a status function. To remind ourselves, Searle believes that status functions are produced through constitutive rules of the form:

[X counts as Y in C]

where X is some thing which counts as some other thing (Y) in some context (C).

The term *constitutive* within constitutive rule is used in that sense adopted in the work of Anthony Giddens (1984). His constitutive cycle was introduced as a means of addressing the intellectual division between an action perspective on the nature of institutions and a structural perspective on the nature of institutions. Giddens believes that these two perspectives on the nature of an institution can be brought together through the idea of structuration. On the one hand, the structure of social institutions is created by human action. Through human interaction, the social structure of institutions is reproduced but may also change. On the other hand, humans utilise institutional structure as a resource in interpreting their own and other people's action. This means that institutions act as a constraint on human action. This cyclical process of structuration is the process through which the order we consider as institution is constituted and reconstituted.

Take the idea of a DOI as an example of an identifier, which in turn is an example of a status function. As a constitutive rule, the relationship between a DOI and the document it identifies might be expressed as:

[X (a DOI) counts as Y (a specific journal article) in C (the registrants and users of the international DOI registry)]

It is also possible to consider lists as status functions in their own right. In other words, the act of creating a list typically involves naming the list. The naming of the list acts as a form of proxy for the common context declared on the members of the list. For example, we might name a list important to the institution of the business and management panel of REF as the list of journals in the Information Management subject area of the ABS. We might further express the members of this list of significance to this institution and its communicants in the following manner:

[Journal of the American Society for Information Science and Technology (JASIST) MEMBER OF <List of journals in the Information Management subject area of the ABS>]
[Annual review of information science and technology MEMBER OF <List of journals in the Information Management subject area of the ABS>]
...

Within this set of binary relations, the subject of each relation consists of an identifier, while the object of each relation consists of the list.

The relation MEMBER OF consists of a membership predicate which serves to form a list of identifiers. However, inclusion in a list also implies an order or ranking within the list. Hence, each subject area within the overall ABS 2010 list is ordered in terms of the 'star' rating associated with journals (from 4 indicating the highest ranked through to 1, the lowest ranked).

This means that particular institutional actors within the UK academy use the formation of the ABS list to constitute or 'declare' the notion of the overall 'quality' of a particular journal. The ranking or ordering of a particular journal within the ABS list serves to 'direct' the formation of further lists by other institutional actors such as the list of publications submitted for the Information Management area by university X to a nominated REF. By implication, the assignment of a particular DOI to this latter list served to declare or constitute the 'quality' of the article referred to. By further implication, the inclusion of four DOIs within this list also served to constitute the declared 'quality' of particular academics working within UK higher education bodies.

Speech Acts

John Searle is first known for his theorisation of so-called speech act theory, which he developed from the earlier work of the British philosopher John Austin. The major claim of speech act theory is that much communication of interest to institutions is accomplished through what Searle, following Austin, refers to as speech acts. Within the previous section, various list-items operate as speech acts. According to Searle, individual speech acts such as this can be viewed from at least three different viewpoints: as a locutionary act, an illocutionary act or as a perlocutionary act. As we shall see, this bears a distinct relationship to our three domains of action highlighted in our model of information situations (see Chapter 1) which we referred to as articulation, communication and coordination.

A locutionary act defines the content of a speech act and is divided further into an utterance act and a propositional act. An utterance act corresponds to the act of physically creating some form from a particular substance. In contrast, a propositional act consists of the act of using such form to refer to or predicate some things. For instance, we may speak the words 'JASIST is a 3-ranked journal on the ABS 2010 list'. As an utterance, this would be considered purely in terms of a number of forms — phonemes formed in the substance of air. As a proposition, such forms would be treated as a series of terms which identify or predicate some things of interest. Hence, JASIST is a term (an identifier) we use to refer to a particular journal.

However, speech acts not only have content, but also have intent. Locutionary acts, as we have seen, can be decomposed as propositional acts and utterance acts, but speech acts are also illocutionary acts. Each speech act not only expresses the proposition being communicated, it also expresses the attitude or 'force' of that being communicated. This is because illocutionary acts are focussed on getting the receiver of the message to do something, to take further action. Indeed, we typically recognise that the intent of some communication has been achieved by observing the actions of the receiver of some communication and seeing whether certain conditions set by the attitude, force or intent of the communication are satisfied. The result here is what is meant by a perlocutionary act.

To summarise, the main idea is that engaging in some communication, such as uttering a sentence, is the performance of an act. Speech acts are acts of communication in which actors create and send messages in an appropriate context with certain intentions, normally to influence the action of the receiver of the message. Although these acts of communication are referred to as speech acts, such acts are not restricted to the use of spoken language and would also be taken to cover written texts and the use of other signs such as gestures, flags, and yes even records. Therefore, to avoid confusion, I prefer to use the more encompassing term *communicative act* from this point forward.

Searle (1970) further maintains that it is possible to formulate five key types of communicative act in terms of differences in the intentions that the actor communicating has, and which he labels as assertives, directives, commissives, expressives and declaratives. These types of communicative act can be distinguished in terms of illocutionary force or propositional attitude (the kind of attitude a speaker has when she says something) and the direction of fit between the world and the propositional content of the communicative act (the word).

For example, in terms of illocutionary force, assertives are communicative acts that explain how things are in the world, such as: 'Our orders have fallen by 10% this month'. In contrast, directives are communicative acts that represent the senders' attempt to get a receiver to perform an action, such as: 'Please ensure that our production target is met next quarter'. Declaratives are communicative acts that aim to change the world through the communication itself, such as: 'This order has been fulfilled'.

The term direction of fit was used by Austin (1962) to refer originally to the relationship between mental states (perhaps rather confusingly called *the word*) and reality (or what philosophers refer to as *the world*). In the work of Searle (1970), the word is expanded to denote the notion of an 'utterance' discussed earlier. Three directions of fit are proposed between an utterance (word) and the world: word-to-world (intended to describe the world), world-to-word (intended to change the world) and null (making some utterance implies that some fitting to the world has already taken place). Each type of illocutionary act, as we shall see in the next section, has a different direction of fit.

The Performativity of Lists

The language-action tradition, approach, viewpoint or perspective has been around for over 30 years, if we take the publication of a paper by Flores and Ludlow (1980) as its starting point. Generally, the term is used to refer to the adoption or translation of a series of ideas from the philosophy of language, particularly the work of Austin, some of the early work of Searle and possibly some of the work of the German philosopher Jurgen Habermas, into the information disciplines (Goldkuhl and Lyytinen, 1982).

The language/action tradition is so called because of its focus upon communicative action and the use of such communicative action by actors to do things. It takes something of an intellectual leap in treating a data structure, such as a list-item, as an act of communication — as a speech act. More precisely, the data structure itself corresponds to an utterance act (Searle, 1970). However, each utterance within a list also corresponds to a propositional act because the status functions comprising the utterance are used to refer to things or to describe things.

However, lists, as we have seen, are not only locutionary acts, they are also illocutionary acts — they not only communicate content, but also communicate intent. Take an example modified from that given by Searle (1983). Assume that a retail manager gives her procurement operative a list of products needed to replenish a particular store. Further assume that these products are referred to by the identifiers P1, P2, P3.... (Searle, 1983). Hence, we might represent this list as follows:

> *[P1 MEMBER OF <Procurement list for store 1>]*
> *[P2 MEMBER OF <Procurement list for store 1>]*
> *...*

Now for the procurement operative each item in her list is an illocutionary act. It directs her to purchase the item referred to by the identifier. The entire list also acts as a directive to the operative. It probably establishes the action-context for the list — to procure items for store 1.

Now consider the same list used by another actor. Assume that the retail manager also employs an external consultant to audit procurement. He is therefore given access to the same procurement list as the procurement operative. The consequence of this is that the audit consultant uses the same procurement list in a different way from the procurement operative. He probably interprets each list-item not as a directive but as an assertive.

We can understand these differences more clearly by considering the direction of fit of these two lists. The procurement operative takes the list to the market and makes purchases to match items on the list. Hence, the list functions as an order or desire and has a world-to-word (list) direction of fit. It is the responsibility of the procurement operative to make the world, in terms of his purchases, match the items on the list (the word).

Suppose the man's activity is tracked by the audit consultant. The consultant writes down everything the operative orders. When both the consultant and the procurement operative return to report to the manager, they have identical lists. However, the function or direction of fit of the two lists is different. In contrast to the operative's world-to-word direction of fit, the consultant's list has a word-to-world direction of fit.

The differences between these two functions become apparent when we examine what happens when an error is made — when a breakdown occurs in the use of lists (we shall look at such breakdowns in more detail in Chapter 6). Suppose the operative fails to procure product P1, but instead procures a different product with the identifier P1.1. In terms of the consultant's list the error is easily corrected. He crosses out the identifier P1 and substitutes the identifier P1.1. However, in the case of the procurement operative, the situation is not so easily corrected. Correcting his list does not change the state of the world.

To reiterate, the consultant's list comprises a set of assertives, which have a word-to-world direction of fit. It is the function of the consultant's list to match reality — it functions as a list of assertions of what happened. In contrast, the procurement operative's list comprises a set of directives, which have a world-to-word direction of fit. It is the responsibility of the procurement operative to make the world match the items on the list (the word).

Within this example of procurement as an institutional process, we have a clear linkage between a list of identifiers, its use for communication and the instrumental actions effected by such communication. However, there is a mysterious thing going on here. In a classic speech situation, the retail manager would be issuing a series of spoken instructions to the procurement operative — 'buy P1, buy P2, …', but in the example described, the list is actually communicating. The logical consequence of this is that it makes sense to think of lists of identifiers as engaging in limited action — as displaying what Cooren (2004) calls 'textual agency'.

Textual Agency

Agency is typically defined as the ability to perform actions that have outcomes (Rose *et al.*, 2005). Agency is imbued to agents or actors, and an agent or actor is seen as anything that can produce an effect or a change in something; what we referred to as a transformation of the world in our model of information situations (see Chapter 1). Clearly much action within contemporary institutions is not enacted by humans but by machines, particularly by IT systems. This means that the concept of agency is particularly problematic for any attempt at explanation which attempts to deal with the relationship between technology and institution. In social determinist accounts, only humans have agency. In technological determinist accounts, technology has agency in the sense that technology influences institutional activity.

Cooren (2004) and others attempt to develop a middle ground where technology or what we referred to as techne in Chapter 1, such as data structures, serve not only to influence, but also to constitute institutional activity. He makes the key argument that 'texts' such as reports, contracts, memos or work orders can be said to be performing action that have outcomes in the sense of producing effects upon the actions of other actors.

In short, texts on their own appear to make a difference to institutions and as such should be considered as having a limited form of agency. To demonstrate this, he provides a number of thought experiments. For instance, imagine a visual sign placed in the reception area of an organisation building. This sign acts in the sense of directing people to do certain things such as swiping their entry pass at the entry gate or visiting reception to authorise their entry. As such, the sign stands in place of particular actions typically undertaken by security personnel responsible for controlling organisational entry. The sign acts to instruct people without the need for security personnel to reiterate the same thing time and again in acts of verbal communication.

The key argument we make here is that we should adopt the stance of considering artefacts such as data structures as displaying the potential to take limited action within the production and reproduction of institutional action. We do not need to conduct thought experiments such as Cooren's to demonstrate the validity of this way of thinking. The power of data structures to act and the importance of designing data structures with such agency in mind is evident in an example cited quite a while ago by the American anthropologist Benjamin Lee Whorf. Whorf came to linguistics from a background as a fire insurance inspector. What first attracted him to issues of language was the way in which workmen he inspected acted in relation to petrol drums, or more precisely to the labels placed upon these drums. Normally, workmen were extremely careful with drums labelled as being *full* of petrol. However, they tended to take a very casual attitude towards petrol drums labelled as being *empty*. In actuality, empty petrol drums are far more dangerous than full drums of petrol. Empty petrol drums are a natural fire hazard because petrol vapours, which remain in the drum for some time after they have been emptied, are extremely flammable. Whorf therefore concluded that there was something about the labels placed upon these drums and what these labels communicated — the concept of *empty* — that was triggering what might be conceived as dangerous behaviour amongst workmen. If the labels had been changed to indicate something like the concept of *danger*, then more appropriate handling of drums might be expected.

In thinking of data structures having agency, it becomes possible to consider lists of identifiers as particularly potent actors in the constitution of institutional order. List-items serve to stand in place of the assertions, commitments, directions or declarations of particular human actors in multiple situations where such actors are not co-present. This idea is indicative of 'the communication as constitutive of organisation' view-point — the idea that 'communication generates, not merely expresses, key organizational realities' (Ashcraft *et al.*, 2009). To demonstrate this further, consider the way in which institutions shortlist, blacklist, whitelist and watchlist people.

Shortlisting, Blacklisting, Whitelisting and Watchlisting

The performativity of lists is evident in a number of English terms — blacklisting, shortlisting, whitelisting and even watchlisting. These terms all refer to commonplace activities driven by the data structure of the list. When shortlisting a group of people for an interview or for a prize, the data structure, the *shortlist* serves to initiate action such as calling someone to interview. The term *blacklist* originated with a list created by King Charles II. The original blacklist consisted of the names of some 58 judges that had sentenced his father, Charles I, to death. When Charles was restored to the throne in 1660, 13 of these judges were put to death, 25 were sentenced to life imprisonment and the remainder escaped punishment. In more contemporary settings, blacklists may be used as data structures shared between financial institutions to prevent persons who have reneged on their debts from obtaining credit. Interestingly, the *whitelist* has been used particularly by trades unions to refer to people held by the union to be suitable for employment within their protected trade. Finally, a *watchlist* is a list of persons or things that some institution deems should be watched for possible action in the future. It has come to the fore in recent times in relation to the way in which law enforcement agencies generate lists of known criminals and terrorist suspects for use in surveillance operations, some of which use technologies such CCTV and facial recognition (see Chapter 12).

Let us look more closely at what is going on with the data structure in circumstances of shortlisting, blacklisting, whitelisting and watchlisting. A blacklist is a listing of identifiers of things, typically persons but possibly objects such as products, which are to be shunned or banned by actors using the blacklist. A whitelist is a listing of identifiers of things that are known, trusted and explicitly permitted to do certain things by actors using the whitelist. A shortlist is effectively a subset of a whitelist, used by actors to identify things that should be interacted with. Finally, a watchlist could be a list of financial securities deemed important to monitor by an investment company or a list of named humans used to direct the activities of law enforcement actors.

A whitelist, shortlist and watchlist is clearly a data structure which prescribes what should happen to those persons or things identified on the list. A blacklist, in contrast, proscribes persons or things identified on the list from certain happenings. Hence, the list of four best publications associated with a particular academic is a shortlist which should be submitted to the research evaluation framework. The list of Jews compiled by Oskar Schindler is also a shortlist of persons selected and trusted to work in his factory. In the US, Japanese Americans were singled out for internment during World War II by shortlisting from the US census data — a practice which in normal times would have been considered illegal. Lyon's (1994) concept of social sorting, which we referred to earlier, is mainly an example of blacklisting — the way in which contemporary institutions make life-critical decisions about individuals on the basis of inclusion or exclusion of personal identifiers on particular lists. Such lists are explicitly devices which serve to sort those persons regarded as members of a particular institutional area and to exclude others, regarded as in some way 'undesirable' (Lyon, 2004).

What is effectively happening here is that actors are not only devolving performance to data structures, they are also imbuing these artefacts with certain powers to make things happen. We return to this issue of data structures and the power with which they are imbued in Chapter 7.

The Ownership of Data

Thus data structures are not only informative, but also performative — they get things done. This idea helps to set a number of issues, which are much discussed in relation to data, in their proper context: data ownership, data control, data privacy, data protection and data security, to name but a few. All these issues, as we shall see, are necessarily interlinked and relate to rights of articulation with regard to data structures. Such rights we refer to as *data rights*. In the current chapter, we consider the issue of data ownership. In further chapters, we shall consider data privacy, data protection, data control and data security.

Can you really own data in the same way that you can own an automobile or a house or an apple? The classic answer to this question is no.

Data are something entirely different from conventional goods because they are replicable — they can be easily copied. This has key consequences for the exchange of goods described as being non-rivalrous. Non-rivalrous goods are goods that when consumed do not affect the supply of such goods. Automobiles, houses and apples are rivalrous. When you purchase an automobile, house or apple, the good transfers from the seller to the purchaser and the supply of automobiles, houses and apples is decreased by one. However, when you exchange data the purchaser gets a copy of the data but the data itself still remains in the hands of the seller. Also, the supply of data as such remains unchanged.

For such reasons, within many legal jurisdictions, such as that in UK common and civil law, there is no legal basis for the notion of data ownership. However, it is noteworthy that concerns over data ownership seem to vary depending on what things the data identifies or describes. There seems an enormous gap in concerns raised about the ownership of personal data as compared to non-personal data. People feel they should have certain rights in relation to data held about them but appear far more relaxed in relation to data created about other things such as property or automobiles.

Within the literature, however, issues such as data ownership are made unnecessarily confusing because of the way in which data is discussed in the abstract rather than in relation to the concrete notion of a data structure. A data structure is clearly a physical representation of data which identifies and describes some thing. It may just exist as a stream of bits resident upon some electromagnetic media, but it still exists physically — it is a material object. Somebody has to articulate this data structure and policies must be developed for access to it and for its transfer or sharing.

This is why modern data management is so important. Data management is a function within some organisation concerned with the management of data structures throughout their life. Such management will involve:

- Data control — establishing policies and procedures concerning who is able to articulate the data structure throughout its lifecycle.
- Data protection — ensuring that adequate protections are in place to ensure that data is used only for declared purposes.
- Data security — ensuring that data cannot be articulated by unauthorised actors.

- Data retention and disposal — maintaining clear policies for the deletion or retention of data structures after their useful life has to come an end, including the archiving of data.

We shall consider each of these important topics in further chapters.

Conclusion

Within this and the preceding chapter, we have attempted to conduct an exercise in sensebreaking by considering the ontological basis of data structures through a close examination of two apparently mundane but related symbolic artefacts — that of the identifier and list. Considered as a data structure, a list consists of a set of list-items, each of which can be considered a binary relation. We also restricted our consideration of binary relations to those containing identifiers, predicated in some way. Identifiers are terms that refer to some instance of a thing across many different information situations. Because of the function they serve, identifiers are particularly important data items within larger data structures utilised by all institutions.

Although not specifically proposed as such within speech act theory, the language/action tradition considers data structures, data elements or data items (such as lists, list-items and identifiers) as speech or more broadly as communicative acts. This means that we can analytically decompose any data structure into a locutionary, illocutionary and perlocutionary act. As a locutionary act, a binary relation can be further considered as both an utterance act and a propositional act. As an utterance, a data structure is some form created from some substance. As a propositional act, the data structure is considered as a set of 'forms' which refer to or predicate some things.

However, data structures as communicative acts are also illocutionary acts. Each data structure not only expresses the proposition being communicated, it also expresses the attitude, 'force' or intent of that being communicated. This is because illocutionary acts are focussed on getting the receiver of the message contained in a data structure to take further action. We recognise that the intent of the data structure as communication has been achieved by observing its perlocutionary effect. In other words, data structures are not only material forms, they serve to inform, which in turn cause people to perform.

Gawande (2010), for instance, argues for the central place of the checklist in improving systems of healthcare. A checklist, like the procurement list we mentioned within the body of the chapter, can be treated merely as a set of descriptions. Each description on Gawande's checklists has a specific intent — they direct multi-disciplinary healthcare teams to do certain things in specific sequences. The end-result, if such lists are successful, is that appropriate procedure is followed in terms of medical intervention. Appropriate medical procedure is likely to contribute, in turn, to successful medical outcomes.

Thus a data structure is a form of substance that serves to inform and perform. In Chapter 5, we look at the role data structures play in performance — in resolving problems of coordination. In Chapter 6, we take the crucial next step in our exploration of data structures and start explaining how data structures help construct and reconstruct institutional order. This is accomplished through the role that data structures play in the generation of institutional facts — a process we refer to as the scaffolding of data structures.

References

Ashcraft, K. L., T. R. Kuhn and F. Cooren (2009). "Constitutional Amendments: "Materializing" Organizational Communication." *The Academy of Management Annals*, 3(1): 1–64.

Austin, J. H. and C. Y. David (2002). "Biometric Authentication: Assuring Access to Information." *Information Management and Computer Security*, 10(1): 12–19.

Austin, J. L. (1962). *How to do Things with Words* (Oxford: Oxford university Press).

Barker, K. (2007). "The UK Research Assessment Exercise: The Evolution of a National Research Evaluation System." *Research Evaluation*, 16(1): 3–12.

Beynon-Davies, P. (2007). "Informatics and the Inca." *International Journal of Information Management*, 27(5): 306–318.

Beynon-Davies, P. (2009). "Neolithic Informatics: The Nature of Information." *International Journal of Information Management*, 29(1): 3–14.

Beynon-Davies, P. (2015). "Forming Institutional Order: The Scaffolding of Lists and Identifiers." *Journal of the Association for Information Science and Technology*. DOI: 10.1002/asi.23613.

Black, E. (2002). *IBM and the Holocaust* (New York: Crown Publishers).

Codd, E. F. (1970). "A Relational Model for Large Shared Data Banks." *Communications of ACM*, 13(1): 377–387.

Cooper, G. and D. Otley (1998). "The 1996 Research Assessment Exercise for Business and Management." *British Journal of Management*, 9(1): 73–89.

Cooren, F. (2004). "Textual Agency: How Texts Do Things In Organisational Settings." *Organization*, 11(3): 373–393.

DOI (2014). *The Digital Object Identifier System Handbook*. Available at: http://www.doi.org/doi_handbook/

Eco, U. (2009). *The Infinity of Lists* (New York: MacLehose Press).

Ezzamel, M. (2009). "Order and Accounting as a Performative Ritual: Evidence from Ancient Egypt." *Accounting, Organizations and Society*, 34: 348–380.

Frost, R. A. (1982). "Binary-Relational Storage Structures." *The Computer Journal*, 25(358–367).

Gawande, A. (2010). *The Checklist Manifesto: How To Get Things Right* (New York: Profile Books).

Giddens, A. (1984). *The Constitution of Society: Outline of a Theory of Structuration* (Cambridge, UK: Polity Press).

Goldkuhl, G. and K. Lyytinen (1982). 'A Language Action View of Information Systems.' *Proceedings of the International Conference on Information Systems*, C. Ross and M. Ginzberg (eds.). (Ann Arbor, Michigan, USA) pp. 13–31.

Goody, J. (1977). *The Domestication of the Savage Mind* (Cambridge, MA: Cambridge University Press).

Keneally, T. (1983). *Schindler's Ark* (London: Coronet).

Kent, W. (2012). *Data and Reality: A Timeless Perspective on Perceiving and Managing Information in Our Imprecise World* (Westfield, NJ: Technics Publication).

Lyon, D. (1994). *The Electronic Eye: The Rise of Surveillance Society* (Cambridge, MA: Polity Press).

Schmandt-Besserat, D. (1978). "The Earliest Precursor of Writing." *Scientific American*, 238(6): 50–59.

Searle, J. R. (1970). *Speech Acts: An Essay in the Philosophy of Language* (Cambridge: Cambridge University Press).

Searle, J. R. (1983). *Intentionality: An Essay in the Philosophy of Mind* (Cambridge, UK: Cambridge University Press).

Rose, J., M. Jones and D. Truex (2005). "Socio-Theoretic Accounts of IS: The Problem of Agency." *Scandinavian Journal of Information Systems*, 17(1): 133–152.

Rosenberg, D. and A. Grafton (2010). *Cartographies of Time: A History of the Timeline* (New York: Princeton Architectural Press).

Tsitchizris, D. C. and F. H. Lochovsky (1982). *Data Models* (Englewood-Cliffs, NJ: Prentice-Hall)

Urton, G. (2003). *Signs of the Inka Khipu: Binary Coding in the Andean Knotted-String Records* (Austin, TX: University of Texas Press).

Usher, S. (2014). *Lists of Note* (London: Canongate Books).

Chapter 5

Coordination Problems

Introduction

Within previous chapters, we have established that data structures are not only formative, but also informative and performative. Within this chapter, we take this insight and apply it to understanding the role that data structures play within systems of coordination. Let us introduce this idea by considering a number of work practices that Reeva Lederman studied surrounding a manual whiteboard used for the allocation of beds within the Intensive Care Unit (ICU) of an Australian General hospital. An illustration of the whiteboard in use within this case is provided in Figure 5.1 (Lederman and Johnston, 2011). Data-items upon this whiteboard were updated by nursing staff continuously throughout their working shift. The observed state of this whiteboard as well as the observed state of the ICU itself were used by nursing staff to make choices as to routine action in relation to bed allocation. For instance, the nurse manager always made a call at 9 am each morning to operating theatres to determine likely demand for ICU beds. This call was always taken in front of the whiteboard and from where all the beds on the ward could be observed, allowing her to routinely act without significant thought.

Situations such as that experienced in the Australian ICU are commonplace across many institutional settings. In Chapter 4, we introduced the domain of coordination that forms one of the three interconnected domains making up our theory of information situations. We hinted in Chapter 4 that coordination is frequently achieved through the performativity of data structures — the ability of data structures to prescribe and

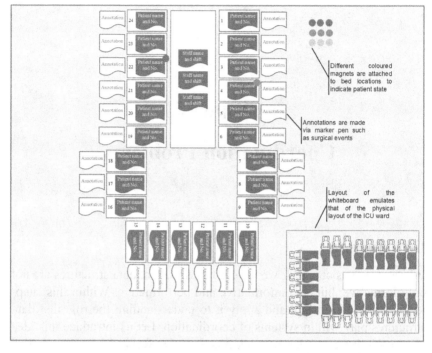

Figure 5.1:   A manual whiteboard used in intensive care.

proscribe action. Blacklists are examples of data structures that proscribe action while watchlists are examples of data structures that prescribe action.

Within the current chapter, we examine the issue of coordination in more detail and in doing so we use what the philosopher David Lewis refers to as coordination problems. A coordination problem occurs when two or more actors have a purpose or goal in common that must be achieved through joint action. Coordination problems, as we shall see, are resolved through conventions of action, particularly conventions which couple articulation of data structures with certain communicative conventions, which in turn are associated with conventions of activity.

Thus many information situations are driven by coordination problems. This is particularly true of areas in which primary action is instrumental work — such as in manufacturing, software production and healthcare. We examine examples from such institutional areas and show

how data structures are critical to scaffolding coordinated activity within delimited institutional domains.

The point we fundamentally want to make in this chapter is that our model of information situations not only offers an explanation of the role of data structures within ways of organising, but also offers constructive ways of thinking about the nature of design in relation to data structures. Data structures cannot merely be designed as physical artefacts — they must be designed in terms of how they communicate and how such communication achieves more effective coordination.

Coordination Problems

The philosopher David Lewis (2002) describes a convention as a regularity in the behaviour of a population of actors and argues that it serves a key function for such a population. For Lewis, conventions solve coordination problems. A coordination problem arises when two or more actors have a purpose or goal in common that must be achieved by joint action. In other words, achieving the goal cannot be achieved by action of a single individual. Instead, two or more actors must coordinate their actions to achieve the goal.

A classic example here is the activity of driving an automobile along some road network. If two drivers are approaching each other along the same road, they both have a common goal: that of passing each other safely. Assuming that the road consists of two lanes, to achieve this joint goal there are actually different ways of achieving a successful outcome. Car A can pass on the left while car B can pass on the right; alternatively, car A can pass on the right while car B can pass on the left. However, to achieve either of these successful outcomes, each driver must engage in joint action with the other; the successful action of actor A depends on the mutual and successful action of actor B.

Therefore, to make coordinated action such as driving an automobile possible, conventions have to be established amongst all road users. Within the UK, drivers are always required to drive in the left-hand lane while in most other countries drivers are required by convention to drive in the right-hand lane. Ruth Millikan (2005) argues that not all coordination relies on convention. If the actors engaging in some joint action are able to gain evidence of each other's likely future actions, then coordination can be negotiated. Only when each partner in a joint action must act before having evidence concerning the likely behaviour of the other actor are coordination conventions, such as the driving example, necessary.

Lewis not surprisingly argues that communication can be used as a major means to negotiate coordination. The actors can reach agreement on coordination through communication rather than convention. However, as we hope we have explained sufficiently in previous chapters, communication itself relies on systems of signs or status functions, which are in themselves sets of conventions. In situations demanding communication between actors remote in time and space, persistent data structures are critical to communication.

Kanban

Let us consider a simple example from manufacturing, similar in nature to that already considered in Chapter 3, where structures of data are used to accomplish information, which in turn facilitates coordination. We shall focus in this section upon a set of data structures used within a set of management practices known as *visual management*. Visual management is typically implemented in terms of the *visual workplace* (Grief, 1991), which employs the idea of using certain artefacts, known as visual devices, situated within work settings to communicate with 'doers' — the actual people performing work within these settings. A visual device is defined by Galsworth (1997) as 'a mechanism that is intentionally designed to share information vital to the task at hand at a glance – so that what is supposed to happen does happen'. The artefacts of the visual workplace are also used to tackle what Galsworth (1997) refers to as information deficits. An information deficit occurs when data does not get shared rapidly, accurately and completely amongst the workforce as soon as it becomes available.

To illustrate how visual management works, we can first look at a set of production practices collectively referred to as pull production or Kanban production. The simplest form of Kanban production works with just two visual devices or what we call data structures — a production card and a move card (see Figure 5.2). Each of these is a physical piece of cardboard on which certain data is recorded. Such cards are placed in plastic sleeves attached to production containers, sometimes called stillages.

Kanban or pull production is really an attempt to resolve a type of coordination problem — how to get the right quantity of material transported along a chain of production units in time for its use within production. To illustrate how it works, consider just the relationship between two

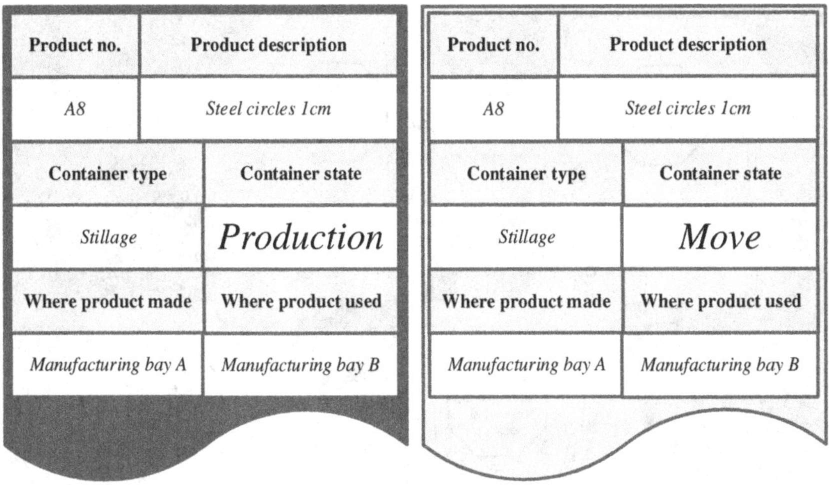

Product no.	Product description		Product no.	Product description
A8	*Steel circles 1cm*		*A8*	*Steel circles 1cm*
Container type	**Container state**		**Container type**	**Container state**
Stillage	*Production*		*Stillage*	*Move*
Where product made	**Where product used**		**Where product made**	**Where product used**
Manufacturing bay A	*Manufacturing bay B*		*Manufacturing bay A*	*Manufacturing bay B*

Figure 5.2: Production and move cards.

production units: production unit 1 and production unit 2. Production unit 1 produces material for use within production unit 2. Full production containers need to be moved from production unit 1 to production unit 2 by forklift truck drivers, but only as and when material is required. And empty production containers need to be moved from production unit 2 to production unit 1 by forklift truck drivers. This cyclical pattern of activity is illustrated in Figure 5.3 as what we refer to as a tabletop prototype (Beynon-Davies, 2021). A tabletop prototype involves positioning various icons on a tabletop to represent various patterns of action. It can be used as a means of documenting analysis of existing patterns of action or specifying the design for a new system of action. The advantage of this design technique is that patterns can be built quickly and thrown away easily.

Let us next look at how Kanban cards are articulated as a pattern of action between these two production units (see Figure 5.4). At production unit 1, when a stillage is full, the production card is removed from the plastic sleeve attached to the stillage and replaced with a move card. A forklift truck driver reads the move card attached to the stillage and moves the stillage to production unit 2. When the stillage is received in production unit 2, the move card is taken out and the material in the stillage is used in production. When the stillage is empty, the move card is placed back in the sleeve. The forklift truck driver reads the card and moves the empty stillage back to production unit 1. The move card is then

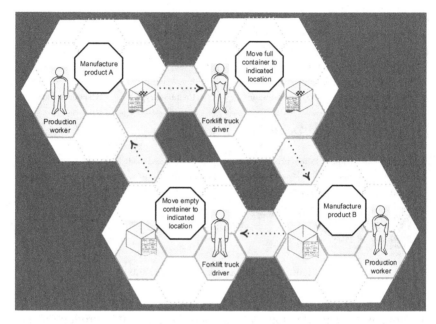

Figure 5.3:   The activity of pull production.

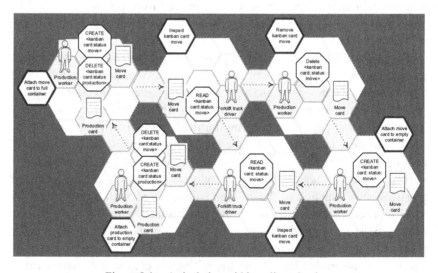

Figure 5.4:   Articulation within pull production.

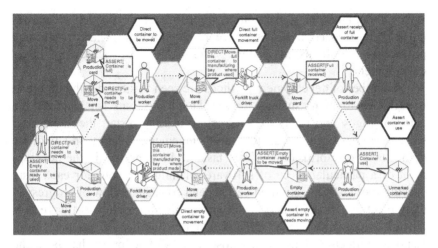

Figure 5.5:   Communication within pull production.

removed from this stillage at production unit 1 and replaced with a production card.

Figure 5.5 illustrates the intervening pattern of communication for
pull production. Acts of articulating data structures communicate various
things to different actors working within this domain of organisation.
Taking a production card out of a sleeve and replacing it with a move card
are acts of articulation. By replacing the production card with the move
card, fellow production workers are informed what has happened and
what should happen. The move card asserts to fellow production workers
that this stillage is full and hence not to add any more material to the stillage. The move card directs the forklift truck driver to move the stillage to
production unit 2.

Scrumban

Next, let us consider a more involved example of the use of visual management within production, from the domain of software development.
Within the last decade or so, a number of changes to practices within
this domain have occurred, which are frequently denoted by the term
agile computing or sometimes agile development. Agile development
emphasises iterative and incremental development, intensive stakeholder

involvement and joint collaboration and cooperation between stakeholders and developers in teams where responsibility is shared. All such properties are focussed on the overall goal of achieving faster development.

A number of development methods are seen to sit under the umbrella of agile development, such as Scrum. The term 'Scrum' is taken from the game of rugby and refers to a formation used to restart the game after some event has occurred, such as an infringement. Scrum works with the definition and prioritisation of key tasks to be done within the development of a particular piece of software, planning sessions for each task, execution of tasks in delimited periods and constant review of progress in daily meetings. Practitioners from within this approach to software production have started to adopt and adapt a number of practices from Kanban production. One of the most successful adaptions has been the melding of Kanban pull-production philosophy as described in the previous section with the agile method Scrum. Ladas (2009) collectively refers to this fusion as Scrumban.

Within his essays on Scrumban, Ladas (2009) refers to a number of possible ways of adapting Kanban principles to agile software development. Within this section, we focus upon the utilisation of a key visual device or physical data structure used to help Scrum work — the Scrumban task board. Ladas describes a simple scenario of applying visual management principles to the Scrum approach based around use of this task board, which has many possible configurations, one of which is illustrated in Figure 5.6. Physically, the task board consists of a grid into which various task cards are placed. Scrum assumes that a particular software product can be broken down into a number of distinct features which can be implemented in a defined unit of time known as a timebox. The main problem of the project manager (often referred to as the Scrum manager or Scrum master) is to effectively allocate various tasks performed in relation to a particular software feature amongst a limited set of defined members of the software development team. It is with this coordination problem in mind that task or feature cards are used.

Vertically, the task board is divided into five major parts of an iterative software development process. Each part comprises a list of one or more cards, up to a maximum defined limit for each list. Feature or task cards are moved across these sections of the board to represent the allocation of work. The To-do section is used to represent the tasks or features that have to be built. When a new feature is first determined it is added to

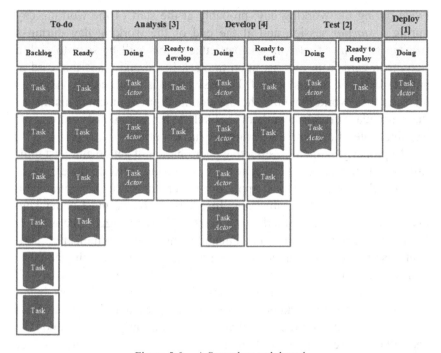

Figure 5.6:   A Scrumban task board.

the backlog list. When it becomes available for development it is added to the to-do ready list. The four other sections of the flow board represent to the Scrum team when a feature is being analysed, developed, tested or deployed. A feature can be done or ready to move into the next stage of this process. When a task is being done, a named Scrumban actor is indicated upon the card. When a task is in a ready state, no actor is indicated as allocated to the feature/task.

One way of thinking about situations such as the Kanban production case we have already considered, as well as the case of Scrumban, is as a *way of organising* — a way of accomplishing joint but mutual action between multiple actors — this is the essence of coordination. However, as we have seen in previous chapters, any way of organising comprise multiple information situations that help constitute mutual action. Information situations couple events of articulation, events of communication and events of coordination.

In the case of Scrumban, actors such as the Scrumban manager and Scrumban workers within the team will inspect the task board at least twice during the working day: probably at the start of the working day during a *startup* session and at the end of the working day during a *washup* session. At such times, particular actors will be seen to pick a Scrumban card from one list upon the task board and place this card in another list upon the task board. The task board is continuously visible to all Scrumban workers within the development environment. This means that particular Scrumban workers are likely to be continuously reading the ongoing state of the entire software production effort.

To properly explain the effective coordination of action amongst multiple actors in cases such as the way of organising software development which is Scrumban, we must apply our understanding of the component elements of information situations. In other words, we must understand that each manipulation of a data structure is likely to trigger one or more informative actions, which fundamentally involve communicative conventions relating manipulations in the articulation domain with manipulations in the coordination domain.

The positioning of particular Scrumban cards upon the task board asserts to Scrumban workers not only where a particular feature is within the overall Scrumban process, but also who is currently working upon the particular feature. This serves to help workers decide on the scheduling of their own work. The figure also shows how the Scrumban manager declares a change of state of a particular feature in two ways to the work group. First, she will move a Scrumban card from a ready list to a doing list. Second, she will annotate the card with an identifier for a particular Scrumban worker. When the nominated worker has completed the task assigned, he will remove his identifier and place the card in a ready list. This piece of articulation serves to declare the completion of a particular task to the group. Figure 5.7 illustrates one information situation from this way of organising.

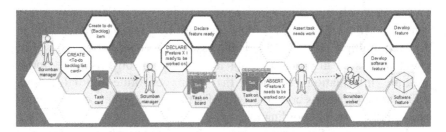

Figure 5.7:   An information situation from the Scrumban domain.

Managing the Semiotics of the Workplace

Within previous sections, we have used our model of information situations to unpack how visual devices such as Kanban cards, task boards and whiteboards are used to achieve coordination. Inherently, in doing so, we have proposed elements of what we might call a design theory for visual management. Such theorisation is important for explaining not only *how* these systems of visual devices work but *why* they are effective in particular situations of work. A well-formed design theory of this nature should also suggest ways in which visual management can be better undertaken in practice to support operations.

We have examined just three of many instances of visual management which have been applied in numerous work domains, such as in manufacturing, software development and healthcare. All such cases have four features in common. The first feature is that these systems involve use of material and typically highly visual artefacts for informative purposes. The second feature is that the physical manipulation of such artefacts in relation to each other is important to informing actors within group work. The third feature is that the overall state of the physical environment in which such manipulation takes place is an integral part of the ways in which actors are informed. The fourth feature is that the manipulation of physical and visual artefacts in a structured environment is particularly important to supporting routine action.

First, in terms of an artefact such as a task card, it is not only important that this artefact affords actors the potential to write upon it, but also that it affords positionability. A task card can clearly be positioned, usually in relation to other such artefacts within lists upon the Scrumban task board. This means that the physical arrangement of artefacts in space as well as the movement of artefacts through space is important to their informating capacity. Informating is a concept coined by Zuboff (1985) to refer to the way in which the manipulation of artefacts '... produces a voice that symbolically renders events, objects and processes so that they become visible, shareable and knowable ...'. Moving a magnetic disk on an ICU whiteboard is a significant and informating act as is the positioning of a task card upon a task board or the placement of a Kanban card upon a stillage.

Therefore, it is incorrect to refer to the key artefacts proposed within the tradition of visual management purely as visual devices because the message conveyed by such devices is frequently sent over other sensory channels besides vision. Hence, as a vocabulary, it is also somewhat cumbersome to refer to the visual workplace or visual management. A more appropriate idea would perhaps be managing the semiotics of the workplace. Semiotics (Noth, 1990), as we have seen, is broadly that discipline which studies signs. 'Visual' devices are best conceived of as specific signs used by specific actors in specific ways of organising work. Such devices, as signs, can exist in various different forms, sensed by actors over a number of different sensory modalities.

The second feature is that the physical manipulation of artefacts such as Kanban cards in relation to each other is important to informing different actors across time. This means that it is important to separate out the act of articulating or forming the artefact from its use for doing something. Within the context of situations in which we are interested, it is important to separate out (at least for the purposes of analysis) the act of placing a task card somewhere from the accomplishment of being informed by this action. There are two main reasons for this: the act of forming an artefact may be accomplished by a different actor from that being informed by the artefact, and the association between the act of manipulating some artefact and the act of being informed by it is an arbitrary one. A certain artefact may hold significance for one actor but not for another. The same artefact may also inform two different actors differently. What turns the accomplishment of being informed into a non-arbitrary phenomenon for particular actors is the notion of a communicative convention. Within semiotics, as we have seen, this process is referred to as semiosis — the process of sign-use or more precisely sign-action-events (Noth, 1990). It is this process of semiosis that seems to be at the heart of the enterprise of visual management.

The third feature is that the structure of the physical environment in which such articulation takes place is also important to informing actors. The entire physical environment forms the 'gestalt' within which artefacts perform as actors (Preda, 1999). From the point of view of visual management, the task board and the associated task cards within the management of agile software development are visual devices. However, such devices form part of a wider visual system or sign-system, which is the entire physical environment within which and upon which actors perform work. In other words, the whiteboard is not the only visual device important to the coordination of work in the ICU setting. As part of the wider visual system of the intensive care unit, the very placement of patients in particular beds upon the ward help inform nurses of appropriate healthcare actions.

The fourth feature is that the manipulation of physical and visual artefacts is important to supporting situated choice. Within the ways of organising we have described, choices of appropriate action seem to be made using a logic of appropriateness. This means that responses to situations are accomplished using direct appreciation of patterns in the working environment together with tacit knowledge of appropriate response. Hence, within the ICU unit, the nurse can make immediate, routine, situated choices (Suchman, 1986) about bed allocation. Within the Scrumban case, software developers can make instant choices about what to work on next, as well as the type of work to be performed and by when. Thus, the structure of the physical environment as well as the structure of informative artefacts enables actors to reproduce the spatial and temporal order of organising within these settings.

Designing Data Structures with Coordination in Mind

The upshot of our close analysis of visual management in terms of our design theory of information situations is that data structures have to be designed with coordination problems in mind. To demonstrate this, let us consider another case from manufacturing, and specifically involving the work of inventory management. This case explicitly demonstrates the way in which an analysis of information situations can be turned into the appropriate design of information situations.

A piece of highly visual and material technology was co-created between the author and a large manufacturing organisation, the Royal Mint, within an action research study (Beynon-Davies, 2013). This large, manufacturing organisation was experiencing problems with a process of checking inventory with the goal of improving stock accuracy at production locations. This routine involved production staff taking a sample stock check with hand scanners on a weekly basis and reporting results back to a central production controller. The problem was that such stock checks were consistently under-reporting stock by as much as 30% as compared to that reported by the central production ICT system used at the plant. Various different actors within the manufacturing plant were convinced that this disparity was an illusion. According to them, stock did not just disappear, the ICT system merely recorded it as missing.

A close analysis of the situation soon identified that a key problem appeared to be that the data supplied by doing the inventory checking had little influence on work practices performed upon the shopfloor. Because of the poor timeliness of reports back from central production planning, production workers could do little to address undercounting or overcounting of stock, making it particularly difficult to track 'rogue' stock in this regard. Suggestions emerged from organisational actors themselves that if data could be used immediately on the ground to make decisions on actions to be taken, then many stock variances could be quickly resolved, leading to consequent improvements in stock accuracy.

To address this situation, a data structure known as a stock flow board was co-created in a design workshop between the author and representatives of various production units (see Figure 5.8). The stock flow board effectively consisted of a wall-mounted white board on which a series of named elements were clearly demarcated. It also included an area for hanging two critical paper reports: a stock location enquiry (STLQ) report printed from the production ICT system and a summary sheet used for recording stock accuracy over a monthly period by production operators. Such boards were placed at each production location (identified by a barcode) within a production unit.

Therefore, to design a data structure, we need to think not only of the structure itself, but also what we want elements of this structure to signify and to whom. We also need to think through the expected activity we want to prescribe or proscribe as the end-result of such communication. Hence, the writing of some description in an action line upon the board asserts to actors within a production shift that a stock anomaly needs to be resolved. This serves to help workers decide on the scheduling of their own work. In particular, the production operator responsible for a particular production location will be directed by this entry. If the stock issue can be resolved, then the production operator will update the completion data-item upon the respective action line. This serves to assert her belief that the anomaly has been resolved. However, it is the responsibility of the shift team leader to authorise completion of a stock action. Hence, this is only declared to be the case to the rest of the team when he or she signs off the action by updating the T/L (team leader) data-item.

Take another example of a designed information situation. A production worker needs to signal to other actors within work that he has been unsuccessful in resolving a particular stock anomaly. To do this, he

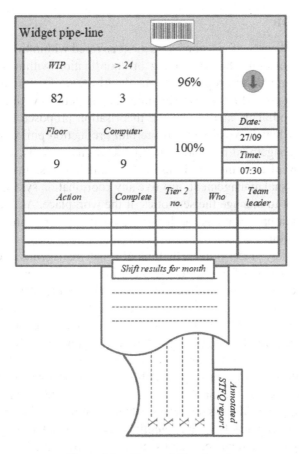

Figure 5.8:   The stock flow board.

updates the T2 (tier 2) data-item of the relevant action line upon the stock flow board. This articulation serves to signal a collective intention, namely, the need to escalate the resolution of this anomaly to a higher layer of management. In Searle's (1970) terms, the articulation of this particular data structure creates an assertion — a statement of belief that something is the case by a particular actor. The team leader treats this assertion as a signal to escalate action. To declare this, he fills out a stock issue card, which he hands over to the production clerk of the particular production unit. This is likely to direct her to perform a more comprehensive stock check across the entire production unit.

Conclusion

We have used cases of visual management covered within this chapter not only to demonstrate the positioning of coordination within information situations, but also to propose that our theorisation of information situations offers a powerful tool for designing data structures with coordinated action in mind. This means that the theorisation proposed not only has potential for better explaining how certain production philosophies such as visual management provide value to operational activity, it also offers a better way of enacting the design of coordination systems much more generally. Visual management, just like any coordination system, provides us an attempt to manage the semiotics of the workplace. As such, a number of explicit prescriptions for designing good data structures fall out of our theorisation.

The first key prescription is to think of visual management not in terms of the management of 'visual' devices but in terms of the management of signs situated within the physical environment of a particular work setting. The material properties of such signs have potential to be perceived by actors in terms of all aspects of an actor's sensory apparatus. In other words, the effectivities of human actors rely upon not only the sensory modality of the visual, but also sound, touch, taste and smell. Properties perceived through any sensory modality are non-arbitrary, meaning that such properties are invariant across situations and hence are observer-independent. Signs also, as material structures within the physical environment of the workplace, have the potential to be perceived directly by actors without any intermediate, conscious, cognitive processing.

The second key prescription involves thinking about 'visual' devices not as purely physical artefacts, but in terms of actors taking action. A way of organising as we have portrayed it is best seen as an ensemble of both humans and artefacts taking action. Hence, 'visual' devices such as manual whiteboards should be understood in terms of not only which actors undertake what articulations with them but for what purpose. In other words, we need to think of such devices not only as physical structures but coupled to the notion of such artefacts as communicative actors.

This leads to the third key prescription, which is to think of physical structures such as whiteboards as instances of data structures. Such structures as signs or sign-systems are typically introduced into the workplace in an attempt to constrain or enable actors through the opportunities they provide for action. However, introducing a data structure as the 'form' of some sign or sign-system into a workplace does not guarantee appropriate action in and of itself. To prove effective such form must serve to inform with the intention to perform. This means that the designers of artefacts such as whiteboards, magnetic tokens and paper cards need to think through how particular articulations of these data structures relate to particular communicative conventions. Designers also need to think about how particular communicative conventions should couple with specific actions of coordinated work.

The fourth and final prescription involves the usefulness of thinking through patterns of action either as-is or as-if or to-be. In other words, we need better ways of thinking through how articulation, communication and coordination occur in existing settings. We also need ways of thinking through what patterns of articulation, communication and coordination we might want to see happen within some work setting. Finally, we need better ways of helping to change ways of organising work using 'visual' devices. In particular, we need ways of communicating the patterns of action expected of particular participating actors in relation to such artefacts within some work setting.

One important exercise in the design of data structures is to think about their life-history. As we shall see in the next chapter, data structures are created by somebody to do something. However, once data structures are created, they are likely to be updated and read by many different actors. Finally, they are either removed from existence or stored away in archives.

References

Beynon-Davies, P. (2013). *Business Information Systems* (Houndmills, Basingstoke, UK: Palgrave Macmillan).

Beynon-Davies, P. and R. Lederman (2016). "Making Sense of Visual Management Through Affordance Theory." *Production Planning and Control*, 142–157. DOI 10.1080/09537287.2016.1243267.

Beynon-Davies, P. (2021). *Business Analysis and Design: Understanding Innovation in Organisation* (London: Palgrave).

Ladas, C. (2009). *Scrumban: Essays on Kanban Systems for Lean Software Development* (USA: Modus Cooperandi Press).

Lederman, R. and R. B. Johnston (2011). "Decision Support or Support for Situated Choice: Lessons for System Design from Effective Manual Systems." *European Journal of Information Systems*, **20**(5): 510–528.

Lewis, D. (2002). *Convention: A Philosophical Study* (Oxford: Blackwell).

Millikan, R. G. (2005). Language: A Biological Model (Oxford: Clarendon Press).

Grief, M. (1991). *The Visual Factory: Building Participation Through Shared Information* (Portland, OR: Productivity Press).

Galsworth, G. D. (1997). *Visual Systems: Harnessing the Power of the Visual Workplace* (New York: AMACOM).

Noth, W. (1990). *Handbook of Semiotics* (Indiana: Indiana University Press).

Preda, A. (1999). "The Turn to Things: Arguments for a Sociology of Things." *The Sociological Quarterly*, **40**(2): 347–366.

Searle, J. R. (1970). *Speech Acts: An Essay in the Philosophy of Language* (Cambridge: Cambridge University Press).

Suchman, L. (1986). *Plans and Situated Actions* (New York: Cambridge University Press).

Zuboff, S. (1985). "Automate/Informate: The Two Faces of Intelligent Technology." *Organizational Dynamics*, **14**(2): 5–18.

Chapter 6

The 'Life' of the Record

Introduction

We began this book with the claim that your life is documented in records, but your life is also lived through records. A biography is an account of a person's life produced by another. However, the average person living in a nation-state does not need a dedicated, written account of one's life — one is already available in the record systems of the state and other institutions. As an account of yourself, your biography is typically told through records held about you such as birth, marriage and death certificates, and these data structures will have been produced by many different actors working within many different institutional domains. Your relationships with others will also be accounted for in such records, and your genealogy is also traced through such records. In more recent times, accounts of where you have been, who you have communicated with and what you have done will also be solidified in records.

Such records are not just passive accounts that aggregate up within biographies and genealogies. As we saw in Chapter 4, records are very much active in the sense that your ability to act as an individual within society is reliant upon records held about you. If you cannot prove certain institutional facts held about you in and through records, you are often prohibited or proscribed from acting in ways you might wish. Therefore, in this chapter we examine the 'life' of a data structure from two complementary directions — how data structures serve to construct institutional facts and how such facts may be changed through the life-history of articulation associated with a data structure.

In Chapter 4, we referred to the active nature of data structures as the performative side of a data structure. We used the idea of a communicative act to understand how data structures can act in the sense of asserting something to an actor, directing an actor to do something, acting as a commitment to future action, declaring that something is the case and finally expressing how actors feel about something. In the current chapter, we move our ideas forward by linking acts of communication to institutional facts. Such institutional facts are critical to the production and reproduction of institutional activity.

It is strange to think that records have lives, but they do — they are created once, amended many times, retrieved sometimes and eventually deleted or archived. Given this life-history, it is important to understand the context in which records are articulated. For this we need the concept of an institutional fact, which in turn relies upon the notion of collective intentionality. These ideas allow us to portray a clear path from physical ontology to social ontology — from theories of physical reality to theories of social reality. In other words, following Searle, we can see clearly how the social or institutional world arises from the bedrock of the physical world.

Because of their critical importance in scaffolding institutional action data structures, and more precisely the data contained within them, have been at the centre of numerous debates concerning their proper articulation. This is particularly true of data held about the person in such data structures. It has become generally accepted that because these data structures identify and describe the person then an individual's right to privacy should be extended to the data structures representing him or her. Data privacy demands that data held about the person should be articulated only in defined ways and that the sharing of such data with third parties should be strictly controlled. Data privacy, as we shall see in this chapter, is normally ensured through some form of data protection legislation.

Institutional Facts and Social Ontology

In Chapter 4, we started to use part of the philosophy of John Searle to help understand how data structures are not just formative and informative, they are also performative. We closed Chapter 4 with the idea that data structures are best considered as having a limited form of agency — they act in a certain critical way within domains of institutional activity.

In Chapter 5, we showed how data structures are critical to the performance of coordination. We open this chapter with the idea that data structures are critical more generally to the performance of institutions because of the way in which they enact institutional facts.

Therefore, to help understand the place of data structures within the formation of institutional order, we need to unpack two further concepts from Searle's theoretical edifice. We need to explain how constitutive rules produce institutional facts and how such institutional facts help constitute (construct and reconstruct) social ontology (institutional reality).

For Searle, institutional facts are the very 'stuff' of social reality and he contrasts such facts with what he calls brute facts. Brute facts are the very stuff of the physical sciences — physics, chemistry and biology — and as such exist independently of human institutions. An example of a brute fact is that *the sun is ninety-three million miles from the earth*. In contrast, institutional facts are matters of culture and convention. They exist only within the context of human institutions, such as *JASIST is considered a 3-star journal on the ABS list* or *John Smith is a British citizen*.

Institutional facts rely on the background of collective intentionality. The term intentionality is often simplistically summarised as 'aboutness' or the relationship between mental acts/states and the external world. According to the *Oxford English Dictionary*, it is 'the distinguishing property of mental phenomena of being necessarily directed upon an object, whether real or imaginary'. John Searle (1983) defines intentionality as the special way the human psyche has of relating to the world. For philosophers, such as Searle, intentionality encompasses a vast range of mental phenomena such as believing, desiring, wishing, knowing, guessing, forgetting and intending. Idioms such as these are referred to as propositional attitudes, since what they have in common is that they are all attitudes towards or about something. Hence, believing is always believing that something is the case and wishing is always wishing for something.

In *Making the Social World*, Searle (2010) adds a further claim: that status functions are created through declarative speech acts. This results from that peculiar property of such declarations, which we have already seen Chapter 4 — that they have both a world-to-word and word-to-world direction of fit. Making a declaration of something unifies the world with the word, as in the classic example in which a judge declares the period of imprisonment imposed on an offender. Sentencing someone in this manner makes the world match the statement. For Searle the same is true of all status functions. Collective intentionality is built from mutual acceptance or recognition of status functions by a group of actors. We, as actors, make something the case by declaration that a given status function X exists.

Thus the social world relies upon collective acceptance of status functions. However, such acceptance by its very nature is not permanent, it is temporary. It relies upon the continual accomplishment by institutional actors of collective intentionality. This is why in the next section, we use the metaphor of scaffolding the institutional order. Data structures such as lists of identifiers (see Chapter 4) are important elements within the institutional order, but they always contain within their application the potential for breakdown of such order.

We use the term *breakdown* here in the sense adopted in the philosophy of Martin Heidegger and utilised by some proponents of the language/action tradition (Winograd, 2006). Such proponents adapt this concept from Heidegger's insistence that things and their properties are not inherent in the world but arise only in an event of breaking down, a process in which human actors undergo an experiential shift in which things change from being *ready-at-hand* to being *present-to-hand*. The classic example of the hammer and the nail is typically used to explain this experiential shift. To a person hammering in a nail, the hammer as such ceases to be foregrounded in perceptual terms. In Garfinkel's (1967) terms, it is seen-but-unnoticed; part of the background readiness-to-hand that is taken for granted. The hammer presents itself as a hammer only when there is some kind of breaking down, such as when it breaks, slips from the hammerer's grasp or bends the nail. The same could be said of our two young fish mentioned in the Prologue. For these fish the water they swim in is ready-to-hand. Only when they are stranded, perhaps on a sandbank, does this substance they exist within become present-to-hand.

In a similar manner a data structure, such as a list, is normally ready-to-hand for most actors. For them it is part of the accepted and mundane background to institutional action. Only when there is some breakdown, such as when the identifier within a list-item fails to identify something or a list-item classifies the wrong thing in institutional terms, do we experience a data structure as being present-at-hand.

Let us get back to the nature of facts. The primary difference between a brute fact and institutional fact relies upon the different status that such facts have in relation to some theory of existence — some ontology.

Brute facts are observer independent. Within a brute fact, the status of the thing referred to has an existence independent of institutions. Indeed, brute facts are independent even of the institution of language. In contrast, institutional facts are observer relative. Within an institutional fact, the status of the thing depends upon a collective attitude or acceptance by the actors concerned that the thing has a certain function. This defines the notion of a status function for Searle.

One might be tempted to use this polar distinction to make claim that institutions deal solely with institutional facts. Institutions, such as manufacturing companies, healthcare organisations or higher education institutions, clearly must deal with both brute facts and institutional facts. Indeed, many things can be referred to and described not only by brute facts, but also by institutional facts. Searle has even acknowledged that whereas brute facts are independent of language, we need language as a system of signs or status functions to represent such facts (Searle, 2006, 2007).

Consider a thing familiar within the institutional context of manufacturing and which we have experienced in an earlier chapter — that of a stillage. Stillages are physical things and as such have an existence independent of the institution. In other words, they can be described in terms of brute facts such as: *a stillage is a steel box being approximately 1 metre in depth, height, and width.* These brute facts can be confirmed by any observer of such objects making such facts observer independent.

However, what is the function of a stillage? A stillage may be a physical structure, but these physical structures are assigned a status within the institution concerned. A stillage is used to store various stages of finished product — 'stock' — within the context of the manufacturing plant. We might even frame the constitutive rule in this case as being:

[A stillage (X) counts as a unit of stock (Y) within the manufacturing plant (C)]

In the same way, treated purely as a material artefact, as a form, a data structure can be considered a brute fact, or more accurately a series of brute facts. In other words, as a sequence of perhaps written letters or numbers, an identifier is observer independent. However, this term can also be treated as both an informative and a performative artefact. As such, this term acts in the capacity of what Searle calls a status indicator. This is because 'we impose intentionality on entities that are not intrinsically intentional. A status indicator is a representational device that allows an entity to represent something beyond its physical features' (Searle, 2006). Hence, a passport number, postcode or a commodity code, as we shall show in Chapter 7, are all brute facts that act in the capacity of status indicators to institutional facts.

The Scaffolding of Lists

We have argued in previous chapters that data structures are critical scaffolding within institutional orders, but we did not consider in any real detail what we mean by such scaffolding. In this section, we examine this notion of *scaffolding* more closely to learn what it tells us about the nature of institutional data structures.

Institutional facts are not of course brought into existence in isolation. Instead, they take their place in what we like to think of as wider scaffolds. A scaffold is a structure used in the construction industry to support the building or repair of physical structures such as houses. One of the most popular types of scaffolding is built from steel tubes and couplers placed upon a series of base plates. Such scaffolding affords the act of construction or repair by numerous actors. We want to use the analogy of data structures as scaffolding in which the articulation of data structures forms the baseplate or 'load-bearing' component. Various 'tubes' of communication are coupled to this baseplate and in turn various 'tubes' of coordinated action are coupled onto 'tubes' of communication. This analogy is visualised within the illustration in Figure 6.1. In this figure, data structures serve not only as 'base-plates' for intra-institutional action, they also serve to scaffold inter-institutional action.

Scaffolding has already been applied analogically through metaphor within areas such as learning theory, child development and distributed cognition. In such areas, scaffolding is a term used to refer to augmentations that allow humans to achieve goals that would normally be beyond us. The scaffold helps structure human action by supporting and guiding it. However, such scaffolding also serves to discipline or guide such action. This idea appears to have a certain synergy with Giddens' constitutive cycle discussed in Chapter 4.

Orlikowski (2006) describes certain characteristics of physical scaffolding that provide insight into the way in which what she refers to as 'everyday knowing in practice' is constituted. It is useful to reflect upon

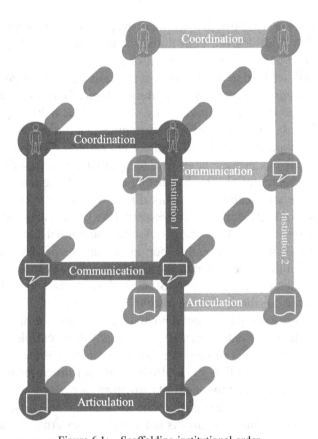

Figure 6.1:   Scaffolding institutional order.

some of these characteristics and apply them to understanding the case of the data structure as material scaffolding for institutional order. According to Orlikowski, scaffolds are temporary, flexible, portable, dangerous, generative and constitutive.

Scaffolds are temporary structures designed to support aspects of construction. Once this aspect of construction is regarded as complete, they are dismantled. Scaffolds are flexible in the sense they are erected in many different situations but adapted to the exigencies of the situation. Scaffolds are portable. They can be quickly and easily assembled and disassembled across many different sites. Scaffolds are dangerous. Because of their temporary, flexible and portable nature, such physical structures are vulnerable to breakdown and failure. Scaffolds are generative in the sense that they augment the process of physical construction. Finally, scaffolds are constitutive in the sense that they play an important part in affording the very act of construction.

Although we tend to regard our data structures as permanent, they are in fact *temporary* structures, with a lifespan typically determined by the duration of the institutional order they scaffold. This helps explain how the life of the data structure, which we examine in a further section within this chapter, parallels the life of institutional activity. The very value of data structures lies in their *flexibility*. As symbolic artefacts, the general principles of representation such as listing and identifying (see Chapter 4) are applicable and adaptable to many different situations. They are particularly *portable* structures in the sense that we can expand and contract data structures to account for many different institutional situations. They are *dangerous* in the sense that our infrastructure of data structures contain within them the potential for breakdown. However, they are necessary because they are *generative* of institutional facts, and such institutional facts are *constitutive* of the institutional order itself.

However, we should be careful not to take the metaphor of scaffolding too far in relation to data structures. Unlike physical scaffolding, which tends to afford the acts of construction or repair to a separate physical structure such as a building, the scaffolding of data structures is a crucial part of the action of institutions. Data structures are necessary to institutions because they are constitutive of the institutional order itself. Hence, the scaffolding of data structures is not something external to the idea of institution — it is critical to the institutionalising process itself.

Data structures are normally ready-to-hand for institutional actors and are initially created typically to scaffold some delimited domain of routine institutional action on the part of such actors. However, over time, such scaffolding is often extended to support other aspects of institutional action not framed by the initial contextualisation of such data structures. This sometimes assumes the status of inter-institutional scaffolding and in such situations the scaffolding of data structures is particularly prone to breakdown. So, let us look at this idea of data breakdown more closely.

Data Breakdowns

Figure 6.2 annotates our model of the scaffolding of data structures with a number of ways in which these structures can breakdown. These various

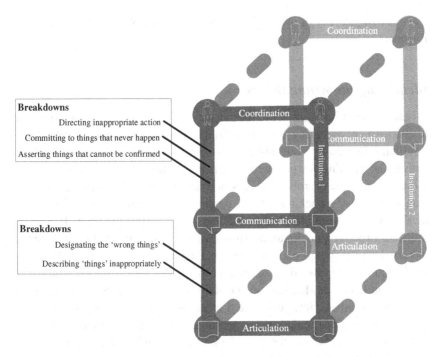

Figure 6.2:   Types of data breakdown.

instances of breakdown can be understood in relation to a certain brittleness in the institutional coupling between articulation and communication
as well as the coupling between communication to coordination. Within
the discussion that follows, we describe practical experiences of problems
in identification and designation as instances of breakdowns in the coupling between articulation and communication. Likewise, we highlight
certain problems with the intention imparted to data structures as breakdowns in the coupling between communication and coordination. The
three-dimensional structure in Figure 6.2 is meant to illustrate that breakdowns can clearly occur not only within intra-institutional scaffolding, but
also across inter-institutional scaffolding, which impact the performance
of institutional actors. Hence, data structures may break down within the
intra-institutional scaffolding of production, but they may also break
down in the inter-institutional scaffolding of activity systems such as the
supply chain. To help ground our discussion of data breakdowns, we provide several examples from an actual study of a supply chain undertaken

by a colleague, Yingli Wang (Beynon-Davies and Wang, 2019), in what follows.

Identifying the wrong things

When an identifier from some data structure fails to identify something or identifies a 'wrong thing' in institutional terms, we experience a data structure that is normally ready-at-hand as being present-at-hand. Consider the activity of packing a truck with orders ready for transportation to a customer from some warehouse. This activity is typically scaffolded by the data structure of a packing list. On receipt by the customer, this list should be able unequivocally to identify products delivered on the truck. However, this data structure may break down in terms of detailing what has happened in relation to dispatch of items. In mechanical terms, this is evident in a mismatch between two data structures, the product identifiers on the packing list and what is detailed on the delivery note handed to the inbound logistics operative. Here, we have a clear example of a breakdown in the coupling between articulation and communication implied by a certain data structure. In other words, there is a lack of coupling between the data structure and what it communicates to diverse actors within this inter-institutional setting — what the packing list asserts as comprising a delivery and what the inbound logistics operative asserts as comprising the delivery.

Describing things inappropriately

Another example of a breakdown is where things might be described in a certain way by data structures, whereas in practice actors know from experience that they should be treated differently. Within a supply chain, for instance, a shipment, might be described by the dispatching company as urgent within data structures transmitted between the dispatching and receiving company. However, frequently the receiving actor for such shipments will request urgent orders to be put on hold at their last mile delivery stage and then change the designation of the shipment shortly after from *urgent* to *normal*. Designating a shipment as urgent should put in train a whole series of special actions by receiving warehousing staff, not least of which is to place the shipment in a priority holding bay for speedy dispatch. However, since experience tells warehouse people that most items designated as *priority items* are later assigned non-priority or normal status, many warehouse staff have become proactive and now locate such stock in non-priority holding bays as a norm.

Asserting things that cannot be confirmed

The example discussed previously of the packing list identifying the wrong things acts as an assertion to actors of things as happening when they have not actually happened. Such an inter-institutional breakdown causes problems further up the chain of action in that the activities of numerous people must readjust to the reference problems of this data structure. As a result, time and effort is expended by actors, both within the dispatching company and receiving company, in addressing aspects of this breakdown. The workarounds (Alter, 2014) used by various actors to reconstitute the institutional order consume unnecessary resource.

Committing to things that never happen

To manage the effective flow of goods through the supply chain, the dispatching company sends a demand forecast (yet another data structure) to the warehousing company, indicating the expected flow of material through the supply chain. The exchange of the demand forecast can be seen to act as a commitment (intent) between critical actors within the two companies. In other words, the act of articulating this data structure serves as a promise that certain quantities of material will flow between the two companies in the future. However, experience of breakdowns in such commitment will cause relevant actors to mistrust and even to ignore such data structures as a means of guiding institutional action.

Directing people to do the wrong things

As a data structure, a picking list generated in relation to a partial order may direct warehouse operatives to do the wrong things. The picking list given to a warehouse operative in this situation might direct him to pick three items identified as item 1, item 2 and item 3. There are three boxes or cases at the designated production location each containing 123. However, the warehouse management system directs the picking operative to pick item 1 from box 1, item 2 from box 2 and item 3 from box 3. This clearly misdirects coordinated action.

Vital Signs

The examples provide a useful initial taxonomy of the sorts of happenings that can go wrong with data structures, whether electronic or otherwise. So, let us use a more detailed case to examine how data structures build institutional facts, how institutional facts help scaffold institutional activity and how the instituting facility of data structures always contain the potential for breakdown.

Evidence suggests that the early detection of medical complications, coupled with the timeliness of response and the competency of clinical response, can have a marked effect on patient outcomes. It is estimated that thousands of lives can be saved by improvements in such factors. Therefore, for more than a century, healthcare workers have been recording a number of vital signs — body temperature, blood pressure, heart rate, etc. — that are used to indicate the medical condition of acute patients and signal the need for medical intervention. Such signs are typically recorded upon medical charts normally placed worldwide within general hospitals at the foot of the patient's bed. In some countries, these charts are typically used to compute scores that can be used as an early warning system to alert medical staff to the development of a number of different medical complications.

However, in many health services, there are several difficulties experienced in the use of such charts. Taking the UK National Health Service as an example, first, there are many different such charts used within this health service, each with a different scoring system. Second, there is inconsistent use of such charts across the health service with many examples of poor use and variable monitoring of vital signs. Third, when medical staff move between different medical units, they must learn to use different charts to monitor the patient condition. This introduces potential for error. Fourth, the lack of standardisation means that it is difficult to provide good training to medical workers in this area.

Not surprisingly, in 2012, a report produced by the Royal College of Physicians (RCoP, 2012) suggested moving to a standardised way of capturing vital signs and of computing an early warning score. The report states:

'... when assessing acutely ill patients using these various scores, we are not speaking the same language, and this can lead to a lack of consistency in the approach to detection and response to acute illness. This lack of standardisation also bedevils attempts to embed a culture of training and education in the assessment and response to acute illness for all grades of healthcare professionals across the NHS.'

Therefore, the working group proposed standardising the chart with its associated procedures across the NHS, including its use within hospitals and ambulances. The key rationale for this change is based on:

'... the need to standardise the approach across the NHS and link the scoring system to clearly defined principles with regard to the urgency of response, the competency of the responders and the organisational infrastructure required to deliver an effective clinical response to acute illness, every time it is needed ... simple things done well can make a huge impact in healthcare ...'

A simplified version of the NEWS clinical observations chart produced by the working group is illustrated in Figure 6.3. Six physiological measurements are used on this chart: respiratory rate, blood oxygen level, body temperature, systolic blood pressure, heart rate and level of consciousness. Each of these measurements is normally made by nursing staff, typically nowadays with the aid of some electronic instrumentation.

Body temperature

Body temperature used to be measured with a thermometer placed within the mouth. Nowadays it is most likely measured using an electronic thermometer inserted in the ear.

Heart rate

Heart rate is normally measured as pulse rate: the number of heartbeats per unit of time, typically expressed as beats per minute (bpm). The typical resting heart rate in adults is 60–90 beats per minute (bpm). Resting heart rates below 60 bpm may be referred to as bradycardia, while rates above 100 bpm at rest may be called tachycardia. Heart rate normally was

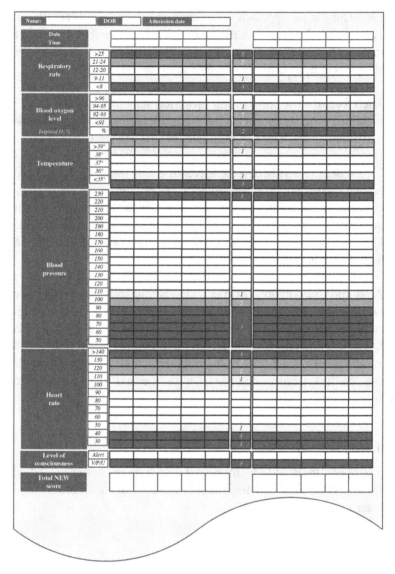

Figure 6.3:   A NEWS chart.

measured manually by a nurse taking the pulse of a patient. Nowadays, patients are likely to have a fingertip monitor inserted or in more serious cases may be hooked up to a heart rate monitor via electrodes attached to the chest.

Blood pressure

Systolic blood pressure is the amount of pressure that blood exerts on vessels while the heart is beating — measured in millimetres of mercury (mmHg). In a blood pressure reading (such as 120/80), systolic blood pressure is the number on the top, while diastolic blood pressure (the blood pressure when the heart is resting) is the bottom figure. If systolic blood pressure is higher than 140, the person has a condition called isolated systolic hypertension. To measure systolic blood pressure, a healthcare worker will usually use a device called a sphygmomanometer. A fabric cuff is wrapped around your arm and then inflated slightly. The blood pressure is measured on a gauge attached to the cuff.

Consciousness

Consciousness is measured as being either alert or responding to Voice (V), responding to Pain (P) or unresponsive (U). The assessment is done through observation in sequence and only one outcome is recorded.

Respiratory rate

Respiratory rate is the number of breaths taken within a set amount of time, typically 60 seconds. It is normally measured when the person is at rest by observing the number of times the chest rises within a minute. Average respiratory rate for a healthy adult varies in the range 12–20 breaths per minute.

Blood oxygen level

Blood oxygen level refers to the level of saturation of the patient's haemoglobin (the protein in the red blood cell that stores oxygen for transportation around the human body). This is now normally measured using a fingertip sensor known as a pulse oximeter, which uses light absorption by the skin to determine the level. Healthy adults should have an oxygen saturation level of 95–100%.

A score between 0 and 3 is allocated to each measurement as they are measured. The score signifies how far the physiological parameter varies from the expected norm. Each score is also colour-coded on the chart to give a visual signal of divergence from the norm — 0 is left white, while 1 is coded green, 2 is coded amber and 3 is coded red. Each of the scores taken at a date/time are then aggregated to form a total NEW score. The physical act of calculating this score by a member of nursing staff is seen as important for setting the attention of nursing on the condition of the patient.

The Informative and Performative Nature of a Vital Signs Chart

The NEWS chart is clearly a data structure and hence according to the theory we have been developing in this and earlier chapters we would expect it to be not only informative — to communicate important things to key actors — but to be performative, to trigger responsive action by such actors.

Clearly the so-called vital signs themselves are brute facts. The body temperature, blood pressure, heart rate, etc. are physiological aspects of an individual that are observer independent in the sense that they can be verified by different actors. However, note that such actors cannot access such brute facts directly. They must measure such facts using certain instrumentation. In doing so they collectively establish a set of signs or status functions to count as or stand for these physical phenomena. For example, we use perhaps the Centigrade or Fahrenheit scale, calibrated into a certain electronic thermometer, to measure body temperature.

We then take the next step to make such measurements truly institutional facts. The various measurements are classified (see Chapter 8) as being in one of three categories — normal (green), as potentially of concern (yellow) and in danger (red). Such institutional facts are then important to what happens next — how this classification triggers healthcare actions by medical staff.

Within published guidance, the performative nature of the NEWS chart is formalised in terms of three so-called trigger levels, which are calculated from the aggregate scores of vital signs. A score between 1 and 4 is categorised as *low*, a score between 5 and 6 or one of the scores for an individual physiological parameter being in the red (3) is classed as *medium*, a score of 7 or more is classed as a *high* score. Such scores are meant to direct the urgency of the clinical response needed as well as the clinical competency of the responder/s.

A low score should prompt assessment by a competent registered nurse who may decide to change the frequency of clinical monitoring or to escalate the degree of clinical care required. A medium score should prompt an urgent review by a clinician skilled in the competencies of acute illness — usually a ward-based doctor or acute team nurse who should consider whether escalating care to a team with critical care skills is required. A high score should prompt emergency assessment by a clinical team/critical care outreach team with critical-care competencies and will normally involve transfer of the patient to a higher dependency care area.

For those scoring zero, the minimum frequency of monitoring should be once every 12 hours. For those classed as low risk (1–4) this should be increased to monitoring once every 4–6 hours. For those classed as at medium risk, monitoring should be conducted hourly and those of high risk should be monitored continuously.

Therefore, to understand a data structure such as a NEWS chart, we cannot merely focus upon the structure itself, such as the two-dimensional data layout illustrated in Figure 6.2. We must understand how differences made to this structure make a difference to the users of such a chart, not only in terms of how the marks made on this chart serve to inform key actors but also how it makes a difference to further actions of such actors.

In other words, to understand the data structure fully, we need to unpack the various information situations in which this data structure plays its role. Each of the trigger levels discussed above can be treated as an information situation. The health worker, usually a nurse, on a periodic basis, takes a vital sign measurement. This involves the nurse in reading the measurement from some instrument. For instance, the nurse might take the body temperature of the patient using an electronic thermometer. The relevant data-item on the chart is then updated by the nurse and acts as a record of this reading. Once all the vitals signs have been recorded in this manner, the aggregate score for the readings is computed and the appropriate data-item on the chart updated.

When recording each reading on the chart, the nurse is making an assertion not only of the measurement taken, but also the category of the vital sign into which it falls. The aggregate score computed for each session of readings effectively acts as a declarative communicative act. The health worker declares the state of the patient's health at a certain date and time through this score. This declaration then establishes the coordination of further activities that will be performed on the patient. If the risk is

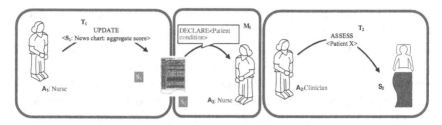

Figure 6.4:   An information situation in the healthcare domain.

categorised as low, then patient monitoring through vital signs continues. If the risk is categorised as medium to high, then various clinicians will be brought into play to make more detailed assessments of the patient's condition and treatment (Figure 6.4).

Thus the vital signs represented on the NEWS chart scaffold a major element of institutional activity conducted by various healthcare workers. Just like any data structure, we might expect aspects of the coupling between articulation and communication as well as that between communication and coordination to breakdown. We shall return to this domain of healthcare in Chapter 9 and consider some actual data breakdowns.

The Typical Lifecycle of the Record

Wheeler (1969a) believes that a record 'may have a career quite independent from that of the person to whom it refers...it may be copied in whole or in part and sent from one institution to another'. Within Chapter 2, we briefly described four different types of articulation that can take place with data structures. As an act of articulation, *create* involves encoding symbols in some new data structure. In contrast, *update* involves recoding certain symbols in some existing data structure. *Read* involves decoding some existing data structure, while delete will involve removing some existing data structure. However, these acts do not occur in isolation — they are component pieces of the career or life-history of a data structure.

Thus acts of articulation are typically enacted within the life-history of a data structure, an abstract representation of which is presented in Figure 6.5. This figure illustrates a series of typical transitions between states within the life-history of a data structure. Data structures usually have a 'birth'. They are created by some actor with some intention

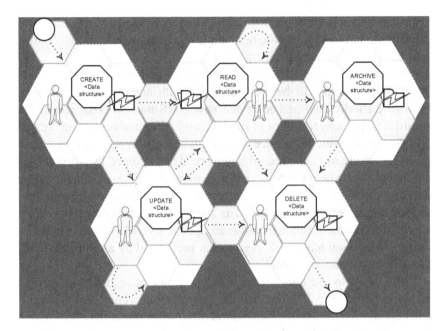

Figure 6.5:   The lifecycle of a data structure.

in mind. Data structures are typically read many times by many different institutional actors because, of course, they communicate about things of interest to such actors. To help actors coordinate their activities, a data structure may be updated many times, again by many different actors. At some point, the things referred to or described by the data structure are regarded by one or more institutional actors as no longer relevant to current or future activity. At such a point, two options become available. Either a data structure is forgotten about, in which case it is deleted, or it is placed in long-term collective memory, in which case it is archived.

Take the example of a patient record within an institution such as the UK National Health Service. This is a large and complex record which mirrors a person's lifelong interaction with this health service. A typical patient record will begin with a surrogate identifier, which in the NHS consists of an NHS number. An NHS number is a 10-digit number such as 485 777 3456 and serves to uniquely refer to one person. The record will then have certain descriptors about the patient which rarely change, such as the name, date of birth and address of residence. This will be followed by lots of data elements which accumulate the life of the patient as an actor that interacts with this institution. Such data elements include health conditions, treatments, medicines, allergies, tests, scans, X-ray results, hospital admissions and discharge data.

Now, consider the life of a patient record within the health service. The patient record will be created by a health administrator following birth of an individual and a unique new NHS number assigned to the record. For persons not born in the UK, an NHS number will be created on first contact with the service when registering with a general practitioner. After its creation, the record will be read and updated by many different actors. So, whenever you visit a General Practitioner, details of the decision made in terms of your treatment and any changes to your prescribed medicines will be recorded as an update to your record. If you are admitted to hospital, this will cause an update, as will your eventual discharge. When you have an X-ray or scan performed by appropriate staff, this will also cause an update.

This leads to the question as to when a patient record is deleted or archived. Most patient records will be archived following a person's death and kept in such an archive for a period of 10 years thereafter. Only at this point will the record be deleted. Can a patient request deletion of their patient record or part of during their lifetime? This right to forget something about the recorded individual is at the centre of a large and complex debate about the rights associated with the record. It is at the centre of the domains of data ownership, data privacy and data protection. We shall examine data protection and data privacy later.

Key Principles

Examining the life of a data structure reveals several crucial points about data structures which we must bear in mind whenever we consider the role of data structures in society.

Data and abstraction

Data structures are constructed artefacts. As Wheeler (1969b) states:

> '... the making, keeping, and reading of records is itself a form of conduct, and indeed an increasingly important one. We actively decide to record some aspects of an individual's behaviour and to ignore others.

To an important extent the actions we later take regarding them will depend upon what we have decided to record. The very record-making process itself then, must be regarded as problematic and we can ask not only for the conditions under which events in a persons life will become a matter of record, but whether it is legitimate for them to become a matter of record.'

The upshot of this is that data structures are always created by somebody or something with a specific purpose in mind — normally to communicate something to some other actors. The act of creating a data structure is not only an act of representation, but also an act of forgetting. Inherent in using a data structure to abstract is the decision of the actor as to what is important to represent and what is not important. For instance, the creator of a data structure such as a passenger name record within the EU records details of a plane trip undertaken by a person and included dates of travel, travel itinerary, ticket information, contact details, travel agent, means of payment, seat number and baggage information. The data structure does not include the purpose of the trip, even though this may be asked of the individual by airline and customers staff.

Informing

Data structures inform intended readers. Data structures are inherently created with an intended reader in mind and this frequently means that the creator of the data structure articulates the facts to be represented to fit the expectations of the intended. Consider the case of Meehan (1986) who studied the record-keeping practices in the policing of juveniles. He argues that what he calls people-processing organisations inherently rely upon both written and oral records to support decision-making about how individual clients are to be treated. However, such records are also used by external agencies to monitor the performance of organisational staff and the organisation as a whole. These conflicting demands influence the type of records kept and the content of such records.

Police officers that Meehan studied routinely made the distinction between three types of 'career' for a routine document in terms of the objective of the written record: internal, external and personal. External documents (such as arrest reports) were accessible and of use primarily to external agencies such as the courts. Internal documents (such as patrol log sheets) were likely to be seen only by co-workers within the organisation. Personal records include the jottings on the police officer's pad, have no organisational status and are used to support the work of the individual. Records with a projected external career have a contractual rather than an actuarial use. An actuarial use seeks to derive a statistical profile. A contractual use may be read as a contract between the organisation and its wider constituency. Hence, an arrest report will be read as accounting to the courts that appropriate standards of law enforcement are exercised.

Meehan (1986) believes that 'This assembling process may involve the selection, recasting, and on occasion, even fabrication of the 'the facts' and the sequence in which they occurred'. An example is provided of the arrest of three youths who were pursued on the ground merely because they were seen at and ran off from an area at which an incident was reported. In the official report, the police officer records coming across them performing a criminal act at the scene and then attempting to abscond. It was explained later that this rendering was a retrofitting to demonstrate that an appropriate arrest was made in the face of a deemable offence. In contrast, the patrol log-sheet was an internal record used for actuarial purposes. The log-sheet summarised the activities (such as calls for service, patrol area checks ...) performed by police officers during their patrol. The record was used primarily by superiors and administrators to manage issues such as productivity. The main problem for the patrol officers is accounting for time spent between official activities such as calls for service that are logged at headquarters. Officers frequently manipulate so-called on-view entries for this purpose such as combining together a series of checks done at different times into one coherent piece of activity. Managers may also issue edicts about patrol-logging practices to attempt to support certain budgetary requests.

The same data structure can also communicate different things to different actors. Another way of putting this is that two or more actors may inform differently on the same data. This is not just that actors may read and focus upon different parts of a data structure. It is because the same data element or item can inform different actors of different things. Reflect back to the example of a procurement operative and audit consultant effectively creating the same list of products in Chapter 4. For the procurement operative, the list-items served as directives to action while for the audit consultant each list-item served as an assertion of a product purchase.

Articulation and communication

Articulation of data structures is always coupled with communication. Updating, deleting and even reading a data structure are all essential parts of communicative acts as are create acts. For instance, updating a data-item which records a person's status will communicate an assertion, which in turn is likely to change certain permissions and obligations associated with a person. Hence, if your status changes to *married* or *parent* then your obligations in relation to the payment of national taxes may change. These changes are associated with the deontology of data structures, a topic which we examine in more detail in Chapter 9.

Design

Data structures have context. An important point is that at some point prior to the enactment of the data lifecycle, data structures must be designed by somebody. However, as I hope to have made clear in Chapter 5, you cannot design a data structure without having a close understanding of the informative and performative context of the data structure. You must understand not only what you wish to communicate with this data structure, but also what you wish to achieve with this data structure. This is why in Chapter 9, we consider how a close understanding of institutional ontology is critical to the proper design of data structures.

Data systems

Data structures exist within wider data systems. A data system consists of a set of data structures and a set of operations which transform or change data structures. Operations in their base form can be defined in terms of the four types of acts of articulation we have considered: create, update, read and delete. Any collection of data structures and operations that articulate data can be considered a data system. Thus Sumerian clay tokens would constitute a data system as would the Inka *khipu*. The old administrative system of using office clerks to maintain a collection of filing cabinets with file drawers and file hangers would be a data system as would a modern electronic database with tables, columns and rows and updated via transactions. A data system also acts as the bedrock for the idea of a physical symbol system, which underlies the notion of a data-driven software actor discussed in Chapter 11.

However, there is an important caveat to all this, namely that the life-cycle of data structures and the data systems within which such lifecycles exist has become much more complex than in the past. This is primarily because many if not most data structures created within modern society are not created by human actors but by artificial actors — i.e. machines. The same goes for updating, reading and even deleting data structures. What is perhaps worse is that the human actors that created the algo-rithms for these software machines frequently do not have a handle on the lifecycle of the data structure articulated by their creations (see Chapter 11).

Data Privacy and Data Protection

It is appropriate at this point to summarise some of the key points about data structures made in this book so far:

- Data are differences made in some substance with the intention to inform — to make differences in the psyche of some other actors.
- Data are typically formed as structures, which are used to code and signal messages. The forming and reforming of such structures is what we have referred to as articulation.
- Such structures are particularly important when articulated in some persistent substance. Persistent data structures are able to code and signal messages to multiple actors across time and space.
- The differences sensed in some data structure form an utterance within a wider communicative act.
- The message formed in some data structure consists of not just con-tent but also intent. Data structures can be used to assert things, direct actors to do things, commit an actor to doing something, declare that something is the case and to express the actor's feelings about something.
- Data structures play a part as key terms within constitutive rules. The data-items within such structures, through collective acceptance, can be taken to count as something else — they form status functions or signs.
- Through this process, data structures scaffold institutional order through the construction of institutional facts that are used in support of coordinated activity.

Because of their critical importance in scaffolding institutional action, data structures, and more particularly the data contained within them, have been at the centre of numerous debates concerning their proper articulation. This is particularly true of data held about the person in such data structures. It has become accepted that, because these data structures identify and describe the person, an individual's right to privacy should be extended to the data structures representing him or her. Data privacy demands that data held about the person should be articulated only in defined ways and that the sharing of such data with third parties should be strictly controlled. At a national and supra-national level, data privacy is normally ensured through data protection legislation.

Countries such as the UK, Sweden and Eire (Ireland) have had a certain level of data protection in place since the late 1980s. This legislation typically seeks to establish certain core principles if organisations wish to articulate data structures that identify or describe the person. It is noteworthy that many such principles are expressed in terms of the collection of data, which as a concept we find problematic (see Chapter 2). We shall therefore express the essence of these principles in terms of obligations placed upon the articulation of data by various institutional actors.

The first principle is that data should be articulated for a specific and declared purpose by organisations. We would interpret this as meaning that the informative nature of the data should be clear — what does the data mean to communicate about the person and what is the intent of such communication? Take a higher education institution that wishes to create student records. To do so, the university will need to declare what attributes of the student it wishes to record and why it wishes to do so. Suppose the university declares that it wished to describe the term-time address of the person. It does so with a clear intention — that of exercising duty of care to the student such as being able to contact the student if they miss a substantial number of classes.

The second principle is that the articulation of data structures that identify and describe individuals should be relevant to the declared purpose. This principle alludes to the performative nature of data structures in implicitly constraining the use of data structures to do certain declared things. In terms of our example, it would be valid for some actor to read the term-time address from this data structure and be informed by this to contact the student about matters pertaining to her academic progress. It would not be appropriate to use such data to send them direct marketing literature.

The third principle is that organisations should maintain accurate and current data on people. Here the focus changes to the articulation of existing data structures and ensuring that such articulation serves to declare 'accurate' institutional facts about the person identified and described. The accuracy of data is a somewhat fluid concept and tends to assume a correspondence view of the data structure, which we discussed in Chapter 2. This is also referred to as a mirror perspective on the data structure, in that it works with the idea that data should accurately *reflect* some observer-independent external reality. According to this viewpoint, data accuracy is a matter of consistency between what a data structure asserts and what is true in the world.

The correspondence or mirror view of the data structure works reasonably well with brute facts — facts held about physical reality. For instance, it is reasonable to assume the idea of consistency between data structures representing the positioning of stars in the solar system and their placing within outer space. These facts can be confirmed by all observers of such physical phenomena. However, the same is not true of institutional facts, such as those that assert institutional attributes of the person. Assertions in this sense correspond to some actors' justified belief that something is the case.

Therefore, within the context of institutions, we believe that it is better to think of a data structure as a set of negotiated collective facts held to be true of something, such as a person. Such institutional facts rely upon a collective acceptance of the existence of certain things for certain purposes. Assume, for instance, we use the identifier of a student number to identify each current student within some higher education institution. The student number serves to assert that the identified person is a valid student within the boundaries of this organisation. As such, the possession of this token enrols this person in the rights associated with students at this institution. However, it also enrols the person in a series of consequent responsibilities such as to behave in a manner specified within the rules and regulations of the institution in question.

The fourth principle is that personal data should be identifiable only for a period and for the purposes for which data is declared. This principle acknowledges that data structures have lives that must be controlled. Policies have to be established for the expected lifespan of a data structure and thereafter for the deletion or archiving of data structures held about the person. Data archiving is often confused with data retention, even within legislation. When data is archived, it is stored for a period, often to meet regulatory requirements of the nation-state, but is not articulated in any way thereafter. When data is retained, also usually to meet regulatory requirements, it may be operated upon and accessed, typically by agencies of the nation-state. Hence, internet service providers as well as many other communication service providers are typically compelled by governments to retain data structures which record the communication activities of their customers. This data is then available to data surveillance operations (see Chapter 12).

Finally, the fifth principle establishes that organisations must ensure that personal data is secured from unauthorised access. This principle clearly establishes the notion that institutional actors must be given appropriate rights to articulate data structures held about the person. This is the issue of data control. It also establishes the need to secure data structures from articulation by actors unauthorised to gain such access — typically actors considered outside of the institution concerned.

The UK's data protection laws have been similar to, but also different from, the data protection laws operated in the 27 other countries of the EU. However, as of May 2018, a set of common data protection laws became applicable for all organisations operating within the EU, wherever they are based. This is known as the General Data Protection Regulation (GDPR) and enshrines the notion that data protection of personal data is now a fundamental right of all citizens of the EU.

The GDPR applies to any forms of data processing or articulation carried out by organisations operating within the EU. It also applies to organisations outside the EU that offer goods or services to individuals in the EU. The GDPR restricts itself to personal data and defines such in terms of any data relating to a person that can be referred to by an identifier (see Chapter 3). The regulation defines three roles in relation to such data: data controllers, data processors and data subjects. A data controller determines the purposes and means of processing personal data. A data processor is responsible for processing personal data on behalf of a controller. A data subject is a person about which personal data is held.

As a data processor, the GDPR places specific legal obligations upon organisations or individuals, such as being required to maintain records of personal data and processing activities. If you are a controller, the GDPR places obligations upon you to ensure your contracts with processors comply with the GDPR.

To be a data controller or processor, you must have a lawful basis to articulate data structures held about persons. Six lawful bases are established in the regulation, and at least one of these must apply whenever you process personal data. The normal state of affairs is that the individual has given clear consent for you to process their personal data for a specific purpose. Alternatively, the processing is necessary for a contract you have with the individual, or because the processing is necessary for you to comply with the law. There are provisions to account for certain exceptional cases which allow articulation where the processing is necessary to protect someone's life or the processing is necessary for you to perform a task in the public interest or the processing is necessary for your legitimate interests.

A series of principles are set out to guide organisations in relation to their data protection responsibilities within the GDPR. These correspond quite closely to the principles discussed earlier, such as data only being articulated in terms of a specified purpose, being adequate and relevant to this expressed purpose, being accurate, held for no longer than necessary and secured from unauthorised access. However, what the GDPR really strengthens in terms of data protection is the rights that a data subject has in relation to the data held about them. These include rights to be informed, have access, to object, the right of rectification and erasure, the right to restrict processing and the right to data portability.

The right to be informed

Individuals have the right to be informed about the collection and use of their personal data.

The right of access

Individuals have the right to access their personal data and can request such access from a data controller.

The right to rectification

The GDPR includes a right for individuals to have inaccurate personal data rectified or completed if it is incomplete. A request can be made for such rectification.

The right to erasure

The GDPR introduces a right for individuals to have personal data erased and a request can be made 'to be forgotten'.

The right to restrict processing

Individuals have the right to request the restriction or suppression of their personal data in certain circumstances.

The right to data portability

The right to data portability allows individuals to obtain and reuse their personal data for their own purposes across different services.

The right to object

The GDPR gives individuals the right to object to the processing of their personal data in certain circumstances, such as in the case of data being used for direct marketing.

Rights in relation to automated decision-making and profiling

Automated decision-making is making a decision solely by automated means without any human involvement (see Chapter 11) while profiling is automated processing of personal data to evaluate certain things about an individual (Chapter 8). The GDPR maintains that you may only carry out automated decision-making where the decision is necessary for the entry into or performance of a contract, or authorised by Union or Member state law applicable to the controller or based upon the individual's explicit consent.

Conclusion

Wheeler (1969) states that, '… a file or dossier is likely to attain a legitimacy and authority that is lacking in more informal types of communication' … 'The file is something we can turn back to again and again, whether the individual to whom the record refers is available or not ... they have a life far beyond the life-span of given individuals'. Thus an understanding of the life of data structures is particularly important in modern institutional life, if only because without such an understanding it is difficult to meet the requirements of data protection and data privacy as well as ensuring effective data control and data security.

Four key ideas have been considered in this chapter. First, that data structures are used to build institutional facts. Second, that such institutional facts serve to scaffold institutional action. Third, that the scaffolding of data structures is always open to breakdown. Fourth, that data structures have a life — they move through various stages of articulation, beginning with their creation and ending with their deletion.

We have argued that making or forming a data structure is a significant part of the way in which modern institutional reality is constituted (Searle, 2010). Data structures take central place in the way in which organisations and society at large form order through the construction of institutional facts which declare states of the world (March and Allen, 2014). Such facts rely upon a background of collective intentionality and are used as a key resource in communicating and reinforcing the nature of institutional order through action.

Just like Bowker and Leigh-Star (1999), the exercise we have attempted here can be seen to employ a meta-level of analysis above that of particular technologies; a way of unpacking the enacted environment within which IT systems are designed, constructed and used. This enables us to understand not only the ways in which order is constituted, but also the ways in which breakdowns (Bødker and Grønbœk, 1991) can occur in contemporary institutional order. However, the work considered in this chapter differs in a number of respects. Bowker and Leigh-Star, for instance, make a convincing case for the place of classification schemes as critical elements of institutional infrastructure. However, their theorisation does not attempt to explain the 'mechanics' of how the data structures reliant upon such classification support and frame institutional action. This has been the objective of the current chapter and we will continue this exercise in further chapters.

Clearly, digital computing and communications technology has made the making and use of data structures much easier. Larger data structures can be built, and such data structures can be manipulated far more quickly than in the past. Hence, it is comparatively easy to search a data structure containing millions of elements in many varied and complex ways in a matter of a few seconds. The practical ease with which modern articulation can occur, linked to the increasing rationalisation of action in modern life, has meant that we rely upon data structures more than at any time in human history. However, the increasing ease with which we can create and manipulate data structures frequently masks much of the nature of these structures as significant artefacts.

Within the current chapter, we have focussed on the way in which the person is instituted through data structures. However, data structures are not, of course, only used for building institutional facts about the person. In Chapter 7, we examine how four other important things are instituted through facts: places, products, times and digital presence. The institutional facts about such things are collected together in registries, meaning that the act of registration is an important part of the mechanics of institutions.

References

Alter, S. (2014). 'Theory of Workarounds.' *Communications of the AIS*, **34**(55): 1041–1066.

Beynon-Davies, P. and Y. Wang (2016). 'Deconstructing Information Sharing.' *International Conference on Information Systems*, Association for Information Systems, Dublin, Eire.

Bødker, S. and K. Grønbæk (1991). 'Co-operative Prototyping: Users and Designers in Mutual Activity.' *International Journal of Man-Machine Studies*, **34**: 453–478.

Bowker, G. and S. Leigh-Star (1999). *Sorting Things Out: Classification and its Consequences* (Cambridge, MA: MIT Press).

Garfinkel, H. (1967). *Studies in Ethnomethodology* (Englewood Cliffs, NJ: Prentice-Hall).

March, S. T. and G. A. Allen (2014). 'Toward a Social Ontology for Conceptual Modeling.' *Communications of the AIS*, **30**(70): 57–62.

Meehan, A. J. (1986). 'Record-Keeping Practices in the Policing of Juveniles.' *Journal of Contemporary Ethnography*, **15**(1): 70–102.

Orlikowski, W. J. (2006). 'Material Knowing: The Scaffolding of Human Knowledgeability.' *European Journal of Information Systems*, **15**(5): 460–466.

RCoP (2012). National Early Warning Score (NEWS): Standardising the Assessment of Acute-illness Severity in the NHS. Royal College of Physicians, London.

Searle, J. R. (1983). *Intentionality: An Essay in the Philosophy of Mind* (Cambridge, UK: Cambridge University Press).

Searle, J. R. (2006). 'Social Ontology: Some Basic Principles.' *Anthropological Theory*, **6**(1): 12–29.

Searle, J. R. (2007). Social Ontology: The Problem and Steps Toward a Solution. In *Intentional Acts and Institutional Facts: Essays on John Searle's Social Ontology*. S. Tsohatzidis (eds.) (Dordrecht, Netherlands: Springer Verlag), pp. 11–29.

Searle, J. R. (2010). *Making the Social World: The Structure of Human Civilization* (Oxford: Oxford University Press).

Wheeler, S. (ed.) (1969a). *On Record: Files and Dossiers in American Life* (New York: Russell Sage Foundation).

Wheeler, S. (1969b). Problems and Issues in Record-keeping. In *On Record: Files and Dossiers in American Life*. S. Wheeler (eds.) (New York: Russell Sage Foundation), pp. 3–24.

Winograd, T. and F. Flores (1986). *Understanding Computers and Cognition: A New Foundation for Design* (Norwood, NJ: Ablex Publishing).

Chapter 7

Instituting Place, Product, Time and Digital Presence

Introduction

The timetable is a ubiquitous data structure in modern society but one which we all take for granted. We forget to remember that a timetable is an artefact with a comparatively recent history. Timetables as data structures are used to commit actors to certain happenings in time — the time a train is expected to arrive at some railway station, the time a plane is due to depart an airport or the time a lecture is due to start or an examination is deemed to finish. Within any one institutional domain, such as a national railway system, the timetable serves to scaffold the coordination of activity not only for passengers but also for other actors such as train drivers and station guards. It informs the train driver of the goals he must meet whereas it informs the station guard of the times he needs to prepare the station platform for. In this sense, timetables as data structures help to institute the very notion of happenings in time for actors within certain domains of institutional activity.

In the last chapter we established that data structures such as timetables are important to instituting facts. The whole point of this is that data structures do not just represent some thing; the act of making a data structure frequently brings the thing into existence for some institution. Hence, as we shall see, a land parcel and, more precisely, the relation of ownership between the land parcel and specific individuals only exists once the place and relation of ownership are registered in something like a land register.

Registers are lists of things, relationships or happenings frequently managed at national and sometimes international level. Hence, most nation-states register not only places, but also births, deaths, marriages and many other things. Some registers record not only things, but also when such things occurred. Hence the notion of time is instituted in registers of records. The important point is that the act of creating some data element in a register, which is typically referred to as an act of registration, is an existential act — a declaration that something is deemed to exist to the institution concerned. The notion of registration is not just a matter of creating a representation of something; the act of registration is effectively a declaration of something — a communication that something is brought into existence.

However, registers are not just important parts of the data infrastructure of nation-states; they are also increasingly important to global digital infrastructure. Therefore, we also look at domain name registries and show how registration of digital presence is critical to scaffolding digital commerce, an area we shall consider in Chapter 10.

We close with an examination of the sharing of data structures which underlies much economic activity within inter-institutional domains such as the supply chain. The sharing of data structures, as we shall see, must be based upon the proper linkage of articulation, communication and coordination. When the coupling between such actions breakdown, then economic activity can be compromised.

The Notion of a Register and Registry

In Chapter 3, we mentioned the important position of identifiers within data structures. An identifier is a data-item used to refer to something of importance to some institution. However, in using the term *refers to* as the relation between the identifier and the object, there is a tendency to think only in terms of an identifier being created once and only if a physical thing already exists. This is the classic view of the data structure in which the structure merely mirrors or represents or corresponds to a pre-existing reality.

What if there is no physical thing to refer to as such, as is the case with institutional things such as contracts, orders, deeds, etc. A better way of thinking about the *refers to* relation in the multifarious ways it can be used with institutional things is to think that the act of reference does not just count as or stand for the thing — it brings the thing into existence for an institution. In other words, the data structure establishes an institutional fact about something. This is why registers and the act of registration is so important to institutions.

Typically, registers are maintained and controlled by registration authorities — or registries for short. Registries are organisations that create and maintain registers. Registers are lists usually maintained on an official basis of things that are held to exist. Indeed, in institutional terms, something does not exist until it has an entry upon a register. The act of registration — of adding a record of something to a register — is effectively a communicative act; in fact, it is a declaration of something. After an entry is made in a register, the thing registered is declared to exist. Registration is an existential act.

In terms of persons, registers are critical for establishing institutional facts such as who someone is, what they are permitted to do or prevented from doing, what they have done, what they own, who they are married to and so on … Hence, if actors wish to undertake many activities, then they must inherently engage with registries of various forms (see Chapter 3). Such registries are sometimes regarded as trusted third parties in that the trust placed in certain activities such as monetary exchange by participating actors is reliant upon the records stored within the registers of registries (see Chapter 10).

The existential status of data structures as a vehicle for institutional facts is the main reason that institutions, even up to the level of nation-states, establish registries with the purpose of maintaining registers of things. In Finland, for instance, four base identity registers are specified by central government: a personal identity register, an enterprise identity register, a building identity register and a land identity register (Rekisteripooli, 2003). These four registers declare citizens, companies, buildings and land parcels to the nation-state.

Registers may simply consist of a list of things assigned a given institutional status. Thus, to start a company in countries such as the UK, you first must register it with a companies registry. Until a record of the company exists in the companies register the company is not deemed to exist and no business activity can be undertaken. Once a company is registered a whole series of obligations become incumbent on the registered directors of the company, such as declaring yearly accounts.

Register entries often consist of a description of events. Take the classic examples of a register of births, marriages and deaths. A birth, marriage or death is an event which affects one or more individuals.

An individual's status changes only when a data element is created within one of these registers. Hence, you are not born, married or die as an event. You are born, married or die to the institution such as a nation-state only when an entry is made in the birth register, marriage register and death register for you. Once an entry exists for you, then your status is declared as a communicative act to all that is given access your record.

Registers also record relationships between things, particularly between people and other things. In a land register, for instance, an entry records a relationship of ownership between one or more individuals and a parcel of land or property. You do not legally own a land parcel or property until a record is made for you in the land register. Likewise, a patent record is required to establish the link between a person or persons and some item of intellectual property. Once such a patent is granted and recorded, then no other individual can make, use or sell similar intellectual property within a defined period.

To solidify our understanding of registers as institutional scaffolding, let us look more closely at four domains where registers are likely to be important to institutional activity. Registers are not just lists of identifiers of place, product, event and digital presence. As we shall see, registers serve to institute the very idea of place, product, event and digital presence.

Identifying Place

To get things done, societal institutions typically have to maintain many different registers of place. Such registers scaffold for institutions the very notion of place. A place is brought into existence through its identification and enacted through the assignment of some identifier, such as an address, to some data-item (Beynon-Davies, 2015), such as:

[<Address> REFERS TO <Place>]

Addresses, as we shall see, scaffold institutional action in several ways. Within the urban landscape of much of the planet, identifiers of place are typically formed as compound signs. By this we mean that they are formed as a compound of a number of significant elements, typically organised in some hierarchical manner. Hence, within much of the Western world, addresses are formed from house numbers, street names, town names or city names and possibly even country names. For instance:

[<12, Friars Road, Dagenham, England, United Kingdom> REFERS TO <Place>]

In doing so, address entries within registers, such as this, serve not only to identify and describe the urban landscape, but also structure activity in terms of the defined architecture of space.

To help manage identifiers within the institutional order of place, many countries have introduced a much more succinct form of surrogate identifier, critical to scaffolding several contemporary institutional contexts. The postcode in the UK, the zip-code in the US and the postleitzahl in Germany all have different forms and work in slightly different ways. In this section we shall therefore focus upon the British postcode as an example of a much wider phenomenon.

Within the UK a postcode is an alphanumeric identifier between five and eight characters long. It consists of two parts divided by a space. The outward code consists of a postcode area and postcode district. The inward code consists of the postcode sector and postcode unit. In contrast, within the US, a zip-code consists of a sectional centre facility code (SCF code) followed by a postal-zone number followed by a hyphen followed by an add-on code.

Postcodes are not simple identifiers. This is because what they refer to in relation to place varies. Within the UK, for instance, each postcode unit can identify a street, part of a street, a single address, a group of properties, a single property, a subsection of some property, an individual organisation or a subsection of some organisation. What is appropriate in each case is often based on the number of packages and physical mail received by the postcode unit. Hence, the following identifier,

[PO16 7GZ REFERS TO <A particular set of residences in Fareham>]

Whereas, the following identifier,

[CF99 1NA REFERS TO <The National assembly of Wales>]

As revealed in their name, postcodes were originally designed as supporting scaffolding for the delivery of letter and parcel mail. They were designed to expedite the delivery of mail by improving the mail sorting process. However, breakdowns still occur within this institutional setting. Mail still gets delivered to the wrong address. Part of the reason for such breakdown revolves around the granularity of the postcode. In other words, a postcode frequently identifies an area of residences rather than a residence. This is part of the reason that Ireland, which never introduced postcodes, introduced instead a more sophisticated form of identification based upon a seven-digit code that uniquely identifies each of its 2.2 million residential addresses (*The Economist*, 2014).

The list of postcodes in current use within the UK is maintained in something known as the Postcode Address File. This register establishes not only the form of identifiers, but also the boundaries of each postcode unit. This list currently serves to enable the identification of approximately 29 million delivery points. However, this list is not a fixed structure. To cope with the continually changing nature of the built landscape within the UK, this list is continuously maintained and periodically updated.

However, postcodes help scaffold various other types of contemporary institutional action beyond the mere sorting and delivery of mail. Many commercial and public satellite navigation systems allow the user to navigate to an address by street number and postcode. This may be life-critical in cases in which an emergency response ambulance needs to arrive within minutes at an incident location. Life insurance companies and pension funds frequently use postcode areas to assess the longevity of customer segments and determine appropriate pricing for premiums and contributions. Car insurance companies frequently use postcode area as a convenient proxy for the risk of events such as theft or accident. Primary healthcare units and secondary schools use postcodes to define the catchment area for their services.

Because of its ubiquity as an identifier of place, postcodes in many institutional areas have become indicators of social status. The perceived linkage between house pricing and postcode area means that residents sometimes campaign to the registration authority of the Royal Mail to change their postcode to that of an adjoining area. Conversely, the catchment area of some desired school, as formed in a list of postcodes, frequently influences house pricing.

The addressing of place is thus not only important scaffolding for the constitution of intra-institutional order, but also critical for effective inter-institutional action. For this reason, many countries have decided that the management of lists of identifiers of place is too important to be left to individual institutions. Denmark, for instance, has one central body which publishes and updates addresses (*The Economist*, 2014). In the UK, the official address register known as the National Address Gazetteer is owned by a private company established in partnership between central and local governments.

The identification of place has been exacerbated in recent times by the rise in location-based services. Some apps utilise the global positioning system (GPS) capability of the smartphone or tablet to identify place and deliver customised services based on such identification. GPS is a network of orbiting satellites that send precise details of their position in space back to earth. These signals are obtained by GPS receivers and are used to calculate the exact positioning of the receiver. A location-based service uses data about location within the provision of some digital service. Therefore, a user might obtain a local weather forecast based on their current location or find Italian restaurants nearby. Certain access devices such as a satellite navigation unit determine location in terms of GPS. Some smartphones also have GPS access. However, for the majority, when using a smartphone, the location of the device is determined in relation to the delay in the signal received from the closest mobile-phone towers (cell-phone towers).

On the ethical front, many worry about the increasing penetration of location-based services and issues of data privacy that arise from this. Although on most mobile phones identification of location can be switched off, most users typically adopt the default setting of on for all apps that need it. This means of course that a whole new data stream is opened up within the data infrastructure of digital commerce (Chapter 10). Institutions can not only capture data about what you are doing with them, but also reference such activity to locations.

Identifying Products

As we shall see in Chapter 10, identifiers are critical to economic activity of various forms. Consider the identification of products. Let us look at an instance which exemplifies many such issues experienced in commerce — the mechanics of using barcodes as classifications of standardised commodity coding and the use of such systems of classification within identifiers for products.

A barcode is a machine-readable representation of a code. Traditionally, barcodes are one-dimensional representations which serve to code data in terms of the widths of lines and spaces between lines. Typically, such a code is used as an identifier for many different things in many different institutional settings. Almost every food retail store, from the largest to the smallest, now sell products that contain barcodes. Patients in hospitals are frequently tagged with plastic bracelets containing barcodes. Books and other forms of document are now given barcodes for ease of tracking. Airline luggage is frequently tracked across the world using barcodes.

The relationship or mapping between a barcode as form and what it refers to is frequently and perhaps confusingly termed a symbology. The most used form of symbology is that to standard commodity coding. The European Article Number (EAN), now renamed as the International Article Number, is widely used in association with a standard for barcoding. As a register, it is maintained by an international agency known as GS1. As a form, it consists of 13 digits in which the first 12 digits code the item and the last digit acts as a check digit. The first three digits of an EAN identify the member organisation to which the product manufacturer belongs. The next three to eight digits identify the manufacturer itself, whereas the last two to six digits identify the product itself.

Strictly speaking a barcode within the realm of commodity coding typically does not identify, it classifies (Chapter 8). In this context, a barcode as an existential object classifies something as a product class. However, barcodes can be used to represent not only commodity codes, but also serial numbers. In this extended form, a barcode can both refer to and classify something:

[12345-5901234123457 REFERS TO <A particular product>]
[5901234123457 ISA <product type>]

Food retail outlets in the European Union use identifiers such as this in various aspects of performance: tracking goods from suppliers, controlling stock in warehouses, managing food displayed within supermarkets and associating products sold with sales made to customers. To facilitate standardisation of data and hence effective analysis of such data for management, many forms of digital procurement will use standard commodity classification coding. Such standard coding schemes may also enable faster searching for an item amongst a range of possible suppliers. Commodity coding involves the assignment of standard codes to item records (at the part number level) and to purchase orders (at the purchase order line item level). Thus a simple coding scheme, in association with its use as identifiers, is critical to a vast amount of organisational communication, decision-making and action within and between contemporary institutions that engage in commerce.

Identifying Events

Data structures are utilised not only to identify places and products, but also to identify happenings or events. Take the simple notion of someone making a fixed line or mobile telephone call. This activity is event-based in the sense that it takes place at a time and has a given duration. When a data structure records time in any form it is said to be *timestamped*. A timestamp is typically a sequence of characters stored as a data-item which serves to identify when a certain event occurred, usually giving date and time of day, sometimes accurate to a small fraction of a second. The term derives from the use of rubber stamps in offices to stamp the current date and time in ink on paper documents. Such a timestamp was normally used to record when the paper document was received.

With the use of automatic digital equipment, timestamping has become an almost universal feature of data articulation. A digital camera will record the time and date at which a photo is taken. A computer will record the time and date of an electronic document being saved. A social media post is likely to have a time and date recorded for the posting.

A good example of the instituting of events is that of product movements. This involves the need to identify not only a product, but also when it moves between various stages of the supply chain. When a product is picked from the warehouse and packed onto some transport, a record is created of this happening. When the transport leaves the warehousing facility, a further happening is recorded. When it arrives at the depot, a timestamped record is created. When it is dispatched from the depot and when it is received by the customer, both such happenings are recorded.

However, let us examine more closely the institutional background to the rise of data structures designed solely with happenings in mind. Timestamping is, of course, only possible because of the collective acceptance of the standard measurement of time.

During the 19th century, increasing industrialisation stimulated the routinisation of activity in work settings. This further stimulated innovations in the standardised measurement of time and space. For effective coordination, instrumental activities need to be referenced in time and space to what we referred to in an earlier chapter as a common ontology. Such referencing demands effective ways of signifying events in time and points in space. Hence, during the rise of industrialisation, the invention of accurate clocks for the signification of time and the invention of accurate maps for the signification of space assumed critical importance.

Just take the notion of time and its importance to scaffolding the activity of institutions. The representation of time in terms of seconds, minutes, hours, days, months and years is clearly an arbitrary set of signs. In other words, it is an invented (cultural) sign-system. We collectively accept that midday is signed as 12 am and midnight as 12 pm but this is purely an arbitrary if convenient convention.

The signification of time in terms of such units serves to aid collaborative action in the sense of providing a common reference point for persons in coordinating their joint action. The measurement and standardisation of time using accurate clocks and the calibration of such clocks in terms of standards such as Greenwich Mean Time were critical to establishing both the concept of time itself and the accurate measurement of other related concepts such as longitude (Sobel, 1996). The accurate measurement of time consequently aided the development of naval exploration, merchant shipping and subsequent world trade. Therefore, time is a critical sign-system in the sense that it is important to the scheduling of human action, has developed a standardised syntax for expressing the meaning of the passage of time and has stimulated the development of a range of technologies for its measurement.

Consider one particularly interesting example of the relationship of time within acts of communication and its performative consequences. Until the advent of the railways in the early 19th century, towns and cities throughout Great Britain kept their own time based upon the rising and the setting of the sun. Travellers across Britain would recalibrate their timepieces as they moved east to west across the country. This meant that the time at Plymouth in the west was 20 minutes earlier than the time kept in London in the east. When travel by stagecoach between these two cities took 22 hours, this had little effect on the activity systems of industry and trade. However, with the rise of the railway network and the speedy travel which it afforded, the need for a common measure of time became essential. First suggested by the Great Western Railway, Greenwich Mean Time or London Time was eventually adopted across the railway network by the mid-1850s. However, it was not until 1880 that Greenwich Mean Time became established in British law as the standard for measuring time across all parts of the country.

This base ontology of time encouraged further innovation such as the invention of the railway timetable, a significant artefact that contributed to the coordination of activity by a multitude of actors such as passengers, station guards, train drivers and number takers in the British railway network (Wolmar, 2007). Early railway companies produced their own timetables for this purpose. However, in 1839, George Bradshaw introduced a single timetable for all the railways in the British rail network. In 1842, this timetable was published monthly, and each issue had over 1,000 pages. The publication ran for over 1,500 editions, the last appearing in May 1961.

As a data structure, Bradshaw's timetable had a page constituting each data element. Each page was presented as a matrix with the stations stopped at along each row, and the columns indicating the times for each possible journey. The page also presented a series of fares for each stage of the journey in several different classes of fare.

Unlike most registers which institute facts about things that have deemed to have happened, the timetable is a register which plots future happenings. Therefore, the timetable does not act here as series of assertions about the world but acts as a series of commitments by a nominated actor (the railway company) to create the events as listed in the timetable in the future. The timetable in this guise is of course an important coordination mechanism not only for passengers but also for other actors such as train drivers and station guards. It informs the train driver of the goals he must meet whereas it informs the station guard of the times he needs to prepare the station platform for. Clearly the scaffolding of this data structure can frequently breakdown. Railway companies today as in the past often commit to things that never happen. In a crowded and ageing railway network, such as that in the UK, trains being late or cancelled are a frequent event.

Identifying Digital Presence

Registers, registries and the process of registration are not limited to instituting physical presence such as place, product and event; they are critical for instituting digital presence, such as in the case of domain name registers. Domain name registers are critical parts of the infrastructure of the World Wide Web.

Domain names initially arose as an attempt to provide meaningful conventions enabling connections to be made between computer systems across the Internet. An Internet Protocol (IP) address is the fundamental way of identifying uniquely a computer system on the Internet. However, Internet users generally find IP addresses difficult to remember. Hence, more memorable identifiers have been introduced which map to IP addresses. Computers attached to the Internet and the Hypertext Mark-up Language (HTML) documents resident on such computers are identified by Universal Resource Locators (URLs).

The syntax of a URL consists of at least two and as many as four parts. A simple two-part URL consists of the protocol used for the connection (such as Hypertext Transfer Protocol — HTTP) and the address at which a resource may be located on the host (such as www.cardiff.ac.uk), typically referred to as a domain name. A domain name is therefore an agreed and structured string of characters that may be used to provide some greater meaning to a URL. In practice, a domain name identifies and locates a host computer or service on the Internet. It often relates to the name of a business, organisation or service and its elements (such as cardiff.ac.uk) must be registered in the same way as a company name.

Any domain name is typically made up of three or more parts referred to as domain levels. Levels therefore provide structure to the domain name. In a URL, domain levels read from right to left: sub-domain, second-level domain and top-level domain (TLD). TLDs consist of either so-called generic top-level domain names (such as .com) and referred to as gTLDs or country codes (such as .uk) and referred to as ccTLDs. gTLDs are also referred to as first-level domain names. Second-level domains serve to further refine the top-level domain name by typically suggesting the type of provider. For instance, .ac indicates an academic institution based in the UK. Sub-domains refer to those domains below the second level and are typically used to refer to a specific content provider. In our example, cardiff signifies the website of Cardiff University.

IP addresses are mapped to domain names by domain name servers. These are computer systems in the inter-network that perform such transformation. For such domain servers to work effectively, standardisation is needed in domain names. Such standardisation has traditionally been in the hands of the US government. However, during the late 1980s and early 1990s, the responsibility for allocating domain names was given to the Internet Assignment Number Authority (IANA). In 1997, IANA and a number of other organisations advocated self-governance in the domain name service and a year later the Internet Corporation for Assigned Names and Numbers (ICANN) was created. The main role of this organisation is to oversee the allocation of domain names and the distribution of addresses by domain name registrars — public and private organisa-tions that exist tasked with maintaining so-called registries: databases of domain names and IP addresses (Mueller, 1998). ICANN therefore has the responsibility for several naming conventions, including gTLDs such as .com and .org and ccTLDs such as .uk and .fr. They also have responsibil-ity for sponsored top-level domain names (sTLDs) such as .coop and .museum and un-sponsored TLDs such as .biz (ICANN, 2007).

IANA originally created seven gTLDs, consisting of strings of three letters taken from the following list: .com. (signifying some form of com-mercial organisation), .org (signifying any type of organisation but typi-cally used to signify public sector or voluntary sector organisations), .gov (initially used to signify government establishments generally but now restricted to refer to US government establishments), .edu (used generally to signify an educational institution internationally), .mil (initially used to signify military establishments generally but now restricted to refer to US Armed Forces establishments), .int. (initially conceived for international entities) and .net (initially used to signify 'networks' and therefore a generic free usage domain).

However, in 'an uncharacteristic lapse of consistency on the part of early Internet designers (Mueller, 1998), IANA established a parallel list of ccTLDs. Part of the reason ccTLDS were introduced and began to be used was because gTLDs gradually began to be perceived internationally as US TLDs (Steinberg and McDowell, 2003). For instance, the original intention was that any educational institution in the world could register itself under the .edu gTLD. In practice, it turned out that, with a few exceptions, only US-based institutions registered under .edu.

The ccTLDs consist of strings of two letters, e.g. .uk, .fr and .es. ICANN clearly states that it does not decide on the status of a country. The verification of countries is therefore delegated to the International Standards Organisation (ISO) and more specifically to inclusion in its ISO-3166 list of country codes. However, there are considerable anoma-lies in the ccTLD naming conventions arising both from inconsistencies in the ISO list and from the presence of early naming agreements estab-lished before the creation of ICANN. The ISO list is derived primarily from a list of country names published by the United Nations, which also assigns unique codes to several inhabited overseas territories. Thus, in 2002 there were 189 countries which had seats in the UN General Assembly but 239 countries on the ISO 3166-1 list. Some countries have also established country codes that conflict with the ISO 3166-1 list

(ISO, 2007). The .uk country code is a notable example in that the specified country code for Britain in the ISO 3166-1 list is .gb. Some 'regions' within this country also have codes established in ISO 3166-1 list. Examples here are .gg (Guernsey), .im (Isle of Man) and .je (Jersey).

Therefore, over time the domain system has been gradually extended, sometimes in an apparent piecemeal manner. For instance, the current ICANN namespace contains 21 registered gTLDs, all of which are open for use as supporting infrastructure for the Internet. At the end of 2006, there were 120 million unique registered domain names in the world (New Media Age, 2007) and, of these, 80 million were generic TLDs. The most used generic TLD was .com, with 62 million domains. There was a 32% increase in domain name registrations in 2006 as compared to 2005. In early 2010, there were 192 million registered domain names with the largest fraction still being in the .com TLD, while in 2020 there were 198 million.

Adding to its complexity, since 2000, several sTLDs have been created, typically backed by some defined community. The named sponsor of an sTLD is delegated the responsibility of administering the domain in the sense that it decides if a person or legal entity can register for use of the domain. Such sponsored domain names include, .aero (signifying the aeronautical industry), .coop signifying cooperative organisations, .museum (signifying museums) and .cat (signifying the Catalan language and cultural community, discussed below).

Also, since 2000 a number of non-sponsored domain names have been created. These are gTLDs, not backed by a community but which operate under the policies established by the global Internet community, directly through ICANN. Such non-sponsored domain names include .biz. (signifying businesses), .info (signifying information resources — an extension of .net), .pro (signifying independent professionals — lawyers, doctors, etc.) and .name (signifying individuals or legal entities that wish to register their names as domains).

Applications for the approval of a new TLD are made to ICANN using a defined process. Decision-making on applications within ICANN is conducted via a series of meetings held by ICANN's board of governors, and within a variety of committees such as the Generic Names Supporting Organisation (GNSO), the At-Large Advisory Committee (ALAC), the Governmental Advisory Committee (GAC) and other so-called constituencies. Representation from various interest groups is included at the committee level. After approving a new TLD domain,

ICANN delegates the administration of issuing it to IANA. Domain names frequently launch with a defined sunrise period, which refers to the period at the launch of a new TLD during which owners of trademarks may register a domain name containing the owned mark.

Data Sharing

We mentioned in Chapter 6 that data structures not only serve to scaffold intra-institutional order, but also are critically important to inter-institutional order. Many of the examples of instituting things through registers highlight the ways in which the sharing of data is critical inter-institutional scaffolding. The common addressing of place, identification of products, calibration of time and registration of digital presence acts as infrastructure allowing actors taking action in different institutional domains to use a common ontology for communication and in order to coordinate their activity.

Much has been written within communities of practice, particularly within the public sector, about both the potentialities and pitfalls associated with the sharing data such as lists of personal identifiers (see Chapter 4) between institutional agencies. The theory developed in this book has allowed us to unpack not only the key function that data structures play, but also some of the inherent dangers that lie within any attempt at articulating such data structures. Hence, we need to understand not only how intra-institutional order is constituted, but also how inter-institutional order relies upon the collective declaration of significance through the scaffolding of data structures.

To demonstrate how data structures are shared between institutions, let us unpack the scaffolding of data structures enacted within a significant aspect of modern-day life — that of using automobiles for personal transportation. The inter-institutional narrative provided here is based on our understanding of a number of directives issued by the European Parliament and Council, which pertain to activities associated with automobile use by European citizens, including the UK at the time of writing.

The simple activity of using an automobile to transport oneself relies upon a complex, entangled order of significant accomplishment. Such order involves the coordinated action of many different institutional actors, which in turn relies upon a network of communicative actions, and which further relies upon a network of actions involved with the articulation of data structures. We first demonstrate how an inter-institutional domain such as this can be unpacked in terms of our theory of the scaffolding of data structures developed in previous chapters. This leads to discussion of a number of potential dysfunctions that arise in the use of lists as institutional artefacts that bind communication and performance within this domain.

First, let us establish something of the ready-to-hand background to this domain which any actor participating in institutional action must utilise. Personal automobiles are clearly produced by automobile manufacturers. As new vehicles, they are then normally sold through established automobile dealerships to buyers. Automobiles are, of course, purchased for the purpose of driving and as such pass into the ownership of persons, but they can only be driven by people who have passed the appropriate driving test. They also need to be parked at various locations in the process of making journeys. At some point in its life, an automobile may be subject to some incident: it may be in a crash, be stolen in its entirety or have its number plates or hub caps stolen. Eventually, the automobile will reach the end of its usefulness and will need to be scrapped and recycled.

However, the activities of personal automobile use demand a complex sequence of communicative acts between various actors, often acting within different institutions. The manufacturer of a new vehicle first must assert to its dealerships that a vehicle that fits a certain description has been manufactured on a certain date and is available for sale. A customer will then direct a dealership that they wish to purchase a car at a price and a sale is struck by the dealership confirming details of the vehicle sold with the customer. The seller of the automobile then must assert to the appropriate registration authority that the vehicle has been sold to a designated person. The vehicle registration authority then declares that the nominated person is the new owner of the vehicle. To insure the automobile against fire, theft and damage, the owner has to both tax the vehicle and prove its roadworthiness. In the case of a new vehicle, roadworthiness is communicated automatically through the manufacturer and dealership. In the case of a car more than three years old, then roadworthiness must be declared by an authorised test centre to the registration authority. If the roadworthiness, taxable status and driving status of the owner can be declared from the vehicle registration authority, then the insurance company can declare in turn that the vehicle is insured for a given period. During its life, the driver may park at some location and be declared to have parked illegally. Also, more serious incidents may occur, such as theft of number plates, which need to be asserted to law enforcement agencies.

Clearly, many acts of communication within this enacted environment will not be conducted in face-to-face communication between actors. Instead, such acts of communication will form data structures within the data systems of various institutions. Such data structures are then exchanged between institutional actors and will be used to inform further performance by such actors.

When a manufacturer produces a new automobile, they are likely to enter a vehicle record into their manufacturing database. This can be considered as similar in nature to entering a new identifier for a vehicle as a list-item into the list of vehicles manufactured by this company. Details from this database will be used to select an automobile by a dealership for sale to the customer. Before sale, the dealership will apply for a vehicle registration number to the registration authority and this number will be placed on number plates positioned on the car. After sale of the vehicle, the two parts of the vehicle registration document are completed by the seller. One part is given to the buyer as proof of purchase, while the other is sent to the registration authority. The registration authority uses part 2 of this registration document to update its ownership and vehicle records and will send the final ownership document to the address of the nominated owner. To drive the car, the owner needs to tax and insure the vehicle. To tax the vehicle, the owner needs to prove ownership through the relevant documents. Also, if it is a car over three years old, then the roadworthiness of the vehicle needs to be verified through a roadworthiness certificate issued by a validated test centre. To insure the vehicle, details are provided to the insurance company of the registration number of the car and the person or persons expected to be driving the car. The insurance company can enquire of the registration authority certain data structures which it uses to confirm details of the vehicle, its ownership and roadworthiness. Provided these are satisfactory, the car insurance policy can be issued. At some point in using the vehicle, the driver may receive a parking ticket; details will be entered as an infringement record in the data structures of the parking agency. When something more serious such as the theft of number plates happens, then an incident record will be entered by a law enforcement agency and an incident number given to the owner for use in claims to insurance companies.

It is noteworthy that the data structures articulated by various actors within this inter-institutional order come in various 'forms'. Some comprise physical tokens such as number plates or tax disks. Others comprise electronic signals such as telephone messages or electronic records such as vehicle or ownership records. Finally, a great deal of tangible documentation is produced within various information situations, such as registration documents or certificates of destruction. The important point is that both the content and intent of communications can be formed in many ways within such institutional patterns. The subtle differences in the way in which such a pattern is constituted amongst various countries of the EU sometimes depends upon the forms of data articulated. For instance, a few years ago the UK introduced a variation to its inter-institutional order which removes the significance of the tangible tax disk as a data structure. The consequence of this change to the form of a tax registration means that the only way of now knowing whether an automobile is taxed or not is to query the electronic records held by the vehicle tax registration authority.

Now consider how this inter-institutional order may breakdown. Agerfalk and Eriksson (2011) describe a scenario taken from the enacted environment of personal automobile transport, based upon an incident reported in the Swedish press. The scenario begins with Lars having his number plates stolen from his blue Toyota Auris, which he duly reports to the police. He then proceeds to order another set of the same number plates from a registered plate supplier, and when they arrive, places them back on his car.

A week or so later, Lars receives a notification from the police that a burnt-out car had been found with his stolen number plates and that this car is now being scrapped. Then Lars received 13 parking tickets for his car through the postal service. He is puzzled since during the period in which these offences occurred his car had been parked outside his house. It becomes apparent, after contacting the police and parking authorities, that the parking tickets were actually incurred by the car with his stolen number plates. Later still, Lars receives notification from his car insurance company that his car insurance policy is now void because they have been informed that his car has been scrapped. This is odd because Lars can clearly see his car parked on his drive!

As we have made the point repeatedly, conventionally data structures are taken to be unequivocal representations of some real-world domain, typically some intra-institutional or inter-institutional domain (Wand and

Weber, 1995). In such terms, an identifier, as a critical part of some data structure, is used to stand for properties of some real world 'thing'. Thus, a vehicle registration number as an identifier is used to stand for properties such as the model, colour and engine size of the vehicle and these properties are seen to represent an actual car in the real world. Such representations, stored in some data structure, are considered facts or propositions which describe the domain of discourse covered by the database. In such terms, two vehicles having the same registration number amounts to a logical contradiction which must be resolved outside of the data system by various actors.

In contrast to this correspondence view of data structures, we have, of course, made the case for treating data structures and their components, such as identifiers, as communicative acts, particularly acts of declaration. As such, an identifier, and the properties it stands for, need relate to not only a physical thing, but also to a conceptual and institutional thing. In the latter case, identifiers and records relate to a whole series of rights, responsibilities, obligations and commitments associated with the thing. Hence, the act of registering ownership of a vehicle puts in train a series of rights such as capability to drive the vehicle on the road and a series of obligations upon the owner to tax, insure and regularly test the roadworthiness of the vehicle. We shall examine how data structures enact such rights in more detail in Chapter 9.

In this case, the scenario of the stolen identifier can be explained as a breakdown in the scaffolding of data structures within the interinstitutional domain described. In the scenario described, two different cars ended up with the same identifier — the same number plates. Since this identifier was recorded in various institutional lists against one particular owner, identified in various different ways within such systems, the rights and responsibilities of this particular owner were essentially 'multiplied' across two things (cars) for the period in which the stolen number plates were used. As far as the parking institution was concerned, for instance, its inspection of ownership records clearly showed that Lars was the owner of the car with the registration BD51SMR. In other words, this particular data structure asserted the institutional fact of ownership. This was sufficient for them to issue parking tickets to the address listed for Lars, and through this to declare that this person had engaged in several parking infringements. More intense scrutiny might have revealed that further designated properties of the car having made the infringement did not match details held within certain data structures.

Likewise, when the car with the stolen number plates was eventually set on fire, the authorised treatment facility, which was given responsibility for scrapping the car by the police, produced a certificate of destruction having first enquired of the registered owner of the vehicle in appropriate data structures. They then notified the registration authority of the destruction of the vehicle, which updated its data structures accordingly. This triggered a declaration to the insurance company listed for the vehicle, which in turn issued a declaration of insurance termination to the registered owner of the vehicle. Great effort was then needed on the part of Lars to unravel these institutional facts and reinstate his previous deontic status: his rights and responsibilities in relation to an automobile.

Conclusion

Lists of identifiers act not only as supporting 'infrastructure' (Bowker and Leigh-Star, 1999) or 'scaffolding' (Orlikowski, 2006) within organisations, but also as institutional objects shared between organisations. The identifiers of people, places and products are critically important scaffolding not only for actions of governance, but also for actions of commerce. Such data is typically held in registers of various forms — basic data systems storing necessary identity data. Because of the criticality of such data structures, many nation-states have made efforts to centralise these registers of identification.

However, lists of identifiers as institutional objects not only serve to constitute institutional order, but also are critical elements within breakdowns in such order. For instance, lists of personal identifiers act not only as critical scaffolding within the inter and intra-institutional order, such lists help form a considerable problematic for modern individuals, organisations and societies (Whitley *et al.*, 2014). Breakdowns in institutional order are evident in the case of the Criminal Records Bureau in the UK (Beynon-Davies, 2011), the ownership of automobiles in the European Union (Agerfalk and Eriksson, 2011) and in the management of foreign students in higher education in Sweden (Eriksson and Agerfalk, 2010).

Breakdowns are an inherent consequence of the ways in which data structures scaffold institutional ontology. In the next chapter, we take a more detailed look at this notion of institutional ontology. We demonstrate how we can construct such ontology from the base principles established in previous chapters, as well as certain principles of abstraction.

This enables us to examine a critical aspect of contemporary data infrastructure with greater precision — that of metadata — which is important not only to the sharing of data, but also other data-driven activities such as surveillance (see Chapter 12).

References

Agerfalk, P. J. and O. Eriksson (2011). The Stolen Identifier: An Inquiry Into the Nature of Identification and the Ontological Status of Information Systems. *International Conference on Information Systems*, July 2011, Shanghai.

Beynon-Davies, P. (2011). *Significance: Exploring the Nature of Information, Systems and Technology* (Houndmills, Basingstoke: Palgrave).

Beynon-Davies, P. (2015) "Forming Institutional Order: The Scaffolding of Lists and Identifiers." *Journal of the Association for Information Science and Technology* **67**(11). DOI: 10.1002/asi.23613.

Bowker, G. and S. Leigh-Star (1999). *Sorting Things Out: Classification and Its Consequences* (Cambridge, MA: MIT Press).

ICANN. (2007). http://www.icann.org/. Retrieved March 2007.

The Economist (2014). *Getting on the Map*, 20 September.

Eriksson, O. and P. J. Agerfalk (2010). "Rethinking the Meaning of Identifiers in Information Infrastructures." *Journal of the Association for Information Systems*, **11**(8): 433–454.

Mueller, M. L. (1998). "The Battle Over Internet Domain Names." *Telecommunications Policy*, **22**(2): 89–107.

Orlikowski, W. J. (2006). "Material Knowing: The Scaffolding of Human Knowledgeability." *European Journal of Information Systems*, **15**(5): 460–466.

Rekisteripooli (2003). *Base Registers in Finland* (Helsinki: Finnish Government).

Sobel, D. (1996). *Longitude* (London: Fourth Estate).

Steinberg, P. E. and S. D. McDowell (2003). "Mutiny on the Bandwidth: The Semiotics of Statehood in the Internet Domain Name Registries of Pitcairn Island and Niue." *New Media and Society*, **5**(1): 47–67.

Whitley, E. A., U. Gal and A. Kjaergaard (2014). "Who Do You Think You Are? A Review of the Complex Interplay Between Information Systems, Identification and Identity." *European Journal of Information Systems*, **23**(1): 17–35.

Wand, Y. and R. Weber (1995). "On the Deep Structure of Information Systems." *Information Systems Journal*, **5**(3): 203–223.

Wolmar, C. (2007). *Fire and Steam: A New History of the Railways in Britain* (London: Atlantic Books).

Chapter 8

Building Ontology

Introduction

Signs are vehicles that enable us to chunk up the complex world around us into convenient categories. Such categories not only allow us to organise our perception of the world, but also help us determine what we do or should do in the world. This is why the Computer Scientist/Sociologist Lucy Suchman (1994) claimed a number of years ago that 'categories have politics'. Suchman made this statement to emphasise the way in which the categories we use to classify things reflect what we believe to be prescribed or proscribed within society. Given that the signs we use to chunk up the world are critical to the way we communicate, our discourse is necessarily likely to reflect and inject our politics — our beliefs about power and how it should be exercised.

Let us ask you a simple question which will demonstrate the power of categories or classification. Ernesto 'Che' Guevara was an Argentine Marxist who played a significant role in the Cuban Revolution. So, *was Che Guevara a terrorist?* Using this sign (terrorist) to stand for this person (Guevara) and classifying or categorising him in this way probably depends upon what end of the political spectrum you are from. If your political attitudes lean towards the Right (another example of classification) then this statement would probably accord with your views. In contrast, if you are at the opposite end of the political spectrum (the Left) you would probably prefer to classify him as something like a *freedom fighter*. We consider the relationship between data structures and power more clearly in Chapter 9. In the current chapter, we concentrate on the essence of chunking up the world through signs and how such chunking provides the basis for institutional ontology.

In previous chapters we made the point that semiosis — sign-activity — is a continuous process in which actors engage the world. Some would even argue that we never engage with the world directly — our engagement is always mediated through signs. Signs, of course, are not isolated entities; they exist in a complex lattice consisting of a mass of other related signs. The way in which a certain sign leads certain actors to accomplish information is often down to its relationships with other signs within this lattice structure.

Signs not only identify and describe, they serve to construct the world. Hence, this notion of a sign lattice, as we shall see, helps provide a way of thinking about the idea of institutional ontology — the things or objects held to exist by a group of actors within some institutional domain. In this chapter, we want to consider how such a lattice might be constructed from base principles established in previous chapters. This will give us a better understanding of the ways in which institutional ontology is constructed from data structures through different but connected processes of abstraction, such as association, generalisation and aggregation. This architecture of abstraction will also allow us to examine more closely the important topic of metadata — data about data. Metadata, as we shall see, is critical to the way in which the contemporary data infrastructure within society is formed.

Objects

Within previous chapters, we used the term 'thing' in a very general way to represent any unit of existence, or more precisely something a set of actors within some institutional domain takes to exist (see Chapter 2). Computer scientists would refer to such things as *objects* and think of the abstraction of such objects as classes of object or *object classes*. We used the terms *object* and *object class* rather informally in previous chapters, but in this chapter we define them more clearly. This will lead us to adopt these terms wherever possible from now on in this book because they provide a more precise vocabulary with which to understand and to build ontology.

So, objects are the component units of some ontology — some set of beliefs common to a set of actors about what reality is. An object is an instance of something of interest to two or more actors within some domain. Objects, as we have seen, may be physical things, such as customers, products, houses, and cars — all these objects have a material form. However, objects may also be events such as a house sale, a customer order, a customer payment or a car service — these events are all timestamped happenings (see Chapter 7). Finally, objects may be institutional things, such as orders, sales, contracts and deeds. Institutional objects may take a material existence, such as a paper form or an electronic data structure, but the objects themselves do not depend on their material form as such. Instead, they rely on a collective acceptance amongst a group of actors that these objects are deemed to exist.

A fundamental property of any object is that it must be distinguishable (see Chapter 1). We must be able to sever some physical or conceptual space and say what is a certain object and what is not that object. In this sense, we might define an object as some aspect of a domain which can be distinguished from other aspects of the domain: something that makes a difference to actors. To differentiate one object from another, we typically assign an identifier (see Chapter 3) to the object and to effectively discriminate each identifier ideally should be unique within the domain in question. For example, assume the domain of interest is a manufacturing plant. We might have a list of identifiers for objects of interest to this domain as follows:

[5342]
[6634]
[9982]
...

As identifiers these signs refer to some distinct object — physical, institutional or an event:

[5342 REFERS TO <object>]
[6634 REFERS TO <object>]
[9982 REFERS TO <object>]
...

Classification and Instantiation

Bowker and Leigh-Star (1999) explore the use of categories within standards established for professional practice. Indeed, they consider the creation and maintenance of classification schemes as a form of work practice in itself. They make the important point that classification helps order human interaction. For them, 'to classify is human'. Classification schemes form an important part of the data infrastructure underlying much human activity and, as such, they are frequently invisible or tacit to actors performing such activity. They are ready-at-hand parts of the way in which actors approach objects. So, let us look at what classification means in terms of ontology.

If you remember from Chapter 3, a constitutive rule is a rule which has the form:

[X counts as Y in C]

Or,

[X stands for Y in C to Z]

where X is some thing which counts as or stands for some other thing (Y) in some institutional context (C) to some actor (Z).

However, in previous chapters, we also introduced certain constitutive rules that are special in nature. In Chapter 3, for instance, we introduced an instantiation or classification rule and indicated that such rules are building blocks for the process of infinite semiosis — the process by which one sign, B, stands for another sign, A. In turn, sign C stands for sign B, and so on. We did this because classification, or its opposite instantiation, is a key example of *abstraction* — taking some sign not to stand directly for something but to stand for another sign. To remind ourselves, as a constitutive rule, classification can be expressed as:

[X ISA Y in C]

The relation *ISA* here may be taken to be a special type of stands for relation in which X is a placeholder for some identifier, while Y is a class or category to which the thing identified by X applies. C denotes the institutional domain in which this classification rule holds. So, we might instantiate (assign some instances to) the identifiers previously listed within the domain of a manufacturing plant in the following manner:

[5342 ISA Product]
[6634 ISA Product]

[9982 ISA Product]

...

The *Y* term in the constitutive rule we have just seen is an *object class*, or class for short, and forms an abstraction of a group of instances or objects. This means that there are normally many objects that correspond to an object class, as is the case with our example of the class *product*. If there are not many instances of something within the domain in question, it is probably not worth actors making the abstraction of an object class.

Generally, a class is something which a group of actors wishes to communicate about. To do so, the group of actors must be able to distinguish instances of some class from instances of some other class. Therefore, a class is an abstraction from the complexities of some domain. When we speak of a class, we normally speak of some aspect of the domain which can be distinguished from other aspects of the domain. Again, something that makes a difference. But now we are working at a higher level of abstraction than an object. An object class is a sign which stands for an object, or more likely a set of such objects, and serves to categorise or classify such objects.

When actually writing of a product such as a galvanised steel lintel or a person such as a lecturer or an event such as a business visit, we are inherently using signs as classes. As we indicated, to speak or write or generally to communicate about some object, we need an identifier to refer to the specific thing we are referring to or identifying (Chapter 3). In such terms, an identifier, as we have seen, is one of the most important of signs. Paul Beynon-Davies is an identifier for me: it singles out me as an object of interest. Lecturer, consultant, academic and author are all signs for classes which apply to me: they are designators for certain concepts that encapsulate a certain space of objects. What we use such classes for is to chunk up the world so that we can communicate about it — discriminate between things and describe such things.

Hence, when we write:

[9982 ISA Product]

we are defining an object (identified as 9982) as being a member of the class product. In one direction, from object to class (9982 to product), we are classifying an object as being an instance of a class: this is the process of classification. In the other direction (product to 9982), we are engaging in instantiation: instantiating (making an instance of) a given class, by listing an object that is encompassed by or covered by the class.

Attribution and Association

Therefore, an object class is an abstraction of the common features of a group of objects. Such features are defined in terms of relationships between the class and its properties and instances as well as relationships between the class and other classes.

When we define the properties of some class, we engage in a process of *attribution*. Attribution is the process of defining a class in terms of its properties or attributes. Consider the notion of a manufacturing product again, perhaps steel lintels. A product is a class here defined by attributes or properties such as product length and product weight.

The constitutive rule for attribution might be written as:

X HASA Y in C

Where *X* is a class and *Y* is an attribute of the class within the institutional domain *C*. This means that we can define a class in terms of a listing of its attributes. For example:

[Product HASA Product Length]
[Product HASA Product Weight]

This way of defining a class through its attributes, properties or features is referred to as an *intensional* definition of the class.

Valuing an Object and Forming an Object Class

In previous chapters, we established that a datum, i.e. a unit of data, is used to represent a fact (typically an institutional fact) relevant to some domain. In terms of the persistent record, a datum is formed by making a data-item correspond to the attribute of some class and assigning some value to this data-item. This means that a data element is typically used to collect together a set of cognate attributes of some class and through so doing builds an instantiation of the class — it represents an object of the defined object class. Thus, we can build a data element or object for the *product* class by listing its attributes and assigning a value to these attributes, such as:

> *[5342 Product Length 10]*
> *[5342 Product Weight 20]*
> ...

This means that the entire listing of objects as data elements serves to form a complete data structure. This data structure serves to represent, through a complete listing of objects, the object class. This way of defining an object class in terms of its objects is said to be an *extensional* definition of an object class. Hence, we might provide a complete extensional definition for our product class by building a list such as:

> *[5342 Product Length 10]*
> *[5342 Product Weight 20]*
> *[6634 Product Length 20]*
> *[6634 Product Weight 40]*
> *[9982 Product Length 60]*
> *[9982 Product Weight 60]*
> ...

Association

However, classes are defined not only by their attributes, but also in terms of their associations with other classes. An association is typically a defined relationship between two distinct object classes. To take an example, as we have seen before from our manufacturing domain, there are likely to be associations between a stillage (a container for a set of product) and a manufacturing location. We first need to define *stillage* and *location* as classes with objects; we have of course already defined the *product* class. We refer to stillage objects through a stillage code and location objects through a production location code. For example:

> *[26641 ISA Stillage]*
> *[26643 ISA Stillage]*
> *[24536 ISA Stillage]*
> ...
> *[PL0102 ISA Location]*

[PL0103 ISA Location]
[PL0104 ISA Location]
...

We then need to build a series of associations between these three classes. This means associating the *product* class with the *stillage* class and the *stillage* class with a *location* class.

[Stillage CONTAINS Product]
[Stillage LOCATED AT Location]
[Stillage MOVE TO Location]

The terms *CONTAINS, LOCATED AT* and *MOVE TO* within these binary relations here are signs we use to refer to linkages between objects in the class *stillage* and objects in the class *product*, as well as objects in the class *stillage* and objects in the class *location*. In other words, we can define relationships of association by extension through building lists of named pairs of object identifiers. Hence, we might have a *contains* list such as:

[26641 CONTAINS 5342]
[26643 CONTAINS 6634]
[24536 CONTAINS 9982]
...

Next, we might build a stock location list, such as:

[26641 LOCATED AT PL0102]
[26643 LOCATED AT PL0102]
[24536 LOCATED AT PL0102]
...

Or a stock movement list:

[26641 MOVE TO PL0103]
[26643 MOVE TO PL0103]
[24536 MOVE TO PL0104]
...

It is noteworthy that two classes, such as stillage and location, can be associated together by more than one relationship. This helps to explain why in building institutional ontology we need a layer of abstraction over and above the layer of institutional facts. The abstraction layer provides context to the institutional facts and represents the collective understanding or acceptance of the facts by actors within the domain. For instance, within our manufacturing domain, it is impossible for actors to be informed by the fact:

[26641 LOCATED AT PL0102]

Without a collective understanding that 26641 refers to a *stillage*, *PL0102* refers to a *production location* and the term *LOCATED AT* stands for an association between the two objects.

Generalisation and Specialisation

So far we have only moved one step up in the process of semiosis by classifying some object or attributing properties to an object or associating one class with another class. We next consider moving further up the hierarchy of semiosis through the process of generalisation. The special constitutive rule here is expressed as:

X AKO Y in C

where X is an object class, described as the sub-class, and Y is its super-class, meaning it is a more general or abstract class than Y. The AKO (short for *a kind of*) relationship represents a form of abstraction known as generalisation or its opposite specialisation. In one direction, from sub-class to super-class, we are generalising from one level of abstraction to another. In the other direction, from super-class to sub-class, we are reducing the level of abstraction, or specialising a class.

Hence, when we state that:

[Lintel AKO Product]
[Crash barrier AKO Product]
...

We are expressing two sub-classes of the *product* class, namely *lintel* and *crash barrier*. The important point here is that sub-classes *inherit* the properties and relationships of their super-class. The analogy being made here is between the transfer of traits through genes and the transfer of properties through specialisation. Hence, declaring a lintel to be a kind of product means that we can assume that it has a weight and length. Also, that it is stored in a stillage at a production location and moved between production locations within the manufacturing plant.

Generalisation is particularly important to many professional practices that involve the standardised naming of things. For instance, it is critical to taxonomy, the science of identifying and naming species or organism. Taxonomy is an important sub-discipline of biology where the taxonomic scheme of biological organisms is organised hierarchically in terms of domain, kingdom, phylum, class, order, family, genus, and species. This amounts to a formalised semiotic hierarchy and allows biologists across the world to communicate effectively. Most libraries also use taxonomy for organising the storage and retrieval of publications. For instance the Dewey Decimal scheme, much used in libraries worldwide, organises publications into 10 main classes. Each main class is then expanded into 10 divisions, and, each division is then expanded into 10 sections.

Aggregation and Decomposition

We can build a substantial part of some ontology with classification, attribution, association and generalisation. However, there is one more constitutive rule that we must exercise — i.e. aggregation or its opposite decomposition. The constitutive rule here is:

X PART OF Y in C

In which X is a class which is part of a wider whole class Y in some domain C.

An aggregation relationship occurs between a whole and its parts and is an abstraction in which a relationship between objects is considered a higher-level object. This makes it possible to focus on the aggregate while suppressing lower-level detail. For example, in terms of the financial domain, we might define a *financial portfolio* class that aggregates together all the financial products making up a given customers interaction with the financial company. In such terms, a *financial portfolio* class can be considered an aggregate of securities, insurance policies and savings accounts. Likewise, a *country* can be considered an aggregate of regions which are aggregates of counties which are aggregates of districts, and so on. In the case of the health service, a *patient history* can be considered as a collection or an aggregate of diagnoses, prescriptions and treatments.

Hence, aggregation relationships compose an object out of an assembly or aggregation of other objects. When we state that:

> *[Railway station PART OF railway]*
> *[Railway line PARTOF railway]*

we are declaring that railways are composed of an aggregation of railway stations and railway lines.

The opposite of aggregation is decomposition. That is, the process of decomposing an object class into its constituent parts. Hence, there is a clear difference between aggregation and generalisation. If two classes are defined in terms of a generalisation relationship, then both sub-class and super-class effectively refer to the same thing, the same group of objects. The super-class is merely a higher-level abstraction of the thing than its sub-class. In contrast, within an aggregation relationship the aggregate, the whole, is different from any of its parts. A financial portfolio is different from an insurance policy and a country is different from a county. A railway is different from a railway line and a patient history is different from a patient treatment.

Institutional Ontology

Let us review where we have got to. A sign lattice helps provide a concrete way of thinking about the notion of institutional ontology and is constructed from objects and classes as well as relationships of attribution, association, generalisation and aggregation.

Objects and classes are signs we use not only to describe an institutional domain, but also to prescribe what can exist within this domain. When we declare *a lintel to be a kind of product* and that *<9982> is a product* we not only identify a product as being of a certain type, we expect through inheritance for it to be described in terms of its length and weight. However, as we indicated in Chapter 4, identifying and describing a product in this way brings this thing into existence for the domain. As far as institutional ontology is concerned, a thing does not exist until it can be signified or named. This is a bit like a wizard from Ursula Le Guin's (1993) fantasy of Earthsea, who can only cast a spell by providing the correct but hidden name for an object.

As Figure 8.1 suggests, signs do not exist in isolation. They exist in a complex lattice consisting of other related signs. The way in which a certain sign has the potential to inform actors is down to its relationships with other signs within the lattice structure. Hence, as we have seen, a stillage only makes sense as a container of product which can be stored at production locations and moved between such locations. Products may be lintels or crash barriers and are part of the wider aggregate of a product line.

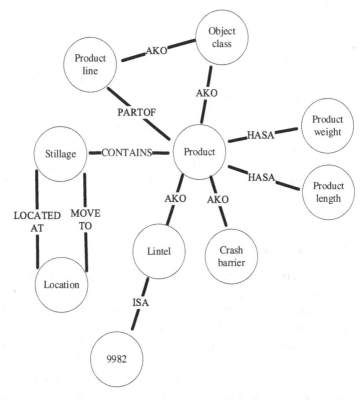

Figure 8.1:   A sign lattice.

Although we have taken great pains within this chapter to unravel the ways in which institutional ontology is built, we should remember that actors taking action within domains, such as the manufacturing domain we have considered, do not think and act with such a formal notion of ontology. Instead, they acquire such ontology through socialisation into the domain and utilise such ontology as an accepted and unexamined part of their surround-world — their ready-at-hand appreciation of the significance of objects. This means that a domain actor's ontological understanding is very much entangled with their use of signs to identify and describe things.

So, how do we arrive at a sign lattice, such as the simple one displayed in Figure 8.1, which describes some domain ontology? There are various ways of doing this. Through intensive investigation of some domain, we can traverse the scaffolding from existing data structures through to communicative acts and the coordinated activities that rely on such practices. Or, we can reverse the scaffolding of data structures by starting with what people do in the domain and then by close study of communicative acts come to an understanding of what people identify and describe.

Unlike human actors, machine actors such as software actors (that we consider in Chapter 11) need some formal representation of the sign lattice appropriate to their performance. As we shall see, to program machines that can perform effectively within institutional domains requires us to supply them with formal representations of sign lattices, such as the one we have been developing as an example. For this purpose, the notion of metadata is important.

Metadata

Our coverage of objects, classes, attribution, association, generalisation and aggregation is designed to expose the component elements needed to form institutional ontology. However, these notions are useful also in understanding an important concept within contemporary data infrastructure — that of *metadata*. Metadata is an abstraction, which helps provide *context* to human or machine actors in their engagement with data.

One of the most straightforward examples of metadata is that of an index. There are many different structures for an index but let us examine one of the simplest — that used at the end of a book, such as the one you are reading. An index is a list in which list-items are composed of at least two data-items. The first data-item is a keyword and the second data-item a page number. This example of metadata — data about data — is used to quickly discover the place or places in which a topic expressed through a keyword is discussed within a book.

Although the prefix meta means *after* or *beyond* in the original Greek, it is conventionally used in English to mean *about*. Metadata might be defined more precisely as data which informs one or more actors about some aspects of underlying data, and as such can be considered a form of abstraction. There are several different types of metadata of which the three most important are structural, descriptive and administrative.

Our definition of a product class evident within the sign lattice in Figure 8.1 is an example of *structural metadata* — data which defines the structure of some other data. In so doing, the metadata maps between aspects of institutional ontology and data.

Metadata was traditionally used in the card catalogues of libraries. Such catalogues contain metadata about books in the library such as author, title, subject classification, etc. This metadata is *descriptive* in the sense of describing certain attributes of underlying data which might be useful in attempts to retrieve such data. In Chapter 4, we considered a simple example of descriptive metadata for an electronic document, such as an academic paper. The document itself is identified by a digital object identifier (DOI) and this is separated from a metadata structure which records changeable things such as the document's current location. However, such a metadata record might also store details such the author, file size, the date the document was created and keywords that describe the document. Metadata for a music file might include the artist's name, the album and the year it was released. A digital image may include metadata that describes how large the picture is, the colour depth, the image resolution, when the image was created, the shutter speed and other data.

However, metadata may also be used for *administrative* purposes in areas such as data control, as we shall see in Chapter 9. Such metadata might consist of the purpose of the data, the time and date of its creation, the creator of the data, where it was created and permissions imposed on articulation of the data such as update, read and delete rights.

The Metadata of the Web

Metadata is particularly important to contemporary technological infrastructure such as the World Wide Web (WWW) or web for short. The web can be thought of as a collection of documents residing on thousands of servers situated on computers around the world. Electronic documents of any form are made up of two types of data: data that represents content, such as text and graphics, and data that describes to ICT or IT applications how the content is to be processed. This latter data is clearly a form of *descriptive metadata*.

Such descriptive metadata consists of a set of embedded tags that indicate how the content is to be presented on devices such as personal computers and tablets. This process of tagging text with descriptive metadata is known as marking up, and the set of tags for doing this comprise a mark-up language. In the 1960s, work began on developing a generalised mark-up language for describing the presentation of electronic documents. This work became established in a standard known as the standard generalised mark-up language (SGML).

SGML is in fact a meta-language: a language for defining other languages, so it can be used to define a large set of mark-up languages. Tim Berners-Lee, the inventor of the web used SGML to define a specific language for web documents known as Hypertext Mark-up Language (HTML). HTML is a standard for marking up or tagging documents that can be published on the web, and can be made up of text, graphics, images, audio clips and video clips. Hypertext documents also include links to other documents stored on either the local HTML server or remote HTML servers.

HTML has undergone a number of versions since it was first introduced in 1991. As suggested above, a HTML document contains both content and tags. The document content consists of what is displayed on the computer screen. The tags constitute codes that tell the browser how to format and present the content on the screen. The general form of this relationship between tags and content is expressed as:

<tagname properties> content </tagname>

The tagname is taken from an established set of keywords established in the version of HTML. Tags are embedded in angled brackets. Certain tagnames and the grammar with which they are used convey specific meanings to web browsers. For instance, in the tag <p align="right">, P is the tagname and acts as an abbreviation for the word paragraph, so this tag is designed to be placed at the start of a chunk or paragraph of text. The word align is a property which can be assigned several values from a limited list. One of these is right, which specifies that the paragraph in question should be right justified on screen. An end-tag </P> is placed at the end of the chunk of text.

The Sharing of Documentation Between Institutions

Metadata is critical to not only for accessing web documents, but also the sharing of data between institutions, which we alluded to in Chapter 7. Data structures such as sales orders, delivery notes, invoices and payment advices, which would once have been on paper, can instead be coded up as electronic messages. To enable the effective sharing of data structures between institutions over digital communication channels, three conditions must be satisfied:

- The digital message comprising the data structure must have a defined format.
- The receiver and sender of the message must agree on its format.
- The message must be able to be sent and read by electronic devices.

These conditions effectively mean that a common and formal ontology must be devised and agreed upon between communicating institutions and the devices they utilise. Historically, a standard for electronic documentation was based on electronic data interchange (EDI). More recently, standards have been defined using a web-based technology known as extensible mark-up language (XML).

One of the main advantages of HTML is its simplicity. This enables it to be used effectively by a wide user community. However, this is also one of its disadvantages. Sophisticated users want to define their own tags, particularly to implement mechanisms for the definition of data structures and the sharing of these data structures. The World Wide Web Consortium developed XML in 1998 (W3C, 2000) to meet these needs. The term extensible means that new mark-up tags can be created by communities of users.

Like HTML, XML is a restricted descendant of SGML. Whereas HTML is used to define how the data in a document is to be displayed, XML can be used to define the syntax (structure) and some of the semantics (meaning) of a document. Thus, for instance, it can be used to specify standard templates for business documents such as invoices, shipping notes and fund transfers. An XML document consists of a set of elements and attributes. Elements or tags are the most common form of mark-up. The first element in an XML document must be a root element. The document must have only one root element, but this element may contain a number of other elements.

Let us use a simple example to illustrate the power of XML as a metadata language. Suppose your company is a coffee wholesaler. You might wish to create XML documents for the exchange of shipping information to your customers. An appropriate root element might therefore be the tag <PRODUCTDETAILSLIST>.

An element begins with a start-tag and ends with an end-tag. The start-tag in our document for the root element would be <ProductDetailsList>. The corresponding end-tag would be <ProductDetailsList>. The corresponding end-tag would be </ProductDetailsList>. Note that tags are case-sensitive in XML. Hence is a different tag from <ProductDetailsList>.

Elements can be empty, in which case they can be abbreviated to <EmptyElement/>. Elements must also be properly nested as sub-elements within a superior element. So, this XML element might be used to define a coffee product:

```
<ProductDetails ID='1234'>
    <ItemName>Kenya Special</ItemName>
    <CountryOfOrigin>Kenya</CountryOfOrigin>
    <WholeSaleCost>20.00</WholeSaleCost>
    <Stock>4000</Stock>
</ProductDetails>
```

Here we have a ProductDetails element with several sub-elements. Definitions for these sub-elements such as ItemName, CountryOfOrigin, WholeSaleCost and Stock are properly nested within ProductDetails.

In terms of our previous notion of a data structure, this would constitute a data element of a product's data structure. Attributes, or what we previously called data-items, are name-value pairs that contain descriptive information about an element. The attribute is placed inside the start-tag for the element and consists of an attribute name, an equality ('=') sign and the value for the attribute placed within quotes. In the coffee producer example, the tag <ProductDetails ID='1234'> contains the attribute ID and the value '1234'.

Traditionally, the structure or syntax of an XML document has been defined in terms of a document type definition or DTD. More recently, the trend has been to use XML Schema to define the structure of an XML document. Such a schema provides the names of all elements, which elements can appear in combination and what attributes are available for each type of element. It can also be used to specify certain rules on data elements such as whether an element is a piece of text or a number, and whether an element has a default value or not.

Conclusion

In their study of classification, Bowker and Leigh-Star (1999) argue that classification schemes are not neutral — '... each category valorizes some point of view and silences another...For any individual, group or situation, classifications and standards give advantage or they give suffering. Jobs are made and lost; some regions benefit at the expense of others.' However, in their important work, they intimate at but never clearly establish the difference between the construction of a formal classification system such as the International Classification of Diseases and the use of such a classification scheme in the making of records. Clearly the construction of a classification scheme involves a multitude of valuation decisions about what categories to include and what to exclude. This is separate from acts of record-making in which things, persons and events are classified through selection of 'appropriate' categories from an existing ontology, perhaps formalised in a classification scheme.

Classification schemes are at the heart of ontology — a set of beliefs common to a set of actors about what reality constitutes. Ontologies are typically implicit or tacit constructs that form an important part of the collective psyche of a group of actors. Within this chapter, we have considered some of the mechanics for building explicit institutional ontology. Such mechanics involve the construction of a sign lattice from objects and classes, as well as from relationships of attribution, association, generalisation and aggregation.

The mechanics of a sign-lattice are useful in understanding the role that metadata plays within contemporary data infrastructure, particularly that underlying the web and the sharing of electronic documentation between institutional actors. Without ontologies of metadata, much of the data infrastructure underlying electronic communications would not be possible.

We began this chapter with a hint as to the relationship between classification or categorisation and power. The way in which we classify things has a bearing on what we believe is possible and not possible. In Chapter 9, we make this linkage more explicit by examining how ontology is related to deontology. Ontology is a theory of reality whereas deontology is a theory of rights and duties. This provides us with a useful hook to examine how data structures are important to not only prescribing what actors can and should do but also proscribing actors from doing certain things.

References

Bowker, G. and S. Leigh-Star (1999). *Sorting Things Out: Classification and its Consequences* (Cambridge, MA: MIT Press).

Le Guin, U. (1993). *The Earthsea Quartet* (London: Puffin Books).

Suchman, L. (1994). "Do Categories have Politics? The Language/action Perspective Reconsidered." *Computer Supported Cooperative Work*, **3**(2): 177–190.

W3C (2000). Extensible markup language (XML) definition. World-Wide-Web consortium. www.w3c.org.

Chapter 9

The Power of Records

Introduction

Soon after the Norman Conquest in 1066, William I sought to consolidate his power by conducting a survey of his new kingdom. This 'Great Description of England' was published as a book, which the common people referred to as the Domesday (pronounced Doomsday) book, because Domesday referred to the day of judgement. This book essentially consisted of a series of data structures which served to document the rights and responsibilities associated with landowners. As such, it served to consolidate William's power and legalise changes made to the kingdom by Norman possession.

Cases throughout history and across cultures such as this reveal that records are not only formative, informative and performative, but also have deontic powers. By this, it is meant that records are important to power and its exercise. More precisely, records, serving as institutional facts, are used to scaffold the rights and responsibilities associated with actors taking action. The records within the Domesday book, for instance, served to declare the rights to property of the new Norman landlords — land that was previously held by Anglo-Saxons. However, the records also served to prescribe the responsibilities of such landowners to provide annual taxes to the king.

Given the central importance of data structures to the scaffolding of the institutional order, it is important that, at the metadata level (see Chapter 8), positive and negative powers are assigned to actors in relation to the articulation of data structures. This serves to define the issue of data control and explains why it has become of increasing concern to institutions. Data control, as we shall see, is a practical response to the need to create and maintain an architecture of deontology in relation to the life (see Chapter 6) of data structures.

Domesday Book — The Book of the Day of Judgement

Let us begin with an elaboration of the Domesday book case. While spending the Christmas of 1085 in Gloucester, William I reportedly had the idea of sending men all over his dominion to find out how much each landholder had in land and livestock, and how much this was worth (Higham, 1993). This exercise was called by many names: The Great Survey, The Inquisition, The Book of Winchester and the Great Description of England. The common people referred to it as the Domesday book and this book was originally held in the King's treasury at Winchester. Later, it was moved to Westminster, London.

Planning for the survey took place in 1085 and the survey itself was conducted in 1086. England at the time was divided up into a series of shires, and to conduct the survey, most shires were visited by a group of royal officers (legati), who held a public inquiry, probably in the great assembly known as the shire court, which was attended by representatives of every township as well as local lords. The unit of inquiry was the Hundred (a sub-division of the county, which then was an administrative entity), and the return for each Hundred was sworn to by 12 local jurors, half of them Anglo-Saxon and half of them Norman.

Domesday names a total of 36,593 places. Apart from the wholly rural portions, which constitute the bulk of its entries, Domesday contains entries of interest for most of the towns of the time. These records include fragments of custumal (older customary agreements), records of the community and food services due, of markets, mints and so forth. From the towns, from the counties as whole and from many of its ancient Lordships, the Crown was entitled to long-held dues in kind, such as quantities of honey.

The Domesday book is really two separate works. The Little Domesday covers the counties of Norfolk, Suffolk and Essex, while the Great Domesday covers the rest of England of the time. Hence, the Northern land under the control of the Scots, and which would become Westmorland, Cumberland and Northumberland, are excluded from the record. Some major cities and towns, such as London and Winchester, are also excluded, presumably because of their size and complexity.

Despite its title, the Little Domesday was a larger record than that of Great Domesday. This is because it contains a record of holdings down to numbers of livestock for each landholder. It has been suggested it was the first attempt at record-making by the Normans, and that the complexity of the record caused changes to be made in the final Great Domesday record.

The Great Domesday book appears to have been transcribed and written up by one man, primarily in Latin but with some vernacular words on parchment. This person was possibly an Anglo-Saxon rather than a Norman because he shows great knowledge of English place names. The Little Domesday Book in contrast appears to have been transcribed by six distinct scribes.

The book is clearly a set of records or data structures that appears to have had a number of purposes. First, it served to document the liability of estates in terms of the Kings Geld — an annual tax levied by the Anglo-Saxon kings and adopted by the Norman conquerors. Second, it served to document the resources of the newly established feudal order in England. Third, and perhaps most importantly, it served to legalise changes made to the kingdom by Norman possession. Because of the way in which the book was structured, it could not have been used primarily for the purposes of tax collection. It is more likely that it was used merely to declare the rights to property of the new Norman landlords.

All this means that we can interpret the acts of representation embodied in the Domesday book as an attempt to communicate and control aspects of the emerging feudal society. Hegemony is the control of one group of actors by another, usually smaller group, of actors. It is probably not too far from the truth to say that whoever controls the important records controls society. Antonio Gramsci (2005) introduced the idea of cultural hegemony — the idea that a ruling class can manipulate the value system within society such that their view of how people should behave becomes the world view of all. The Domesday book is clearly an example of the way in which a hegemony of representation was used to establish or to substantiate a hegemony over physical resources. But what are the mechanics of such a hegemony of representation? To establish this, we need to extend the notion of ontology with that of deontology.

Ontology and Deontology

In previous chapters, we established how data structures are critical to forming institutional ontology. For Searle (2010), institutional ontology is an instance of social ontology which is different from, but which builds upon material reality (physical ontology).

As we have emphasised a number of times, data structures not only refer to and describe things of interest to the relevant institutions, they bring such things into existence for such institutions — they scaffold the institutional reality or ontology. However, the ways in which facts are instituted in relation to such things is not only a matter of ontology, it is also a matter of deontology. The term *deontic* is derived from the ancient Greek *déon*, meaning that which is binding or proper. Such binding is provided through power and its exercise. This means that data structures not only scaffold institutional order through the ways in which they institutionalise facts (Searle, 2010). Such facts are critical to scaffolding the powers associated with actors taking action within both intra- and inter-institutional orders.

As we have seen, a data structure (X), or more likely a data-item or data element within a larger data structure, serves to counts as some institutional thing (Y). The *count as* relation between X and Y relies upon a collective acceptance amongst institutional actors of this so-called status function. But Searle then extends this to include the notion of certain powers to do things associated with a status function. Searle originally proposed several broad categories of status functions — symbolic, deontic, honorific and procedural — but has now argued that all such status functions actually collapse into the base form of the deontic.

Within philosophy more generally, deontology is the branch of ethics dealing with duty, moral obligation and moral commitment — sometimes seen as rule-based ethics. It involves broadly the search for rules with which to lead a moral life. However, Searle switches the focus from the individual to the way in which collective intentionality establishes such rules or norms for individuals to follow. Many such rules, as we have seen, are centred around the presence or absence of data-items or data elements within larger data structures.

Any deontic status function is assumed to have the structure (S does A) 'because power is always the power to do something or constrain someone else from doing something, the propositional content of power status functions is always in part that (S does A) where "S" is to be replaced by an expression referring either to an individual or a group, and "A" by the name of an act, action, or activity, including negatives such as refraining or abstaining …' (Searle, 1995).

Thus Searle extends the collective acceptance of some status function with a related deontic status upon the X term which he expresses as (S has P (S does A)). Here, S an actor within some institution is granted power P within a certain domain of action A. P can be either positive power (rights, permissions, authorisations) or negative power (obligations, duties, responsibilities). For example, we accept (S, the bearer of X [five-dollar bill], is enabled [S buys with X up to the value of five dollars]). We might also collectively restrict the power assigned to some individual or group, as in the case of: we accept (S is required [S does A]). For instance, we accept (S the person to whom X [parking ticket] is issued, is required [S pays a fine within a specified period]).

As we have seen in previous chapters, a data-item such as an identifier, and the properties it stands for, need relate to not only a physical thing such as a person but to a conceptual and institutional thing, such as a picking item. In this case, the identifier, and the data structure of which it is a part, relate to a whole series of rights, responsibilities, obligations and commitments associated with the thing. Hence, the act of placing a product code on a packing list puts in motion a series of responsibilities that serves to frame certain institutional actions undertaken by nominated institutional actors. This means that the articulation of particular data structures, data elements or data-items carries with them not only ontological assumptions (about what things are seen to exist), but also deontological assumptions (about not only what actors are expected and enabled to do but also what they are prohibited from doing) (Searle, 2005).

Zimmerman (1975) cites an interesting example of the power that we invest in data structures. He quotes the case of a person applying for public assistance who indicated to her caseworker that she could not find the necessary citizenship papers that would be used to verify her age and, as a consequence, her eligibility for certain forms of assistance. Instead, she had copied her birthdate onto a slip of paper and handed that as verification to her caseworker. The case worker could not accept this data structure as proof of her age. Zimmerman comments that: '… not just any piece of paper will do for establishing the objective and factual grounds for administrative action. What is it that confers upon a particular piece of paper its authority for the determination of matters of fact?'

The answer to Zimmerman's question lies in the status invested in certain data structures, which invests them with certain rights on behalf of the holder. Relating this to the articulation of data structures, we might express the deontic status of a data structure in its entirety as:

[*We (the institution(s)) accept: actor (S) articulating (X) → has power (P) → S does/does not do action (A).*]

One convenient and simpler way of thinking about this is that the articulation of a data structure comprises a communicative act which serves, in turn, to prescribe or proscribe certain acts of coordinated performance on the part of designated institutional actors. For instance, if you have a passport then you as the identifiable actor can travel freely between certain countries. If you have an associated visa, then you are enabled to travel to the country described in the document for a prescribed period. Possession of these two data structures, passport and visa, grant to you (prescribe to you) the holder certain powers to travel. Lack of such possession proscribes you from doing these things:

[*Actor (S) possesses a UK passport (X) → has permission to travel to countries (L) → S travels to country (Y) where Y MEMBER OF L*]

Likewise, if you hold a European driving licence, then you are enabled to drive certain defined classes of vehicle within the countries of the European Union:

[*Actor (S) possesses an EU driving licence (X) → has permission to drive within countries (L) → S drives across country (Y) where Y MEMBER OF L*]

In many countries around the world, such as India, possession of a national identifier is required to access government services:

[*Actor (S) is identified by identifier (X) → has permission to access government services (L) → S accesses government service (Y) where Y MEMBER OF L*]

The Deontology of Data Structures

Let us build up a larger example which demonstrates the interweaving of ontology and deontology within matters of institutional order. We shall also use it to rehearse elements of the theorisation that we have developed so far.

To remind ourselves, data structures help form institutional order through constitutive rules of the form: X (some data-item) counts as Y (some other thing) in C (some institutional context) (Chapter 4). An identifier forms the X term in a status function when it serves the function of referring to some unique instance of a 'thing'. We also expressed the general form of a 'refers to' relation in the following terms:

[*<Identifier> REFERS TO <Thing>*]

The 'thing' referred to might be a physical thing, such as:

[*<Personal name> REFERS TO <Human>*]

Or an institutional thing, such as:

[*<NHS No.> REFERS TO <Patient>*]

In Chapter 6, we considered the national health service (NHS) number as an important identifier. So, the term 943/476/5919 is an identifier if it counts as a specific 'thing' in some institutional context. In this case, the context is the UK NHS and the identifier is an NHSNo. On creation, this identifier brings into existence an institutional thing — a patient for this institution.

Since identifiers do not describe things, constitutive rules need to work within a process of iterative application. The X term at one level within some constitutive rule is likely to have been a Y term at a lower level within some other constitutive rule. Furthermore, the C term is typically a Y term (or perhaps a series of Y terms from earlier stages of the iteration). Searle (2000) provides the following example of this process:

'I make noises through my mouth. So far, … there is nothing institutional about noises as such. But, as I am a speaker of English addressing other speakers, those noises count as the utterance of an English sentence; they are an instance of the formula 'A counts as Y in C'. But now, in an utterance of that English sentence, the Y term from the previous level functions as an X term at the next level. The utterance of that English sentence with those intentions and in that context counts as, for example, making a promise. But now that Y term, the promise, is the X term at the next level up. Making that sort of promise in those sorts of circumstances counts as undertaking a contract ... Furthermore, we can suppose that that sort of contract, in those sorts of circumstances, counts as getting married. And then, getting married in turn counts as qualifying for all sorts of benefits, obligations, rights, duties, and so on'.

It is evident from this example that the process of iterative application is critical to the way in which actors use status functions to constitute institutional reality. One particularly important way of doing this within contemporary institutions is to assign certain identifiers to defined lists. For example, an important example of such a list for a UK general hospital is its admissions list. Hence, we might add a NHSNo to this list.

[943/476/5919 MEMBER OF Admissions List of hospital (Z)]

The act of creating such a list-item brings the denoted institutional 'thing' into existence — through a type of communicative act which Searle (1970) refers to as a declaration (see Chapter 3). By making this list entry, an individual is instantiated as a particular 'thing' — an in-patient at a general hospital (see Chapter 8).

[943/476/5919 AKO In-patient]

It is also possible to consider lists as status functions in their own right. In other words, the act of creating a list typically involves naming the list. In doing this, the list acts as a proxy which stands for the institutional context of the status functions making up the list. Hence, other related lists are clearly important for the healthcare institution described, such as the list of registered nurses working at the hospital. A given nurse identifier here counts as part of this list:

[26643 MEMBER OF <list of registered nurses working at hospital (Z)>]

[24526 MEMBER OF <list of registered nurses working at hospital (Z)>]

[33442 MEMBER OF <list of registered nurses working at hospital (Z)>]

[36234 MEMBER OF <list of registered nurses working at hospital (Z)>]

...

But now add a third list to this institutional scaffold:

[26643 CARE ACTION-10 943/476/5919]
[24526 CARE ACTION-22 944/456/5619]
[3342 CARE ACTION-10 922/475/5915]
[36243 CARE ACTION-22 923/456/5219]
...

Here, we have an association (another type of counts as relation) (see Chapter 8) between two sets of identifiers — a nurse identifier and a patient identifier. These list-items help form the association between a set of identifiable registered nurses undertaking actions of healthcare on registered in-patients. Such a list is likely, in practice, to be a partition of a list of nursing care actions undertaken across wards of this general hospital.

Hence, through a process of iterative application of status functions within wider data structures such as lists we start to form an institutional ontology. This is because lists such as this are necessary parts of acts of communication. They help form the content of communicative acts. However, communicative acts, as we have seen, also have intent, as assertives, directives, commissives, expressives or declaratives (Searle, 1970). Such patterns of communication are critical to doing things, such as providing healthcare.

Take the list of care actions provided above. For a nurse, each list-item within this list would probably be seen to constitute an assertive (see Chapter 3). When someone creates such a list-entry, it states the belief that a particular care action has been performed upon a defined patient by a defined nurse. Hence,

[36243 CARE ACTION-22 923/456/5219]

Asserts that nurse 36243 undertook care-action-22 (issuing prescribed medication) to patient 923/456/5219.

However, consider this list in alternative terms as a series of care plans for patients. In this rendering, each list-item has clearly the same content but different intent. Now each list-item acts as a directive for a nurse to perform a particular care action on a particular patient. In this case, nurse 36243 is directed to issue prescribed medication to patient 923/456/5219.

Now let us see how such a list is relevant to making sense of a breakdown (see Chapter 5) in institutional order at one UK hospital. After the death of an elderly patient at this hospital, the family questioned the healthcare provided by its nursing staff. Their expressed concerns were later substantiated at an inquest, which led to a public inquiry and to the eventual prosecution of the nurses concerned for professional negligence.

The nurses identified in this case were initially suspended for bad record-keeping. It was eventually shown that these nurses had falsified care records, similar in form to the care list discussed previously. However, what does bad record-keeping and falsification mean in terms of our theorisation? In this case, it appears that nurses were recording incidents of care provided to a patient when these actions had not taken place. They were asserting things that never actually happened. Here, we clearly have a breakdown in the institutional order related to the scaffolding of lists and identifiers. But why is the use of lists of status functions to lie (Eco, 1977) necessarily a breakdown? For that, we need to unpack not only the institutional ontology of this case, but also its institutional deontology.

We have argued in Chapter 3 that lists are particularly used within the modern world to enact, through the presence of personal identifiers, enrolment of people within particular systems of coordinated action or to prohibit enrolment of certain actors in such systems. Enrolment in the large involves answering the question, in relation to a system of coordinated action, *how am I expected to perform and how will others perform towards me?*

As we have seen, entry of a person through an identifier upon an appropriate list is often used to instantiate that person as having an institutional role, such as an in-patient or registered nurse. As such, the existence of the list-item privileges individuals with rights and responsibilities in relation to activities in a system of coordinated action. For instance, referring to a person through an institutional identifier presumes that this identifier exists as an entry upon some institutional list. The presence of such an identifier serves to scaffold the role of the referred to person, such as that of a taxpayer. This assigned identity will enrol the individual in a whole range of rights and responsibilities in the systems of action associated with fiscal matters. It will also entitle the individual to access services provided by the tax authorities of a nation-state. But a list entry may not only enrol persons; it may also prohibit such enrolment for individuals within systems of activity. Hence, if you as an individual appear as an identifier on a credit rating blacklist, this will prevent you from obtaining credit from financial institutions that use such lists to direct their activity (see Chapter 4). Lists are therefore critical, as we have seen, to the institutional process which Lyon (2009) refers to as social sorting. They not only enable certain actors to take actions within a certain institutional context, but may also serve to prohibit certain actors from taking certain actions within such contexts.

The breakdown in institutional order within healthcare described relies upon the interweaving of deontology with ontology. This modification of a constitutive rule declares the so-called deontic status of the status function: the rights, duties, obligations, authorisations, permissions, etc. which come with use of this function. Hence, within the context we have been considering:

[*We (the NHS) accept: the person (S) with registration as a nurse (X)* → *is obliged (P) to provide care to patients* → *S provides care (A) and makes a record of such care (Y)*]

The phrase 'we accept' here is meant to indicate collective intentionality (Searle, 1983) — the idea that we all as part of some institutional domain collectively declare something to be the case. According to Searle, this is the fundamental basis of institutional ontology and deontology more widely. But note, there are a number of data structures evident in this example of the interweaving of ontology and deontology. The power assigned to a person is dependent on her being registered as a nurse. Without a data structure of such a nurse referred to through an appropriate identifier upon a nursing register (see Chapter 7), the person is prohibited from practicing nursing. With such a registration, the person can perform nursing but is expected or obliged to provide care to expected standards and, of course, to make continuing records of such care.

Nurses clearly make lists of care actions not only to coordinate their individual action with other healthcare professionals, but also to account for their actions to other nurses and healthcare professionals. However, as a necessary side effect, through the creation of such data structures, they continuously reconstitute the deontic status associated with their role of registered nurse. This means that we collectively expect nurses to have delivered the care as recorded in the data structures they create. When the established institutional facts as represented in such data structures do not correspond with or couple to directed action, then we have an instance of a breakdown in the institutional order. This is an example of asserting things that cannot be confirmed, in this case because they did not actually take place.

Revisiting Domesday

Let us next build an ontology of the Domesday book as we know it and then upon this bedrock speculate about how the deontology of this data system was enacted — what it was used to prescribe or proscribe. We shall simplify by considering only part this ontology here to make it manageable for discussion. However, the principles we shall establish apply to the whole of this institutional ontology.

First, we need to establish the object classes (see Chapter 8) important to this ontology — the categories of things of interest to the Norman conquerors. Two such object classes appear particularly important, that of a landlord and that of a land holding:

[Landlord AKO Object class]
[Holding AKO Object class]

Not surprisingly, these object classes are associated together. The association relationship implements the institutional function of ownership:

[Landlord OWNS Holding]

Then we need to define the attributes of each object class, in something like the following manner:

[Landlord HASA Person Name]
[Holding HASA Year Surveyed]
[Holding HASA Year Levied]
[Holding HASA No Of Ploughs]

The Domesday book itself consists of a number of entries, each of which establishes a set of institutional facts derived on the basis of a collective acceptance of this ontology. For instance, one such set of facts concerns a holding owned by the Bishop of Worcester, a newly established Norman overlord:

[Bishop of Worcester ISA Landlord]
[Loxley ISA Holding]
[Bishop of Worcester OWNS Loxley]
[Loxley No Of Ploughs 3]
[Loxley Year Surveyed 1068]
[Loxley Year Levied 1068]

These facts served to establish a number of aspects of ontology. The institutional facts identify persons such as the Bishop of Worcester deemed-to-be landlords in the kingdom and Loxley deemed-to-be delimited holdings of land. In associating a landowner with a holding, the book thus served to prescribe changes made to the kingdom by Norman possession. It was particularly used to declare the rights to property of the new Norman landlords, such as the Bishop of Worcester. Such facts also detail the land deemed to be owned by these named persons and the extent of such land in terms of the number of ploughs used to work the land. Such records in turn served to prescribe the liability of each landlord to payments of the Kings Geld — the annual tax levied by the king.

So, the articulation of a data structures within the Domesday book comprised a series of declarations, which in turn prescribed certain acts of coordinated performance on the part of members of the kingdom. If you were named in the book as a landowner, then you were expected to pay to the king an annual tax on your holding of land:

[Actor (S) named in entry (X) → *is expected to pay a levy of (L)* → *S pays levy (L)]*

The Control of Data

We mentioned earlier that the Domesday book is an example of the way in which a hegemony of representation was used to substantiate or account for a hegemony over physical resources. This means that hegemony as a system of control is not limited to issues of physical resources; it also applies to data structures. In Chapter 4, we explored the issue of *data ownership* and concluded that, although intuitively attractive, it is practically difficult to support the notion of certain actors owning either data or more specifically data structures. The main difficulty is that unlike the physical resource of land, as evidenced in the Domesday book, data is replicable and non-rivalrous. When land is exchanged, the physical resource passes from seller to buyer, or as is the case in the years immediately following the Norman Conquest, land transferred from Anglo-Saxon lords to Norman lords. When data is exchanged, in contrast, the data remains in the hands of the seller. If a copy is made of part of the Domesday book and given to some shire administrator, the data still remains in the book held in Westminster.

However, as we have seen in Chapter 7, the notion of data privacy, particularly in relation to personal data and records, is a much easier notion to develop policy and practices to support. Legislation which implements principles of data protection is one way of doing this. The General Data Protection Regulation of the EU, as we have seen, grants data subjects certain rights in relation to records held about them.

The ICT industry is excellent at generating lots of terms that are frequently confusing — often because as signs they stand for much the same thing. The control of data is one such example and is referred to by different terms depending upon who you talk to. Hence, data control has a part to play within data management, data administration, data governance, information governance and ICT governance, to list just a few of the relevant terms.

We have spent much time in previous chapters, including the current one, making the case for an ontological reversal in relation to data structures. Data structures do not represent the institution, they are constitutive of the institution. Data structures scaffold communication by institutional actors and through this help construct and reconstruct institutional activity. However, within this chapter, we have also established that records are important to power and its exercise. Records as institutional facts are used to scaffold the rights and responsibilities associated with actors taking coordinated action. They serve to prescribe or proscribe certain actions for certain actors.

Given the central importance of data structures to scaffolding institutional order, it is important that at the metadata level (Chapter 8), positive and negative powers are assigned to actors in relation to the articulation of data structures. This we think is a much more focussed way of thinking about the governance of data and is what we take to mean as *data control* or data governance here. Data control amounts to the need to create and maintain an architecture of deontology in relation to acts of articulation associated with the life (Chapter 6) of data structures. If we take the position that whoever controls the data controls the institution, then the critical importance of data control becomes apparent.

The literature also uses lots of terms to refer to rights of articulation being exercised over data structures. Data assets, data areas and data stores are just three of the terms used to refer either to specific data structures controlled or to a set of cognate or related data structures over which control is exercised. The actors that have rights of articulation are also referred to as data owners, data stewards, data processors and data controllers.

We shall try to distil the essence of data control by simplifying the vocabulary somewhat, while also relating it to our theorisation of the scaffolding of data structures that we have developed in previous chapters. The issue of data control is best expressed as defining certain roles for actors which have certain articulation rights over certain data structures. Such an architecture of data roles granted certain data rights should provide answers to the following minimal set of questions associated with the life of a data structure:

- Who is able to *create* a data structure/data element/data-item about something?
- Who is able to *delete* a data structure/data element/data-item about something?
- Who is able to *update* a data structure/data element/data-item about something?
- Who is able to *read* a data structure/data element/data-item about something?

The assignment of data rights effectively declares the deontic status of a data role as a status function. Such data rights come in two forms — positive and negative. Positive data rights are defined for data roles in terms of the articulation of data structures and effectively act as data permissions to do certain acts of articulation. In contrast, data responsibilities assign negative powers in the sense of prohibiting the defined data role from doing certain things with data structures.

Every data role must be defined in terms of at least one data right. In practice, a given data role will have rights defined for several acts of articulation on a number of different data structures. So, data protection legislation expects that there should be an audit trail from data roles to data structures; that only named data roles are expected to be able to create, update and delete data which refers to persons. This we might express in terms of the following deontic rule:

[*We (the institution) accept: the person (S) registered as data role (X)* → *is permitted (P) to create/update/delete data structures which refer to persons (L)* → *S creates/updates/deletes data structure (Y)*]

This highlights a crucial split within the domain of articulation. For most things represented by data structures, the issue of ownership is relatively non-controversial in the sense that articulation of such data structures remains unquestioned and unchallenged. Hence, a manufacturer will create data structures that identify and describe the products they produce and ship to customers. It is only the manufacturer, or most likely administrators within this institution, that will be given rights to create, update and delete records about such things. Customers may want to track delivery of products ordered or perhaps in the case of foodstuffs be able to trace the provenance of their production. This effectively means granting certain rights to read product records to a data role declared on customers.

The most controversial of areas clearly concerns the control of data structures built about the person or about what happens to the person. This issue has come to the fore in relation to the practices of digital commerce giants such as Google, Facebook and Amazon that create, update, read and sometimes delete billions if not trillions of data structures, which represent their customers and their actions, over comparatively short periods of time. We shall consider what this data amounts to and how this data is used in Chapter 10. As we shall see, there are an increasing range of challenges to the hegemony of data operated by such Internet giants.

Conclusion

As we have seen, identifiers are for Searle key instances of status functions. Such status functions are constituted through rules which construct institutional facts and which in turn, through their capacity to declare states of the world, help form the very notion of institutional order. However, within our discussion, we have implicitly argued that status functions serve to scaffold institutional order in different ways or modes. We have primarily focussed on the importance of identifiers as status functions which serve to locate a 'thing' in time and space (see Chapter 3). But we have also introduced the idea of status functions which designate or describe (see Chapter 4). Finally, we have talked of the deontic aspect of status functions. Status functions not only serve to identify and describe, they also serve to prescribe (and sometimes proscribe) a range of rights and responsibilities assigned to actors within some domain of action.

In this sense, it is possible to think of status functions more widely as signs fulfilling several different modes in the constitution of institutional order (Morris, 1946). Three modes, we feel, are particularly important for constructing both intra-institutional and inter-institutional scaffolding: identifiers, designators and prescriptors. Identifiers are signs used to reference some thing or object in time and space. Hence, the personal name *Paul Beynon-Davies* identifies me the author. In contrast, designators are signs used to signal properties or attributes of something. Hence, I am designated by my age, which is 63 at the time of writing. Finally, prescriptors are signs used to signal appropriate responses on the part of the actor to particularly significant things. Hence, declaring myself as the author of this written work entitles me to certain rights of intellectual property.

Within our account of the ways in which data structures scaffold institutional order, we have inherently thought of status functions or signs in these three ways. In other words, status functions or signs act in one of three modes: as things referring to other things, as things describing or predicating other things and as things prescribing (or proscribing) action-responses by actors to certain things.

As we have suggested in this chapter, identifiers and designators appear critical to the constitution of institutional ontology. Through their capacity to refer to and describe things of interest to institutions, they bring such things into existence for such institutions. In contrast, prescription (including proscription or prohibition) seems to us to be the essence of institutional deontology. Status functions or signs are typically used to assign roles to actors (including artefacts) and through such assignment to impart both positive and negative power to such actors in terms of current or future action.

However, as we have indicated in our model of information situations, these three modes are not discrete but are typically coupled in the scaffolding of institutional order. Articulation of a data structure typically implements the identification and designation of things. Such identification and designation is typically important to recognition of an institutional thing as being enrolled into a particular institutional role. Such an act of enrolment, in turn, typically using some role name within data structures, prescribes or prohibits the future action of the identified and designated thing within a particular pattern of institutional order.

In the next chapter, we look at how the scaffolding of data structures such as ledgers is critical to the infrastructure of commerce and more particularly to the infrastructure of digital commerce. Without the scaffolding of data structures both within and between institutions, the idea of commerce, particularly at a global scale, would not be possible.

References

Eco, U. (1977). *A Theory of Semiotics* (London: Macmillan).

Gramsci, A. (2005). *Selections from the Prison Notebooks* (New York: Lawrence and Wishart).

Higham, N. J. (1993). "The Domesday Survey: Context and Purpose." *History*, **78**(253): 7–21.

Lyon, D. (2009). *Identifying Citizens: ID Cards as Surveillance* (Cambridge, MA: Polity Press).

Morris, C. W. (1946). *Signs, Language and Behavior* (New York: Prentice-Hall).

Searle, J. R. (1970). *Speech Acts: An Essay in the Philosophy of Language* (Cambridge: Cambridge University Press).

Searle, J. R. (1983). *Intentionality: An Essay in the Philosophy of Mind* (Cambridge, UK: Cambridge University Press).

Searle, J. R. (1995). *The Construction of Social Reality* (London: Penguin).

Searle, J. R. (2005). "What is an Institution?" *Journal of Institutional Economics*, **1**(1): 1–22.

Searle, J. R. (2010). *Making the Social World: The Structure of Human Civilization* (Oxford: Oxford University Press).

Zimmerman, D. H. (1975). Fact As a Practical Accomplishment. In *Ethnomethodology: Selected Readings*. R. Turner (eds.) (Harmondsworth, UK: Penguin), pp. 128–143.

Chapter 10

Scaffolding Commerce

Introduction

The increasing embeddedness of ICT infrastructure within commercial institutions enables rapid flow of trading activity accompanied by rapid flows of money around the world, 24 hours a day, 365 days a year. This infrastructure is hence a critical enabler of globalisation — the interconnected systems of commerce around the world. It also means that difficulties experienced in certain local markets more rapidly diffuse their effects to others than in the past. For instance, many analysts believe that the speed and extent with which the 2008 financial crash occurred was largely due to the increased data connectivity of global financial markets.

In this chapter we utilise the theoretical framework developed in previous chapters to provide critical insight into several important ways in which data structures are used within the modern global economy. Many fundamental economic concepts such as ownership, purchasing, credit and debt are facilitated through data structures such as deeds, orders, invoices and contracts.

We focus within this chapter upon the critical role that data structures play in scaffolding the institutional domains of finance and trade. We start by considering the nature of money as a status function facilitated through data structures. This leads to an examination of the crucial notion of a ledger — a data structure which underlies the whole notion of accounting and finance, but which has applications much more widely. Usually, a ledger acts as a register of transactions and this allows us to explain applications of a recent technology known as the blockchain. However, rather than following the hype surrounding this technology, we correctly place it as a novel data structure with some potentially interesting institutional applications.

Given that the infrastructure of modern worldwide commerce is reliant upon data structures, we conclude the chapter with a look at securing data infrastructure.

The Notion of Commerce

Commerce is an institutional system involving the exchange of goods and services between economic actors — buyers and sellers. Given what we have established in previous chapters, as an institution we would expect commerce to be scaffolded by data structures of various forms. Consider Figure 10.1, which is a much-simplified tabletop model of how the simple exchange of certain goods between two economic actors involves the creation and update of several data structures — orders, delivery notes, payment advices, invoices, payment requests and payments.

This sequence of articulation and communication runs in something like the following manner. An order is first created by a buyer and transmitted to a seller. This data structure communicates what is to be bought and perhaps the quantity of items needed to the seller. The seller delivers the ordered goods, but also transmits a delivery note with them. This delivery note confirms what is delivered to the buyer. Let us assume here a type of commerce known as credit commerce in which the seller invoices the buyer for payment after the goods are delivered. The buyer is then likely to create a payment advice committing them to payment by certain means. Parallel to this, a payment request is created and submitted to a financial intermediary. Following receipt of this directive, the intermediary then updates the financial accounts of both buyer and seller.

The thing to note from this illustration is that the activity of exchanging physical goods demands a significant amount of both articulation and communication. Each phase within the exchange of goods enacts an information situation in which a data structure is articulated, and this data structure then communicates something to the economic actors involved in the exchange. Without such communication, further activity, such as the distribution and handover of goods, cannot occur.

Clearly, the exchange of goods is only part of the activity system of commerce, which in the round will involve pre-sale, sale execution, sale

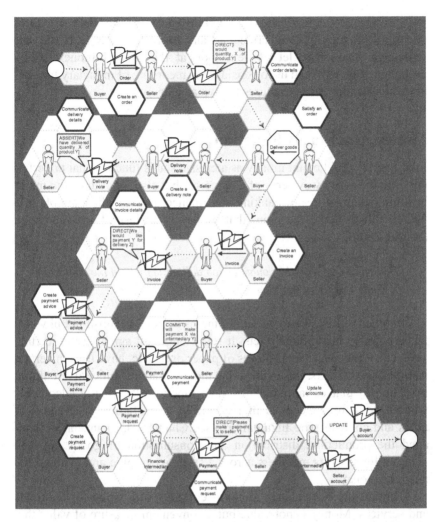

Figure 10.1:   Data structures within acts of exchange.

settlement and after-sale activity. Pre-sale activities are those occurring before a sale, such as advertising and customer enquiries. Sale execution refers to those activities involved in the actual sale of the product or service, such as ordering or picking the product. Sale settlement refers to those activities involved with the completion of a sale, such as payment. After-sale activities enact after the customer has bought the product or service, such as handling complaints.

In both pre-sale and after-sale activity, many further data structures will scaffold activity. But. crucial to any exchange activity is the sale settlement phase. So, let us next look at the role of money within exchange. This will lead us to consider the recording of monetary transactions in specialist data structures known as ledgers.

Money as a Status Function

John Searle would count money as a classic status function that underlies not only the activity systems of commerce, but also, of course, the major institutional structures of banking and finance. He uses the example of a US$10 bill to make the point that money is an institutional invention (Searle, 2006):

> *[This piece of paper (X) counts as ten dollars (Y) within the context of the United States of America (C)]*

In other words, money as an artefact is used to establish not physical facts, but also institutional facts. It relies on us all agreeing that certain artefacts or tokens, such as pieces of paper or plastic, have uses in certain institutional contexts. It is evident that money is an institutional or cultural invention in that certain societies have functioned perfectly adequately without both the concept of money and its instantiation in artefacts of notes and coinage. The Inka empire (see Chapter 2), for instance, managed the production, distribution and consumption of goods between many millions of its members across a large geographic area without the need for money.

There is also a tendency to confuse money with value — i.e. goods and services. Money is not value but a convenient measure of value that is useful within economic exchange. We can demonstrate the difference between money and value quite easily with a simple thought experiment. Imagine you are alone on a desert island and sitting on a wooden chest. Within the chest there are one million pounds sterling in bank notes. What is the value of the banknotes to you? The answer is of course that it is worthless as money but might have some worth as fuel to put on a fire and to keep you warm at night.

Economists argue that money serves three major and interdependent functions: a unit of account, a medium of exchange and a store of wealth. As we have mentioned, as a unit of account, money serves as a measure of the worth associated with goods and services. As a medium of exchange, money must be able to facilitate the exchange of goods and services between economic actors. As a store of wealth, units of money must be consistently valuable in the sense of being able to be exchanged for goods and services.

Each of these functions is sufficiently abstract to allow us to think of and treat money as essentially data held in data structures. Money within contemporary institutional life is essentially a set of data structures held in the ICT systems of financial intermediaries such as banks and building societies. Monetary exchange involves just the articulation of certain data structures accompanying the flow of goods and services between buyers and sellers. The sale settlement phase of commerce, as we have seen, is scaffolded through the articulation of two data structures. The bank account of the seller is updated by writing a new data element to it, which increases the monetary balance of this data structure. Likewise, the bank account of the seller is updated with a data element and its balance decreased.

This also helps us understand the growth in the cashless society and the rise of so-called digital currency. Money traditionally has been given physical form as tokens of value — banknotes and coins. But, in many economies worldwide, the number of economic exchanges performed using physical banknotes and coins (cash) is declining as more and more people use tokens such as credit and debit cards to electronically withdraw monies from their bank or credit account in payment for something. Companies such as Apple have also introduced means by which people can use their smartphones and other mobile devices to pay for things. Bitcoin, as we shall see, is a digital and crypto currency consisting solely of records held within digital wallets held on computing devices.

Transactions

So, money is represented and exchanged in financial data structures, such as bank accounts. A bank account in its simplest form is merely a *list* of financial transactions, typically ordered in sequence of time. This begs the question — what is a transaction? In business terms, a transaction is an event that typically has some monetary impact. In terms of data structures, a transaction is some package of work that has some impact upon one or more data structures.

We shall find some common ground between these two notions of a transaction. Within commercial infrastructure, a transaction can be seen as a package of acts of articulation, each of which changes the state of one or more financial data structures. Through such articulation work, transactions establish institutional facts about the financial state of some economic actors or economic activity. Such institutional facts typically communicate assertions about money as a measure of the worth of some economic exchange, but they also communicate declarations of ownership in relation to units of worth.

Take the example of a simple banking transaction, as described in the previous section, in which a monetary exchange occurs between two economic actors — typically taking the roles of a debtor (buyer) and creditor (seller). As we have seen this transaction works with two data structures — the account held by the debtor (account A) and that held by the creditor (account B). As a package of articulation, the transaction is likely to consist of at least two updates to the data structures involved — adding a new data element to the debtor account and adding a corresponding data element to the creditor account:

Update<Account A: create debit data element>
Update<Bankaccount B: create credit data element>

The whole point of bundling acts together as a transaction is to establish the principle that either all the actions within the transaction are enacted or none of the acts are enacted. If only part of a transaction is enacted, then it is rolled back and attempted again. Computer scientists refer to this as the *atomicity* of a transaction. Hence, if we only debit one account but fail to credit the other account, we roll the transaction back and start again. By this means we ensure that multiple acts of articulation required to enable a proper economic exchange are all enacted properly. Without this notion of the atomicity of transactions, commerce would suffer numerous data breakdowns.

Transaction Costs

There is an interesting side effect to this idea of a transaction. One of the key questions that has concerned economics for many decades is why the economy is populated by a number of business firms. Classical economic theory would in fact predict that the economy should consist exclusively of a multitude of independent, self-employed people who contract with one another in complex networks of exchange. Transaction costs, or what given our model of information situations we might more accurately refer to as coordination costs, are critical to providing answers to this so-called question of the nature of the firm. Coordination costs also help explain the critical importance of data structures and associated data systems to commerce.

The economist Ronald Coase (1937), way back in the 1930s, used the idea of transaction costs or coordination costs to develop a theory as to when certain economic tasks would be performed by firms and when they would be performed by the market. Transactions, as we have seen, amount to articulation work performed against data structures. In the past, such work would be performed by clerks of various forms. For instance, in 1874, the notable case of the railway clearing house in the UK employed 1,325 clerks in handling up to 4.9 million transactions concerned with ticketing and haulage (Bagwell, 1968).

In the digital age, much articulation work associated with transactions is, of course, performed by ICT infrastructure. Nevertheless, whether the articulation is performed by human or machine, every transaction incurs a cost, which is fundamentally concerned with ensuring the coordination of multiple actors within certain domains of activity. In terms of commerce, coordination costs are those costs associated with the coordination of multiple actors engaged in the exchange of goods and services. Within this domain of activity, coordination costs typically amount to the costs of data processing necessary to coordinate the work of people and machines in enacting economic exchange.

For example, when buying or selling a financial security within some stock market, a commission is normally paid to a broker; the commission is a coordination cost of undertaking a deal on the stock market. Or consider purchasing a textbook. The 'costs' in such a purchase not only include the price of the book itself but also the energy and effort expended by certain actors in finding the most appropriate textbook for the most appropriate price from the most convenient bookselling outfit, whether online or offline.

The net result of this is that, as Coase noted, there are a number of coordination costs to using any exchange network for the trading of goods and services. Coordination costs for Coase are to be contrasted with production costs. Production costs are those costs involved in the creation, distribution and consumption of value. Such costs are associated with the costs of transforming something into something else or transporting something from one place to another or consuming something. However, acts of 'production' are always associated with acts of coordination — meaning that production costs always come with coordination costs attached.

This idea led him to suggest that firms as institutions will arise when they can arrange to produce what they need internally and thus reduce their coordination costs. This theory has also been used to attempt to explain why firms engage in relationships with other firms and what form such relationships take. This is fundamentally an issue of how the organisation controls its activities: does it perform them in-house or does it farm them out to other organisations within the wider value-network? This will only occur when the costs of coordination are much lower than the costs of production.

The Ledger as a Data Structure

Without transactions and the costs of making such transactions, the discipline of accounting would not exist. This is because accounting devotes much of its activity to recording and manipulating business transactions and as such is an activity that generates necessary transaction or coordination costs for the firm. Accounting for things has been around probably since the days of the clay tokens mentioned in Chapter 1. To remind ourselves, in around 8,000 BCE within ancient Sumer, a given clay token of a certain shape and sometimes with certain markings was used to stand for one unit of something such as an amphora of wine. A series of clay tokens was wrapped in a clay envelope and then baked. This clay envelope could be interpreted as one of the earliest forms of transaction — it probably recorded a series of things transferred between one economic actor and another in ancient Sumer.

Accounting is a profession heavily concerned with the articulation of special-purpose data structures. An accountant will record and articulate financial transactions using data structures known as journals and ledgers. Financial transactions are first entered in a journal — a mere listing of such transactions in the time-order in which they occur. Such records written to a journal are then used to update a ledger. Transaction entries added to a ledger are described as being *posted* to the ledger and these are typically posted in chronological order. A ledger is typically an aggregate of one or more separate accounts, each of which may be regarded as a data

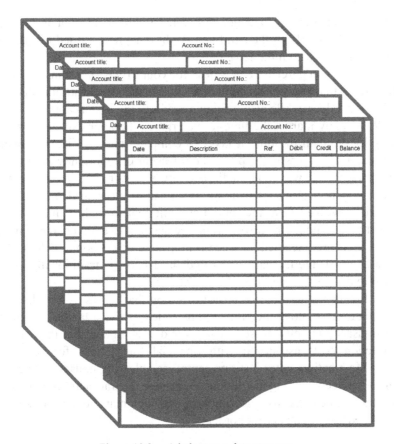

Figure 10.2: A ledger as a data structure.

structure in their own right. This cube-like structure is illustrated in Figure 10.2.

As we have seen, transactions are entered either as credits to an account or debits from an account. Each transaction is dated, described and referred back to the original journal entry. A cumulative balance is also typically held for each account.

Within the articulation of transactions in journals, accounts and ledgers there are numerous opportunities for data breakdowns, such as the mis-posting of transactions from journals to accounts within the ledger. To help reduce data errors or breakdowns in financial work, Benedetto Cotrugli invented the double-entry accounting in 1458. Double-entry accounting is any bookkeeping system that involves both a debit and/or credit entry for transactions. In simple terms it works in the following way — whenever one account is debited, another account is credited within the ledger. Both the debit and credit must be recorded together as one transaction within the ledger.

Suppose you purchase a new desk for your office for a sum of £1,000. This means that you write a debit of £1,000 to the office furniture account within the ledger, while also writing a credit to the cash account.

Within any market the time to undertake a trade or exchange is normally longer than the time it takes to complete the associated financial transaction. This is why the process of clearing is important within financial markets and why intermediaries between economic actors exist to perform such clearing. In banking and finance, clearing denotes all the activities involved from the time a commitment to trade is made to the time at which money is moved from one account to another. When many transactions are executed between a multitude of economic actors, then some form of intermediary or trusted third party is traditionally established to administer the flow of transactions.

A financial intermediary is an institution that serves as a middleman between diverse economic parties. It provides a service facilitating financial transactions between such parties and it is argued that they reduce transaction costs associated with financial transactions for economic actors Most nation-states institute centralised clearing houses as intermediaries between banking institutions to manage the transactions associated with trade. There are also clearing houses which manage the transactions associated with trade across borders.

Digital Currency

As we have seen, payments through use of a debit card or a smartphone are not truly cash payments because the enactment of a financial transaction by these means requires the participation of a financial intermediary to store and transfer funds for you. As a direct result, data are gathered about the payments you make by such intermediaries within their ledgers. True cash transactions can be undertaken without the need for a financial intermediary and without any data being recorded about the transaction. This explains why in most countries there is a hidden economy that is still driven by cash transactions. It also explains why governments worldwide are very keen to reduce the number of such cash transactions as their continued use makes it extremely difficult to track things like a person's income and consequently how much income tax they should pay.

This is where the notion of digital currency or digital cash comes in, of which the most prominent example is Bitcoin. The invention of Bitcoin is attributed to a character who calls himself Satoshi Nakomoto, but who has never actually been identified. His idea was to create a digital currency (sometimes referred to as a cryptocurrency because the process of creating bitcoins involves cryptography) that was not backed by national governments and not administered by any financial intermediaries. In 2009 the first Bitcoin network came into existence, when the first opensource Bitcoin client was issued, and the first block of bitcoins 'mined'.

Bitcoins are stored in digital wallets held on computing devices such as personal computers, tablets, and smartphones. A digital wallet is just a data structure, which records the number of bitcoins held. When bitcoins are used in economic transactions, the transactions are checked by a network of 'miners', who effectively validate transactions and add them to a distributed ledger known as the blockchain, which we describe next. The 'miners' are rewarded for their computational work with the potential for earning new bitcoins. So, new money is generated as a natural by-product of using digital currency in the system of exchange.

The Blockchain

A big impetus to digital currency has involved technologists looking for ways of letting organisations and individuals make and verify financial transactions without the need for a controlling central authority, such as a financial intermediary

In previous chapters we have used lists as an example data structure. It should therefore come as no surprise to find that the blockchain is a form of list known as a linked list. Within a linked list, a list item is made up of two parts: the content of the list-item and a pointer either to the previous list-item or to the next list-item in the list. The list-items within the blockchain are referred to as blocks and the pointers within each block are computed using a hash function. Each block will store a series of transactions.

A hash function is a function which maps a data-item of arbitrary size into fixed-size values. To explain this, suppose you use a series of personal names as identifiers for people. A hash function might transform a name such as John Smith into a hash value of 01, whereas the name John Doe might produce a hash value of 04. The hash pointers effectively create a chain of links between list-items — hence the name blockchain (Figure 10.3).

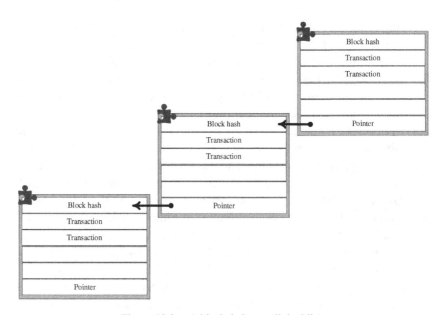

Figure 10.3:   A blockchain as a linked list.

Blockchains are particularly used to build distributed ledgers. A distributed ledger is not stored in one place but distributed across many sites within some computer and communications network. The reason for this is that a way of controlling a distributed ledger can be built, which removes the need for a central controlling registry such as a clearing house. Another advantage claimed for the blockchain is that it has the potential to reduce fraud as every transaction is recorded and available for viewing on a public register.

To summarise then, a blockchain is so-called because as a data structure it is made up of many data elements known as blocks, which are chained together in chronological order through computing hash keys. A new record, such as financial transaction, is placed within a given block. The block is then broadcast to the nodes of the blockchain network. These nodes all either approve the transaction as valid or one or more nodes reject the block as invalid. Only a validated block can be added to the blockchain, which is updated across all nodes within the network.

The blockchain as a technology relies on the following elements (Figure 10.4). First, a set of declared participants must situate themselves upon some communication network and share some common

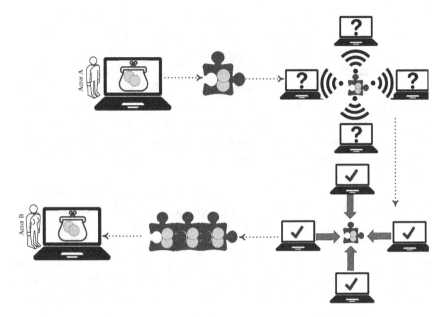

Figure 10.4: Components of the blockchain.

communication protocol such as Transmission Communication Protocol/ Internet Protocol (TCP/IP). Each node on the bitcoin network stores a common data structure known as the blockchain. A common consensus function is used to verify transactions and preserves the immutability of the blockchain. This means that transactions cannot be changed once entered on the blockchain.

The blocks of a blockchain are effectively data elements of the larger data structure. A new transaction forms a data-item that is added to a designated block within the blockchain. The block is then broadcast to the nodes of the blockchain network. These nodes either all approve the transaction as valid or one or more nodes reject the block as invalid. Only a validated block can be added to the blockchain, which is updated across all the nodes within the network.

Bitcoin relies on using the blockchain as a register of both money and financial transactions. Bitcoins are held in digital wallets and these form part of the blockchain. A block within the blockchain is equivalent in size to a text message, held on your mobile phone. There are different forms of blockchain. Bitcoin implements a permission-less blockchain, meaning that anyone can participate and contribute. Each blockchain is unique to each participant in the blockchain network, but personal details of the 'owner' of a designated blockchain are not recorded in it.

When bitcoins are used in a transaction, then the digital signature of the user is attached to the blockchain as confirmation and to prevent duplication of transactions and 'forgery'. But these digital signatures are also not stored in the blockchain. Thus the blockchain provides to bitcoin some interesting properties. No central government banks are required to issue bitcoin. No financial intermediaries are required to manage monetary transactions using bitcoin. The parties to economic transactions conducted in bitcoin cannot be identified.

Figure 10.4 illustrates two actors using bitcoin and the blockchain. Actor A wants to transfer a sum of money to actor B. The transaction is represented as a block and the block is broadcast to every party in the block. All parties in the network approve the transaction is valid. The block is added to the chain providing a transparent and indelible record of transactions made between actors participating in the network. Finally, the sum of money is transferred from actor A to actor B by updating the digital wallet of actor B.

Disintermediation Through the Blockchain

The blockchain as a technological infrastructure is not limited to bitcoin. This form of distributed register is being proposed as a way of implementing data structures for different communicative purposes and for supporting different types of coordinated activity. As we have discussed in Chapter 7, a register is a list of things held important by some institution or group of institutions. Within current practice, registers are maintained by registration authorities or registries for short. If actors wish to undertake many activities, they inherently engage with registers of various forms. An entry on such a register either prescribes certain activities or proscribes certain activities. Hence, to be able to drive a car, you need to be recorded on a driver licence register, while if you are on a sexual offender register, you are prevented from working in certain areas, such as with children or vulnerable adults. The blockchain has been proposed as a form of disintermediation in the sense that registration intermediaries may no longer be necessary for such institutional domains. The function served by the intermediary is assumed by the blockchain infrastructure.

Take the idea of a contract, which is a legally binding document that recognises and governs the rights and duties of parties to an agreement to exchange goods, services or money. Effectively, a contract is a data structure which communicates a series of commitments made by parties to the contract. In 1997 the legal scholar Nick Szabo (1997) realised that a distributed ledger, such as that implemented in the blockchain, could be used for smart contracts in which the list-item stores code which, when executed, implement the various phases of a contract.

Consider a scenario in which a rental contract for a house or apartment is implemented as a smart contract. Suppose actor A wishes to rent an apartment from actor B. Actor B creates a smart contract that acts not only as a series of commitments, but also implements various contractual obligations, such as to pay rent on a given rental date each month. Whenever actor A pays rent in some digital currency, he gets a receipt automatically stored in the smart contract. Actor B gives you the digital entry key, which comes to you by a specified date. If the key does not come on time, the smart contract releases a refund to actor A. If actor B sends the key before the rental date, the smart contract holds the release of both the rent and the key until the rental date arrives.

Data Security

Effective digital commerce demands the storage and transmission of data through data structures. However, this electronic data infrastructure opens up a range of security threats which include:

- **Electronic theft and fraud:** For example, Someone falsely updating corporate data with the aim of defrauding their employer, or a hacker making an illegal entry into a database system and extracting corporate data without permission.
- **Loss of confidentiality:** Such as an unauthorised person viewing information on confidential corporate policies and disclosing it to outside agencies.
- **Loss of availability:** For instance, a database system becoming unavailable because of a natural disaster such as fire and flood, or a human-generated disaster such as a bomb attack.
- **Loss of personal privacy:** When an unauthorised person views personal data someone wished to be kept private.

- **Loss of integrity:** When data is corrupted, by a software virus or a software or hardware failure.

Many such threats amount to breaches of data infrastructure. Data breaches (sometimes referred to as data spills or data leaks) are one of the most worrying concerns for contemporary institutions. A data breach is an incident in which data is lost, destroyed, corrupted or disclosed. Data breaches also include incidents in which data has been accessed without proper authorisation (Chapter 9) or the data is made unavailable through encryption, the application of ransomware or accidentally lost or destroyed.

Since the early 2000s, there have been hundreds if not thousands of data breaches impacting upon millions of people across the world. Data breaches, particularly of personal data, have an impact on the trust that users place in certain institutions and can lead to substantial loss of business for companies. Because of this, many countries require institutions to report data breaches to the centralised data controller of the nation-state, such as the Information Commissioner in the UK.

As we have made plain in this chapter, data form the lifeblood of modern business and commerce. Given the embeddedness of ICT infrastructure within business activity, it is not surprising to find that there are an increasing level of ICT-related crimes such as data breaches. There are also an increasing number of measures, many of them technological, that organisations take in response to this increase in data-related deviance. In this section, we look at a range of such measures designed to ensure data security.

Data security is a critical issue in modern societies and economies because of the increasing use of remote communication through the transmission of data structures such as transactions. As we have made plain in the current chapter, digital commerce cannot occur without the transfer of transactional data and the storage of data as data structures within data systems. Among the problems this creates are the need to ensure the privacy and protection of personal records, the ability to authenticate the parties to a transaction, securing the transmission of data and the risks of unauthorised access to data systems. In this sense, data security amounts to a bringing together of many issues considered in previous chapters.

In Chapter 6, we considered how ensuring the privacy of personal data is now a legal requirement in many countries. Privacy of data is normally ensured by defining the key purposes to which data is put and ensuring that only authorised persons are able to articulate data structures throughout their institutional lives (see Chapter 9). In other words, only authorised people should have access to data structures.

Authorisation of the articulation of data relies upon a prior process of authentication. This means that users of ICT systems need to be authenticated, as do parties to an electronic transaction. In general, messages should only be exchanged between parties whose identity has been confirmed in some way. Typically, this involves the use of personal identifiers, as discussed in Chapter 3, and is sometimes referred to as personal identity management.

As mentioned in Chapter 3, within face-to-face communication between business actors, personal identity is signified through natural signs such as appearance (how a person looks), behaviour (for instance, how a person speaks) or names (for example, personal names and nicknames). Within forms of mediated communication, such as when a person emails a company, such forms of natural identifier are not available. In substitute, mediated communication tends to use surrogate or artificial identifiers. Examples of surrogate identifiers are codes (such as customer numbers), tokens (such as credit cards) or knowledge (such as PINs and passwords). More recently, there has been increasing interest in biometric identifiers. A biometric is a machine-readable measurement or more readily a series of measurements of some bodily characteristic or behaviour such as an iris scan, a fingerprint or a DNA pattern. These measurements can be used to build a unique profile of an individual; this profile can serve as a strong identifier in situations of remote communication.

Hence, when using an online banking website, a customer is likely to be required to enter a range of identifiers to access the services of the website such as a customer number, a password and possibly even aspects of personal knowledge, such as the name of a person's father. Certain banks have now introduced further levels of authentication such as issuing card readers to their online customers or sending access codes to registered mobile devices.

In sharing data structures between institutional actors, only the parties to a transaction should have access to data. Such parties should not be able to deny that they have taken part in some transaction. and the sender of a message cannot deny that they have sent it. This is known as non-repudiability and is a property important to in any commercial transaction. Within contemporary ICT systems, this amounts to fundamentally automation of a common-place business convention.

The data in any message needs to be encrypted. For thousands of years, human societies have invented ways of ensuring the secrecy of data structures transmitted as messages. Encryption involves a double, sometimes a triple, encoding and decoding of data. As we have seen in Chapter 2, the message transmitted by a sender needs to be coded as a set of differences in some medium and a decoding of such differences by the receiver of the message. An encrypted message involves a further process of coding and decoding, typically using some algorithm (see Chapter 11) and an associated key (see Chapter 12).

A very simple form of encryption consists of taking the letters of the alphabet and replacing each one with a letter from a cipher alphabet. The cipher alphabet is the key. The encryption and decryption algorithms detail the method of substitution. For instance, if this key is used to encrypt 'et tu brute?'

Plain: a b c d e f g h I j k l m n o p q r s t u v w x y z
Cipher: j l p a w I q b c t r z y d s k e g f x h u o n v m

the coded message would read 'wx xh lghxw?'

Encryption ensures some privacy if only authorised people have access to the key, but a cryptologist can still use logic to decipher this kind of simply encrypted message, so more complex algorithms are used in practice. We shall return to encryption again in Chapter 13, when we consider its role in relation to systems of surveillance.

Conclusion

In Chapter 5 we saw how coordination is achieved through conventions of communication. Many of the conventions of financial accounting surrounding modern business and trade were invented in renaissance Italy and soon populated the countries of Western Europe. The same is true of associated data structures such as journals, accounts and ledgers that were invented to scaffold this activity. Such conventions as well as associated data structures are now, of course, embedded or translated into contemporary ICT systems. Significant conventions surround purchases of goods and services, sales of goods and services, receipts and payments. These conventions become encoded in contemporary ICT and data infrastructure. Part of the reason that common software packages can be used for financial accounting is that such conventions are well established on a global scale.

Coordination in financial markets is normally achieved by intermediaries, But the increasing penetration of ICT has led to a disintermediation in commerce. As we shall see in Chapter 11, more and more software actors are taking over the role of intermediaries between organisations and between individuals. Many technology giants are modern intermediaries, which act as conduits through which we feed our data. As we shall see in Chapter 12, they can generate an economic surplus from this purely by harvesting our data and through this both monitor and predict our economic activity.

References

Bagwell, P. S. (1968). *The Railway Clearing House in the British Economy 1842–1922* (London: Allen and Unwin).

Coase, R. H. (1937). "The Nature of the Firm." *Economica*, **4**(16): 386–405.

Searle, J. R. (2006). "Social Ontology: Some Basic Principles." *Anthropological Theory*, **6**(1): 12–29.

Szabo, N. (1997). "Formalizing and Securing Relationships on Public Networks." *First Monday*, **2**(9). DOI 10.5210/fm.v2i9.548.

Chapter 11

Data-Driven Actors

Introduction

In the 1970s, two computer/management scientists Alan Newell and Herbert Simon (1996) proposed the concept of a *physical symbol system*. This idea was developed as background theory to what Newell and Simon originally referred to as the *Sciences of the Artificial*. The concept was also critical in formulating the so-called *physical symbol system hypothesis*: that a physical symbol system has the necessary and sufficient means for generating intelligent action. This is seen to be one of the founding principles of the field of Artificial Intelligence, which we examine in this chapter. A physical symbol system consists of physical patterns, which can be combined into structures and manipulated to produce new structures. Data structures are classic examples of physical symbols. But can these structures be manipulated to generate intelligent action? This sets the scene for the current chapter — our examination of data-driven actors.

We have made the point many times in previous chapters that data structures are crucial for scaffolding instrumental communication and that in turn such communication scaffolds coordinated activity. But there is something missing or something we have taken for granted within this account. What we have missed out here is the notion of a decision and the act of decision-making. Decisions provide the important linkage between communication and coordination. This is the reason we placed a symbol conventionally used to signify decision-making — that of a decision diamond — at the heart of actors within our illustration of information situations (Figure 11.1). This is meant to suggest that actors use decision

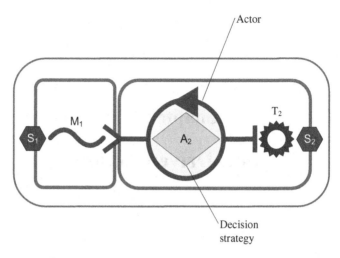

Figure 11.1:   Decisions within information situations.

strategies to make decisions — to choose between alternative courses of action.

Figure 11.1 also makes clear that the outputs of action rely upon decisions, but decisions rely upon the inputs of messages. Within Figure 11.1, actor A_2 senses message M_1 and based on its decision strategy effects transformation T_2. The crucial point we make in this chapter is that coordinated activity relies upon decisions made on the basis of communication — whether internal or external. But communication relies in turn upon the articulation of data. This helps explain the linkage of decisions to data and why many decisions made in contemporary society are data-driven.

Pretty much everything seems to be data-driven in modern society. This particularly applies to machine actors — non-human actors that take decisions and undertake activity based on such decisions, which affect many human actors. We focus on software actors within this chapter and consider two main types of such actors — algorithmic and heuristic actors. We shall examine how data fed to these software actors enable them to 'learn' algorithms or heuristics that implement decision strategies. As we shall see, this developing field of machine learning has heightened the central role that data plays in modern institutional life. Machine learning offers promise for improving activity in many areas but also has many problems.

Decisions and Control

Let us first try to clarify what we mean by a decision and why we have decisions. This is another area which many take for granted. Decisions, as we shall see, give us an entry-point into considering the notion of psyche and mind, which is so central to the discipline of Artificial Intelligence.

At its most basic, a decision is a choice made by some actor between alternatives. This suggests that, in terms of any one actor, there are two elements to any decision, the alternatives to choose from and the process of making some choice. Let us simplify and think of the choice that an actor has to make as the selection between alternative activities. To make such choice we must be informed about the features and likely consequences of alternatives. This demonstrates how decisions provide the linkage between communication and coordination.

To explain further, let us build a simplistic model of decision-making based upon the relationship between representation, communication and control. This will help us expand upon the notion of a decision strategy — a component element of our model of information situations (Figure 11.2).

At an abstract level, any actor can be considered an entity that acts and reacts to its environment in terms of some decision strategy. This way of envisaging an actor thinks of it as a system which is controlled by a control mechanism or process embedded within it. For such a control process to work effectively, it must have three things: resources to deploy

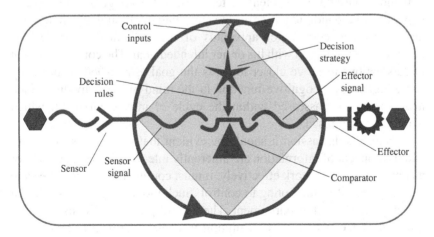

Figure 11.2: A control process embedded within our model of the actor.

to regulate the behaviour of the system in a desired direction; control inputs which implement the purpose or goal of the system; and control signals enabling the process to monitor and instruct operational processes.

The control process ensures defined levels of performance for the system through the use of a number of control inputs. This sets the key decision strategy for the controller. Such a decision strategy then works in interaction with three other key elements of a control process: sensors, comparators and effectors. Sensors, as we have seen in Chapter 1, are processes that monitor changes in the environment of some system or in the system itself (sensed signals) and send further signals to comparators. Comparators compare signals from sensors against some decision strategy and on this basis make some decision to send signals to effectors. Sometimes referred to as actuators or activators, effectors cause changes to the state of some aspect of the environment surrounding the system.

Many elements from this conception of control of the action-space of some actor have already been introduced in previous chapters. In Chapters 1 and 2, for instance, we introduced the ideas of the sensory and effector apparatus of some actor. We argued that embodied communication is reliant on these two types of apparatus. However, all action is reliant upon some notion of control in which actors continually sense their environment and effect changes in their behaviour in response to such sensations. To make this point, consider the simple act of some human walking through some space. Walking is a controlled accomplishment because it demands continual adjustment in terms of some set goal. The sensory apparatus of the individual senses the environment through touch, hearing and sight. The comparator apparatus of the individual compares the actor's current position with his or her intended goal. The comparator then effects actions to move closer towards the goal established probably by some higher-level cognitive function in the mind of the individual. Such action is again reassessed within the cycle of movements from which walking is composed.

From this discussion it should be evident that the process of control and the concept of information are inherently interlinked. For instance, for a control process to work effectively, it must continually monitor the state of the system it is attempting to control. Such monitoring occurs through sensing signals in its environment. The control process must also contain a model of the system it is attempting to control. Critical to this model will be some 'measures' of performance. Signals transmitted from the monitoring process are compared against this model. Further signals are then transmitted back to the system to maintain the system's performance within parameters defined by this model.

Decisions and Communication

Within the discipline of cybernetics, communication is always coupled with the control of action (Wiener, 1948). Taking a cybernetic view of actors, as we have done in the previous section, enables us to make a distinction between internal and external communication and its influence upon control.

Internal communication is thought, particularly conscious thought. We think, at least consciously, using signs. Peirce's semiotics, which we have discussed previously, is proposed not only as an account of language use, but also as an account of thought or cognition. This is because all thought is in signs and all signs are in thought. According to Peirce, 'The only thought ... which can be possibly cognized is thought in signs. But thought which cannot be cognized does not exist. All thought, therefore, must necessarily be in signs' (Houser and Kloesel, 1992, p. 24).

This quote suggests that for Peirce signs are not things or structures, but events or actions taken with things. Consider the colour *red*, as a sign. The notion of colour relies upon 'actions' or processes of sensation, perception and cognition. These interrelated processes correspond closely to aspects of Peirce's metaphysics which he termed as firstness, secondness and thirdness. Humans can sense through their sight organ light in the wavelength range 620–750 nanometres (nm). This is firstness, which corresponds to undifferentiated qualitative experience or *sensation*. Such sensation can be used to distinguish this form of light from another form of light in a different range of the visible spectrum, perhaps 450–490 nm. This secondness (*perception*) corresponds to the ability of some actor to relate one thing to another or to differentiate one thing from another and relies upon the actor's ability to perceive similarities and differences between phenomena. Finally, both forms of light may be classified as colours and tokens used to denote one perceivable colour from another. This is thirdness (*cognition*). If the commonality between two things is itself regarded as a thing, then we have a case of thirdness.

So, the sign *red* relies upon the ability of a human sense organ to discern light in the wavelength range 620–750 nm. Such discernment allows a person to distinguish one colour in this wavelength from another colour in the wavelength 450–490 nm. Finally, both forms of light may be classified as colours and tokens used to denote one perceivable colour from another, such as red and green.

Such thought or thinking through signs is particularly used to decide between alternative courses of action by individual actors. A decision can be regarded as a form of internal communication, almost like a directive to oneself. An actor asks of him, her, or itself, *what should I do next?* The decision is the response to this internal message following the accomplishment of information. Hence, in the encounter of an early mammal with a red berry, the actor might decide to eat it and does so because it has acquired the association between the redness of berries and their ripeness and perhaps also their suitability for eating. A human driver will rely on the signs *red* and *green* and their associations with other signs such as *stop* and *go* to coordinate their actions with fellow drivers at traffic lights.

External communication is different from internal communication because of the externalisation of things (see Chapter 1). External communication must involve the articulation of data structures between two or more actors. Clearly external communication is directed at communicating content and intent to one or more actors and as such is important for group or collective decision-making. Therefore, communicating for action is critically important because it is the catalyst for collective decision-making, which in turn facilitates coordination.

Take a decision from the institutional domain of emergency response. In Figure 11.3, a call-taker consults with a paramedic dispatcher in the ambulance control room by asserting details of the emergency incident to her. The paramedic dispatcher based on this message then directs the call-taker to classify (see Chapter 8) the incident as either a category A incident, a category B incident or a category C incident. Based on this communication, the call-taker decides what to do next. If the call is classified as category A (life-threatening) or category B (non-life-threatening but requiring medical response) then the call-taker proceeds to enter details of the incident into the incident ICT system. The creation of an incident record within the data system acts as a declaration that an incident has occurred and that as a consequence it must be responded to by the emergency response service. If the call is classified as category C, then no record is created, and an incident is not declared. Instead, the call-taker directs the caller to some other non-emergency healthcare provision.

Any point at which a decision must be made, such as the one represented in Figure 11.3, effectively serves to control the flow of action. The

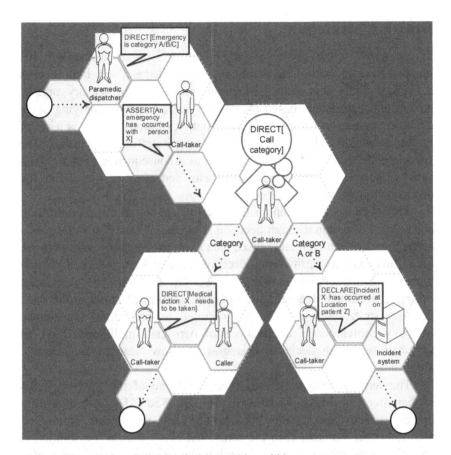

Figure 11.3: Collective decision-making within emergency response.

output from a decision is normally one or more communicative acts which attempt to control the behaviour of other actors. Directives and commissives are particularly important to the control and coordination of activity — people ask other people to do things and people either agree or disagree to do what is asked.

However, decision-making is of course not solely an individual activity. Decision-making within domains of organisation typically involves collective activity. Such collective decision-making relies upon a wider range of communicative acts such as assertives and expressives. Actors need to assert a position in relation to some decision or express how they feel about something. The negotiation of collective intention from individual intention is a critical part of what we mean by coordination.

Decision Strategies

To summarise, within our developing model of information situations, the place of actors is central. An actor can be modelled at a very high level as a cyclical entity that senses its environment through sensory organs. Actors make decisions based on what is sensed and by applying some decision strategy to sensory data. The output of any decision is a set of further actions which the actor effects using its effector apparatus. The success or otherwise of the action taken as a consequence of some decision is likely to be evaluated by the actor and may serve to refine the decision strategy of the actor concerned.

Therefore, decisions demonstrate the linkage between communication and control of action through decision strategies. A decision strategy is a set of functions which relate sensed data to effected actions. Within lower organisms, such as earthworms, decision strategies are inherited. Within higher organisms, such as humans, decision strategies are sometimes inherited but mostly learned. Traditionally, within ICT applications, such decision strategies would be programmed as procedural algorithms. In many contemporary applications of Artificial Intelligence (AI), as we shall see, such decision strategies are now 'learned' as heuristic algorithms.

The term algorithm derives from the name of the mathematician Mohammed ibn-Musa Al-Khwarizmi (750–850 AD). An algorithm amounts to some specification for solving a class of problems. Traditional algorithms are procedural in the sense that every step in the solution is specified. This means that the algorithm can theoretically be represented visually as a flowchart. And, if you follow the steps of the specified procedure, then a solution to the problem is guaranteed. In a heuristic algorithm, you do not specify the steps to a solution. Instead, you specify a set of rules of thumb, which when applied may or may not get you a solution.

Algorithms, whether heuristic or procedural, are typically used to implement the decision strategies of various software actors in the modern digital economy. The algorithms of procedural and heuristic decision strategies are typically transparent, meaning that they can be understood. In a procedural algorithm, the steps to a solution can be clearly followed. In a heuristic algorithm, the rules of thumb applied to reach a solution can be inspected. However, in many contemporary situations, the way in which these algorithms work to drive machine actors is impossible to understand because of the way they are built. To understand this, we need to unpack the general notion behind data-driven AI.

AI and Mind

The term artificial intelligence, or AI for short, refers to the attempt to build computing systems that can act intelligently. However, as we shall see, this is not the same as saying that such devices have a psyche, which enables them to communicate internally — to think. The beginnings of AI began with some speculative work published by Alan Turing in 1950 within a paper entitled *Computing Machinery and Intelligence*. In this paper, he argued that artificially created entities might one day be able to generate sufficient intelligence to pass as human. In the same article, he suggested a test by which one might assess the intelligence of such a machine — a test which he referred to as the *imitation game* — but which has become known more generally as the Turing test.

The Turing test consists of two actors A and B, which are interrogated by means of written questions by another human actor, C. One actor B is a human actor, while the other actor A is the machine actor. Actor C does not know which actor is the machine, and which is the human. A and B are required to provide written responses to a series of questions set by C. C must decide, purely based on the responses to such questions, which is the machine actor and which the human actor. If C cannot make this decision, then the machine is regarded as demonstrating intelligence.

The general point made by the imitation game is that we can only judge the intelligence of something through the actions that it is capable of. This is similar to Peirce's test for a sign — that a sign can only be judged as a sign in terms of its consequences. The entity that is the motive force for action, including sign-action, is of course *mind*. From certain actions, we can infer the presence of mind or psyche — that minds generate intelligent action.

In the 1960s, Herbert Simon and his colleague Alan Newell proposed the so-called physical symbol system hypothesis, which relates machines to mind. This states that a physical symbol system has the necessary and sufficient means for generating intelligent action. We know that brains can be considered physical symbol systems. Brains generate symbols through electrical activity conducted within an extremely complex network of neurons. And, we know, at least as far as Peirce is concerned, that symbols are the component elements of thought, which is the outward expression of mind, or at least conscious mind. The key consequence of the physical symbol hypothesis is that it should be possible to generate mind from different stuff than biological brains, such as the stuff of computing machinery.

The sort of intelligence that a machine would need to demonstrate in the imitation game demands that it has complex, cognitive abilities, which generate the phenomenon we generally refer to as conscious mind. The search for building such abilities into machines continues in an area generally referred to as strong AI, sometimes broad AI. When I began work in AI in the 1980s, researchers held much promise for strong AI and many predicted at the time that machine intelligence would pass Turing's test easily within a decade. Nowadays AI researchers are much more circumspect and admit that they are nowhere close to generating the sort of higher-level cognitive abilities that most humans display with current strong AI technologies.

So why is AI such a hot topic at the time of writing? This is because the area has taken a less ambitious but much more productive path in recent times. This path begins with the recognition that much more limited forms of intelligence are clearly displayed by organisms with less complex cognitive abilities than humans. The philosopher Daniel Dennett (1996) convincingly argues that the idea of there being only one type of mind equivalent to that displayed in *Homo Sapiens* is a mistake. He sees mind and indeed the process of mind (consciousness) rather as an evolutionary process. He further proposes as a consequence of the evolutionary nature of mind that complex organisms, such as humans, actually have a sedimentation or layering of minds, from the most simple found in lower organisms such as earthworms, to the most complex found in higher organisms such as *Homo Sapiens*.

Now a link to cybernetics — the science of control — mentioned earlier. Mind, for Dennett, is effectively a control system. The purpose of mind is to produce future — the ability to produce decisions as to possible actions and to test such decision moves against some environment. This must sound familiar, as it underlies the nature of information situations as we have defined them.

The baseline for the presence of mind is where we have some entity with a body that is self-sustaining (hence the arrow in Figure 11.1) and which is distinguishable from some environment in which it exists. However, there is no interaction between such an entity and its environment. An isolated chromosome is an example of such an entity.

The next step is the evolution of an *actor*, an entity that can sense aspects of its environment through its sensory apparatus and can manipulate aspects of its environment through its effector apparatus. Between its sensory and effector apparatus, there is a set of invariant functions which enable the entity to produce a set of fixed responses to given stimuli. This is the most basic form of decision strategy. The entity has no memory and hence cannot learn and modify its decision strategy. A single-cell bacteria (protozoa) is an example of such an entity. It can sense aspects of its environment (such as the presence of sugar) and effect rotation of its flagella (tail) to move towards the source of the sensation.

The next level of mind possesses some form of memory, and such memory allows different forms of decision strategy to be stored. This opens up the possibility that certain decision strategies can be learned rather than inherited in the sense that the actor can evaluate the result of an action, reinforce one decision strategy over another and store this within memory. An earthworm is an example of such an entity.

What we think of as human mind builds upon these lower levels of mind to include higher-level cognitive functions such as selective attention and the ability to work towards and shift between multiple goals. This means that the actor can exercise some selective control over both its sensory and effector apparatus. It is also able to shift its attention to work on different tasks in the achievement of multiple goals. All this eventually leads to the development of an inner environment in which actors can select amongst possible actions by testing such actions against the inner environment and observing results. This inner environment then becomes a precondition for self-consciousness — the ability that an actor can recognise itself as a distinct entity that is able to plan future behaviour.

Weak AI

As we mentioned, the claims made for the impact of artificial intelligence have usually missed the mark — sometimes by substantial margins. For example, in 1958, Herbert Simon made the claim that within 10 years a digital computer would be the world's chess champion. In 1970, Marvin Minsky, a renowned AI researcher, made the claim that in eight years we would have a machine with the general intelligence of an average human being. Perhaps because of claims such as this and their failure to deliver, research into strong AI suffered a severe cutback of funding in the late 1980s.

However, the notion of various levels of mind and consequent differences in intelligent action opened a whole new agenda of so-called *weak AI*. Weak AI seeks to build working but much more limited minds capable of acting intelligently but in much more limited domains than that proposed within the imitation game. Many of these software minds implement heuristic algorithms of various forms to perform limited action in very well-defined domains. For instance, an online tool which awards you a loan such as a mortgage on a house based on the answers you provide to its questions. Or a machine mind which recognises your voice and exercises a limited set of activities based upon the commands you give it. Or a surveillance system which automatically 'reads' your car's number plate and issues a fine to you (the driver) when you cross into a congestion zone. Or finally even a more sophisticated machine mind which can drive an automobile by itself.

Within the digital economy, software actors clearly now act in many domains relatively autonomously of human intervention. Companies like Facebook use such algorithms to decide which posts from friend and family we should see. Software actors working for Google skew search results depending upon your location and browsing history. Companies like Walmart tailor prices using factors such as user's choice of browser, operating system and purchase history.

However, the increasing use of such actors within the digital infrastructure for many activities originally performed by humans is of concern to many. Some believe that the decision strategies embedded within automated mortgage application systems contributed to the financial crash of 2008. More worryingly, these software actors when targeting high-risk borrowers disproportionally awarded high interest rates to minority groups in the US, such as African Americans and Latinos. More worryingly still, the US National Security Agency used certain algorithms to determine, in the absence of specific data, whether someone was not a US citizen and hence open to surveillance (Chapter 12).

Data-Driven AI

The sort of intelligence that a machine would need to perform effectively in the imitation game demands it having complex cognitive abilities which generate what some refer to as an adaptive mind. Many researchers have become convinced that it is theoretically impossible to program any form of mind from scratch. Instead, they pin their hopes on building an

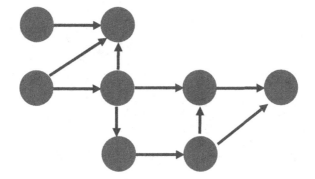

Figure 11.4:   A network as a data structure.

entity that can evolve some kind of 'mind' through learning conducted upon large datasets. Such machine learning relies upon a construct known as a neural network or *neural net* for short.

As the name implies, a neural net can be regarded as a network, which is a form of data structure. Within mathematics, a network is a special type of graph consisting of a set of nodes or vertices joined with a set of edges or links. Neural nets are directed graphs in the sense that the edges or links within the graph are ordered in the sense that each edge represents a specific direction from one node or vertex to another. In Figure 11.4, for instance, there are 8 nodes represented by circles with 10 directed vertices between them. The direction of each vertice is indicated with an arrowhead.

The *neural* in the term neural net refers to the attempt to simulate aspects of the brain as a biological system using a physical symbol system modelled on the idea of a directed graph. Hence, to give it its correct title we should refer to this data structure as an artificial neural network, which is modelled on a biological neural network. Within a biological neural network, neurones or neurons act as nodes and axon–synapse–dendrite connections act as links between neurons. A typical neuron consists of a cell body known as the soma, many dendrites and a single axon. The axon and dendrites are filaments that extrude from the soma. Signals are transmitted along connections as small electrical charges. Neurons are electrically excitable cells that are triggered when the potential of the charge received by dendrites reaches a certain level. When this occurs, the neurons transmit an electrical charge along its axon to a synapse. A synapse constitutes a connector between the axon from one neuron and the

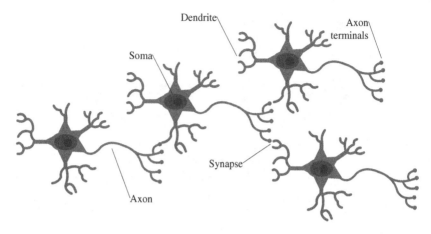

Figure 11.5:   A biological neural network.

dendrite from another neuron. Signals travelling across synapses cause excitation of further neurons in the network (Figure 11.5).

An artificial neural net simulates a biological neural net in the following manner. A node in an artificial neural net is programmed to have several input links but only one output link. Each input link is assigned a weighting which effectively amplifies or dampens the contribution of that link to the receiving node. These input weightings are summed by the node and passed through its so-called activation function, which determines whether or to what extent the node should output a signal to other linked nodes in the network.

As a data structure, an artificial neural net must be trained against data which identifies and describes things of interest in some restricted domain. Effectively training a neural net means developing a classification function (see Chapter 8) for some things of interest. For instance, you might want to train an artificial neural net to be able to distinguish between spam email and not spam email in terms of an email filter. Alternatively, you might want to identify a potential fraudster from a legitimate person in financial fraud detection or an unhappy customer from a happy customer in customer relationship management. To do this you need a data set for your chosen categories and need to label each instance of data within your data set with the appropriate category or class, such a spam email. This approach to training an artificial neural net is known as supervised learning. However, artificial neural nets can also

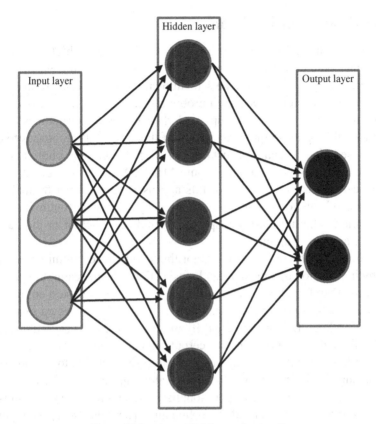

Figure 11.6:   An artificial neural network.

learn by clustering or grouping based upon similarities or differences identified by the net in masses of unlabelled data. This is known as unsupervised learning.

Practical artificial neural nets are built not as one massive network but from three interconnected layers of nodes (Figure 11.6). The input layer is fed data appropriate to describing the range of differences found within a certain domain. The output layer defines appropriate and different responses in terms of a defined set of inputs. One to many hidden layers implement the heuristic algorithm of the net by forming linkages between certain inputs and outputs. The links between nodes in the net adjust weightings assigned to links based upon a comparison of inputs to outputs.

The Opacity of Decisions

The notion that an artificial neural net can implement higher levels of mind has come under intense questioning. However, even if we acknowledge the capacity of neural nets to implement lower-level minds, they have certain problems. One such problem is that the neural net is only as good as the data it is trained upon. Certain biases or 'prejudices' in the data feed through into the construction of the net and its responses to certain sensed phenomena. For instance, in 2015, the Google photo app categorised a certain photograph of some African Americans as gorillas. The photo categorisation function of this app used a neural net trained on a large set of categorised images acquired by Google through its photo application. The net merely displayed prejudices inherent in the dataset that it was trained upon.

Another problem is that the algorithms embedded within neural nets are by implication opaque to outside inspection. The net cannot explain its 'reasoning' and the heuristic algorithm itself is frequently too complex to analyse. There is not a procedure or set of rules to be inspected in an artificial neural net. It is hence very difficult to validate and verify the way in which the net acts in response to certain inputs. Humans can account for their actions but a data-driven AI-actor currently is unable to provide such an account. This is because, of course, although an artificial neural net develops a function which operationalises the classification of things, it does so in a way entirely alien to humans. The classification of things performed by an artificial neural net relies upon the generation of mathematical patterns within the data structure of the net itself. These patterns are not signs which humans would understand.

The fact that a data-driven AI actor cannot explain itself to other actors is a significant break on the deployment of these actors within domains such as healthcare where, for instance, it is essential to explain to patients the basis on which some diagnosis of a medical condition has been reached. Some see the opacity of data-driven actors as disruptive to the very idea of accountability, which is of course a central principle underlying most legal systems.

Insidious Actors

Something that is insidious is unpleasant or dangerous and develops gradually without being noticed. We want to argue in this section that certain software actors that we rely upon in many areas of life are potentially insidious because of the way in which they have gradually occupied cornerstones of digital infrastructure without really being noticed. Such actors have particularly occupied a space of data articulation that we take for granted — that of data retrieval.

There is perhaps an over-focus in the literature upon data-driven AI actors. It is still true to say that many software actors do not operate via neural nets trained by machine learning. Instead, they implement conventional procedural algorithms, or explicit decision rules represented as decision tables or decision trees. A simple example here is one used to decide upon the discount to be offered a customer when renting a car. Figure 11.7 illustrates this algorithm as a decision table, which effectively implements a set of decision rules that automatically applies appropriate discounting to a car rental based on data supplied by the customer.

The software actor in the case of car rental discounting is a lone actor. Now consider the case where many such data-driven software actors take action within a wider domain of institutional action. Many of the ICT systems used for security trading by the big economic actors such as market makers have facilities which augment the trading activity of human actors. Such systems use complex algorithms or 'business rules' embedded within the systems to perform automatic trading of securities in certain situations. A simplification of one such a rule might be of the form: *if the offer price of share S amongst a group of market makers M falls below a certain specified level L then sell P percent of the security holding.*

Car group	Compact											
Rental period	Day				Week				Month			
Loyalty member	Yes	Yes	No	No	Yes	Yes	No	No	Yes	Yes	No	No
>3 days in advance	Yes	No	Yes	No	Yes	No	Yes	No	Yes	No	Yes	No
0%			X	X				X				
5%		X					X					X
10%	X					X					X	
15%					X					X		
20%									X			

Figure 11.7: A decision table.

Depending upon the area of trading, the application of such automation can cover between 30% and 80% of normal trading activity. Much of this trading activity may be performed completely independently of human intervention.

Now assume that a range of such machines maintain a similar range of such business rules. The sale of a particular security by trading machine A, if done in sufficient quantity, is likely to affect the average offer and bid price for this security amongst other market makers. It is also likely to trigger sales of such shares by other traders, both human and non-human, which has the consequential effect of lowering the share prices even further. Hence a positive or reinforcing loop is established between humans and machines within the trading network.

Some have argued also that the latency associated with automated trading has tended to exacerbate the frequency and size of stock market bubbles and crashes. Latency refers to the time taken for a message transmitted from a sender to reach a receiver. The speed with which data such as the offer price of shares is transmitted has a direct effect on the speed with which a financial actor can respond. This speed — which in the case of automated trading can be measured in milliseconds — allied to common behaviour programmed into automated trading systems is seen to contribute to reinforcing cycles of selling behaviour (crashes) or reinforcing cycles of purchasing behaviour (bubbles).

Unless we have access to the procedural algorithm, decision table or decision rules employed by the software actor the decision strategy is still opaque because as intellectual property they are not open to inspection. What is worrying is that the uncritical use of such software actors and the decisions they take for us may be removing many of the essential skills seen to be required by citizen-actors to engage not only with the economy, but also with civil society more widely (see Chapter 12). To make this point let us examine a key actor in the global economy — that of the Google search engine. You may not have thought of it in precisely this way, but the Google search engine makes decisions on your behalf and supplies the data on which you will be informed. But how do you really know that this is the data you want, require, or need?

The Google Search Engine

Google was founded by Larry Page and Sergey Brin while they were students at Stanford University, on the back of research they were both conducting on improving the algorithms underlying search engines. A search engine is an ICT system which searches for web documents matching a set of keywords entered by the user. The search results are generally presented in a list and are often called hits. Search engines work by storing data about content, which they retrieve from HTML documents. This content is retrieved by a web crawler or spider — a piece of software which follows every link on a website and records what it finds. The contents of each page are then analysed to determine how it should be indexed. Data are then stored in an index for use in later queries. A query can be a single keyword or a set of keywords. Keywords are matched against index entries and a listing of the best-matching content is produced.

When a user enters a query into a search engine, the engine examines its index and provides a listing of best-matching web pages according to its criteria. The usefulness of the search engine depends on the relevance of the results it gives back. While there may be millions of web pages that include a word or phrase, some pages may be more relevant, popular or authoritative than others. Most search engines employ methods to rank results to present what the algorithm reckons are the best results first. But hang on, how do we know that these are the *best* of the results that we want? How is best computed? In comes the algorithm.

While at Stanford University, Page and Brin developed an algorithm known as PageRank which underlies the operation of the Google search engine. As we have mentioned, Google uses webcrawlers to continuously build and maintain data structures which describe links between web documents. The web documents are in fact nodes in a large and complex network, as discussed earlier. PageRank analyses the links emanating from and pointing to web documents. It then assigns a numerical weighting based on this analysis which ranks each document examined. The algorithm treats links in a similar manner to academic citations. Generally, the larger the number of citations of an academic paper, the more important it is considered by the academic community. In a similar manner, PageRank ranks a document as particularly relevant in terms of some keyword if it has many links to it.

In the early years of the web, there were many different search engines available. Google now dominates and is the most visited website in the world, handling over 1 billion queries per day and generating over 24 peta-bytes of data per day. This means that Google acts as the primary gatekeeper into the products and services offered online — what some see as a potential monopoly situation. A monopoly is a situation in which one producer controls supply of a good or service, and where entry of new producers is prevented or highly restricted. Some worry that Google's dominance of web search (and the associated marketing opportunities) is fast becoming a monopoly position, which may not be good for a digital economy. It is a bit like saying that the only way you have of buying goods and services is by visiting one and one only high-street store.

Google is not only a gatekeeper, it is of course a decision-maker. When we use a software actor such as Google to do something for us, we are devolving our decision-strategy to the machine. But in devolving data retrieval to algorithms, are we missing anything? Well, the obvious thing to say here is that algorithms, whether they be artificial neural nets or procedural programs like Google, always use proxies of human concepts such as *quality* or *relevance* to direct their search. The Google search engine is somewhat unusual in that the algorithm it uses, at least at its core, is available for inspection by outsiders. As mentioned, PageRank works by counting the number and quality of the links to a page. It then uses this to provide a proxy estimate of how important a page and its corresponding website is. The underlying assumption built into this algorithm is that more important websites receive more links from other websites. But this approach has its drawbacks, as we shall see in Chapter 12.

Conclusion

Non-human actors, particularly software actors, are ubiquitous in our contemporary information society. Many such non-human actors are data-driven in the sense that they take decisions and undertake activity based on data fed to them. The algorithms at the heart of such non-human actors make algorithmic decisions based on procedural or heuristic decision strategies. Traditionally such algorithms had to be programmed up-front and are transparent but more recently such algorithms are now learned by software actors trained on large datasets and are frequently opaque to outside inspection and evaluation.

AI began with the attempt to prove the physical symbol hypothesis. This is the suggestion that intelligence could be demonstrated in a construct built from stuff other than human brain tissue. Such intelligence could be tested and verified through some form of imitation game. Indeed, certain AI systems have performed well in certain imitation games conducted in very narrow domains of expertise, such as in playing chess, the game of Go or double jeopardy. But the vast majority of successful AI to date operate with narrow or weak AI — using heuristic algorithms to conduct intelligent action in very narrow circumstances.

Some still hold out hope for the increasing power of minds developed through machine learning on big data, a topic for Chapter 13. Many software actors are now engaged in data surveillance, the topic of the next chapter.

References

Dennett, D. C. (1996). *Kinds of Minds: Towards an Understanding of Consciousness* (London: Weidenfeld and Nicholson).

Houser, N. and C. Kloesel (eds.) (1992). *The Essential Peirce: Selected Philosophical Writings* (Bloomington, US: Indiana University Press).

Simon, H. (1996). *The Sciences of the Artificial*, 3rd edition (Cambridge, MA: MIT Press).

Wiener, N. (1948). *Cybernetics* (New York: Wiley).

Chapter 12

The Mechanics of Echo Chambers

Introduction

We made great play in Chapter 2 of the substance of communication and made the distinction between persistent and non-persistent data structures in terms of this. Sound is clearly a substance for the transmission of non-persistent messages, but the message can be made to persist for a longer period through the phenomenon of echoes. An echo is a sound that is repeated because the sound waves are reflected back off smooth, hard objects in the same way as a rubber ball bounces off the ground. The echo is used as an analogy within the modern context to refer to the reverberation of persistent messages through data structures created in social media. A consideration of this forms the backbone for our current chapter.

There is a tendency evident in much literature to portray any technology as inherently value-neutral. In other words, technology is portrayed as something necessarily separate from economic, social and political systems. Proponents of this viewpoint maintain that it is only through the uses to which technology is put that certain positive or negative effects emerge from such technology within economic, social and political systems.

It should be evident from the account we have developed in previous chapters that we take issue with this viewpoint, at least as far as it concerns data structures as technology. Technology is a designed and constructed system of artefacts. As such, any technology, including data structures, is inherently value-laden in the sense that certain implicit choices as to the purpose of such artefacts are implicitly or explicitly embedded into the makeup of technology.

Data structures, as we have seen, are vehicles for communication. It should therefore come as no surprise to find that the modern phenomenon of social media is reliant upon the scaffolding of data structures, just like other institutional domains. Just like many other aspects of ICT, social media is a technology for creating information situations. Social media, as a facility for articulating data structures for communication, as we shall see, has come under the spotlight for both good and bad reasons. For instance, it has been seen not only as a catalyst for coordinating political protest, but also as a vehicle for dissemination of extremist views. Some have even claimed that social media is undermining the very notion of civil society because of the way in which this technology facilitates mis-information, disinformation and malinformation. Certain characteristics of social networks, such as the network effect, strong and weak links and social capital make social media particularly attractive to business, as a prime medium for electronic marketing, particularly viral marketing. However, social media is also impacting upon other areas of the digital environment, such as the digital polity.

The key aim of this chapter is to deconstruct the technology and uses of social media in terms of our theory of information situations. We wish to examine the use of social media for communication and coordination and what it contributes to supporting social networks online. However, as we shall see, in many areas, social media does not seem to be supporting open and rational debate about key issues essential for civil society. Instead, it seems to be a force for polarising viewpoints and solidifying such viewpoints through the phenomenon of echo chambers.

What is Social Media?

You as the reader of this book are probably a heavy user of social media. However, what exactly is it and where did this modern phenomenon come from? The term social media was first used to describe a number of sites and tools using the web open standard infrastructure directed at facilitating collaboration and coordination amongst dispersed actors. The dominant tools of social media were created in the early to mid-2000s.

LinkedIn was founded in 2002, Facebook was founded in 2004, YouTube was founded in 2005 and Twitter was founded in 2006.

Having said this, it is quite difficult to pinpoint precisely what is meant by social media. The term is often used to refer to any means for creating digital content and sharing this content via both strong and weak links within online social networks. Therefore, to understand the value of social media we first need to examine these three features of social media — digital content, online social networks and strong and weak links — in more detail.

Digital Content

The term content, in a digital context, was first used to refer solely to documents or web pages held on websites. As we have seen, a web page is a data structure coded in HTML (Chapter 10) and consists of two parts: the content and the tags. To remind ourselves, consider a simple piece of HTML:

<title>This is a title</title>

The content here is the string of text '*this is a title*', while the tag is the keyword, in this case *title*, placed between angled brackets. The tag tells a web browser to display the piece of text on the screen in the format of a title.

We all know that content upon a web page is not restricted to text and can now contain, images, video and audio. All such media demand different formats for the construction of data structures. Nowadays, the term content has expanded even further to refer to all forms of goods and services that can be represented in digital form as data. Movies are a good example as are music tracks. Both movies and music can now be created as data structures, distributed as data structures and consumed as data structures.

The real breakthrough occurred when such digital content could be user-generated. As we all know, digital content is now easily created or captured using both fixed and mobile access devices. However, perhaps more importantly, such content can be shared or distributed in several different ways to other actors, e.g. by posting to a website or by messaging to nominated individuals. This means that digital content can spread rapidly through online social networks.

Social Networks

In Chapter 11, we explained how the notion of a network can be considered a data structure consisting of a set of nodes joined with a set of links. In Chapter 11, we used this to explain the concept of an artificial neural network. A social network, in contrast, is a network in which the nodes are actors, and the links are social bonds of various kinds such as kinship (family), friendship and acquaintanceship. Certain properties of social networks are important for the members of such a network. These include the size of the network, density of the network, the strength of a network's links and the cliquishness of the network.

In Figure 12.1, two different social networks are visualised upon a tabletop with mannequins representing actors and directed lines as friendship bonds. Nine social actors are labelled A through I and friendship icons are placed between certain actors to represent the links in this network. As social bonds, friendship links are reciprocal, meaning that if A is a friend of B then B is also a friend of A (Lazarsfeld and Merton, 1954). This is why the links in the networks illustrated in Figure 12.1 have an arrow at each end.

The actors in network 1 and network 2 remain the same. What varies between these networks is not only how the links are placed, but also the density of the network. The density of a social network refers to the number of links in the network and is a function of the connectivity of the network — how many actors are connected with how many other actors. Hence, network 2 has a greater density than network 1. As we shall see, the density of a social network is one determinant of the value of the network to its members.

Social networks have been in existence ever since *Homo Sapiens* emerged as a distinct species and are one way of conceiving of the concept of community in concrete terms. The links within a social network are just one way of thinking about the multitude of ways one actor interacts with other actors. If no interaction occurs between two actors, then no link exists. This means that links are maintained through action, particularly through communication. Other things can of course spread through a social network — such as a virus like COVID-19 — indeed, viruses rely

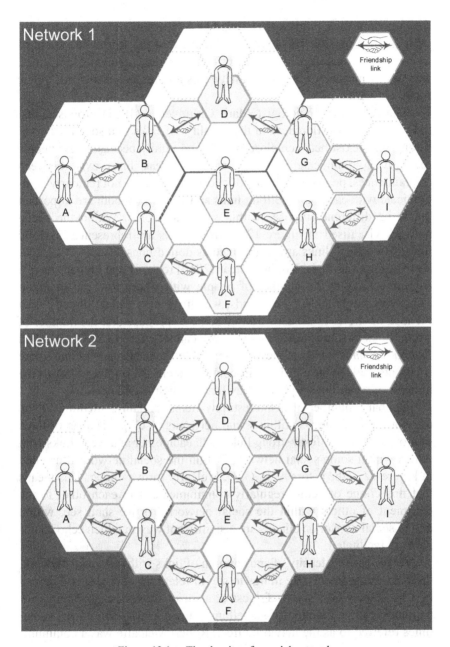

Figure 12.1:   The density of a social network.

for their transmissibility upon a number of features of social networks, such as their density. This explains why most of the worldwide attempts to control the spread of the virus, prior to the development of vaccines, was to disrupt face-to-face social networks and replace them with online social networks.

The American sociologist Mark Granovetter (1973) proposed that there are usually differences in the 'quality' of links in a social network. Strong links exist between close friends and family because these people regularly communicate with one another. Weak links exist between acquaintances, people who know of one another but do not regularly communicate with each other. Strong links and weak links both are important but serve different purposes within social networks. Within the social network visualised in Figure 12.2, strong links are represented as solid lines, while weak links are represented as dotted lines.

The anthropologist Robin Dunbar (2010) reckons that humans have a cognitive limit to the number of people with whom one can maintain stable social relationships or bonds, which we may equate directly with the idea of strong links. This has led some to propose that the number of strong links in someone's social network cannot exceed 150 — so-called *Dunbar's number*. This suggests an upper limit to the density of one's core social network of strong links. In contrast, there is no upper limit to the number of weak links a person may have in their social network.

Dunbar's number also interestingly helps explain something of the development of cliques within social networks. A clique is a set of three or more actors who form strong links with each other and weak links with others within some social network. Within the social network illustrated in Figure 12.2, the actors A, B, G, D, E clearly form a clique. This means that this clique of actors regularly communicate with each other to the detriment of others within the social network. As we shall see, within online social networks, cliques are a significant way in which echo chambers are facilitated.

As well as the density of and strength of links within a social network, there are some interesting things to say in relation to the size and spread of a social network. The usefulness of a social network as a resource for its members is a function of something known as *Metcalfe's law*, sometimes referred to as the network effect. Robert Metcalfe was a communication engineer who proposed this law originally in relation to electronic communication networks. The law states that the value of a communication network to a user is proportional to the square of the number of users

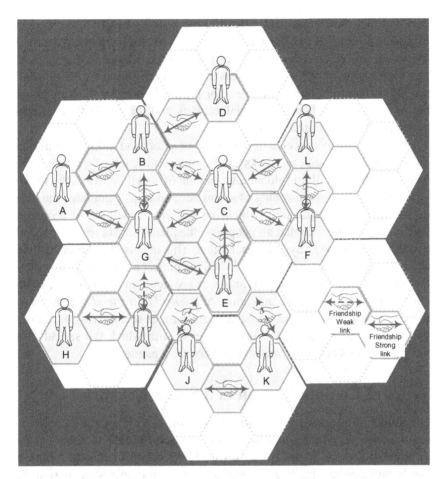

Figure 12.2: Strong and weak links in a social network.

or members of the network. The same principle appears to apply to a social network. What this is suggesting is that the value of participating in a network for a given member grows exponentially with the number of the members of the network.

When visualising social networks through a discipline known as social network analysis, certain actors appear to play a more important role within the network than others. This can typically be understood in terms of the number of other actors having links to this actor (a bit like the basis of the PageRank algorithm discussed in Chapter 11). When such a number is high in comparison to co-actors then the actor is a *hub* for links between many different actors. Within the social network illustrated in Figure 12.2, actor B is clearly a hub in that five other actors have strong links with this actor. Actor B also serves to bridge between two cliques in this social network through the weak link between B and C. As we shall see, this notion of a hub or bridge actor is a useful way of thinking about the role of an *influencer* in a social network and the power they hold to persuade through communication.

It is possible to conceive of the spread of actors and links as encircling the planet, with social networks interjoining with each other across the world. We might call this global interlocking of social networks the *social mesh*. This idea of the meshing of social networks has stimulated the idea of six degrees of separation, which has become something of an urban legend. This is the idea that all people on the planet are six or fewer social connections (links) away from each other. This means that theoretically a chain of 'handshakes' can be established to connect any two people within the global social mesh in a maximum of six steps. In other words, I can connect to you through the maximum of *a friend of a friend of a friend of a friend of a friend of a friend*. Such a meshing of social networks across the world also explains, of course, the ease with which the spread of a virus such as COVID-19 can quickly become a pandemic.

Types of Communication in a Social Network

Our model of information situations is a useful starting point for considering the ways in which social networks are used by their members to do different things. A social network clearly opens up means by which a single message can be disseminated to many actors in a short period. In other words, each link between actors within a social network opens up a channel for the enactment of many information situations. However, such information situations may be directed at achieving different things; the messages sent by actors will be sent with different intentions. Therefore, it is useful to think through and distinguish between four key types of communication that may be enacted through any social network, distinguished in terms of the purpose of the communication.

We mentioned in Chapter 3 that we are interested primarily in this book in instrumental communication — communication that gets things done. Actors seek to assert, direct, commit, declare or express through such communication. Instrumental communication, as we have seen, is important to the coordination of work but it is also significant as a motive force in other areas such as in organising political protest. Social networks can be a source for instrumental communication, such as directing people to view some indicated content online or making commitments to attend some protest event.

However, it is true to say that much communication conducted within social networks serves a much more social than instrumental function. Commonly referred to as 'small talk' (or more formally as phatic communication) this form of communication helps bind people together in social networks. In other words, phatic communication has more of a social function than an informative function. [*How are you?*] as a message sent to a friend along with an appropriate response such as [*I'm fine thank you, and you?*] is an example of phatic communication. The purpose of such phatic communication is to make people feel good and through this to solidify links within their social network. Animal scientists compare such communication in humans to the grooming activities performed by primates, such as chimpanzees. As we shall see, phatic communication is extremely important to the production and reproduction of what some call social capital.

There is room, however, for at least two other types of communication that are clearly evident within online social networks and do not fulfil the purpose of either instrumental or phatic communication. These are forms of persuasive and inflammatory communication. Persuasive communication has the purpose of not getting some actor to do something but of changing or sometimes solidifying the 'mind' of the actor upon some particular issue. Persuasive communication is, of course, at the heart of marketing messages targeted at people. However, persuasion exercised through electronic messages is also at the heart of the phenomenon of *fake news*.

Nevertheless, many messages sent and received through social media are not designed to effect action, to bind people together or to persuade people of something. Instead, such communication is intended to insult and through so doing to hurt and divide people. Such is the nature of defamatory or inflammatory communication, the purpose of which is to defame a person or to incite unrest amongst certain groups. Such communication is at the heart of online phenomenon such as trolling and cyber-bullying.

The Value of Social Networks and Social Media

So, why do we have social networks? What value do such networks hold for their members besides as a vehicle for one-to-many communication?

The answer to such questions is sometimes framed in terms of the concept of social capital and its associated features such as reciprocity and trust.

Over 20 years ago, the US sociologist Robert Putnam (2000) wrote an influential book called *Bowling Alone*. This book described what he referred to as the decline in social capital amongst the population of the mid-West in the US. Social capital is the set of resources available to individuals that participate in dense networks of social relationships. One of the most important of such resources is *reciprocity*, the notion that if you do something for me then you can call on me to do something for you in the future. Note, that this is entirely different from economic exchange as described in Chapter 10. Within economic exchange, I will give you something or do something for you only in return for some financial capital.

Another important resource made available through social capital is *trust*. Trust is a belief in the integrity or surety of another. Generally speaking, you are more likely to trust people in your social network that you are linked to in strong relationships, such as your relatives or close friends rather than strangers or acquaintances. This also means that you are more likely to believe what other members of your social network say about something than what strangers say. This is because trust is transitive, meaning that if you (C) trust what member B tells you and B trusts what member A tells him then you are likely to trust what member A says in turn. This is a critical reason that marketing people are so interested in online social networks and why memes are so easily transferred through online social networks.

Clearly, the key difference between a social network and online social network is that in an online social network interaction is facilitated through information technology and can be conducted remotely. Actors within the online social network communicate through the transmission of electronic messages containing digital content. Social media as we have seen is the attempt to build and support social networks through the application of ICT. Interestingly, when online social networks first emerged, academics started a debate about whether online social networks truly constituted social networks. In the contemporary context, we would probably need to ask a number of alternative questions, such as how much do people communicate any longer face to face as compared to remotely and are most information situations in which actors participate now conducted remotely? It is certainly true to say that the global pandemic has undoubtedly increased the amount of online communication and hence increased the importance of maintaining social networks through data communication.

Therefore, to summarise, social media is particularly used as a means of creating and sharing digital content, but it is also now used as an infrastructure for communication, particularly phatic communication, through various forms of electronic message. This helps explain why organisations from the private sector to the voluntary sector are interested in social networks and the social capital they generate. It also helps explain why social media, which is founded on the idea of online social networks, is such a fruitful bedrock for much recent organisation activity.

You would tend to infer both from the network effect and the distinction between strong and weak links that social media is important to maintaining strong links — particularly as more and more people are geographically dispersed and use social media to communicate on a regular basis with each other. However, social media may also be important to developing weak links as well, because weak links are important to social and economic opportunities. Interestingly, the higher you climb the career ladder, the more important weak links become. This explains why high-ranking business people spend so much of their time 'networking'. Because they know that job opportunities are not usually communicated via strong links but through weak links — by acquaintances.

Therefore, social media sites such as Facebook and LinkedIn offer a number of things to their members. The value of Facebook to its members lies primarily as a tool to build and maintain strong links with people in an online social network. However, the size of its membership also offers its membership opportunities to explore and develop weak links. In contrast, LinkedIn is a social networking site which specialises in professional matters. As such, the usefulness of being a member of LinkedIn is the opportunity afforded by communicating over and developing weak links.

On the opposite side of the fence, business is interested in online social networking for a number of reasons. Business seek to exploit the network effect to more effectively market its goods and services. It also uses social media to search for and recruit new staff and to crowdsource new ideas as a means to innovate. However, because of the growth in social media, there is an increasing range of occasions when social media is used for informative and instrumental communication. Enterprises use social media to facilitate collaboration on things such as project work. Adverts assert the properties of some product or service through social media. People can direct others to attend events such as 'flash mobs' and people can commit to attending through electronic messaging.

Memes

More recently, social media is often touted as infrastructure for the transmission of memes. So, what is a meme? First it should be said that the term *meme* is used in a much narrower way within social media circles than originally proposed by the inventor of the term. Within social media, memes tend to refer solely to an idea spread through some communication medium such as images, videos or electronic messages. However, let us look at its original conception that is much larger and gives us a better way of understanding the link of this concept to a central idea of the current book — the power of data structures.

The term *meme* first appeared in Richard Dawkin's book *The Selfish Gene* (1976). He coined it to refer to a unit of cultural transmission or unit of imitation. Dawkins coined the term meme as a shorter and catchier version of the term mimeme, which derives from the Greek word *mimema* meaning something imitated. He particularly liked the term meme because of its poetic resonance with gene. He argued that memes jump from brain to brain by a process of imitation. We also see a resonance with the idea of a seme — another term for a sign.

Dawkins sees memes as one example of a higher-level concept which he refers to as a replicator. A replicator is any construct that is able to produce copies of itself such as a living organism, an idea (meme) or a program such as a computer virus. Dawkins argues that a gene is a replicator while organisms such as mice, elephants and trees are vehicles for replicators. For Dawkins, a replicator is 'anything in the universe of which copies are made.' Successful replicators, he argues, must have three key properties: fecundity, fidelity and longevity. Replicators need not last forever. They need only last long enough (longevity) to produce additional replicators (fecundity) that retain structure intact (fidelity) through the process of replication.

Susan Blackmore (1999) takes the pragmatic view of memes as behavioural replicators that are carried around and protected by vehicles or interactors: human beings. She also refers to clusters of memes that are replicated together as memeplexes. Blackmore defines the meme as 'instructions for carrying out behaviour, stored in brains (or other objects)

and passed on by imitation'. Memes are thus proposed as a second replicator along with genes.

The term meme suggests that replication of behaviour occurs through
a process of mimesis or imitation. However, mimesis is clearly not the
sole process of replication of behaviour. The 'instructions' for behaviour
must also be passed on by communication between two or more actors.
Our whole education system is founded on the belief that instruction can
primarily be delivered through communication. Semes are hence perhaps
a third replicator and in the guise of data structures are important to the
reproduction of institutions. A seme is a term from linguistics which has
been used in various ways. It has been described as the minimal unit of
meaning in human languages or more broadly as anything that stands for
something else. In the latter sense, this is the classic concept of a sign,
which we have considered in some detail in previous chapters.

Truth and Lies

Our model of information situations has till now assumed that the
message transmitted by actor A to actor B is held to be *true* by actor A.
We take this notion for granted but the notion of truth is slippery and has
consumed philosophers for hundreds if not thousands of years. We do not
need to get into this debate here but just need to present an account of
truth-seeking and truth-making consistent with the notion of status functions or signs as explored in previous chapters. This will then help us
examine some of the more troubling aspects of social media, which play
games with the concept of truth, such as fake news and echo chambers.

For Charles Sanders Peirce, there is an inherent linkage between
signs, inquiry, meaning and truth. We hinted at in Chapter 3 that Peirce is
oft quoted as founding father of the philosophy of pragmatism (Atkin,
2016), which holds as its central maxim that for any sign to be meaningful
it must have practical consequences. In terms of this maxim, Peirce provides an account of both meaning and truth. If we do not consider a sign
to have any practical bearing, then it does not have any meaning. Hence,
for Peirce, this pragmatic maxim is a tool for the analysis of meaning.
It is designed to help us make our signs as clear and meaningful as
possible.

For Peirce then to know that something is indeed a sign, we apply the
pragmatic test of whether the making of differences in a certain substance

(Chapter 2) makes a further difference in turn, typically within the psyche of some actor (Bateson, 1972). In other words, we must judge any potential sign in terms of its consequences, whether it has any practical bearing on some situation. For example, suppose some actor makes some data such as adding a 'thumbs-up' sign to some digital content. This making of some difference only constitutes an action within a wider sign-event. We can only judge the 'thumbs-up' as a sign if it communicates something to some other actor and by doing so causes some difference to the cognition of this actor. We might also judge the result of such communication, in turn, in terms of differences made to the consequent behaviour of that actor, perhaps to changes in the content viewed and further distributed by this actor.

It is clear from this that the meaning of the 'thumbs-up' token in this situation is bound with certain beliefs held by actors interacting with this artefact. For Peirce, a belief is a habit of action (Bacon, 2012), which implies that to establish the meaning of a belief, we must examine the habits it produces, in turn. We would call such habits conventions (see Chapter 5). Peirce maintains that we continually utilise certain unquestioned beliefs, prejudices or habits because they facilitate current action. However, such beliefs are always open to question and may be revised or relinquished at some point if they are no longer found useful. Inquiry is therefore a continuous process of *securing belief* (Hookway, 1985). Secure beliefs must rely on a community of inquirers scrutinising certain beliefs and testing them in relation to action. Such scrutiny is initiated by doubt in the certainty of certain beliefs by a community of inquirers. A belief is therefore that which one would be prepared to act upon, whereas a doubt is a sense of uneasy dissatisfaction experienced when acting according to a belief that does not result in expected consequences. Therefore, inquiry is a matter of securing beliefs that are free from doubt. Inquiry does not aim at truth per se, but security from doubt.

This seems to suggest that Peirce does not support a notion of true belief, which is incorrect (Gallie, 1952). It is apparent from his work that he supports the notion of real things whose character is independent of opinions about them — this appears very similar to the notion of brute facts as proposed by John Searle. He therefore assumes that a process of inquiry can be devised in which the truth of certain beliefs can be fixed by a community of inquirers. This means that the existence of real things can be established or 'fixated' in a continuous and an enacted consensus of beliefs held about them. Reality is thus not determined by a community of inquirers; reality is that to which the community of inquirers is led through inquiry.

Truth in this sense is some *justified belief* held by one or more actors and is normally critical to assessments of the validity of messages sent between one actor and another. The eminent scholar of signs Umberto Eco (1977) interestingly defined the study of signs — semiotics — as 'the discipline studying everything which can be used in order to lie'. This is because signs, as the component elements of messages, are not only used to *inform*, but may also be used to *misinform, disinform* and *malinform*. Misinformation is a false message sent by an actor to one or more other actors without this actor knowing the message asserts something untrue. Here, there is a mismatch between what the actor believes and the world. Disinformation in contrast is a message sent by an actor to one or more other actors knowing that such a message is false and typically sent with the intent of influencing the receiver's behaviour. Malinformation is a false message sent by an actor to one or more other actors with the deliberate intent of causing harm to some individual or institution (Wardle, 2020). Information, as well as its shady sisters, are all critical to understanding how the data technologies of social media are reshaping the concept of the news.

There appears to be a certain synergy here between notion of truth and lies messaged through data structures and the idea of data breakdowns considered in Chapter 6. Such breakdowns can occur in the interinstitutional scaffolding of data structures and two important types of such breakdown are asserting things that cannot be confirmed and directing people to do the wrong things. Disinformation and malinformation are clearly types of data breakdown in which processes of essential and continuous inquiry important to securing belief within communities of actors are suspended or ignored.

Fake News

What is news? The secret is in the name — news is reported new happenings by somebody. News is therefore a data structure, typically a report or set of reports. The other major characteristic of news is that the content is broadcast, meaning that one source can send the report or reports to many potential readers. This leads to the question of who decides what is a new happening, how they choose to report it and who decides to receive it? Ever since the 17th century printed periodicals, known collectively as newspapers, have dominated the making and dissemination of news. In this sense, newspapers were the first major content industry and journalists the first true content producers. The structure of newspapers have changed little since that time, consisting of a series of written articles, with each article consisting of a headline followed by connected text.

News then is traditionally a set of true messages broadcast to a large population of readers by some news-producing organisation. In this sense, the news organisation acts as a gatekeeper to content. Journalists decide on not only what is newsworthy, but also how to investigate it, validate it and report it. Traditionally, much trust has been placed in the Western news media and it is often seen as comprising an important element of civil society.

More recently, however, the shape of the news has been changing with the rise of social media and the growing penetration of online social networks. The first significant change is the change from gatekeeper-generated content to user-generated content. The reporting of events is no longer the sole preserve of traditional news organisations. Pretty much anyone with a mobile device and access to communications infrastructure can now report happenings. The second major change is that from the broadcasting of content to the narrowcasting of content. No longer does news reporting need to be transmitted over traditional media channels, it can be distributed to delimited and targeted populations through online social networks. The last major change is the shift in the consumption of news. As a generalisation, the young appear to have abandoned conventional channels of news production and are getting much of their news content through social media.

However, with such changes comes many challenges. One of the most significant is that of ensuring the veracity (truthfulness) of what is reported as news. Traditionally, journalists are required to test and prove the validity and verifiability of what they report. They are also potentially held to be accountable for any news they report, sometimes in law. Nowadays, pretty much anybody can report anything as happening and being true without any recourse to standards of news-making or for that matter to litigation.

As probably the most prominent example of social media, Facebook has come under fire for acting as a platform for patent untruths broadcast as 'fake news'. A lie wrapped up as Facebook content on the website or as a message sent through their online social network can travel around the globe in a matter of minutes. Such untrue messages can have nasty consequences in terms of the actions taken as a result of them. More worrying is the claim that increasing use of social media serves to demote rather than promote open, rational debate.

The 2008 presidential election in the US is credited as being the first election in which social media was used for political campaigning. In March 2018, Facebook came under intense criticism for apparently collecting data from its members which it passed on to the company Cambridge Analytica. This company is claimed to have used this data to help develop strategy for the Donald Trump campaign for the US presidency.

The disruption of the news as a major content industry and the demise of truthful reporting is not the only issue arising from the increased use of social media. For example, many people have been caught exercising bullying behaviour through online social networks, not just in schools but also in workplaces (cyber-bullying). This often goes hand in hand with trolling — the posting of inflammatory and sometimes abusive content on social media. Social media messages and content are sometimes deliberately controversial and insulting to generate a reaction from their readers. It must also be remembered that such messages are frequently not produced by humans but by bits of data-driven software, sometimes referred to as chatterbots or chatbots. Such 'bots' are increasingly being used by business to disseminate advertisements, but also more worryingly as agents of cyberwarfare (see Chapter 13).

Echo Chambers, Online Cliques and the Decline in Civil Society

Walter Sinnot-Armstrong (2018) reckons that there is an increased polarisation of views in societies worldwide. It is somewhat paradoxical that the increased ability to communicate in countries such as in the US and the UK appears to have contributed to this state of affairs. Increased access to communications infrastructure and the ability this provides to communicate with many persons remotely was originally expected to lead to less polarisation. However, since the early 2000s, it appears that the opposite of this is happening. Social media seems to be encouraging both the development and solidifying of cliques within online social networks.

Polarisation of views is fuelled by many factors but one of the most significant appears to be the ways in which social media sites mechanise

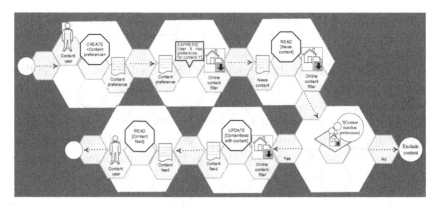

Figure 12.3:   Mechanics of an echo chamber.

confirmation bias. This is the tendency for actors to look for and be informed by data that is consistent with one's existing beliefs. It is evident that users of social media, particularly through the infrastructure of online social networks, seek out and communicate with people having similar views (Colleoni *et al.*, 2014). Such views then 'echo' around the clique reinforcing the viewpoints of its members.

Here is how some see this happening. A generic pattern of action is illustrated within Figure 12.3, evident within social media sites such as Facebook's newsfeed function. A content user X enters a series of content preferences into the content function of some online site. These preferences act as an expression of the type of content that X would like to see. The site content filter continually reads content published on the web and decides whether or not such content matches X's preferences. It then proceeds to update X's content feed only with content that matches preferences. This has the potential effect that the content reinforces rather than changes the attitudes, viewpoints and prejudices of user X. Not surprisingly, this is sometimes referred to as the 'echo chamber effect' — the content site echoes back to the user what the user wants to read.

However, online cliques can also serve to increase levels of polarisation. A clique, as we have seen, is a set of three or more actors who form strong links with each other and weak links with others within some social network. Cliques form typically through the process of homophily (Aiello *et al.*, 2012), the tendency of individuals to bond with and communicate with similar others. The presence of homophily has been found in hundreds of studies of social networks, both offline and online. Such increasing cliquishness amongst online social networks is worrying because it appears to contribute to decreasing levels of rational dialogue. A healthy civil society thrives on a diversity of viewpoints and the civility of dialogue; so, is such under threat?

The German philosopher Jürgen Habermas (1998) argues that a society's traditions (conventions) are not necessarily in the best interest of individuals. The consequence of this is that individuals need to be able to question and change these traditions. They can do this by reasoning together in the sphere of civil society, which builds consensus, brings about change and strengthens society as a whole. Therefore, Habermas argues that a healthy society is one in which communicative reason is used to negotiate and enact continuous change. Since society is a matter of conventions of action, such action should be subject to continual inspection and to critique through communicative reason.

Some have claimed that the increasing use of social media serves to demote rather than promote open, rational debate in contemporary society. This does not augur well for civil society, which in the large can be understood as the individuals and organisations within a society that are independent of government. Civil society is also used to refer to the space for collective action around shared interests, purposes and values, generally distinct from government and commercial for-profit actors.

One way of thinking of civil society which ties in with many themes discussed in the current chapter is as a multitude of actors each 'voicing' opinions through communicative acts. Traditionally, such communicative action would take place face to face in numerous different venues. The classic idea here is of the agora, which means in ancient Greek *a gathering place*. The agora was typically a large open space placed at the centre of the polis or city-state. Within the agora, citizens of the polis could come together to engage in and listen to debate and through this to form collective decisions relating to the future actions of the state.

The agora has no contemporary in the modern nation-state, many of which emerged during the 18th and 19th centuries. As mentioned, persistent communication took off in the paper media of the 18th, 19th and 20th centuries in the guise of newspapers and broadsheets. In such data structures, writers could not only report on the happenings of the day, they could offer their viewpoints on matters pertaining to the state. The rise of modern electronic media such as social media means that communicative acts are now enacted through the articulation of electronic data structures of various forms.

A key premise of a healthy civil society traditionally relies upon the notion of free speech — a principle that supports the freedom of an individual or a community to articulate their opinions and ideas without fear of retaliation, censorship or legal sanction. The term *freedom of expression* is sometimes used as a synonym for free speech but includes any act of seeking, receiving and sending ideas as messages, regardless of the medium or substance used to form such messages. Freedom of expression is recognised as a human right under Article 19 of the Universal Declaration of Human Rights. However, freedom of expression is a two-edged sword — should people have freedom to disinform. misinform or malinform?

Conclusion

Within this chapter, we have attempted to deconstruct some of the mechanics of social media. A social media message of any form is a data structure and as such plays a constituent part in generating many contemporary information situations. Such data structures, as digital content, are distributed around online social networks, potentially to many other actors. Just like any data structure, such a social media message has both content and intent. In terms of instrumental communication, the intent of a social media message is typically an assertive but the veracity of many such messages is frequently open to question. Many social messages are not designed to get things done but are much more directed at bonding participant actors together through friendship, kinship or acquaintance-ship. Some are designed to persuade, and many have the intent of inflaming or insulting persons.

As infrastructure for articulating data structures for communication, social media has been cast as both good and bad technology. We have considered a number of such viewpoints within this chapter such as casting social media as a vehicle for organising political action, the dissemination of extremist views and as infrastructure for fake news. It is tempting in this sense to view social media as an inherently value-neutral technology, but we must be careful. We must remember, as we explore in the next chapter, that the providers of social media technology have a different intent from the users of such technology. They provide such technology purportedly for free. However, there is a price to be paid and the currency in which this price is paid is in personal data.

References

Aiello, L. M., A. Barrat, R. Schifanella, C. Cattuto, B. Markines and F. Menczer (2012). "Friendship Prediction and Homophily in Social Media." *ACM Transactions on the Web*, **6**(2): 1–33.

Atkin, A. (2016). *Peirce* (London: Routledge).

Bacon, M. (2012). *Pragmatism* (Cambridge: Polity Press).

Bateson, G. (1972). *Steps to an Ecology of Mind* (New York: Ballantine Books).

Blackmore, S. (1999). *The Meme Machine* (Oxford: Oxford University Press).

Colleoni, E., A. Rozza and A. Arvidsson (2014). "Echo Chamber or Public Sphere? Predicting Political Orientation and Measuring Political Homophily in Twitter Using Big Data: Political Homophily on Twitter." *Journal of Communication*, **64**(2):317–332. DOI:10.1111/jcom.12084.hdl:10281/66011.

Dawkins, R. (1976). *The Selfish Gene* (Oxford: Oxford University Press).

Dunbar, R. (2010). *How Many Friends Does One Person Need? Dunbar's Number and Other Evolutionary Quirks* (London: Faber and Faber).

Eco, U. (1977). *A Theory of Semiotics* (London: Macmillan).

Gallie, W. B. (1952). *Peirce and Pragmatism* (Edinburgh: Pelican Books).

Granovetter, M. (1973). "The Strength of Weak Ties." *American Journal of Sociology*, **78**(6): 1360–1380.

Habermas, J. (1998). *On the Pragmatics of Communication* (Cambridge, MA: MIT Press).

Hookway, C. (1985). *Peirce* (London: Routledge and Kegan Paul).

Lazarsfeld, P. F. and R. K. Merton (1954). Friendship as a Social Process: A Substantive and Methodological Analysis. In *Freedom and Control in Modern Society*, M. Berger, T. Abel and C. H. Page (eds.). (New York: Van Nostrand), pp. 18–66.

Sinnott-Armstrong, W. (2018). *Think Again: How to Reason and Argue* (Pelican: London).

Putnam, R. D. (2000). *Bowling Alone: The Collapse and Revival of American Community* (New York: Simon and Schuster).

Wardle, C. (2020). "A New World Disorder: Our Willingness to Share Content Without Thinking is Exploited to Spread Disinformation." *Scientific American Specials*, Fall.

Chapter 13

The Modern Panopticon: Data and Surveillance

Introduction

The issue of contemporary surveillance is frequently associated with a type of building developed as a concept by the philosopher Jeremy Bentham in 18th-century Britain. The *panopticon* was a building consisting of a rotunda of rooms with a central inspection house at its centre. The term *panopticon* derives from the Greek *panoptes*, which means all-seeing. The inspection house at the centre of the rotunda allowed all residents of the building to be observed by a single person. Bentham believed that his panopticon was applicable to many institutional settings, such as schools, hospitals and asylums. However, the idea was developed most fully in relation to the design of prisons.

Bentham considered the panopticon not just a building but an associated system of control. Clearly, it was physically impossible for a single guard to observe all prison cells within the panopticon at once. However, since it was impossible for inmates to know when they were being watched, Bentham believed that they would be motivated to act as though they were being watched at all times. In this way, inmates would feel compelled to regulate their own behaviour in ways expected by the institution.

Many authors have discussed the use of data for surveillance purposes as something approaching the modern panopticon. Some refer to our panoptic society as the *surveillance society*. The argument here is that we no longer need physical structures such as a rotunda to make certain actors all-seeing. Actors with access to data infrastructure and crucially the data structures making up this infrastructure, can observe, at a distance, the activities of many other actors and can potentially utilise this all-seeing capacity to control what such actors do and say.

Surveillance is typically defined as the close observation of a person or group, usually because that person or group is under suspicion of something by somebody. This is the classic rationale for agencies of the nation-state to monitor persons or groups in a society suspected of engaging in deviant activity. Because of its role as a scaffolder of institutional action, the data structure, or the meta-data (Chapter 8) which describes it, takes centre stage within attempts to build the modern panopticon.

Surveillance has a history probably as long as the notion of the state. However, the infrastructure of data surveillance really came into its own during the Second World War. For this reason, we spend some time explaining some of the mechanisms of surveillance innovated by two establishments known as station X and station Y in the UK during this major conflict. This allows us to see how and why data surveillance has become the dominant way in which intelligence is conducted in the modern world.

However, data surveillance is no longer an activity performed by agencies of the nation-state. Data surveillance plays a much more mundane and accepted role within our interactions with digital companies. Some even believe that data has become the new oil within capitalist economies. Others warn of the dangers inherent in the data surveillance infrastructure that the digital giants have built.

Station X and Y

To help understand the role of data in surveillance, as well as the growth of what many refer to as the *surveillance society* upon the base of contemporary data infrastructure, let us first turn to a classic case from the Second World War. This case is important because of the ways in which not only the technologies but also the institutions of surveillance were innovated.

The Second World War was a 'wireless' war. The fast military movement of machinery, men and equipment demanded constant radio intercommunication between units, generally using transmission by Morse code. Morse code is of course a method of coding a message as a sequence of bits: dots and dashes or zeros and ones. Such coding was originally invented as a means of economically coding messages in terms of a series of electronic pulses transmitted over telegraphic wires. By the 1930s radio or 'wireless' telegraphy adopted Morse code as a standard method for coding within tele-communication. Military messages were encrypted by the German armed forces using a complex electro-mechanical device known as the Enigma machine.

Radio communication, Morse code and encryption all form the necessary background to a key system of importance to this period: the intelligence work provided by the Government Code and Cypher School (GCCS) conducted at Bletchley Park in the UK during the entire period of the Second World War (Smith, 1998). This code-breaking and intelligence establishment was referred to as station X. We shall also discuss the inter-related role of a tele-communications network known as station Y to Allied intelligence and operations. The names station X and Y were not given to emphasise the secret nature of the work: they were merely the 10th and 11th (in Roman numerals) sites acquired by British intelligence for its wartime operations.

GCCS as an organisation was initially established in 1919 but was moved to Bletchley Park some months prior to the outbreak of the Second World War. It eventually became the largest intelligence establishment of its kind (Aldridge, 2010). We deliberately refer to GCCS as an intelligence unit or establishment rather than its more common designation as a cryptanalytic or code-breaking establishment. This is because, as we shall see, while code-breaking was one of its critical roles, it occurred within a larger system of intelligence-gathering and processing. At its height, GCCS employed over 10,000 people and recruited some of the best minds in Britain at the time. For instance, Alan Turing (Leavitt, 2007), one of the founding fathers of Computer Science, worked at this code-breaking establishment for a number of years, and one of the first programmable computers, the Colossus, was built at Bletchley Park (Copeland, 2004).

Ever since humans invented technologies for recording and transmitting messages, there has been potential for other humans to intercept and read such messages. Hence, human societies have invented a number of related technologies to ensure the secrecy of data transmitted as messages. The encryption and decryption of messages is a system of activity that has been undertaken in human societies for many thousands of years to ensure the privacy of such messages (Singh, 2000). The information technology of encryption may almost have as long a history as the invention of artefacts for signification. For instance, there is evidence of the use of encryption in Egyptian hieroglyphics dating back 4,000 years.

Securing data messages can be seen as a development of the standard model of communication (Chapter 1), involving a double or triple encoding and decoding of data. An unencrypted message is normally referred to as a plain text message because of its historical association with the written word. This plain text message is first encrypted using a particular algorithm and an appropriate key that specifies the exact details of a particular encryption. The encrypted message is typically referred to as cipher text. At the receiver end, the algorithm is applied as a decryption method using another key. This reveals the plain text message to the receiver.

Encryption ensures the privacy of data because the encryption and decryption of the message is dependent on the key that is issued to authorised actors in the communication — it forms part of a 'communication protocol'. Two basic approaches for encryption are normally employed in this augmented communication process known as symmetric and asymmetric key encryption. In symmetric key encryption, sometimes known as private key encryption, the same key is applied at both ends of the encryption process. This means that the key is agreed in advance between the sender and receiver of the message. This was, as we shall see, the fundamental approach adopted by the German armed forces, with a configured Enigma machine acting as both the symmetric key and the encryption/decryption algorithm.

The Enigma Machine

An Enigma machine transposed the letters of the words of a message into other apparently random configurations of letters depending upon the way the machine was configured. Once configured, the sender of the message typed in his message letter by letter into the machine on a keyboard. A display on the machine indicated the transposed letter following each keystroke. The cipher text was copied down and sent as a message in Morse code by a radio operator to a receiver. The receiver was expected to set up his Enigma machine in the same configuration as the sender and typed in the transposed message into his machine to get the decoded or plain text message. Therefore, in order to perform successful decryption, the receiver needed three things: the cipher text of a given message, an Enigma machine and knowledge of how the machine should be configured.

The Enigma machine hence looked very similar to a typewriter of the day and consisted of several components: a plug board, a light board or display, a keyboard, a set of rotors and a reflector. Both the sender of a message and the receiver of the message needed to manipulate or configure two of these components — the rotors and the plug board — in the same way to enable communication. A given rotor contained one-to-one mappings of all the letters in the alphabet. Rotors could be removed and set in one of six possible orders. The actors in a communication first had to select the order of the three rotors to be used from a possible set of five rotors. The plug board allowed for pairs of letters to be re-mapped before the encryption process started and after it ended. This was enabled by plugging together the relevant holes on the plug board with a set of six cables.

The basic Enigma machine was invented in Holland but taken up and adapted in 1918 by Arthur Scherbius in Berlin. Originally designed as a commercial machine for enciphering business communications, it was eventually adopted by the German Wehrmacht for military operations. An Enigma machine enciphered a message by using what is referred to as a substitution cipher: performing a number of substitutions or replacements for each character of a plain text message into a cipher text message. Because the Enigma machine achieved such substitutions automatically through electrical connections, it held a number of advantages over hand encryption and decryption. First, it required no special skills on the part of the sender or receiver of the message. Second, encryption and decryption could be performed much more quickly than possible by hand. Third, and most importantly the makeup of the Enigma machine ensured that a high level of security could be associated with communications traffic.

When a key was pressed on the keyboard, an electrical current passed through each component and made a circuit. The electrical current first went through the plug board, then through the three rotors and into a reflector which reversed the current, back through the three rotors, back through the plug board and onto the display. The circuit made caused the appropriate encrypted letter to be lit. Following this process, the rotors rotated in sequence. In other words, the right-most rotor completed a revolution, causing the middle rotor to rotate one position, and so on.

The German armed forces believed at the time that the astronomical number of different ways the machine could be configured would ensure that it would be impossible for the code to be cracked quickly enough by the Allies for effective responsive action. In a three-rotor Enigma machine, there were six possible orders in which the rotors could be positioned. Each rotor could be set in one of a possible 17,576 settings (26 × 26 × 26) giving 105,456 possible states. The plug board allowed 15,012 changes of circuit. Hence, the total number of possible settings (the variety) for a basic Enigma machine was of the order of 15,018 (McKay, 2011).

Because effective communication was reliant on both sender and receiver configuring their machine in the same manner, each day units in the German military forces were given instructions on how they should configure their Enigma machines. This configuration involved changing rotor positions on the machine and plugging connections between pairs of letters on its plug board. Configuration settings were distributed to members of the German armed forces as pre-printed settings sheets. This determined how the rotors should be set and which letters should be connected together on the plug board. Each setting applied to a 24-hour period and a setting sheet generally contained a month's worth of settings.

However, such sheets did not detail one crucial piece of information: the starting position at which the chosen rotors should be set. The principle was that each message should be sent with a different start position. Different methods were employed for doing this. The simplest was as follows. The sender first set the machine in the base configuration for the day. The rotors were then turned to a start position selected by the operator such as the positions GSX — this was the message key. Then the operator keyed in this string of three letters twice and noted down the string of six transposed letters that appeared on the display — say JMGVEB. This string of six letters was transcribed into the preamble of a message. The rotors were then reset to the message key and the full body of the plain text enciphered and transcribed. The complete message including the preamble was then handed over to a radio operator for transmission.

At the receiving end, an Enigma machine had been set to the same base configuration. The first six characters of the encrypted message were then keyed in, producing a double occurrence of the message key — GSXGSX. This indicated how the rotors should be set. Once set, the rest of the message could be decrypted.

Data Interception and Articulation

Radio signals as data are broadcast as waves of electromagnetic radiation and as such are amenable to interception by any actors having suitable technology to tune in to appropriate radio frequencies. The work of Station X was therefore reliant on a network of wireless receiving stations, known as the 'Y' service or Station Y, situated both around the UK and in the colonies, which intercepted on a continuous basis the radio signals (referred to as signals intelligence or Sigint) from German armed forces. These Y service stations were operated by different branches of the British Armed forces as well as the Post Office and the Metropolitan Police. Each such station therefore tended to concentrate on one particular type of communication traffic. For instance, the main Navy intercept sites in the UK were at Scarborough and Winchester, while the main Army Y station was at Fort Bridgelands near Chatham in Kent.

The task of carefully logging all radio messages from particular sources was performed by thousands of wireless intercept officers. The messages received were passed on from the Y service by tele-printer (tele-writer) or by courier to station X. Sigint actually came in two major forms: encrypted radio communications and unencrypted radio communications. The interception of low-grade unencrypted communications traffic between actors such as pilots in the German Luftwaffe proved important in the Warning Network of RAF Fighter Command during the Battle of Britain (Beynon-Davies, 2009b). Station X was organised in terms of a number of pairs of huts, each pair specialising in communications from a major segment of the German armed forces. For example, Hut 8 was the German U-boat Enigma decrypt hut and Hut 4 was its associated naval intelligence unit. To improve the levels of security, each hut acted independently of each other. Workers in each hut knew little of the work of other huts.

Many accounts of the work of GCCS focus solely on code-breaking. However, this essential code-breaking work occurred in a wider intelligence system. The operation of the huts differed and changed during the course of the War. However, it is possible to identify a number of activities common to the operation of GCCS consisting of intercept control, code-breaking, the production of plain text messages and the fusion of information derived from messages into a general picture of intelligence. There was also an important background activity involved with the management of records.

The first activity was that of intercept control. This was manned by a small complement of staff 24 hours a day and was in constant touch with its designated Y stations. The purpose of this unit was to ensure that the coverage of radio frequencies and radio networks was coordinated. Hence, instructions were issued to Y stations as to what to cover for a particular day and with what priority. Messages received by a particular hut were first examined to see if there was any intelligence that could be obtained before code-breaking commenced. This was then passed on with the messages themselves to the code-breaking function.

Code-breakers rarely deciphered an entire message themselves. Early decryption of the messages passed on from the Y service relied on manual code-breaking involving a systematic search for the occurrence of statistical patterns in cipher text that could act as levers for interpreting the content of such messages. These were known as 'cribs'. For instance, in a statistically significant number of instances, a letter in a piece of cipher text would by chance end up as being substituted with the same letter twice. Early Polish codebreakers of Enigma referred to these occurrences as 'females' and set about the task of analysing which of the 105,456 combinations of rotor orders and settings resulted in 'females' using an Enigma machine. Having identified these combinations, they were crafted onto a series of perforated sheets. The punched holes in such sheets indicated the positions in which a combined rotor order and setting resulted in a 'female'. These sheets could then be used as decryption devices by placing them one above the other and shifting them around atop a light table until a beam of light shone through a particular series of perforations. Using this approach, it was possible to determine Enigma rotor settings for a particular day.

Later decryption relied on the development of an electro-mechanical device known as a Bombe, so named because of the ominous ticking noise it made while searching for rotor positions. This device, which was designed by Alan Turing on the basis of earlier devices created by Polish code-breakers (SebaqMontifiore, 2004), enabled the automatic rejection of millions of incorrect possibilities very quickly: a typical Bombe 'run' taking something of the order of 15 minutes. These machines were given instructions in what was known as a 'menu' constructed by the code-breakers. The menu was configured in a Bombe machine by the physical movement of component elements performed by members of the women's contingent of the Royal Navy. In essence this constituted 'programming' the code-breaking machine.

Once the key had been discovered, the Enigma configuration and the encrypted message were passed to operators of type-X machines. These were effectively mock-ups of the Enigma machine itself. Once a type-X machine was configured, the encrypted message was typed upon it to produce the decrypted message. This was then pasted up and literally pushed into its associated intelligence hut along a connecting corridor.

However, decrypts produced in this manner were rarely in the form of clear German plain text. Instead, messages were typically constructed of a mixture of jargon and contractions familiar to communicants within particular segments of the German armed forces (Brunt, 2006). Hence, decryption of a message in and of itself was insufficient to determine its meaning.

The Keeping of Records

To facilitate code-breaking activity, record-keeping facilities were established by the intelligence units attached to particular code-breaking units, which took two main forms. First, factual indexes were built which recorded data about specific topics such as military equipment and formations. Second, reference indexes were used to identify the meaning associated with strings of characters such as abbreviations and acronyms that appeared in decrypts. One index of abbreviations used by a branch of the British Armed forces contained over 10,000 abbreviations and 16,000 equivalents by the end of the war in Europe (Brunt, 2006).

Such records were stored as vast card indexes and were critical to the correct interpretation of a decrypted message. They also suggested appropriate inferences given the presence of particular signs in a message. For instance, the OKM index (Oberkommando der Kriegsmarine) used by Naval section intelligence in Hut 4 enabled intelligence officers to make sense of a message such as 'Betr.OKM/1 Sk1 e B. Nr. 20345/43: Aufgabe ausgehuehrt' (Brunt, 2006). This could be interpreted using both factual and reference indexes as referring to a mine-laying operation.

In effect such indexes began to constitute a form of 'corporate memory' and as such could be considered an early form of knowledge management (Prusak, 2000). They allowed not only speedier work on the part of knowledgeable intelligence staff but were essential in supporting the work of an expanded collection of less knowledgeable staff recruited during the course of the War. For such purposes, an attempt was made to make copies of certain indexes for various intelligence sections. However, certain indexes were so volatile that they soon went out of date. This strikes a chord with contemporary problems of records management.

The Contribution of Station X and Y

Before interpreted messages could be transmitted to the Armed forces, they were prioritised. Highly urgent messages were tele-printed immediately. Less urgent messages were tele-printed within four to eight hours. The least urgent messages were bagged together and sent by courier.

What is interesting is that in the early years of the War, Station X experienced much difficulty in getting their intelligence taken seriously and used constructively by commanders of the British Armed forces. This was partly due to distrust on the part of commanders of the Armed forces with intelligence produced from a new and non-partisan intelligence organisation. It was also due to difficulties in getting intelligence in a timely manner to the persons that needed it. Hence, special intelligence units manned by members of the Armed forces and directly liaising with Station X were established later in the War, sometimes on the frontlines of the conflict.

In popular conceptions of the work of Bletchley Park, Station X tends to be associated solely with Enigma intelligence. In practice, German armed forces used other electro-mechanical forms of encryption which stimulated the design of more sophisticated forms of code-breaking technology. For instance, 'Tunny' was the name given by Station X to a system of tele-printer or tele-writer encryption (Copeland, 2004). Tunny consisted of an attachment to a tele-printer, known as a Lorenz machine, which automatically encrypted the outgoing stream of electronic pulses or automatically decrypted incoming messages from another tele-printer with a Tunny attachment. The Tunny or Lorenz machine was both more sophisticated and less cumbersome to use than the Enigma machine. Use of Enigma for any one communication, for instance, generally demanded six persons: two signals operators, two enigma operators and two signals assistants involved with writing down and passing on coded and decoded messages. In contrast, Tunny needed just a sender operator and a receiver operator. For this reason, Tunny was typically reserved for high-grade messages, such as for communications traffic between German high command and army group commanders.

Just before the Allied invasion of France, the first programmable computer known as Colossus was built by Tommy Flowers and his team from the Post Office and installed at Station X with the express purpose of breaking the codes associated with Tunny communications traffic. Eventually 10 machines were to be installed at Station X. Consisting of large arrays of thermionic valves, such machines, which constituted the first examples of semi-programmable electronic computers, enabled the cracking of complex codes in a matter of a few minutes.

The intelligence provided by station X was critical to the effective deployment of military operations both on land, on the sea and in the sky. For instance, it contributed to the successful protection of Allied ship convoys during the Battle of the Atlantic, defeat of Field Marshall Rommel's army in the North African desert, victory against the Italian navy at the Battle of Matapan and the successful planning of the invasion of Europe by the Allies in 1944 (Briggs, 2011).

In contrast to the high prominence of signal intelligence to successful Allied operations during the Second World War, interest in the supporting role of signals intelligence in both military and civilian operations by observers and documenters of the intelligence services declined rapidly after the War (Aldridge, 2010). This is interesting in light of the fact that investment in GCHQ, the successor to GCCS, actually increased after 1945 and has in fact continued to consume the largest share of investment amongst the intelligence services by UK government. What is also interesting is the shift in focus by Sigint services after the end of the Cold War from monitoring military, governmental and diplomatic communications to the monitoring of domestic and business forma, justified largely in terms of a new control crisis — the fight against terrorism. In such terms, the emphasis has changed from decryption operations to the utilisation of vast data storage facilities and associated data analytics technologies to construct informative patterns from persistent data (Chapter 14).

The Surveillance Society

In 2006, the office of the information commissioner in the UK published a report on the surveillance society (Wood *et al.*, 2006). It opened with the words, 'We live in a surveillance society ... In all the rich countries of the world everyday life is suffused with surveillance encounters, not merely from dawn to dusk but 24/7'. The report placed the rise of such a society not in an attempt to build George Orwell's *Big Brother* but as a natural consequence of Capitalism's push for greater and greater efficiencies in administration. More on this push later.

But what exactly is surveillance? The report defines it as 'the purposeful, routine, systematic and focused attention paid to personal details, for the sake of control, entitlement, management, influence or protection...' So according to this definition surveillance is very much tied to personal data and the structures which hold such data — to data such as CCTV images, biometrics and records of telephone calls.

Roger Clarke (1994) calls this reliance of surveillance upon data and data structures *dataveillance* — we shall refer to it as data surveillance. Our coverage of the Station X case demonstrates that data surveillance clearly relies upon a number of features. First, one set of institutional actors engage in communication remotely — through tele-communication of double-encoded messages over communication networks. Second, another set of actors undertake the interception of such messages and store such messages in persistent data structures. Third, persistent messages are decoded by a third set of actors. Analysis of such messages by yet another set of actors is used in support of certain activities such as military operations or counter-terrorism.

Therefore, the surveillance society relies upon surveillance data, but it is noteworthy that data surveillance is often an ambivalent concept. For instance, surveillance of the populations of most nation-states during the COVID-19 pandemic was generally seen to be a public good, because the purpose of such surveillance was protection of the population. In contrast, data-driven surveillance of employees within the workplace is generally seen as morally suspect, because its purpose is one of close monitoring for control.

On 31 March 1990, the Ministry of State Security, otherwise known as the Stasi, was disbanded in East Germany. At its height this organisation ran some of the most intrusive of surveillance operations in the world. Its enormous archive assembled data structures on over six million people, and it has been estimated that this data was held in up to 48,000 filing cabinets. Among an estimated 271,000 employees the Stasi had at least 174,000 informants, which would have been about 2.5% of the working population of East Germany at the time. To monitor the population the Stasi steam-opened letters, copied them, filed them and sent them on.

They also went into homes when people were out and bugged them and tapped into the telephone infrastructure of buildings.

However, this surveillance infrastructure is archaic as compared to the possibilities afforded by the data infrastructure of the modern nation-state. For instance, former head of the US national security agency and CIA, Michael Hayden, admitted that US agencies such as the CIA already use metadata as the basis for selecting targets for drone strikes around the world. So how does this work? Take the case of the Snowden revelations. Edward Snowden was an employee and subcontractor of the Central Intelligence Agency (CIA) in 2013 and while working for them copied and leaked highly classified documents from the National Security Agency (NSA). These documents revealed surveillance programs conducted on a global scale by the NSA with the cooperation of telecommunication companies and European governments.

An analysis of these documents by major news outlets in the US, the UK and Germany exposed a series of surveillance practices centred around the NSA but also conducted by intelligence agencies in various countries. The first revelation was that the vast majority of telephone companies in the US were providing metadata associated with their phone records to the NSA. An NSA programme called PRISM allowed this organisation to require Internet companies such as Google, Facebook, Microsoft and Apple to provide metadata on their users and activities. Apparently, the UK equivalent of the NSA, the Government Communications headquarters (GCHQ), which occupies the contemporary institutional space of Bletchley Park, had a systematic programme of tapping into fibre-optic cables around the world and passing this signals intelligence onto the NSA. XKeyscore was revealed as a tool the NSA uses to search 'nearly everything a user does on the Internet' through data it intercepts across the world.

Encryption, as we have seen, is a major way in which the senders and receivers of data attempt to prevent their messages being read and interpreted. Modern forms of data encryption are much more sophisticated than that discussed in relation to the Station X case. This, of course makes the surveillance activities of agencies such as the NSA much more difficult and helps explain why the NSA has employed a range of approaches to circumvent widely used encryption technologies. It has been shown to force communication companies to install backdoors in their software, hack into servers and computers and promote the use of weaker and hence more open encryption algorithms by communications operators.

The Snowden files revealed the presence of an elite hacker team code-named Tailored Access Operations (TAO). TAO is brought in when the NSA cannot find intelligence or needs more detailed data on a target than that available through its normal surveillance programme. This unit apparently hacks into computers worldwide and infects them with malware. The NSA also had other tricks up its sleeve including the ability to infiltrate links connecting Google data centres, without the knowledge of Google. The NSA intercepts millions of text messages every day. Other documents revealed that the NSA can crack cell phone encryption, allowing the agency to more easily decode and access the content of intercepted calls and text messages.

Surveillance is not of course purely a phenomenon of the Western world. Many non-Western countries engage in surveillance operations of their populace, typically through government agencies similar in form to the Stasi. For instance, the Chinese communist party has initiated a series of programmes collectively known as social credit. This is an attempt to regulate the social behaviour of Chinese citizens by monitoring both their online and offline behaviour through data structures of various forms. Such behaviour might include being financially fraudulent but might also include violating traffic regulations or even playing loud music or failing to sort your household waste for recycling properly. Those deemed to have infringed normal expected conventions of Chinese behaviour are placed on blacklists (Chapter 4). Certain data from such blacklists may then be made public and even displayed online or at public venues. Blacklists are then used to proscribe those persons deemed to have low social credit from participation in many areas of Chinese life. For instance, blacklisted persons may be banned from certain aspects of travel or excluded from admissions to certain public institutions such as schools.

There are a number of important elements which we can glean from cases such as this about the nature of the contemporary surveillance society. Modern surveillance is based upon the notion of signals intelligence, very similar in nature to that used by Station X during the Second World War. Signals intelligence relies upon the transmission of data structures as messages between diverse actors globally. Such data structures come, of course, in numerous different forms — as fixed line telephone calls, cell phone calls, electronic mails, electronic documents, texts and tweets. Most of these messages are transmitted over the common data infrastructure of the Internet and the Web. Some of these data structures are double encoded using encryption algorithms.

However, the main substantial change since the end of the Second World War is the 'direction of gaze' of intelligence agencies such as the NSA, GCHQ or the Ministry of State Security in China. Nowadays, the direction of signals intelligence is not only outward at signals transmitted and received by foreign powers, but also inward at signals created and received by citizens of the state. The gathering of such signals intelligence is made easier not only by the ways in which data structures are transmitted as messages, but also by the way in which metadata is recorded whenever a message is sent and received.

Knowing the power of data surveillance many nations have enacted legislation to solidify its position within the state apparatus. For instance, in 2016, the UK government of the time enacted the Investigatory Powers Act, which effectively is a mechanism establishing the surveillance powers of the police and the intelligence agencies in the UK. The act specifies the basis for law enforcement agencies to carry out targeted interception of communications, bulk collection of communications data, and bulk interception of communications. Communication service providers must store internet connection records of their users for up to one year, which can then be accessed by police and security agencies on provision of a warrant, except in the case of a serious crime.

Such powers are important because whenever you do something online over the Internet and perhaps through the Web, data structures are created which identify and describe your activity. In other words, personal traces are left of your activity. Of critical importance is the metadata associated with any electronic communication. Metadata is important to surveillance because of the way it instantiates critical elements of the ontology (Chapter 8) of communicative practice adopted amongst a collective of actors.

For instance, the metadata associated with a telephone call includes who is called, who is calling, the date and time of the call, the duration of the call and, if you use a mobile phone, the location from where the call is made. Likewise, a tweet has a mass of associated metadata such as the creation date and time, the author of the tweet, the author's location, number of users the author is following and number of followers of the author. Note that such metadata is different from the content of the call or tweet itself, which of course may also be stored as a record or intercepted and stored as a consequence of such interception.

Personal Traces

The value of data and metadata obtained through surveillance lies in the fact that it helps instantiate elements of institutional ontology (Chapter 8) as it pertains to persons. This refers to the ways in which actors within institutions such as companies as well as intelligence agencies link and cross-reference a multitude of data-items derived from various different sources of data, but all linkable to a common ontology. Such data-items, if collected along with the metadata which describes them, enables such actors to make inferences about the current behaviour of the person or predictions about the future behaviour of the person based upon the objects, classes and relationships of the relevant ontology.

Using such ontology, the dispersed bits of data collected about a person can be used to build a classification (Chapter 8) of that person. On this basis institutional actors may try to predict the behaviour of the classified person — such as purchasing preferences on the part of an online company or leanings towards to terrorism on the part of intelligence agencies. The metaphor used here is of trails or tracks left in digital space by persons, from which profiles of persons can be assembled and various inferences about their current and future behaviour drawn.

Let us simplify and explain the principles of such inference built upon institutional ontology using elements of the theory we have developed previously.

According to John Sowa (2000), the Internet is a giant semiotic system. This is because it is possible to think of the Internet as a vast network of machine actors, such as computers and other digital devices, engaging in communicative action through signs. Just like in any communication, within any one act of communication over this network one computing device is the sender of some message and another technological actor is the receiver of a message. To enable such communication both sender actors and receiver actors are identified with an internet protocol (IP) address. Each computing device on the Internet has an IP address such as 2001:0:9d38:6ac8:1c48:3b1c:b1c2. There are an estimated 40 billion IP addresses globally at the time of writing, each referring to a specific node in the global communications network:

[<IP address> REFERS-TO Computing device]

To send some message from one device to another over the Internet, the message is first divided into structures known as packets. Each packet is given the IP address of its common destination and is then directed to its destination, sometimes via different routes, by devices known as *routers*. At the destination or receiving device the message is re-constituted into its original form.

Web communications operate as another layer on top of internet communications and use identifiers for Web documents known as universal resource locators or URLs:

[<URL> REFERS-TO Web page]

Whenever you request a web page through a browser it generates a request message which is sent to the Web server holding the Web page identified by the relevant URL. This means that the IP address of the requester is available to the Web server servicing the request. This data is typically stored by the Web server in a data structure known as a log file. The Web page is then sent as a message from the Web server to the requester:

[<IP Address> REQUESTS <URL>]

Now suppose the person clicks on a link within the Web page. A request will again be sent to the Web server and a record made of the request by the server. In this manner a series of traces of a person's Web activity are left as records on the Web server.

Now, it is likely that the Web page will have been tagged with some metadata which describes the content of the page:

[Web page Description <Keyword, Keyword, Keyword>]

Keywords taken from such a description are likely to provide a proxy of the interests of the actor identified by the IP address:

[<IP address> Interest <Keyword>]
[<IP address> Interest <Keyword>]
...

So what uses are made of such data structures? Well, the data can be used by the Website to manage future interactions with you, the user. This data can also be shared with other providers to enable them to customise their future marketing messages to you, the consumer. An intelligence agency might have more subtle uses for such data such as assessing whether your interest in particular topics suggest a leaning towards terrorist activity.

But note that it is not you that is actually identified in these log records. It is your IP address — the node in the Internet that you use. But wait a moment, there are a number of ways that personal identifiers (Chapter 3), such as your personal name, might be inferred from an IP address. When an IP address is assigned to a computer or other digital device then the physical location of the hub to which the IP addresses are assigned is registered in a metadata registry (Chapters 7 and 8). Knowing an IP address then it is relatively straightforward to generate a place — a physical location — usually down to postcode or zip code granularity (Chapter 7):

[<IP-address> REGISTERED <Postcode area>]

A message can then be sent to the IP address requesting the name of the host computer. This will typically return something like a domain name — the top-level of a URL (Chapter 7). Domain names, as we know, have to be registered in a domain name registry and a simple lookup of this registry using the domain name should respond with the name of the registrant:

[Person REGISTRANT Domain name]

So, let us review the traces made in the institutional ontology so far:

[<IP address> REFERS-TO Computing device]
[<URL> REFERS-TO Web page]
[<IP Address> REQUESTS <URL>]
[<IP-address> REGISTERED <Postcode area>]
[Person REGISTRANT Domain name]
   ...

We know from Chapter 7 that a limited number of properties are co-located within a postcode area:

[Property LOCATED <postcode-area>]

We also know that the ownership of properties is registered in another registry, something like a land registry perhaps. From this we should be able to make a match between:

[Person OWNS property]
[Property LOCATED <postcode-area>]
[<IP-address> REGISTERED <Postcode area>]

To infer:

[<IP-address> REFERS-TO Person]

Having inferred this institutional fact we can, of course, infer many other things:

[Person REQUESTS <URL>]
[<Person> Interest <Keyword>]
[Person LOCATED <postcode-area>]
...

We have spent some time on this rather simplistic scenario just to show how the ontology of the Internet and the Web can be traversed to identify the person, and from this to establish many other things about the person. But of course, there is a far shorter route to gaining your personal data and assembling data profiles. Suppose that you use a website to purchase something. To do so you register with the website, meaning that you create a personal record for the company owning the website, perhaps consisting of your name, address (including postcode) and telephone numbers (mobile and home).

[Person HASA Name]
[Person HASA Address]
[Person HASA Postcode]
[Person HASA Mobile telephone number]
[Person HASA Home telephone number]

Now suppose you forget to read the small print of the privacy agreement which states that the website may share data given to them with

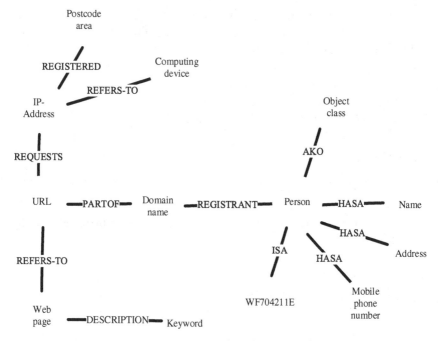

Figure 13.1:   A personal profile as a sign lattice.

other providers, not including surveillance agencies. At some point of time, this data profile is shared with another provider who is able to access data held about you with communications providers. Knowing someone's mobile phone number, for instance, opens up a whole range of further traces — texts, tweets and Facebook messages.

Both routes through institutional ontology enable us to build a profile of the person which may be represented as something like the sign lattice (Chapter 8) illustrated in Figure 13.1.

Surveillance Capitalism

In 2016, *The Economist* magazine published a report entitled 'the world's most valuable resource is no longer oil, but data'. Since that time, it has become almost commonplace to make the following analogy: data flows like oil from numerous sources. Data is an essential resource like oil for capitalism, and particularly for commerce, as we have seen in Chapter 10. Energy can be extracted from oil, while information can be 'extracted' from data. Oil powered the industrial economy while data powers the information economy.

The power of data, as we have seen, is fundamentally linked to its capacity to make inferences and fuel predictions about the future actions of people. The rise of business, web and marketing analytics suggests why data is said to be the new oil because data is increasingly useful and hence valuable to companies. Transactional data gathered about people's activities is particularly valuable in areas such as marketing research. This explains why much of your Web surfing activity is tracked (Chapter 8). There is no such thing as free software. Apps supplied by companies such as Google create data about the behaviour of their users. This is the return companies receive for supplying the software to you.

The sociologist Shoshana Zuboff (2015) has argued that the growing centrality of data to economic activity, as is evident in many of the commercial applications of social media (Chapter 12) and mobile commerce, is creating a new form of capitalism that she calls *surveillance capitalism*. Surveillance capitalism generates new forms of capitalist production based upon not the direct production of goods and services but the collection and analysis of large amounts of data gathered about people and what they do. This data is used not only to understand but also to predict human behaviour, with normally the intention of influencing its course.

The way in which this works is illustrated in Figure 13.2 and involves two cycles of action. Within the lower cycle, we have seen that when actors undertake online actions then behavioural data is created about them (Chapter 8). Data structures are formed about a person's web accesses, purchases, Facebook messages, tweets, etc. This behavioural data has traditionally been used to enact service improvements, such as providing more personalised services for the participating actor. Hence, Amazon uses data gathered about your use of the Amazon website to suggest further purchasing options to you as a customer.

However, Zuboff writes of another loop which forms the upper cycle in Figure 13.2. This begins with the surplus data gathered from actor online behaviour, which is used through the application of certain software products to make predictions of the behaviour of actors in defined markets. This enables online companies to build new markets in the prediction of future behaviour, which they then sell on to other companies. The lucrative revenue opened up by this new line of business provides the basis for such companies to take greater control over the data

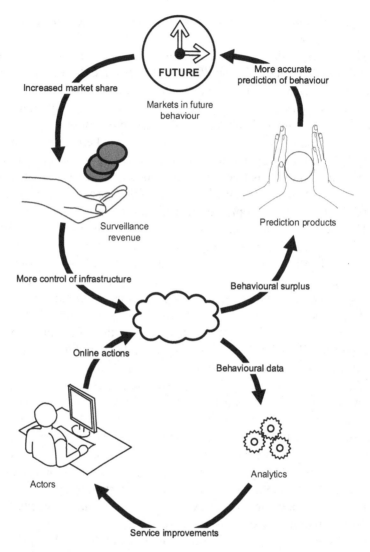

Figure 13.2:   Surveillance capitalism.

infrastructure utilised by consumers, which, of course, drives greatest levels of data articulation by these consumers.

Zuboff identifies the rise of surveillance capitalism with the realisation made by Google that the data gleaned from users of its search engine was a valuable surplus resource, which it could analyse and exploit.

In fact, this insight was actually realised much earlier by financial services companies such as Visa and American Express. Such companies harvested transactional data gained from their customer's use of their credit cards and began to sell this on to direct marketing companies (Lauer, 2020).

Whenever it emerged, this set of practices, Zuboff feels, is ethically suspect. She believes that this represents a novel market form with a distinct logic of capitalist accumulation. Industrial capitalism exploited nature while surveillance capitalism exploits human nature. What is more insidious is that the construction of mass data has been done largely without the consent of data subjects to whom the data applies. She believes that this form of capitalism erodes an individual's rights to self-determination, because in interacting with others through digital infrastructure the software is able to nudge your behaviour in certain ways based upon the data it knows about you.

The concept of the 'nudge' was proposed by Richard Thaler and Cass Sunstein in their book *Nudge: Improving Decisions About Health, Wealth, and Happiness* (2009). It influenced many approaches to government policy and implementation in countries such as the UK and the US. A nudge is a way of providing indirect suggestions and positive reinforcement to influence both the decision-making and action of actors.

Thaler and Sunstein (2009) define their concept in the following way:

> A nudge, as we will use the term, is any aspect of the choice architecture that alters people's behavior in a predictable way without forbidding any options or significantly changing their economic incentives. To count as a mere nudge, the intervention must be easy and cheap to avoid. Nudges are not mandates. Putting fruit at eye level counts as a nudge. Banning junk food does not.

One of the most frequently cited examples of a nudge is the etching of the image of a housefly into the men's room urinals at Amsterdam's Schiphol Airport, which is intended to improve the aim of users and consequently to reduce the need to clean up spillages.

Nudges are ubiquitous in software infrastructure, relying upon technologies such as SMS text messages, email, push notifications, mobile apps, and gamification to encourage people to take desired actions. Nudges can also be built more directly into interfaces to organisational information systems and can influence the way in which people interact with e-government applications, trade financial products online, buy products in online shops and book hotel rooms on mobile booking apps. Such digital nudges can also, of course, be linked to digital response on the part of the receiver, allowing institutions to learn about the success of their nudging strategy. For example, suppose a crowdfunding site wished to increase the amounts of money pledged by people willing to invest. A 'choice architect' could design the interface to present the desired reward option as the default option or pre-populate the input field with a particular value. The site can then measure the number of persons who responded in the desired manner.

Conclusion

We began this chapter with a description of Bentham's panopticon, a structure which enabled one actor to be all-seeing — to potentially observe the activities of all other actors occupying the building. The Internet and the Web were not originally established with this purpose in mind. However, as data infrastructure their contemporary use by companies and intelligence agencies makes them much more powerful versions of Bentham's idea of a panopticon. If you remember, Bentham believed that it is not important for an actor using the panopticon to observe everyone at once. It is only important that the observed know that the panopticon exists and hence that they may be observed, and as such will be motivated to act in ways expected of the constructors of the panopticon. This, of course, is the danger at the heart of the surveillance society — the notion that data surveillance becomes a mechanism for centralised control of the populace.

Everybody worries about the potentiality of surveillance within the modern state. But few, until recently, have worried about the companies, normally US in origin, that operate major chunks of our digital infrastructure. As we mentioned in this chapter, data is often seen as the new oil within capitalism, but this comes at a price which we all pay in terms of surveillance. Surveillance is 'the purposeful, routine, systematic and focused attention paid to personal details, for the sake of control, entitlement, management, influence or protection ...' We can probably live with its use for improvements made to the services provided to us and in the ways data affords protection in times of crisis, such as the COVID-19 pandemic. But we all baulk at its use for social control and subtle influencing of behaviour, whether by government or commercial enterprises.

The next chapter begins our examination of constituent elements of what some have begun to refer to as data science. In Chapter 14, we look at the way data structures are aggregated and analysed using classical statistics. In Chapter 15, we look at a central phenomenon of the contemporary data-driven age — that of big data.

References

Aldridge, A. J. (2010). *GCHQ: The Uncensored Story of Britain's Most Secret Intelligence Agency* (London: Harper Press).

Beynon-Davies, P. (2009b). "The 'Language' of Informatics: The Nature of Information Systems." *International Journal of Information Management*, **29**(2): 92–103.

Brunt, R. (2006). "Special Documentation Systems at the Government Code and Cypher School, Bletchley Park, during the Second World War." *Intelligence and National Security*, **21**(1): 129–148.

Briggs, A. (2011). *Secret Days: Codebreaking in Bletchley Park: A Memoir of Hut Six and the Enigma Machine* (London: Frontline Books).

Clarke, R. (1994). "Human Identification in Information Systems: Management Challenges and Public Policy Issues." *Information Technology and People*, 7(4): 6–37.

Copeland, J. B. (2004). *The Essential Turing* (Oxford: Oxford University Press).

The Economist. (2017). "The World's Most Valuable Resource is No Longer Oil But Data." *The Economist*, 6 May.

Lauer, J. (2020). "Plastic Surveillance: Payments Cards and the History of Transactional Data, 1888 to Present." *Big Data and Society*, 1–14.

Leavitt, D. (2007). *The Man Who Knew Too Much: Alan Turing and the Invention of the Computer* (New York: W.W. Norton).

McKay, S. (2011). *The Secret Life of Bletchley Park: The History of the Wartime Codebreaking Centre by the Men and Women Who Were There London* (London: Aurum Press).

Singh, S. (2000). *The Science of Secrecy* (London: Fourth Estate).

Smith, M. (1998). *Station X: The Code Breakers of Bletchley Park* (London: Pan MacMillan).

Sowa, J. F. (2000). "Ontology, Metadata, and Semiotics. Conceptual Structures: Logical, Linguistic, and Computational Issues." *ICCS 2000*, Ganter, B. and Mineau, G. W. (eds.) (Berlin: Springer, p. 1867).

SebaqMontifiore, H. (2004). *Enigma: The Battle For the Code* (London: Phoenix).

Thaler, R. H. and C. S. Sunstein (2009). *Nudge: Improving Decisions About Health, Wealth and Happiness* (Harmondsworth: Penguin).

Wood, D., K. Ball, D. Lyon, C. Norris and C. Raab (2006). *A Report on the Surveillance Society*. (Wilmslow, UK: Office of the Information Commissioner).

Zuboff, S. (2015). "Big Other: Surveillance Capitalism and the Prospects of an Information Civilization." *Journal of Information Technology*, **30**: 75–89.

Zuboff, S. (2019). *The Age of Surveillance Capitalism* (London: Profile Books).

Chapter 14

Counting Heads

Introduction

In Chapter 8, we considered mechanisms of abstraction that are important to the formation of institutional ontology. Aggregation is one of these key abstraction mechanisms that we return to in this chapter. To remind ourselves, aggregation is the mechanism by which we collect a set of units or parts and form them into a mass or whole, which can be treated independently. Aggregation is important because it is fundamental not only to the idea of statistics, but also to the growing areas of big data, data analytics and the whole notion of a data science. Within the current chapter, we focus upon statistics, while in Chapter 15, we look at big data.

Statistics is a branch of mathematics devoted to the collection, analysis, interpretation and presentation of masses of numerical data. Statistics is also now seen to be an important part of the infrastructure of data science. Within statistics, aggregation as a term tends to be used in a slightly modified sense than we have used previously to refer to the combination of many numerical measurements taken from a population of *parts* into one or more summary measures. These summary measures are then taken to stand for certain features of the *whole* aggregate.

We have no intention of providing a primer of statistics in this chapter, and indeed we are not qualified to do so. However, whenever people speak of data and particularly of inferring things from data, they frequently equate data and inference with statistics. Therefore, in this chapter, we merely wish to unpack or deconstruct some of the fundamental principles on which this mathematical discipline is based. We want to explore some of the bedrock upon which statistical activity takes place and do so in terms of the theorisation we have been developing. This will serve as a useful basis for our exploration of some of the infrastructure associated with big data and data science in Chapter 15.

The word *statistics* is derived from the Latin word *status* or the Italian word *statista*, meaning, respectively, political state or government. Statistics has its origin in census (head) counts taken by ruling elites of their populations for thousands of years. In Chapter 2, we saw how the Inka took regular censuses of members of their empire, while in Chapter 9, we referred to the Domesday book as one of the earliest attempts to survey a medieval kingdom. However, the very notion of state-istics as the counting of things such as persons and the mathematical analysis of such counts for certain purposes only really emerged in the 18th century in response to the needs of the newly industrialising nation-states. Originally, the term statistics was restricted to data created about features of the state, such as details of the citizen population. The term was later expanded to refer to collections of aggregate data of all types, including the analysis and interpretation of such data.

Our aim in this chapter is to establish the necessary truth that the analysis of data in any form must be based upon a firm understanding of the ways in which data structures are made. We want to make the point, recognised by any good statistician, that a statistic is only as good as the data it is built upon and indeed that it is impossible to interpret an aggregate measure properly without understanding the making of data structures that scaffold this analysis. We use two cases to evidence this important point — one historical and one contemporary.

The historical case examines a certain study made by one of the founding fathers of Sociology, Emile Durkheim. Over 100 years ago Durkheim published a book which he believed would prove an exemplar of how Sociology should focus upon the study of what he referred to as social facts. Such social facts describe phenomena that are external to individual experience; having an existence in and of themselves and not bound to the actions of individuals. He further thought that such social facts should be derived by quantitative means and analysed through summary statistics. As we shall see, such claims were fraught with difficulties which centre around a misunderstanding of the scaffolding of data structures produced for administrative purposes at the time by the French state.

The writing of the current book took place within the midst of the COVID-19 pandemic. Therefore, it is appropriate that we examine the ways in which statistics were used during the pandemic by governments to take policy action. We specifically look at the case of counting people testing positive for coronavirus and those held to have died as a result of contracting the virus. The ways in which data structures were constructed of COVID tests and COVID-related deaths is a cogent example of the way in which data structures scaffold both policy and action. The critical lesson we take from this case is that because the scaffold of data structures in this case was somewhat weak, the actions taken could not be as focussed as perhaps they might have been. The case serves to provide further evidence of the critical role that the design of data structures and the associated processes of making such data structures plays within the contemporary institutional order.

Data Structures and Statistics

In Chapter 8, we examined the notion of ontology and began constructing ontologies using the ideas of objects, classes, attributes and various relationships of abstraction. In Chapter 3, we considered the importance of identifiers, particularly personal identifiers for institutions. Statistics is no different to other institutional domains, which rely upon the scaffolding of data, which in turn instantiates ontology. Indeed, statisticians, as we shall see, frequently traverse the existing scaffolding of data structures within and between institutions.

Therefore, let us first make the rather obvious point that to do statistics you must have data formed in structures. Such data structures must both identify and describe objects of interest (see Chapter 8). The entire set of such objects identifiable within some delimited domain is normally referred to within statistics as the *target population*.

Consider the most commonly used example of doing statistics — through a census of some human population. At its most basic, a census is typically a count of all the people in a country, region or locality. Usually, a census will not only count heads, but will also build data structures that identify individuals and record attributes of persons such as their age, sex, ethnicity, occupation, etc.

The notion of a census as a listing of people or things seems to be pretty much universal across human cultures in which states have formed. Indeed, as we have seen in Chapter 1, there seems some suggestion that a listing of people and other things is inherently associated with the rise of the state in the sense that human innovations such as cities, the rise of agriculture and the keeping of records seemed to have emerged in tandem.

Hence, there is evidence of the collection of census data in the system of clay tokens studied by Schmandt-Besserat and dating between 8,000–3,000 BCE (Beynon-Davies, 2009) (Chapter 1). However, the first documented census was undertaken by the Babylonians over 5,000 years ago. Records suggest that such a census was undertaken every six or seven years and counted the number of people and livestock, as well as quantities of butter, honey, milk, wool and vegetables. In Chapter 2, we have seen that, among the Inka in the high Andes, assemblages of knotted string were significant artefacts (Beynon-Davies, 2007). At the provincial level, the Inka used *khipu* within annual censuses of the population. Census data included records of births, deaths, marriages and other changes of a person's status. Individuals of each sex were assigned to one of ten categories corresponding not with their chronological age but to their stage in life and ability to perform useful work. Separate *khipu* were apparently kept for this purpose by each province.

The backdrop of this is that to do statistics (such as producing and analysing a census) we first must design some data structure that defines (as precisely as we can) the list of things or objects we are interested in. Inevitably, in terms of institutional ontology (see Chapter 8), such a structure defines the object class we are interested in. For a state census of its population, the object class would be a person or perhaps a citizen of a country. Each data element entered in this data structure will comprise a representation of one instance or object of the object class. In turn, each object is defined in terms of common attributes defined for the data structure and each attribute is made a data-item of the data structure. Therefore, we might give each citizen a unique identifier and define further data-items such as age, sex, ethnicity, age, etc.

However, note that there are other institutional domains in which the complete population of objects represented through data structures is available for analysis. Much making of statistics works with official records of things, often utilising the data structures making up registers (Chapter 6) of things, such as births, marriages, deaths, car registrations, criminal offences, etc. By definition, such registers represent a complete listing of important events pertaining to persons. The statistics performed on these existing data-sets are considered in later sections. As we shall see, Emile Durkheim effectively used the register of deaths maintained by the French state. Counting COVID deaths relied on record-making such as on cause of death certification performed by physicians.

Therefore, the typical aggregate considered within statistics is that of a population of objects, which we should potentially be able to identify and describe using data structures. Traditionally, building data structures which represent things in an entire population is regarded as infeasible, because of the large amount of data that would need to be articulated. This means that, for most of its history, the discipline of statistics has worked with the assumption that we must instead produce a *sample* of our chosen population.

Sampling data involves articulating data structures in a slightly different way than that required for entire populations. First, we must create a structure for data which defines the object class we are interested in sampling. This follows the same procedure of defining a list of the data-items we wish to represent data about. However, unlike a full population, we must now also build a list of instances of our chosen class, which is smaller, normally considerably smaller, than the list comprising the entire population of instances or objects of the class. Then, we must create data elements to populate our data structure, and in so doing form our sample data-set.

Where a full population of data elements is not readily available, then a subset of data elements derived from the notional population is normally produced via a survey. In both the case where data structures are produced officially and in the case of data structures produced via a survey, the same general point applies. We must be clear as to how the records are made — either by officials or by survey personnel. This is a principle we examine more closely in a later section.

As a relevant contemporary example, suppose our population comprises all those people in a particular country that has tested positive for COVID-19. We know that we can build a list of this population because a data structure is updated by each health authority with the name and contact details of the infected person as part of the testing regime. Suppose now that we wish to know how many of these people adhered to the self-isolation protocol established for those having coronavirus. This is not a data-item built into the data structure built for the population in question. It is not feasible for us to contact all such persons and ask this question so instead we decide to build a sample. We know that members of this population are distributed all over the country. Therefore, we perhaps decide to select persons from each health authority data structure proportionate with the number of persons resident in each area. We then contact people within the sample and ask them in confidence whether they self-isolated after having a positive test and for how long.

Population and Sample

The idea of sampling from a population relies upon a central principle of statistical thinking — that the values assigned to data-items and which are taken to represent attributes of the things listed as a population tend to be distributed in a predictable way amongst members of that population (Spiegelhalter, 2019). This distribution is often referred to as a normal distribution or a Gaussian distribution, after the 19th century mathematician Karl Friederich Gauss who deduced its shape. This distribution tends to be visualised as a central peak with gently sloping sides as in Figure 14.1.

Let us assume that we wish to build a list of the entire human population of some country. Suppose perhaps for reasons of public health, we wish to record physical attributes of humans within this population, such

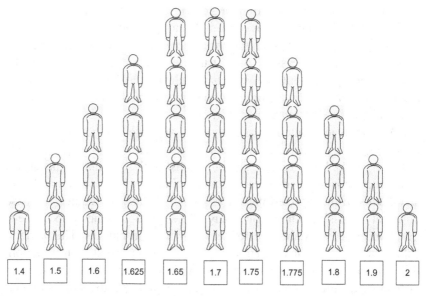

Figure 14.1:   A normal distribution of heights amongst a human population.

as the height and weight of each individual. This was something one of the founders of modern statistics, Lambert Quetelet, did. Quetelet is noteworthy for promoting the use of statistics in the social sciences. He developed his idea of social physics, that social phenomena could be described and analysed in terms of statistical trends. He was also an early proponent of anthropometry — the idea that detailed measurements should be made of human physical traits — and proposed that such human traits were distributed according to a Gaussian distribution. Through this, he developed the idea of the average man, whose attributes are valued close to the mean along a range of measured variables. This led him to propose that normal variation provided a basis for the idea that populations produce sufficient variation for artificial or natural selection to operate.

Anthropometry was of course central to the development of criminal identification within the Bertillon case (see Chapter 3) and is the foundation of modern biometrics. Anthropometry is also much used within medicine. Quetelet established a simple measure for classifying people's weight relative to an ideal for their height. This proposal of a body mass index (or Quetelet index) has endured with minor variations to the present day. Anthropometry is also the driver behind ergonomics. Sometimes referred to as human factors, it is an applied science devoted to understanding how people and things interact and to use such understanding to develop principles of good design for products such as chairs or interactive computer software.

Now back to distributions. If we were to plot the heights of individuals (in metres) amongst our population, then we would find that a small minority of people are very short (perhaps having a height around 1.4 metres) and a minority are very tall (perhaps having a height around 2 metres). Likewise, if we were to plot the weights of humans within this population, we would find a small minority of people who are extremely heavy and a minority who are very thin. Most individuals would clump in the middle of the distribution — approximating a *normal* height (such as 1.7 metres) and weight for individuals in the country in question. Hence, the Gaussian curve is also referred to as a normal distribution curve. Such a distribution for human heights is illustrated in Figure 14.1.

However, let us suppose that we do not have the resources to conduct a full census of all the persons in our population but wish to build a sub-list of persons, which we call a sample. To be a true sample, at least as far as statistics is concerned, then the distribution of values assigned to attributes within this sub-list must reflect or mirror the distribution of values within the general population. When this is the case, the sample is said to be *representative* of its population. Thus representative here means that the distribution of values produced by a sample will closely match the distribution of values in the entire population. Hence, if we were to take a sample of the general population and plotted the height of persons within this sample, then we would expect that the distribution of this attribute would closely match that of the general population.

We established earlier that to begin to do statistics (in the sense of producing aggregate measures of a population), we first must design some data structure which defines (as precisely as we can) the list of things or objects we are interested in as well as the attributes of the class to which the objects generalise. But note a certain flaw in our account so far. Without knowing how an attribute is distributed in the population (such as height or weight) we have chosen, we cannot say for sure whether our sample is representative of it or not. We might produce a sample with many very tall people or many very short people. This is where the assumption of randomness comes in. The assumption is made, which has proven valid in cases of samples above a certain size in terms of their population, that a sample of things chosen at random from a population will be representative of that population.

Assuming that we can plot the Gaussian curve of a certain attribute from our sample, then we can summarise this distribution in a number of ways. What we are actually doing here is taking one value to stand for an aggregation of values derived from our sample. Two of the most common examples of summary data are the mean and the range. There are in fact a number of different types of mean but let us consider the simplest, that of the mode or modal value. The mode is the most common value that occurs in the list of values. It will be the peak in a Gaussian curve — such as 1.7 metres in Figure 14.1. The range is the difference between the smallest value in a list and the largest value in the list — which is 0.6 from Figure 14.1. It provides an inkling of the spread of some attribute amongst the population.

Brute Facts and Institutional Facts

Data structures, as we have seen, are used to establish facts and in Chapter 6, we introduced two types of facts established through data structures. Brute facts are the very stuff of the physical sciences — physics, chemistry and biology — and as such exist independently of human institutions. Such facts are established through measurement of the physical world, such as the orbits of the planets in the solar system or the composition of the human genome. In contrast, institutional facts are matters of culture and convention. They exist only within the context of human institutions and indeed serve to declare things to exist within domains of activity. Hence, when a contract is declared between two economic actors, then certain prescriptions and prohibitions are brought into play for such actors.

The height and weight of individuals assert brute facts about individuals. In other words, providing we can collectively agree a system of signs for measurement, such as using metres or feet for this purpose, then we can represent and communicate, in an observer-independent way, the values for these data-items appropriate to listed individuals. Two observers can mutually agree how tall or heavy a particular individual is, and these measurements can be plotted for an entire population. However, statistics is not only interested in the physical attributes of people. It is also interested in institutional attributes such as one's political affiliation or marital status. It may also be interested in people's opinions and expectations, such as who somebody might vote for in the next general election or what they expect a government to do in terms of policy options.

So, let us consider two other important attributes of individuals gathered in a national census — a person's *socio-economic status* and a person's *ethnicity*.

Consider first how we might measure or value the data-item of ethnicity. To do this we must agree a list of acceptable values that the data-item can take. Take the list of values used in the UK census. People have to assign an ethnicity to themselves from the following list and record this on the survey questionnaire:

- White.
- Mixed/Multiple ethnic groups.
- Asian/Asian British.
- Black/African/Caribbean/Black British.
- Other ethnic group.

Building a record of a person's ethnicity clearly establishes an institutional fact. For the purposes of the census, we collectively agree not only upon the appropriate categories for ethnicity, but also how the process of classification using such categories should occur, in this case by self-selection.

The Office of National Statistics in the UK provide eight categories for socio-economic status, coded as 1 through 8:

1. Higher managerial, administrative and professional occupations.
2. Lower managerial, administrative and professional occupations.
3. Intermediate occupation.
4. Small employers and own account workers.
5. Lower supervisory and technical occupations.
6. Semi-routine occupations.
7. Routine occupations.
8. Never worked and long-term unemployed.

The point here is that such socio-economic categories are arbitrary in the sense there is no direct relationship between the sign and the object represented. This does not mean that the categories have no purpose in mind. The categories are assigned by the institution, the state in this case, and applied in classification for the state to gain an understanding of the range of different ethnic backgrounds and occupational groups evident amongst the UK population. This is essential for policy actions such as understanding the need for welfare, health and economic actions to be taken in different parts of the country.

It is interesting that the COVID-19 pandemic raised the question of why apparent high rates of deaths were evident amongst certain ethnic groups. Speculations spread about the possible genetic predisposition of certain ethnicities to detrimental effects of COVID-19 infection. A closer analysis of the aggregate data began to show that one's socio-economic category was a better predictor of not only your likelihood to catch the infection, but also to suffer serious consequences from the infection. This was, of course, because the categories applied to ethnicity and socio-economic status overlap amongst the UK population. Certain ethnicities are over-represented among certain socio-economic categories.

A Cautionary Tale — Durkheim and Suicide

The point made in the previous section shows that statistics clearly relies not only upon assumptions relating to the ontological status of data structures, but also upon assumptions relating to the validity of processing data in certain ways. As we have seen, this primarily means aggregating data, which involves the gathering together of data and the representation of such aggregate data using summary measures. Within this section we revisit a well-cited controversy surrounding the aggregation of data based upon institutional practices that affect the scaffolding of data structures.

Over 100 years ago, one of the founding fathers of sociology, Emile Durkheim, published an influential book simply entitled *Suicide* (Durkheim, 1976). He intended this book as an example of how Sociology should focus upon the study of what he referred to as *social facts*. This was a term he used to describe phenomena that are external to individual experience, having an existence in and of themselves and not bound to the actions of individuals.

Durkheim proposed that even the most apparently individualistic acts, such as suicide, are to be regarded in aggregate (as suicide rates) to be observer-independent social facts. Sociology's task was to discover the qualities and characteristics of such social facts, primarily through quantitative means. Statistics implicitly relies upon the idea that the social world can be relatively easily quantified based on 'facts' collected about it. Hence, Durkheim pioneered the analysis of statistics in support of sociological reasoning. In *Suicide*, for instance, Durkheim explored the differing suicide rates among Protestants and Catholics and explained the lower suicide rates amongst Catholics at the time in terms of the stronger levels of integration and social cohesion among Catholics than amongst Protestants.

Within contemporary institutions, we have made the case in previous chapters that records are equally and typically treated as 'facts' about things of interest to the institution. Many years after the work of Durkheim, a branch of sociology known as ethnomethodology started to critique many of the assumptions employed by Durkheim. For Garfinkel, Cicourel and others, social facts are not objective but are instead reliant upon a set of subjective human accomplishments and practices (Cicourel, 1974). As evidence of this, they focussed upon the practices or 'methods' people use in record-making and record-keeping of various forms. They argued that the process of producing a record of something is an accomplishment or a set of practices that serves to create the social order. Practical reasoning is utilised by relevant actors, for instance, in decisions pertaining to defining delinquent behaviour in the creation of criminal records by police officers or the registration of a person's death as a suicide by coroners.

A suicide rate is clearly a summary fact based upon the aggregation of data, and as a social fact was treated by Durkheim as objective — indicating a necessary correspondence between data and reality. The ethnomethodologists showed that such social facts are reliant upon the scaffolding of data structures. In the case of suicide, various professional groups accord the status of suicide to suspicious deaths. In the process, they assign a category or classification to this event based upon an interpretation of the likely intentions of the dead actor and thus create an appropriate data structure to instantiate this institutional fact.

Let us look at this accomplishment of making records more closely, using the example of a record of a suicide. Consider the case in which a given police officer or medical practitioner is called to the scene of a death. Such actors are imbued by society with the authority to make the key decision as to whether the death was 'suspicious'. In coming to this decision, they look for 'evidence' that accords with their 'common sense' definitions about what constitutes a 'suspicious' death. Hence, they might ask themselves questions such as:

- How did the person die?
- Was the victim alone at the time of death?
- Was there a note left with the body or was some other message made prior to death?
- What was the victim's 'state of mind' immediately prior to death?
- Were elaborate preparations made by the victim?

If answers to such questions confirm the conception of 'suspicious death', which such officials hold, then an inquest into the death is called at a Coroner's Court. The coroner then becomes the most important actor, insofar as he or she now must come to a decision about whether the death was a suicide.

Garfinkel (1967) argues that coroners in coming to the categorisation of suicide in the case of an equivocal death typically use a form of practical reasoning reliant on a myriad of cues present in the 'remains' of the dead.

'That death they use as a precedent with which various ways of living in society that could have terminated with that death are searched out and read "in the remains"; in the scraps of this and that like the body and its trappings, medicine bottles, notes, bits and pieces of clothing and other memorabilia — stuff that can be photographed, collected and packaged. Other "remains" are collected too: rumours, passing remarks, and stories — materials in the "repertoires" of whosoever might be consulted via the common work of conversations. These whatsoever bits and pieces that a story or a rule or a proverb might make intelligible are used to formulate a recognizably coherent, standard, typical, cogent, uniform, planful, i.e. professionally defensible, and thereby for members, a recognizably rational account of how the society worked to produce those remains.'

What Garfinkel is imputing here is that the Coroner is likely to engage in similar forms of practical reasoning to actors such as the police or the medical profession. Hence, if a person was found hanging and alone, had left a note explaining his actions and was suffering depression prior to his death, the coroner is probably likely to declare such a death to be a suicide. Such practical reasoning is built around notions of collective intentionality, particularly about the likely causes of suicide and the expected behaviour of a suicidal person. It is also built around a human's capacity to empathise — to take the role of or 'walk in the shoes of' another.

If one or more of the answers to such questions cannot be determined, then the coroner must weigh the evidence in favour of a suicide verdict, or not. For example, consider the case of a woman in which there appears to have been a history of depression as well as evidence of suffering financial problems. The person's death was caused by a head-on car crash with a wall, but no note was found with the victim. However, the victim is a Catholic and she comes from a Catholic family. The coroner herself is a Catholic and the court is being held in a Catholic country. All parties are therefore aware that the Catholic Church views self-murder as a sin.

In such a situation, the coroner may not declare a suicide, perhaps explicitly citing the lack of clear evidence such as a suicide note, but also implicitly considering the likely consequences of her decision upon the victim's relatives. A data element is therefore added to the register of deaths which records 'death by misadventure'. On entry of this list-item, the coroner declares the form of death.

Of course, individual acts of articulation, such as this, when manipulated as aggregates may serve to communicate certain things about the state of the world. When all such acts of communication are aggregated together in state-istics, it might appear evident that Catholic countries have lower suicide rates than Protestant countries.

Take another example in this vein but with strategic consequences. During the Battle of Britain in 1940, intelligence from both sides contributed to strategic and operational decisions. A crucial part of such intelligence were counts of aircraft, particularly estimates as to total number of enemy aircraft and reporting by pilots of the number of enemy aircraft shot down. In terms of total aircraft, the Luftwaffe consistently underestimated the overall size of the RAF fighter command while the British consistently overestimated the size of the German Luftwaffe. During the battle itself, British RAF pilots and German Luftwaffe pilots self-reported numbers of enemy aircraft shot down. Both sides consistently over-reported the actual number of enemy aircraft shot down. These two factors led to the Luftwaffe mistakenly believing that RAF fighter command was virtually eliminated and contributed to the strategic mistake of shifting bombing targets from airbases to sites of industry.

Counting COVID-19

The key lesson we take from the cases such as Durkheim's analysis of suicide is that we need to be always aware that the inferences we make from data must be based on a firm understanding of the ways in which data are made. Data used within statistical activity is typically 'collected' through surveys and using questionnaires. However, the ways in which surveys are conducted and questions asked of respondents influence what can be inferred. Also, as in the case of Durkheim's *Suicide*, counts can be made against data collected for administrative purposes, such as the total number of tests for COVID-19 issued in the UK. In such situations, great care must be taken in interpreting statistics such as simple counts produced from the aggregation of data contained within such data structures. This is because counts used in statistics inevitably rely upon processes of classification conducted by actors. To ensure consistent articulation of data structures, clear definitions concerning how classes are formed from instances must be arrived at and agreed upon amongst a community of actors.

To make this point, let us elaborate upon the relationship between an event such as the death of a certain person and the classification processes that precede declaring the cause of such a death. As we have seen, in most nation-states, deaths are declared through data structures such as death certificates. Death certificates as data structures are used worldwide not only to declare that a death has occurred, but also to assert reasons for such a death. Death certificates obtain their deontic status because they can only be signed-off (declared) by certain nominated persons such as doctors, medical examiners or coroners. However, making records of the causes of death are never easy. This proved particularly difficult during the COVID-19 pandemic. So, let us examine how the list of persons declared to have died as the result of COVID-19 was compiled in various countries around the world. As we shall see, various countries classified COVID-19–related deaths in vastly different ways and many countries changed their basis for counting such deaths during the pandemic itself.

Making the judgement that COVID-19 caused the death of a person is often difficult because many persons contracting this virus and who subsequently died had a range of other medical conditions such as coronary artery disease or kidney disease. In the UK, the government initially took the decision to count as a COVID-19 death any person who died in hospital at any point in time following a positive COVID-19 test. What is first noteworthy about this is that, unlike other countries such as Germany, the UK authorities initially did not include deaths in care homes but only deaths in hospitals. Germany counted deaths in care homes only if it followed a positive COVID-19 test, but Belgium included deaths suspected by a doctor that coronavirus was involved. Clearly, this variation in the way in which COVID-19 deaths were classified and recorded made comparisons between these countries extremely difficult, if not impossible at the time.

What made things even worse was that governments changed their method for counting COVID-19 deaths as the course of the pandemic progressed. For instance, the UK changed the basis of its definition some months into the pandemic from those persons dying at any point after a positive COVID-19 test to only counting those persons dying up to 28 days following a COVID-19 test. This change in definition actually reduced the national figures at the time of change by more than 5,000.

Comparisons of counts from COVID-19 records are also difficult to make even within the same country. For instance, it is impossible to compare the count of COVID-19 infections produced in the first wave of the pandemic (March, April, May of 2020) in the UK against counts produced in the second wave (September, October, November of 2020). Any such comparison would be suspect because the number of tests available increased in the second wave as compared to the first. Indeed, testing continued to increase in the third wave of the outbreak (December, January, February of 2021), making comparisons with counts made in the second and first wave extremely difficult.

Let us assume that two countries agree on a similar way of classifying COVID-19-related deaths. Another problem then emerges because the way in which an aggregate measure such as a death or fatality rate is presented can cause confusion. Such confusion can make the death rate from the virus in two countries appear vastly different, even if their populations are dying at the same rate. Two aggregate measures give different impressions of the progression of a disease and may illicit different policy action.

One measure often used is known as the *case fatality rate* and is the proportion of people who die having tested positive for the disease. This is the measure adopted during the pandemic by countries such as the UK. However, this contrasts with another measure known as the *infection fatality rate,* which is the proportion of people who die after having the infection overall. To demonstrate the difference this makes, suppose 100 people are infected with COVID-19. Ten of them develop severe symptoms and so are admitted to hospital, where they test positive for the virus. The other 90 remain untested for the virus. One of the hospital patients then dies from the virus; the other 99 survive. This would give a fatality rate of one in 10, or 10%, but the infection fatality rate would be just one in 100, or 1%.

From the theory established in previous chapters it should come as no surprise to find that the way cases are counted is influenced by the making of data as measurement. In terms of the COVID-19 pandemic, this means that the way in which the testing regime is organised has an influence on how death rates are calculated. Those countries that test only those persons admitted to hospital or those persons displaying symptoms of the disease will display apparent higher rates of fatality from COVID-19 than those countries that test the less-ill or even asymptomatic cases (those persons not showing any signs of infection).

This does not negate the importance of this exercise because counting COVID-19–related deaths is typically used as some form of proxy measure for the effectiveness of public health control within a nation, region or locality. However, what was even more important during the pandemic were the records made of COVID-19 tests (particularly the positive results). Aggregate measures produced from such data were used to implement public health actions such as national and local area lockdowns.

Consider some of the problems experienced in the making of such test records. Throughout the pandemic, a number of problems emerged in the testing regime exercised in the UK. Throughout the pandemic, testing of the general population proved impractical because of the vast numbers involved. Therefore, tests were first restricted to those persons admitted to hospital or a resident in a care home suspected of having contracted the virus. This was later expanded to those persons showing symptoms of the virus in the general population.

Consider this scenario — a pupil in a school displays symptoms of the virus, gets tested and has a positive result. The school is informed and immediately orders all 30 pupils in the same class to self-isolate for 14 days. None of these pupils show any symptoms of the virus and hence do not get tested. If they could get tested and prove negative, they would be able to return to their critical schooling. The same applies to adults in the workplace. Therefore, the lack of good data in this case is a direct cause of problems in access to education and in return to workers within the wider economy.

This is yet another example of the agency of data structures and hence their importance to effective institutional action. Let us examine this in a little more detail. Within countries such as the UK, one of the most prominent policy interventions was the intention to track persons infected, trace those persons who had been in close contact with the infected person and to demand that this group of persons self-isolate for a nominated period. This seems an eminently sensible response to managing the epidemic and is a clear example of the way in which data is so critical to action. A person with symptoms of the disease takes a COVID-19 test and comes back with a positive result as recorded. This record drives a number of trace activities which involve communicating with those persons that have been in close contact with the person during the time he has had the disease. When records are built for such persons and they are used to communicate with such persons then certain prohibitions result — namely that they must self-isolate for a period of time. But note that all this works on the basis of collective acceptance of prohibitions of certain data structures such as a COVID-19 test. Many persons testing positive may choose not to self-isolate.

Data Science

The term *data science* was originally coined in the late 2000s and is now widely used. However, like most signs what the term data science refers to is a moving beast. In other words, what data science comprises depends on who you ask? In 2009 Hal Varian Google's chief economist at the time described some of the skills required of the data scientist — 'The ability to take data – to be able to understand it, to process it, to extract value from it, to visualise it, to communicate it ...' (McKinsey, 2009). There is now some core consensus that data science clearly focuses upon developing methods and technologies for engaging with what some have referred to as the data deluge [Chapter 1] – the large amounts of data created in modern society and the correspondingly large data sets that need to be managed and analysed arising from this. It is sometimes seen as an interdisciplinary area which is attempting to develop a unified view of data appropriate to the diverse areas of statistics, data analysis, machine learning, big data, mathematics and computer science. Yet another viewpoint characterises data science in terms of a lifecycle model with interlinked activities including data capture, processing data, maintaining data, analysing data and communicating data.

The key problem is that, as we have seen, all of these viewpoints appear to work with a limited viewpoint on data, which we referred to in previous chapters as the conventional ontology of data structures. We have hopefully made the case that this viewpoint tends to straitjacket approaches developed for engaging with data and in some cases leads us astray in designing good ways of making data and drawing inferences from it.

We think it important to establish a programme to try to define the prospects for a data science that is informed not by the conventional ontology of data structures but by a social ontology of data structures. Any valid data science must recognise the way in which data structures scaffold institutional action. Data structures are made by actors within acts of articulation. Data is not neutral or objective but valued. It is directed at achieving communication, and such communication is entangled with the rights and responsibilities imbued to actors through data structures.

Conclusion

In this chapter, we have shown how any inferences drawn from statistics are only as good as the data aggregated through data structures in such statistics. To make any sensible inferences, we need to have a detailed understanding of how data structures are made — for what purpose and by whom. The main reason that Durkheim's inferences drawn from official statistics are potentially suspect is because Durkheim treated social facts as brute facts rather than institutional facts. A suicide is only deemed as such when a certain privileged actor classifies a certain death in this manner and declares this event through making a record such as a death certificate. Hence, when we examine the processes by which the making of suicide records occur, we must be careful as to what aggregate statistics drawn from such data tells us.

In the next chapter, we shall see that the modern phenomenon of big data does not usually work with samples and populations familiar within traditional statistics. It also does not work with methical instruments such as surveys but instead works with whole populations of existing data generated from a number of diverse sources, integrated together to form massive data-sets upon which algorithmic analyses can be conducted. However, this does not mean that the lessons gleaned within this chapter are not equally applicable to this recent data phenomenon. As we shall show, big data, just like traditional statistics, relies upon the mechanics of data structures scaffolding institutional order.

References

Beynon-Davies, P. (2007). "Informatics and the Inca." *International Journal of Information Management*, **27**(5): 306–318.

Beynon-Davies, P. (2009). "Neolithic Informatics: The Nature of Information." *International Journal of Information Management*, **29**(1): 3–14.

Cicourel, A. V. (1974). Police Practices and Official Records. In *Ethnomethodology: Selected Readings*. R. Turner (ed.) (Harmondsworth, UK: Penguin).

Durkheim, E. (1976). *Suicide: A Study in Sociology* (New York: Free Press).

Garfinkel, H. (1967). *Studies in Ethnomethodology* (Englewood Cliffs, NJ: Prentice-Hall).

McKinsey and Co. (2009). *Hal Varian on How the Web Challenges Managers*, 1 January.

Spiegelhalter, D. (2019). *The Art of Statistics: Learning from Data* (London: Pelican).

Chapter 15

A Social Ontology of Big Data

Introduction

Deoxyribonucleic acid (DNA) is a nucleic acid that is generally described as containing the genetic 'instructions' used as the motor of organisation amongst all known living organisms. As we mentioned in the prologue, DNA is often considered as a code, since molecules of this acid contain instructions needed to construct other components of cells, such as proteins and RNA molecules. DNA is made up of chemical building blocks known as nucleotides, which consist of three parts: a phosphate group, a sugar group and one of four types of nitrogen base.

In terms of structure, Figure 15.1, DNA consists of two long chains or polymers of nucleotides, with backbones made of alternating sugar and phosphate groups joined by ester bonds. Attached to this backbone, in which two strands run in opposite directions to each other, are the bases. The four types of nitrogen base are: adenine (usually symbolised as A), guanine (G), cytosine (C) and thymine (T). The order or sequence of bases code biological instructions. For example, the sequence ATCGTT might code for blue eyes, whereas the sequence ATCGCT might code for brown eyes.

Each DNA sequence that codes for a protein is known as a gene. Proteins are complex molecules that do most of the work in constructing and maintaining organisms. The size of a gene may vary greatly, ranging from 1,000 to 1 million bases. In 1984, the Human Genome Project was established as an international scientific research project with the goal of determining the base pairs that make up human DNA, and of identifying

Figure 15.1:   DNA as a physical structure.

and mapping all of the genes of the human genome. Work began in 1990 and completed in 2003. The complete DNA code or genome for a human contains about 3 billion bases chunked into some 20,000 genes. As we shall see, the human genome was the original big data (structure).

Big data has been big news for some time, not only in the popular press, but also within academia. This is true not only of the information disciplines (Abbasi *et al.*, 2016), but also within business and management. Much of this literature looks at the way big data has changed or is likely to change key areas and practices such as the nature of capitalism (Zuboff, 2015), management (McAfee and Brynjolfsson, 2012) and strategy (Constantinou and Kallinikos, 2015).

In this last full chapter, we wish to examine the nature of big data itself using the theoretical framework we have developed in previous chapters and which we have referred to as the scaffolding of data structures. In more specific terms, we want to critique the often-purported notion that the 'data' in big data is in many ways distinct from the 'data' in small data. The technologies of big data were developed originally in the physical sciences as an attempt to handle large collections of physical or brute facts, such as those important to the Human Genome project (Collins *et al.*, 2003). We wish to question in this chapter the generally held assumption, particularly by technologists, that big data technologies can be transferred, in a relatively unproblematic manner, into domains dealing primarily with social or institutional facts.

Kitchin (2014) has reckoned that there is an urgent need to critically examine the epistemological foundations of big data. However, any epistemology (theory of knowledge) is heavily reliant upon ontology (theory of existence). The idea of building new approaches to knowledge construction is heavily reliant upon an understanding of how the world is constituted, and how it is legitimate to engage with the world through data. We agree with Kitchin (2014) that many of the claims made for a new epistemology emerging from big data are open to question, but we want to show how they are questionable because of the way many contemporary practitioners of data science frame the relationship between data and reality, particularly social reality. In this sense, we want to provide an understanding of the micro-dynamics of social or institutional data as a means of providing more precision to certain existing critiques of big data.

We first consider what the literature tells us big data is, and to do this we utilise a key feature analysis. We then make no apologies for reviewing what we know of the nature of data as it is portrayed conventionally in technology areas such as ICT. As we have seen, this worldview believes that a necessary and unequivocal correspondence exists between data and reality (Kent, 2012). Big data, we shall see, in the large adopts this notion of data as objective facts. This leads us to the question of what our view of data structures as institutional scaffolding for social ontology says about big data and related exercises.

In previous chapters, we have unpacked the scaffolding of data structures largely using Searle's theory of social ontology. Within the current chapter, we wish to utilise the complementary viewpoint founded within the Semiotics of Charles Sanders Peirce, which we introduced in Chapter 3, and which supports similar conclusions as to the role that data structures play as institutional scaffolding. We demonstrate the veracity of our conception of such scaffolding by unpacking several of the 'should-have' features of big data and show how they necessarily rely upon notions of social ontology founded in institutional scaffolding.

What is Big Data?

Big data is a difficult term to pin-down precisely as it involves many things. When people attempt to define big data, they normally do so in terms of certain characteristics of data itself. Big data applications are normally defined in terms of three core features — data volume, data variety and data velocity. Several tangential features are also sometimes seen as important to big data such as data resolution, data relatability, data flexibility, data indexicality and data exhaustivity (Kitchin, 2014). Not all examples of big data display these features. In addition, big data clearly builds upon small data, if only by using conventional databases as data sources. Some also include within definitions of big data features associated with the analysis and presentation of data. Data analytics is the activity in which data sets are examined using complex algorithms to reveal patterns in the data. Sometimes people include the capacity to visualise such patterns in various ways (data visualisation) within definitions of big data. Some even see big data as belonging to a coherent subset of Computer Science which they call Data Science. Data science is devoted at least in part to building better analytics and visualisation on the back of big data.

Therefore, the way in which big data is defined typically uses a feature-based approach (Kitchin, 2014). It is useful to think of two types of such features: must-have features, which the majority of the literature uses to define this phenomenon (data volume, data variety and data velocity) and, should-have features, which only certain literature adds to the mix (data resolution, data relatability, data flexibility, data indexicality and data exhaustivity), to name but a few. It is interesting that Kitchin and McCardle (2016) analysed 26 data sets describing themselves as big data and while all displayed elements of data volume, data variety and data velocity, only a handful displayed both must-have and should-have features.

The core or must-have features of big data applications are summarised in Table 15.1. The size of data-sets used within big data applications is very large (data volume), frequently constituting terabytes, petabytes and sometimes even exabytes of data (see chapter 1). The sources

Table 15.1:   Key features of big data applications.

Feature	Description	Must-have/ Should-have
Volume	The size of the datasets used is very large, frequently measured in terabytes, petabytes or even exabytes and zetabytes of data.	Must-have
Variety	The sources of data are diverse, frequently meaning that big data must handle multiple structures for data.	Must-have
Velocity	The speed with which data is collected, processed and output for analysis approaches real time.	Must-have
Resolution	Data has fine granularity, aiming to be as detailed as possible.	Should-have
Relatability	Data in one dataset should be relatable to that in other data sets.	Should-have
Flexibility	Both the structure and size of data can expand easily and rapidly.	Should-have
Indexicality	Data is uniquely identifiable.	Should-have
Exhaustivity	Whole populations of data, rather than samples of data, are collected, stored and analysed.	Should-have

of data are diverse (data variety), frequently meaning that big data applications must handle multiple structures for data. The speed with which data is articulated — i.e. created, updated and read — has rapidly increased (data velocity), leading to data sensed, recorded and analysed almost in real time. These must-have features of big data tend to be cited in all attempts to define this phenomenon. In this sense, big data is defined in terms of the size and variety of datasets as well as the speed with which big data is processed.

Should-have features are additional characteristics of big data cited sometimes in much more limited literature (Table 15.1). In terms of features which some think are important to big data, data can now be handled in fine-grained detail (data resolution). Data is also uniquely identifiable to designated people or things (data indexicality). New technologies enable whole populations rather than samples of data to be collected and stored (data exhaustivity). Data in one dataset is relatable to that in other data sets (data relatability). Finally, both the structure and size of data can expand easily and rapidly (data flexibility).

The Conventional Ontology of Data and Data Structures

In our search through contemporary literature on the subject, it is evident that what is mostly absent from accounts of big data are attempts to deal with the ontological basis of data. This, of course, has been the primary objective of the current work. We infer from this that data, as accounted for within much of contemporary data science is assumed to be unproblematic (see Chapter 14) in the sense that such data provides an unequivocal, objective account of reality. This stance, as we shall see, is particularly evident in common attempts made by data scientists to undermine the notion of *structure* within data.

The concept of data is clearly central to big data, but within applications of this phenomena, data is still treated from what we referred to as the correspondence view — the viewpoint that data mirrors an external reality. Within previous chapters we have taken a contrary position and established the way in which data structures 'scaffold' institutional order. We have argued that data structures act as crucial internal scaffolding in the continual reconstruction (building and repair) of contemporary institutional order. Such artefacts serve to represent and communicate aspects of institutional order. Nevertheless, they also afford people access to numerous systems of activity that make up institutional order.

In this section, we examine the nature of data from these two alternative positions: the conventional position in which data is considered a form of representation which merely supports institutional action and a viewpoint derived from Peircean semiotics, through which data is considered an important element within the accomplishment of signs. This latter viewpoint is important because it suggests that data as vehicles for signs serve not to support but to constitute institutional action. This leads to a demonstration that these different viewpoints on data suggest different ways in which we should think about big data — not only in terms of its promises, but also in terms of its perils.

Most current conceptions of the notion of data either explicitly or implicitly utilise a view of reality consistent with that evident in the work of Bunge (Wyssusek, 2006), in which reality (including institutional reality) is considered an organised collection of objective and observable things of interest. The conventional viewpoint also tends to adopt a related Fregean view of 'language' (Lyytinen, 1985), which proposes that statements in some formal language, such as those encapsulated in a set of data structures, correspond to objective facts about some real-world domain such as some section of institutional reality. For example, from this viewpoint, the population of students from some university on industrial placement comprise a collection of objective and observable 'things'. Student data held in various data structures by a university correspond to objective facts about the current state of student placement within this university.

In the conventional view of a data structure, such as a student placement record, the elements within the record represent propositions about 'things' in some real-world domain. The institutional reality is also assumed to be observer-independent, meaning that it is the same for all actors. Hence, a data-item such as a student identifier serves as a proposition about these 'things' within the university. Within formal logic, data-items as propositions may take only one of two values, namely, true or false. Within data management, any data element or data-item written with concrete arguments is assumed to be true (Gallaire and Minker, 1978). This implies that the state of a data structure, such as an industrial placement file, at any given time consists of true statements about the real-world domain it represents — in this case, the students on industrial placement from some academic school. This so-called correspondence view of truth implies that there is a necessary separation between institutional reality and data structures. It also suggests that a data structure is a representation taken to correspond to some real-world thing, or more likely a set of things important to some institutional reality.

Now consider data and data structures from an alternative perspective: that of the semiotics of Charles Sanders Peirce (Mingers and Wilcocks, 2017) which we considered in Chapter 3. From this perspective, data is a component element within the accomplishment of signs. To remind ourselves, a sign for Peirce is something (representamen) which stands to somebody (interpretant) for some other thing (object). The representamen is the signifier, sign-vehicle or representation. The object is the signified or referent; that which is represented. The interpretant is the concept or the meaning of the symbol formed through some process of interpretation by some actor. For Peirce, the sign only exists within this triad of elements or through the accomplishment of this triad. In other words, the sign is not in any one of its component elements. Nor is it in all three together as a 'structure'. Instead, the sign emerges in the mutual coupling of all three component elements within the process or accomplishment of sign-use or semiosis.

Consider the case of a data structure of student placement records from this perspective. Assume that one data-item within this data structure comprises a student identifier (see Chapter 3). The student identifier is the representamen for Peirce. It serves to stand for some other thing — an instance of a human, which is the object. However, the act of referring to an object using a representamen calls into existence a particular interpretant, namely a certain institutional concept or category for informing actors, that of perhaps a placement student.

In this process of performing these actions, we open up further levels of semiosis. For instance, in categorising an individual as a placement student, we imply further action consequences, such as an expectation that these individuals will be working with an organisational partner in a defined job for a defined duration. In other words, we will need to employ further signs (partner, job, duration) to make sense of this particular sign.

The direct consequence of this perspective on data is that data and data structures are not something separate from institutional action but constitutive of institutional action. The signs we use to make sense of institutional reality serve not to merely support institutional reality but to produce and reproduce (constitute) such institutional reality. In other words, data structures do not just record data, they do things. By creating a new student placement record, the institution brings into existence a new institutional thing (a placement student), and in doing so opens up a potentially further series of actions that it will need to signify, such as registration of the placement, monitoring of the placement and perhaps grading the placement.

Thus, the articulation of data structures such as student placement data structures is critical to communicating intention to multiple actors, who, based on such communication, coordinate their activity. For instance, to gain access to the teaching at a university, you must have a valid student record, which as a data structure contains an identifier: a student number. This data-item uniquely refers to a 'thing' within this institutional domain, namely a person. However, the crucial point is that this institutional token is created because it scaffolds communication and coordination between dispersed actors, frequently working in different parts of the institution. The student number serves to assert that the identified person is a valid student within the boundaries of this organisation. As such, the possession of this token enrols this person in the rights associated with students at this institution. However, it also enrols the person in a series of consequent responsibilities such as to behave in a manner specified within the rules and regulations of the institution in question. Serious infringement of such institutional rules will probably enact the removal of this token from the identified person, which will scaffold some communication and coordination, such as a declaration of the person as an unfit person to be a student and consequent barring from student premises and activities.

Scaffolding Big Data

The cases of Durkheim's masterwork *Suicide* and counting COVID-19 discussed in Chapter 14 illustrate some key lessons arising from the scaffolding of data structures, which are relevant to a critique of many contemporary big data practices. All data is necessarily created in acts of articulation either by humans interacting with machines or by machines programmed to create data structures in particular ways. Much of the data generated in modern societies refers to humans and their actions and as such constitute institutional not physical facts. Within any act of articulation, implicit or explicit decisions are made about what to represent and how to represent it. Data is always an abstraction of the world (see Chapter 8) as we know it and created with a specific intention or purpose. Nevertheless, institutional data is always a social construction in that it relies upon the collective acceptance of what is significant as well as how to record it. The consequence of this is that the masses of data collected as institutional facts within big data applications should be treated with great care. Statisticians have always cautioned that any aggregation of data and the inferences drawn from such aggregation should be based on a careful understanding of the scaffolding of data — how data structures upon which the aggregation relies were created and for what purpose (Huff, 1954).

One of the key points we were trying to make in Chapter 14 is that data is not readily available to be collected, aggregated and analysed. Data has to be made by institutional actors following institutional practices. There is an adage which we can paraphrase as 'not everything that counts can be counted, and not everything that can be counted counts'. Take two contemporary examples of this. A hospital boasts that 100% of the patients that enter its doors have successful medical outcomes and it has medical records to prove this. However, this hospital rejects the sickest of patients. Likewise, a school boasts of the high academic achievement of its pupils in national examinations, but what if the school admits the only the brightest of pupils? So, are the hospital and school counting the right things here?

The whole point of course is that the articulation of data structures not only informs actors, but also leads them to perform. Making inferences (sometimes automatically) from large collections of institutional facts should be done judiciously and with great care because such facts are used to drive further action by institutional actors (McKinney and Niese, 2016).

Take the example of criminal records, which we considered in Chapter 3. Criminal records are created in acts of articulation — people deciding what is significant to represent as well as how to represent such significance. Hence, a given act of performance might be classified as an act of deviance through the creation of a certain data structure. Such data structures are later used as a resource within communicative acts. They are particularly used to communicate the belief (assertion) that a deviant act has taken place and on this basis to (declare) that somebody should be classified as a criminal or not. On the basis of this institutional scaffolding, certain persons make decisions and take action such as accepting or prohibiting someone from doing something — such as taking on a job as a teacher or a nurse.

So, a record created by one actor for one explicit purpose can be used by another actor for another purpose entirely, Wheeler (1969) argues, '...since individuals may accumulate records in several different locales, and since the records themselves may be transferred, records from various sources may be combined in myriad ways, often without the knowledge of the person whose fate they may be helping to determine'. Let us consider a scenario which illustrates this point. John is nine years old. He has been learning about alcohol abuse in one of his school lessons. John is a disruptive pupil in class, so his teacher holds a meeting with him to see if he needs extra support. In this meeting, John claims that his mother is an alcoholic; he also mentions that his father is in prison. When John is 14, he gets into a fight with some youths and he ends up with a caution from the police. Some 10 years later, John applies for a job with one of the UK central government agencies and supplies his national insurance number as part of this process. A background-screening program, which involves the sharing of data structures between government agencies, picks up on a history of alcohol abuse and criminal activity in his family. He does not get the job.

So, data structures are not only made by institutional actors, once they are made, they act independently of such actors, sometimes in ways not intended in the original act of creation. Cicourel (1974), for instance, in a series of studies conducted many decades ago, argues that the construction of official records by the police rely on practical knowledge and reasoning, particularly the use of everyday categories such as the 'strange', 'unusual', 'wrong', etc.

> 'How the day-to-day activities of the police, probation, and other officials associated with the courts or detention facilities produce information that becomes part of an official file on the juvenile … is not understandable without reference to the improvised but 'normal' rules and theories utilized by officials. The rules and theories … have their roots in common sense or folk typifications making up law-enforcement officials stock of knowledge' (Cicourel, 1974).

He further cautions about constructing rates of delinquency from police records without an understanding of the practical methods police officers use on the ground to categorise and record different types of delinquency: 'If the routine procedures and ideologies of police and probation officials filter juveniles into various categories and courses of action, then the researcher's construction of tables based upon structural information must reflect the typifications employed by officials'.

Criminal records rely on two key acts of articulation. First, the victim of a crime must be prepared to come forward and provide evidence of the crime. Second, a law enforcement officer must be prepared to open up a criminal record and classify the event accordingly. In many areas, these two acts are open to much variation. For instance, in cases of sexual assault, there is a known under-reporting of such crimes by victims. Even when such crimes are reported to law enforcement agencies, many such records are declared unfounded, signalling that no further investigation is required. This classification may be based on officers making practical judgements about the veracity of claims or the likelihood of future criminal prosecution. If law enforcement agencies have their performance measured in terms of ratios of crimes recorded to crimes solved, it makes sense for actors within such institutions to make practical judgements only to record as crimes those likely to be resolved.

This has much similarity with processes of white-listing and black-listing, which which we considered in Chapter 4 — the way in which contemporary institutions make life-critical decisions about individuals on the basis of inclusion or exclusion of personal identifiers on particular lists. Lists articulated in this manner are explicitly devices which serve to sort those persons regarded as 'eligible members' of a particular institutional area and to exclude others, regarded as in some way 'undesirable' (Lyon, 2004). However, such classification has practical consequences. This record-making frequently serves to reinforce existing structures of social and economic exclusion within society and the economy

Take the notion of a credit rating. The construct of a credit rating is typically formed from an aggregation of data recorded about a person's financial activity. However, this data is then typically used to make decisions that affect that person's future financial activity, such as access to loans. More worryingly still is the notion of *social credit*, which is developing as a data construct in certain countries around the world and which is reliant upon many big data practices. This amounts to monitoring people's online behaviour and scoring people's social as well as economic credit. Hence, for example, being friends with lowly rated social credit people might lower your social credit score to such an extent that algorithms prohibit you from doing things like obtaining certain state benefits.

Re-examining the Features of Big Data

In this section, we examine the key features of big data in terms of our understanding of the scaffolding of data structures. The features of data volume, data variety and data velocity are largely concerns of the mechanics of data. Modern technologies allow larger amounts of data of various structures to be stored and articulated rapidly. Larger here can mean data elements identifying all things within a target population or describing through attributes a vast number of features of something. Hence, all customers of a company might have data elements created which identify them while in the human genome project one person's entire genetic code would be described. In contrast, data resolution, data relatability, data flexibility, data indexicality and data exhaustivity are features that rely upon the intentionality associated with everyday and organisational actors taking action. These features, as we shall see, are hence subject very much to matters of social ontology.

Data resolution

Data resolution refers to the objective of big data applications being as detailed as possible. The issue of data resolution is often operationalised in terms of the notion of data granularity, which refers to the level of detail at which data is recorded. The greater the granularity of data, the deeper the level of detail. However, granularity is normally very much a social construct in most data applications. As we indicated previously, it is impossible to represent and store everything because representation (the act of creating some sign-vehicle) is necessarily a process of abstraction. It involves decisions made by institutional actors (people or machines) about what is appropriate and often feasible to represent as well as how to represent it. For instance, airlines may store details of your seating position on journeys but not your choice of meal. Clinicians may choose to classify your condition as type 1 diabetes but not to record aspects of your lifestyle. Parcel delivery companies are likely to identify delivery points based upon data at the level of post-code or zip-code, and not in terms of GPS coordinates. All these examples demonstrate the linkage between data and action. Institutional actors normally create facts at a certain level of detail to enable further action.

Data relatability

Data relatability refers to the objective that the data in one dataset should be relatable to that in other data sets. Because of the way in which data is stored within contemporary big data applications, the issue of data relatability is often problematic. This helps explain why in many accounts of the advantages of big data, the issue of data relatability appears to be the feature most open to sacrifice. To relate one data structure to another relies typically upon some institutional framing of not only what things can be referred to, but also what it is appropriate to associate, classify or aggregate (Chapter 8). For instance, it is normally deemed acceptable to associate a data structure containing details of a person's occupation to another data structure describing a person's health. It would not be appropriate to relate the occupational record to a data structure storing the eating habits of occupants of a zoological garden, even though records from such different institutions might contain common data such as personal names. In conventional data management, the issue of data relatability is resolved or realised in an information model. In essence, what we considered in Chapter 8 was the component elements of an information model. Such a model can be resolved into the data structures important to some institutional domain as well as the relationships between such structures. Such an information model, we have shown in previous work

(Beynon-Davies, 2017), is reliant upon an understanding of the communicative practices appropriate to some institutional domain, which is, of course, very much a matter of social ontology.

Data flexibility

Data flexibility refers to the objective that both the structure and size of data should be expandable easily and rapidly. However, ideas about how it might be appropriate to extend data both in structure and size (volume) is very much reliant upon aspects of social ontology. In terms of size, flexibility is clearly a function of data exhaustivity — how much data is needed to cover the entire population of 'things' that data is meant to represent. In terms of structure, flexibility is a function of granularity, how many data-items are needed to describe a 'thing' completely in terms of its properties or attributes. Therefore, both exhaustivity and flexibility rely upon an understanding of social ontology.

Constraints on flexibility and exhaustivity are often not a technological matter but imposed by social institutions. Hence, the idea of data protection restricts certain data being represented about the individual. As we covered in Chapter 9, there is an ongoing debate about what data should be collected about the individual and her activities as part of what Zuboff calls surveillance capitalism (see Chapter 12).

Data structure

Big data technologists frequently argue that the applications they build do not rely upon the notion of structure. To explain this a distinction is frequently made within the technological literature between structured and unstructured data. Examples cited of structured data are records stored in a relational database consisting of defined data elements with defined data-items. Examples cited of unstructured data are documents, emails, images and videos.

This distinction is somewhat artificial because all data to be data must have structure (see Chapter 2). All data must have structure in being formed from a consistently applied set of differences made in some substance. All data needs data structures for representation, storage and analysis. And all data must be structured in playing its part in the accomplishment of significance (semiosis) by institutional actors, whether such actors be people or machines.

So, an electronic document is likely to have a schema which defines its structure, and images have to be captured and stored using defined formats such as jpg or gif. What technologists are really doing here is making a distinction between levels of analysis that have to performed upon data to generate institutional facts. Within so-called structured data, a great deal of the ontology of the data is embedded within the way data is organised, and may even be defined systematically in some metadata. In contrast, within so-called unstructured data, work (sometimes significant work) must be performed on the data to re-engineer aspects of ontology.

Let us work through an example here to help explain this point. Take a simple data profile of the person — this can be represented as a record with data-items name, age, marital status, address, land-line telephone number and mobile phone number. To ask questions of this data, such as how old the person is or whether he is married, you merely must retrieve the value held in the data-item age or the data-item marital status. The way in which this data is organised reflects its overarching ontology.

Now imagine that this same data is represented as a piece of text, perhaps implemented as an email or an electronic text. This might consist of:

> [*John Doe is fifty-five years old. He lives on 24 Crawshay Street, Canton, Cardiff. John is married to Eileen and has four children. His land-line number is 029294563 and his mobile phone number is 0777643256*]

To ask the same questions of this piece of text (what is John's age and marital status) a great deal of prior analysis must be done on the text to derive implicit rather than explicit ontology. The program used to implement the questions must work out that things such as that the phrase 'fifty-five years old' refers to someone's age and that to live on somewhere indicates someone's place of residence. Therefore, the distinction between structured and unstructured data is not really about structure but about the level of existing ontology and analysis needed.

Data indexicality

Data indexicality refers to the objective that data is uniquely identifiable. Clearly indexicality relies upon the social notion of identification — the deemed relationship between some identifier and what it indexes (see Chapter 3). Things or objects that are regarded as distinct or unique from other things (identity) is fundamental to notions of existence. The idea of indexicality is one of the three fundamental modalities of a sign identified by Peirce — the other two being symbolism and iconicity. A sign is an index if the presence of the representamen co-occurs with the object either spatially or temporally but whose interpretant is reliant upon the context in which the sign is used. For instance, words such as *I*, *here* and *this* are typically indexical, relying upon who is using them and in what setting. Hence, what is indexical within any institutional domain is critically dependent on social ontology.

Data exhaustivity

Finally, data exhaustivity refers to the objective that whole populations of data, rather than samples of data, should be collected, stored and analysed. However, as we alluded to in Chapter 13, this notion of data exhaustivity relies upon the notion of what is considered a population and its proper extent.

Take the population of all British citizens. Clearly the population here relies upon the social construct of citizenship — who is deemed a member of some nation-state, such as the UK. However, as we have argued previously, citizenship is reliant upon a sophisticated scaffolding of data structures such as passports or identity cards (Chapter 4). Therefore, there is a circularity of referencing here in ideas of data exhaustivity. A population is defined in terms of the differences drawn amongst a group of objects, which in turn serves to define the data required to exhaustively cover the population.

However, and more critically if we take any data to be an act of creation by people or machines, then all data because of its basis within representation is inherently 'sampled'. As Kitchin (2014) states:

> '...though Big data may seek to be exhaustive, capturing a whole domain and providing full resolution, it is both a representation and a sample, shaped by the technology and the platform used, the data ontology employed and the regulatory environment, and it is subject to sampling bias. Indeed, all data provide oligoptic views of the world: views from certain standpoints, using particular tools, rather than an all-seeing, infallible God's eye view.'

This comment is really about the limitations of the correspondence view of data structures, which we have covered exhaustively in other parts of the book.

Conclusion

The key conclusion to be taken from this chapter is that dominant conceptions of what big data is relies upon an ontology based in a misconceived worldview of what data constitutes, particularly within institutional settings. We propose that if one examines applications of big data, the data within big data is not ontologically different from the data in small data. The datasets may be larger, have more variety in terms of source and structure and collected more rapidly than in the case of small data applications. However, the nature of data itself remains the same as do the challenges of its analysis (McKinney and Niese, 2016).

In previous chapters, we have argued that to provide any generic definition of what data is, we must engage with the notion of difference. Data are differences made in some substance by some actor that make a difference, in the sense of informing some other actor. This definition of data is consistent with the Peircean notion of a sign, which, in contrast to a Saussurian view of the sign, involves a triadic relation between the differences made in some substance (representamen), what makes a difference (object) and how this informs some actor (interpretamen).

However, there is a point to be made that ontologically data used to build physical facts are subtly different from data used to build institutional facts. As we have seen, much of Searle's (2010) theoretical edifice of social ontology relies upon the distinction and relationship between brute facts and institutional facts. The primary difference between a brute fact and institutional fact relies upon the different status that such facts have in relation to some theory of existence — some ontology.

Brute facts are independent of the observer because they represent material things and happenings within the physical world. Within a brute fact, the status of things referred to has an existence independent of institutions. In terms of an institutional domain, such as student placement, for instance, brute facts constitute the ontology of physical things such as human beings and their places of work. In contrast, institutional facts relative to the observer. Within an institutional fact, the status of the thing (or things) referred to depends upon a collective acceptance by the actors concerned that the thing has a certain function. This means that institutional facts exist only within the context of human institutions and are brought into existence through collective acceptance by actors within such institutions that certain things can be taken to stand for certain other things. Institutional facts are important because they serve to constitute the institutional domain itself as a social ontology. Institutional facts serve to constitute institutions and data structures scaffold processes of institutionalisation.

For instance, within the institutional practices of medical emergency response (Beynon-Davies, 2017), what constitutes or should constitute a patient and what constitutes a true emergency and thus a valid emergency incident is a continuous source of sense-making for participating actors. An emergency call only becomes a medical emergency and consequently an emergency incident through the ways in which actors such as paramedic dispatchers triage events. Just like the classification of an event as a suicide by a coroner, an emergency call only becomes the institutional fact of an emergency incident if it is deemed sufficiently 'serious' to warrant dispatch of an ambulance.

Big data began with and is still much used for the scaffolding of physical facts such as gene sequencing or the positioning of constellations. However, much of what is published about the promises of big data relates primarily to the scaffolding of institutional facts (McAfee and Brynjolfsson, 2012). In such domains, data cannot be separated from institutional practices of articulation, which include not only the creation of data structures, but also the aggregation of such data structures for analysis (Chapter 13). There are hence clear dangers in making inferences from aggregates and through algorithms that are opaque to inspection, where processes of articulation and sometimes communication are lost.

Our micro-analysis of the ontological foundations of big data presented here lends support to existing critiques of the developing assumptions on which the new data science is being built (Zuboff, 2015). For instance, there is a strong likelihood that the application of big data applications will not serve to disrupt societal infrastructure as is sometimes claimed by many data scientists (Mayer-Schonberger and Cukier, 2013). Instead, it will serve to preserve existing processes of institutionalisation already developing within societies globally. For instance, and as we have seen Chapter 13, Zuboff has demonstrated the way in which large tech companies employing big data institute practices of surveillance which have become normalised within society, but which infringe many traditional notions of the individual's right to privacy and self-determination.

References

Abbasi, A., S. Sarker and R. Chiang (2016). "Big Data Research in Information Systems: Toward an Inclusive Research Agenda." *Journal of the Association for Information Systems*, **17**(2). DOI: 10.17705/1jais.00423.

Beynon-Davies, P. (2017). "Declarations of Significance: Exploring the Pragmatic Nature of Information Models." *Information Systems Journal*, **28**(4): 612–613.

Cicourel, A. V. (1974). Police Practices and Official Records. In *Ethnomethodology: Selected Readings*. R. Turner (eds.) (Harmondsworth, UK: Penguin).

Collins, F. S., M. Morgan and A. Patrinos (2003). "The Human Genome Project: Lessons from Large-scale Biology." *Science*, **30**(5617): 286–290.

Constantinou, I. D. and J. Kallinikos (2015). "New Games, New Rules: Big Data and the Changing Context of Strategy." *Journal of Information Technology*, **30**: 44–57.

Gallaire, H. and G. Minker (1978). *Logic and Databases* (London: Plenum Press).

Huff, D. (1991). *How to Lie with Statistics* (London: Penguin).

Kent, W. (2012). *Data and Reality: A Timeless Perspective on Perceiving and Managing Information in Our Imprecise World* (Westfield, NJ: Technics Publication).

Kitchin, R. (2014). "Big Data, New Epistemologies and Paradigm Shifts." *Big Data and Society*, **April–June**: 1–12.

Kitchin, R. and G. McCardle (2016). "What makes Big Data, Big Data? Exploring the Ontological Characteristics of 26 Datasets." *Big Data and Society*, **January–June**: 1–10.

Lyon, D. (2004). *Identity Cards: Social Sorting by Database*, Internet Issue Brief No. 3 (Oxford University: Oxford Internet Institute).

Lyytinen, K. J. (1985). "Implications of Theories of Language for Information Systems." *MIS Quarterly*, **March**(9): 61–74.

Mayer-Schonberger, V. and K. Cukier (2013). *Big Data: The Essential Guide to Work, Life and Learning in the Age of Insight* (London: John Murray).

McAfee, A. and E. Brynjolfsson (2012). "Big Data: The Management Revolution." *Harvard Business Review*, **October**: 61–69.

McKinney, E. H. and B. D. Niese (2016). "Big Data Critical Thinking Skills for Analysts — Learning to Ask the Right Questions." *22nd Americas Conference on Information Systems*, San Diego, CA, USA.

Mingers, J. and L. Wilcocks (2017). "An Integrative Semiotic Methodology for IS Research." *Information and Organization*, **27**(1): 17–36.

Searle, J. R. (2010). *Making the Social World: The Structure of Human Civilization* (Oxford: Oxford University Press).

Wheeler, S. (Ed.) (1969). Problems and issues in record-keeping. In *On Record: Files and Dossiers in American Life* (Russell Sage Foundation, pp. 3–24).

Wyssusek, B. (2006). "On Ontological Foundations of Conceptual Modelling." *Scandinavian Journal of Information Systems*, **18**(1): 63–80.

Zuboff, S. (2015). "Big Other: Surveillance Capitalism and the Prospects of an Information Civilization." *Journal of Information Technology*, **30**: 75–89.

Epilogue

An institution is a data structure's way of making another data structure.

Revisiting Our Aims

I have been engaging with issues of data, its use and effects for over 40 years. My doctoral research focussed on the better handling of masses of textual data in a time before the World Wide Web. I then spent some years as a technologist concerned with building software infrastructure to manage burgeoning amounts and a myriad of different forms of healthcare data. Having moved back into academia, my attention in teaching, research and consultancy turned to the technologies of databases and database management systems, the methods of modelling data and the synergies between databases and a branch of AI known at the time as expert systems. More recently, I have moved somewhat away from a pure focus on technology to what I hope is a deeper and more enlightened outlook on data. Over two decades ago, I became interested in the strange questions of why we have data in the first place, what does data do in practice for us and why do people often experience problems with data, even in the age of mass communication and ubiquitous technology. Answers to these questions were not easy to come by and so in attempt to achieve some clarity I had to look to areas beyond my original technological area of expertise. From a quite prolonged period of searching amongst diverse literature, I have come to some firm conclusions about what I believe to be some of the fundamental properties and consequences of this mysterious stuff we call *data*. This book is an attempt to impart what I have learned.

It soon became apparent to me that to examine closely the nature of data you must focus upon the mechanics of data — how data is formed and articulated in data structures. Starting from such first principles as bedrock, it then becomes possible to explain how much of the institutional infrastructure of contemporary society is built directly upon an infrastructure of data structures. We have tried in this book to develop a theory of data structures that better explains their critical place within societies, increasingly on the global scale. Data structures are a human invention that date back to our prehistory and appear to mirror the rise of other human inventions such as agriculture and the state. Perhaps because of their long history as background infrastructure within society (a term we have used to also encompass the economy and polity) we have all become overly complacent in their consideration. They are treated as mundane artefacts with little influence upon our everyday existence beyond representing things such as people, places, happenings (times) and products. And, as such, we have become somewhat complacent in the use of such artefacts. We increasingly build technological artefacts upon this infrastructure without seeking to critically examine the nature of this exercise.

The Central Theory

Let us summarise the central backbone of theory that we have developed within this book. The overall purpose of such theory is to provide better explanations of the linkages between data (structures) and society. Within various chapters we have demonstrated how such theory helps us unpack, in a much clearer way, not only the numerous benefits that data structures hold for institutions, but also the difficulties inherent in the very notion of a data structure.

Information situations

The fundamental principle is that the place of data structures within society can only be understood within the wider information situations (Figure E.1) in which data structures play a key role. Information

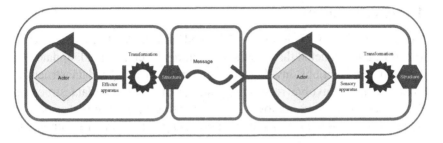

Figure E.1:   Our model of information situations.

situations consist of three fundamental and coupled domains of action: articulation, communication and coordination. These three domains provide different lenses with which to view the nature of data structures.

The formative aspect of a data structure

Articulation is action directed at the *formative* aspect of a data structure — the physical form that a data structure takes. Data comprises differences made in some physical substance. The making of such differences by one or more actors is what we mean by articulation. Actors articulate physical substance to form structures using their effector apparatus. Some of these structures are data structures.

Data structures

A data structure is a form for organising data. A data structure is a form created in some substance that serves to inform and perform. The structure in a data structure is typically hierarchical. Data structures consist of data elements, which in turn consist of data-items. Data structures may be persistent or non-persistent, depending upon the substance in which differences are made. This difference in form triggers a number of consequential differences in the ways in which data structures can be used within information situations. There are certain advantages to the use of persistent data structures, which include that these externalised objects can be manipulated by multiple actors, at different places and at different times. This turns individual memory into collective or social memory.

Acts of articulation

The domain of articulation can be defined in terms of four basic acts of transformation enacted through data structures — create, read, update and delete. Create actions involve encoding new data in a data structure. Update actions involve recoding existing data within a data structure. Delete actions involve removing some existing data structure or part of from existence. Read actions involve decoding data from an existing data structure.

The life history of data structures

Data structures have a life history within their institutional setting. Data structures are created by somebody to do something. However, once data structures are created, they are likely to be updated and read by many different actors. Finally, they are either removed from existence or stored away in archives. It is likely that many different actors within any one institutional domain will articulate the same data structure over its life, sometimes for different purposes.

The informative aspect of a data structure

Communication is action directed at the *informative* aspect of a data structure. The form of some physical structure is sensed by the sensory apparatus of one or more actors. The sensed physical state of structures serves to communicate, through acquired conventions, some message to such actors. These actions take place in what we refer to as the communication domain. A message produced through any communicative act has both content and intent. The content of a message consists of things identified and described. The intent of a communicative act is to assert, commit, direct, express or declare something to one or more actors.

The performative aspect of a data structure

Many information situations are driven by coordination problems. A coordination problem occurs when two or more actors have a purpose or goal in common that must be achieved through joint action. Coordination problems are typically resolved through conventions of action, which couple articulation of data structures with certain communicative conventions, which in turn are associated with conventions of activity. Coordination is action directed at the *performative* aspect of a data structure. Messages act as stimulus to activity in fulfilment of joint goals, which typically involves the transformation of some further structures by actors. Some of these transformed structures may be further data structures.

Cycle of enactment

Acts of coordination, communication and articulation are coupled, meaning that in practice, acts of coordination contained within a coherent pattern of institutional activity are closely coupled to a parallel stream of communication and articulation. Without such coupling, the effective coordination of the activity of a multitude of dispersed actors would not be possible. Therefore, articulation, communication and coordination form a continuous cycle of enactment — which we have referred to elsewhere as the enactment of significance (Beynon-Davies, 2011).

In unpacking information situations in this manner, one might think our scheme somewhat contrived. 'But surely everything is action?' you might say. Why do we need this distinction between coordination, communication and articulation as action?

The three types of act may seem on the surface to be the same, but note some differences. First, there is a difference in the actors enacting various acts. Any communication, for instance, must necessarily involve one actor creating data and another actor reading data. Second, there is a necessary time delay between the act of intending to form some data, forming the data, sensing the data, interpreting the data, and deciding to further act upon it. Performing (coordination), forming (articulation) and informing (communication) are necessarily distinct but interlinked processes. Each such process may take a second, a minute, an hour, days or possibly even weeks. For instance, the act of creating a record may take place some weeks before this record may be read and acted upon, potentially also by a different actor than the one who created it.

Scaffolding institutions

Our major claim is that, through this cycle in which actors enact information situations, institutional ontology is scaffolded. This analogy of data structures as scaffolding is one in which the articulation of data structures forms the baseplate or 'load-bearing' component. Various 'tubes' of communication are coupled to this baseplate and in turn various 'tubes' of coordinated action are coupled onto 'tubes' of communication.

Institutional facts

Data structures take central place in the way in which institutions and society at large form order through the construction of facts that declare states of the world. Data structures, data elements and data-items are used to build both physical facts and institutional facts. Data-items are status functions that act as placeholders for values. The value of some data-item (X) counts as some physical or institutional thing. Institutional facts not only represent things, but also bring such things into existence for institutions. Various things can be instituted in such manner through data structures, including persons, places, products, times (events), and digital presence.

Deontology of data structures

Within our account of the ways in which data structures scaffold institutional order, we have inherently thought of status functions or signs in three distinct ways. Status functions or signs act as things referring to other things, as things describing or predicating other things and as things prescribing (or proscribing) action-responses by actors to certain things. This means that data structures not only build ontology, they have deontology. Data structures are used to prescribe what actors can do but also proscribe or prevent actors from doing certain things.

Breakdowns with data structures

Breakdowns are an inherent consequence of the ways in which data structures scaffold institutional ontology. As institutional scaffolding, there are a number of ways in which data structures can breakdown, including identifying the wrong things, describing things inappropriately, asserting things that cannot be confirmed, committing to things that never happen and directing people to do the wrong things. These instances of breakdown can be understood in relation to a certain brittleness in the institutional coupling between articulation and communication as well as the coupling between communication to coordination.

Three Examples

The central claim made in this book is that information situations, having the component parts illustrated in Figure E.1, are universal across all areas of institutional activity; those that have occurred in the past, those happening in the present and those that are likely to happen in the near future. Take three examples of such information situations from different settings and situated in the past, present and future.

Figure E.2 illustrates how bed management was enacted in the intensive care unit of an Australian hospital prior to computerisation (Lederman and Johnston, 2017). Here, a ward nurse articulates a coloured, magnetic token in relation to a magnetic whiteboard. The state of the whiteboard records the current state of action in relation to bed management on an intensive care unit. The positioning of this token upon the whiteboard is read by another actor, namely another ward nurse, and it informs her to move (admit) a patient to a designated bed for treatment. The patient is then moved to the requisite bed.

Figure E.3 illustrates an information situation situated within a current area of commercial activity — that of supermarket retail over the

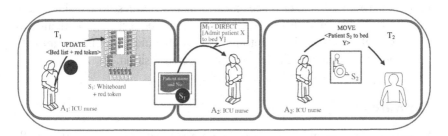

Figure E.2:   An information situation from healthcare.

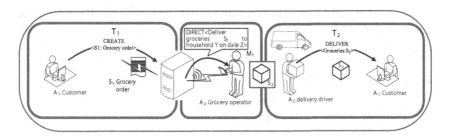

Figure E.3:   An information situation from online grocery.

Figure E.4:   An information situation from driverless cars.

Internet and web — sometimes referred to as online grocery (Beynon-Davies, 2017). Here a customer creates an online grocery order on some digital commerce website. This order communicates to some grocery operator to pack and deliver the indicated groceries to a specified location on a specified date. This triggers a grocery delivery to the customer by another actor, namely a delivery driver.

Finally, Figure E.4 illustrates an information situation in the near future where driverless electric cars may be shared amongst a pool of passengers in a large urban area such as metropolitan London. In this scenario, a carpool passenger places a car transport request to the shared car indicating pickup and drop off locations. This request communicates to the car itself, causing it to automatically schedule the journey into its movements and execute the trip in the directed fashion.

Domains

However, we make no claims for the completeness of our coverage with this theory. Because of the way in which data structures are so embedded within institutional life, it is impossible to cover in one book all the ramifications of the linkage between data (structures) and society. Within the current work we have touched upon the following domains in which data structures have an important part to play:

- The formation of collective memory.
- The enactment of personal identity.
- The listing and sorting of persons and things.
- The debate over ownership of data.
- The role of data in the distribution and exercise of power.
- The importance of controlling the articulation of data.

- The ways in which data is used to build institutional ontology.
- The importance of ensuring the privacy of personal data through data protection legislation.
- The way in which data control is a practical response to the need to create and maintain an architecture of deontology in relation to the life of data structures.
- The ways in which data drive automated decision-making by software actors.
- The infrastructure of data supporting commerce.
- The need to base the design of data structures in a detailed understanding of institutional ontology.
- The important place metadata takes in scaffolding inter-institutional ontology.
- The basis of data aggregation and inference in the making of data structures.
- The centrality of data in acts of surveillance.
- The place of data in continuous inquiry, the securing of justified belief and the execution of effective civic action.
- The importance of data to both the making and execution of effective policy.
- Data as the base plate in contemporary technologies such as big data and machine learning.
- The prospects for a better-informed data science.

However, in a way, we have only touched upon the tip of an iceberg in this current work. Data will continue to be both essential and problematic to the ways in which societies develop into the future. Let us briefly outline some important scenarios that demand closer examination.

Richard Buckminster Fuller, the 20th century American polymath, is best known for his invention of the geodesic dome. However, Fuller believed that design was an attitude or orientation needed to confront some of humankind's greatest problems. Such problems are sometimes referred to as the grand challenges of our age — such as increasing population, feeding the planet, managing water resources, reducing inequality and tackling climate change. Buckminster Fuller believed that a design orientation is important because the solutions to many such problems demand that we organise ourselves differently — such as reorganising our patterns of water conservation and consumption as one way of better managing our finite source of freshwater. Therefore, the key message here is that whenever we change our ways of doing things such as this, we inherently design. Within this book, we have tried to the make the case for considering data, and more precisely data structures, as a crucial element of all forms of organisation. Hence, if we are to change our ways of organising, we will inevitably have to better engage with the design of data and the structures within which they deliver agency.

Thus if there is one thing you can take away from reading this book, it is that data is important because it is critical to effective action. This is clearly evident in the way data has proven important in managing the COVID-19 pandemic (see Chapter 14). It might be argued that many of the deleterious consequences of the blunt instruments of national and local lockdowns might have been avoided if a more effective system of tracking and tracing infected individuals through their social networks was available earlier within Western countries. The COVID-19 virus, just like any virus, shows no respect for national borders. The data which attempted to map the transmission of the virus is typically collected within nation-states but clearly also needs to cross borders. But this, of course, demands that international standards for the classification of the objects and classes relevant to this institutional ontology and their instantiation within data structures are agreed and implemented.

As we indicated in Chapter 11, data-driven software actors are already ubiquitous in many institutional domains. Many important decisions that affect us all are delegated to such artificial actors. However, the transparency of both the data used by such actors and the decision-making which this data drives is open to question. We clearly need not only better ways of making the information situations utilised by such data-driven actors transparent, but also a better understanding of the role that such data-driven actors play within society at large. The aim is clearly not to remove such actors from institutional action but to better design and evaluate such actors and the data they rely upon.

If data science is to become a true and effective science of this wondrous stuff we call data, then it must not focus solely upon the wonders of articulation exercised through information technologies. It must not take the nature of data for granted but examine closely what this fundamental stuff it deals with actually is. Our exploration within this book leads us to believe that this would undoubtedly cause a reframing of the ways in which data science is conceived and conducted. For instance, as we indicated in Chapter 9, data by its very nature is never neutral and is always contested since it reflects our viewpoints and prejudices — both our understanding and engagement with the world. Data is always a reflection of how we choose to chunk up the world and why we push one categorisation of things rather than another. This does not mean that we ignore the fact that data is essential because it is a critical resource with which to organise ourselves better. It merely means that we both think of, create and work with data structures with some model of information situations in mind. It means that we always have to design and operate data structures with clear intentions to do things — *to make a difference with differences.*

An Institution Is...

So, to end, let us return to the sensebreaking exercise we set in the Prologue. If you remember, we came up with a curious adage there — that *an institution is a data structure's way of making another data structure.* This is actually an adaptation of an earlier quote by the pioneer of zoosemiotics (the study of animal communication) — Thomas Sebeok (1972) — who placed at the centre of this discipline the idea that '[Life is] is only a sign's way of making another sign.' As we hinted at in the Prologue and considered in more detail in Chapter 15, anyone with a basic understanding of human biology would now acknowledge that the constitutive element of life — DNA — could be regarded as a sign with the implicit purpose of creating more signs of life — more DNA.

In Chapter 12, we referred to Richard Dawkins' (1976) notion of a replicator, with which he characterised the notion of both a gene and a meme. Replicators need only last long enough (longevity) to produce additional replicators (fecundity) that retain structure intact (fidelity) through the process of replication. We have argued throughout this book that just as DNA is the primary biological replicator, data structures, as collections of signs or semes, are key replicators within institutional domains.

Traditionally, data structures are treated as merely *mirrors* of institutional life — reflecting back to institutions, or more precisely to actors within such institutions, what has happened, what is happening and sometimes even what is likely to happen. It is presumed through this that data structures *correspond* to the institutional reality they represent. However, the term *represent,* as we saw in Chapter 1, does not do full justice to the role data structures play within institutions. Data structures not only record what has happened, is happening or will happen — they make things happen and, in this sense, scaffold the very notion of institution.

Data structures scaffold institutional action, but such action inevitably serves to recreate data structures in the sense that institutional activity of any form generates lots and lots of data structures. Without such data structures, the institution would cease to operate effectively and in certain circumstances would cease to exist. So, *an institution is a data structure's way of making more data structures.*

This book was written in the year 2020 in the midst of the COVID-19 pandemic. In North America someone with perfect eyesight is said to have 20/20 vision — in Europe we have a much more boring 6/6 denotation of perfect vision. These figures relate to letter charts used in standard eye-tests by optometrists. The first number refers to the distance at which a chart is viewed (20 feet or 6 metres) and the bottom number refers to the distance at which a person with perfect eyesight can see each letter on the chart clearly. Therefore, a record of 20/20 vision is a sign of perfect vision. Perhaps we can hope that our collective experience of the year 2020 will cause a change in how we envision our future — that the year 2020 will provide us all with a 20/20 vision for the future. We very much agree with Shoshana Zuboff (2019), who recently wrote, 'If the digital future is to be our home, then it is we who must make it so'. This book has been an attempt to provide greater clarity to questions that relate data to society, which is only one of the many stepping stones we will need to travel into a digital future where we can all feel at home.

Paul Beynon-Davies
Rhondda, South Wales
April 2021

References

Beynon-Davies, P. (2011). *Significance: Exploring the Nature of Information, Systems and Technology* (Houndmills, Basingstoke: Palgrave).

Beynon-Davies, P. (2017). "Characterising Business Models for Digital Business as Patterns." *International Journal of Electronic Commerce*, **22**(1): 98–124.

Dawkins, R. (1976). *The Selfish Gene* (Oxford: Oxford University Press).

Lederman, R. and R. B. Johnston (2011). "Decision Support or Support for Situated Choice: Lessons for System Design From Effective Manual Systems." *European Journal of Information Systems*, **20**(5): 510–528.

Sebeok, T. A. (1972). *Perspectives in Zoosemiotics* (The Hague: Mouton).

Zuboff, S. (2019). *The Age of Surveillance Capitalism* (London: Profile Books).

Bibliography

Abbasi, A., S. Sarker and R. Chiang (2016). 'Big Data Research in Information Systems: Toward an Inclusive Research Agenda.' *Journal of the Association for Information Systems*, **17**(2). DOI: 10.17705/1jais.00423.

Agerfalk, P. J. and O. Eriksson (2011). The Stolen Identifier: An Inquiry Into the Nature of Indentification and the Ontological Status of Information Systems. *International Conference on Information Systems*, Shanghai.

Aldridge, A. J. (2010). GCHQ: *The Uncensored Story of Britain's Most Secret Intelligence Agency* (London: Harper Press).

Ascher, M. and R. Ascher (1997). *Mathematics of the Incas: Code of the quipu* (New York: Dover Publications).

Ashby, W. R. (1956). *An Introduction to Cybernetics* (London: Chapman Hall).

Ashcraft, K. L., T. R. Kuhn and F. Cooren (2009). 'Constitutional Amendments: 'Materializing' Organizational Communication.' *The Academy of Management Annals*, **3**(1): 1–64.

Austin, J. H. and C. Y. David (2002). 'Biometric Authentication: Assuring Access to Information.' *Information Management and Computer Security*, **10**(1): 12–19.

Axelrod, R. (2006). *The Evolution of Cooperation*. Revised edition (New York: Perseus Publishing).

Bagwell, P. S. (1968). *The Railway Clearing House in the British Economy 1842–1922* (London: Allen and Unwin).

Baskerville, R. L., M. D. Myers and Y. Youngjin (2019). 'Digital First: The Ontological Reversal and New Challenges for IS Research.' *Management Information Systems Quarterly*, **44**(2): 509–523.

Bateson, G. (1972). *Steps to an Ecology of Mind* (New York: Ballantine Books).

Beniger, J. R. (1986). *The Control Revolution: Technological and Economic Origins of the Information Society* (Cambridge, MA: Harvard University Press).

Beynon-Davies, P. (2007). 'Informatics and the Inca.' *International Journal of Information Management,* **27**(5): 306–318.

Beynon-Davies, P. (2007). 'Personal Identity Management and Electronic Government: The Case of the National Identity Card in the UK.' *Journal of Enterprise Information Management,* **20**(3): 244–270.

Beynon-Davies, P. (2009). 'Neolithic Informatics: The Nature of Information.' *International Journal of Information Management,* **29**(1): 3–14.

Beynon-Davies, P. (2011a). *Significance: Exploring the Nature of Information, Systems and Technology* (Houndmills, Basingstoke: Palgrave).

Beynon-Davies, P. (2011b). 'The UK National Identity Card.' *Journal of Information Technology (teaching cases),* **1**(1): 12–21.

Beynon-Davies, P. (2011c). 'Information on the Prairie: Signs, Systems and Prairie Dogs.' *International Journal of Information Management,* **31**(3): 307–316.

Beynon-Davies, P. (2015) 'Forming Institutional Order: The Scaffolding of Lists and Identifiers.' *Journal of the Association for Information Science and Technology.* DOI: 10.1002/asi.23613.

Beynon-Davies, P. (2017a). 'Characterising Business Models for Digital Business as Patterns.' *International Journal of Electronic Commerce,* **22**(1): 98–124.

Beynon-Davies, P. (2017b). 'Declarations of Significance: Exploring the Pragmatic Nature of Information Models.' *Information Systems Journal,* **28**(4): 612–613.

Beynon-Davies, P. (2021). *Business Analysis and Design: Understanding Innovation in Organisation* (London: Palgrave).

Beynon-Davies, P. and R. Lederman (2016a). 'Making Sense of Visual Management Through Affordance Theory.' *Production Planning and Control,* **28**(2): 142–157. DOI 10.1080/09537287.2016.1243267.

Beynon-Davies, P. and R. Lederman (2016b). 'Theorising Visual Management Through Affordance Theory.' *Production Planning and Control.*

Beynon-Davies, P. and Y. Wang (2016c). 'Deconstructing Information Sharing.' *International Conference on Information Systems,* Association for Information Systems. Dublin, Eire.

Beynon-Davies, P. and Y. Wang (2019). 'Deconstructing Information Sharing.' *Journal of the Association for Information Systems* 20(4). DOI: 10.17705/1. jais.00541.

Black, E. (2002). *IBM and the Holocaust* (New York: Crown Publishers).

Blackmore, S. (1999). *The Meme Machine* (Oxford: Oxford University Press).

Bødker, S. and K. Grønbæk (1991). 'Co-operative Prototyping: Users and Designers in Mutual Activity.' *International Journal of Man-Machine Studies,* **34**: 453–478.

Boland, R. J. (1987). The In-formation of Information Systems. In *Critical Issues in Information Systems Research.* R. J. Boland and R. A. Hirschheim (eds.) (New York: John Wiley), pp. 363–394.

Bowker, G. and S. Leigh-Star (1999). *Sorting Things Out: Classification and its Consequences* (Cambridge, MA: MIT Press).

Brachman, R. J. (1983). 'What ISA Is and Isn't: An Analysis of Taxonomic Links in Semantic Networks.' *Computer*, **16**(10): 30–36.

Briggs, A. (2011). *Secret Days: Codebreaking in Bletchley Park: A Memoir of Hut Six and the Enigma Machine* (London: Frontline Books).

Brunt, R. (2006). 'Special Documentation Systems at the Government Code and Cypher School, Bletchley Park, during the Second World War.' *Intelligence and National Security*, **21**(1): 129–148.

Cicourel, A. V. (1974). Police Practices and Official Records. In *Ethnomethodology: Selected Readings*. R. Turner (eds.) (Harmondsworth, UK: Penguin).

Clarke, R. (1987). 'Just Another Piece of Plastic In Your Wallet: The 'Australian Card' scheme.' *Computers and Society*, **18**(1): 7–21.

Clarke, R. (1994). 'Human Identification in Information Systems: Management Challenges and Public Policy Issues.' *Information Technology and People*, **7**(4): 6–37.

Coase, R. H. (1937). 'The Nature of the Firm.' *Economica*, **4**(16): 386–405.

Cohen, M. (2005). *Wittgenstein's Beetle and Other Classic Thought Experiments* (Oxford, UK: Blackwell).

Cole, S. A. (2001). *Suspect Identities: A History of Fingerprinting and Criminal Identification* (Cambridge, MA: Harvard University Press).

Collins, F. S., M. Morgan and A. Patrinos (2003). 'The Human Genome Project: Lessons From Large-Scale Biology.' *Science,* **30**(5617): 286–290.

Conklin, W. J. (2002). A Khipu Information String Theory. In *Narrative Threads: Accounting and ecounting in Andean Khipu*. J. Quilter and G. Urton (eds.) (Austin, TX: University of Texas Press), pp. 53–86.

Constantinou, I. D. and J. Kallinikos (2015). 'New Games, New Rules: Big Data and the Changing Context of Strategy.' *Journal of Information Technology*, **30**: 44–57.

Cooren, F. (2004). 'Textual Agency: How Texts Do Things In Organisational Settings.' *Organization*, **11**(3): 373–393.

Copeland, J. B. (2004). *The Essential Turing* (Oxford: Oxford University Press).

D'Altroy, T. N. (2002). *The Incas* (Oxford: Basil Blackwell).

Darwin, C. (1998). *The Expression of Emotions in Man and Animals*. 3rd edition (Oxford: Oxford University Press).

Dawkins, R. (1976). *The Selfish Gene* (Oxford: Oxford University Press).

Dennett, D. C. (1996). *Kinds of Minds: Towards an Understanding of Consciousness* (London: Weidenfield and Nicholson).

Derrida, J. (1971). 'Signature, Event, Context.' A communication to the Congres Internationale des Societes de Philosophie de Langue Francaise. Montreal, Canada.

DOI (2014). *The Digital Object Identifier System Handbook.*

Dunbar, R. (2010). *How Many Friends Does One Person Need? Dunbar's Number and Other Evolutionary Quirks* (London: Faber and Faber).

Durkheim, E. (1976). *Suicide: A Study in Sociology* (New York: Free Press).

Eco, U. (1977). *A Theory of Semiotics* (London: Macmillan).

Eco, U. (2009). *The Infinity of Lists* (New York: MacLehose Press).

Ekman, P. and W. V. Friesen (1971). 'Constants Across Cultures in the Face and Emotion.' *Journal of Personality and Social Psychology*, **17**(2): 124–129.

Eriksson, O. and P. J. Agerfalk (2010). 'Rethinking the Meaning of Identifiers in Information Infrastructures.' *Journal of the Association for Information Systems*, **11**(8): 433–454.

Ezzamel, M. (2009). 'Order and Accounting as a Performative Ritual: Evidence from Ancient Egypt.' *Accounting, Organizations and Society*, **34**: 348–380.

Flores, F. and J. Ludlow (1980). Doing and Speaking in the Office. In *Decision Support Systems: Issues and Challenges*. G. Fick and R. H. Sprague (eds.) (Oxford: Pergamon Press), pp. 95–118.

Forsyth, F. (2011). *The Day of the Jackal* (London: Arrow).

Gallaire, H. and G. Minker (1978). *Logic and Databases* (London: Plenum Press).

Galsworth, G. D. (1997). *Visual Systems: Harnessing the Power of the Visual Workplace* (New York: AMACOM).

Garfinkel, H. (1967). *Studies in Ethnomethodology* (Englewood Cliffs, NJ: Prentice-Hall).

Gawande, A. (2010). *The Checklist Manifesto: How To Get Things Right* (New York: Profile Books).

Giddens, A. (1984). *The Constitution of Society: Outline of a Theory of Structuration* (Cambridge, UK: Polity Press).

Goldkuhl, G. and K. Lyytinen (1982). 'A Language Action View of Information Systems.' *International Conference on Information Systems*, C. Ross and M. Ginzberg (eds.). (Ann Arbor, MI), pp. 13–31.

Goody, J. (1977). *The Domestication of the Savage Mind* (Cambridge, MA: Cambridge University Press).

Gramsci, A. (2005). *Selections From the Prison Notebooks* (New York: Lawrence and Wishart).

Grief, M. (1991). *The Visual Factory: Building Participation Through Shared Information* (Portland, OR: Productivity Press).

Habermas, J. (1998). *On the Pragmatics of Communication* (Cambridge, MA: MIT Press).

Higham, N. J. (1993). 'The Domesday Survey: Context and Purpose.' *History*, **78**(253): 7–21.

Hobart, M. E. and Z. S. Schiffman (1998). *Information Ages: Literacy, Numeracy and the Computer Revolution* (London: John Hopkins University Press).

Hoopes, J. (ed.) (1991). *Peirce on Signs: Writings On Semiotic By Charles Sanders Peirce* (London: University of North Carolina Press).

Houser, N. and C. Kloesel (eds.) (1992). *The Essential Peirce: Selected Philosophical Writings* (Bloomington, US: Indiana University Press).

Huff, D. (1991). *How to Lie with Statistics* (London: Penguin).

Keneally, T. (1983). *Schindler's Ark* (London: Coronet).

Kent, W. (2012). *Data and Reality: A Timeless Perspective on Perceiving and Managing Information in our Imprecise World* (Westfield, NJ: Technics Publication).

Kitchin, R. (2014). 'Big Data, New Epistemologies and Paradigm Shifts.' *Big Data and Society*, **April–June**: 1–12.

Kitchin, R. and G. McCardle (2016). 'What Makes Big Data, Big Data? Exploring the Ontological Characteristics of 26 Datasets.' *Big Data and Society*, **January–June**: 1–10.

Latour, B. (2005). *Reassembling the Social: An Introduction to Actor-Network-Theory* (Oxford: Oxford University Press).

Lauer, J. (2020, January). 'Plastic Surveillance: Payments Cards and the History of Transactional Data, 1888 to Present.' *Big Data and Society*, 1–14. DOI: 10.1177/2053951720907632.

Le Guin, U. (1993). *The Earthsea Quartet* (London: Puffin Books).

Leavitt, D. (2007). *The Man Who Knew Too Much: Alan Turing and the Invention of the Computer* (New York: W.W. Norton).

Lederman, R. and R. B. Johnston (2011). 'Decision Support or Support for Situated Choice: Lessons for System Design From Effective Manual Systems.' *European Journal of Information Systems*, **20**(5): 510–528.

Lewis, D. (2002). *Convention: A Philosophical Study* (Oxford: Blackwell).

Lyon, D. (1994). *The Electronic Eye: The Rise of Surveillance Society* (Cambridge, MA: Polity Press).

Lyon, D. (2004). 'Identity Cards: Social Sorting by Database.' *Internet Issue Brief No. 3*, Oxford Internet Institute, Oxford University.

Lyon, D. (2009). *Identifying Citizens: ID Cards as Surveillance* (Cambridge, MA: Polity Press).

Lyytinen, K. J. (1985). 'Implications of Theories of Language for Information Systems.' *MIS Quarterly*, **9**: 61–74.

Lyytinen, K. J. and R. Hirscheim (1988). 'Information Systems As Rational Discourse: An Application of Habermas's Theory of Communicative Action.' *Scandinavian Journal of Information Systems*, **2**(1/2): 19–29.

Mann, C. M. (2005). 'Unravelling Khipu's Secrets: Researchers Move Towards Understanding the Communicative Power of the Inca's Enigmatic Knotted Strings Which Wove An Empire Together.' *Science*, **309**(5737): 1008–1010.

March, S. T. and G. A. Allen (2014). 'Toward a Social Ontology for Conceptual Modeling.' *Communications of the AIS*, **30**(70): 57–62.

Marshack, A. (2003). *The Art and Symbols of Ice Age Man. Communication in History: Technology, Culture and Society* (Boston: Pearson Education).

Mattesich, R. (1989). 'Accounting and the Input-Output Principle in the Prehistoric and Ancient World.' *ABACUS*, **25**(2): 74–84.

Mayer-Schonberger, V. and K. Cukier (2013). *Big Data: The Essential Guide to Work, Life and Learning in the Age of Insight* (London: John Murray).

Mcafee, A. and E. Brynjolfsson (2012). 'Big Data: The Management Revolution.' *Harvard Business Review*, **October**: 61–69.

McKay, S. (2011). *The Secret Life of Bletchley Park: The History of the Wartime Codebreaking Centre by the Men and Women Who Were There* (London: Aurum Press).

Mckinney, E. H. and B. D. Niese (2016). Big Data Critical Thinking Skills For Analysts — Learning To Ask The Right Questions. *22nd Americas Conference on Information Systems*, San Diego, CA, USA.

McKinsey (2009). Hal Varian on how the Web challenges managers. 1 January, McKinsey Consulting.

Meehan, A. J. (1986). 'Record-Keeping Practices in the Policing of Juveniles.' *Journal of Contemporary Ethnography*, **15**(1): 70–102.

Millikan, R. G. (1984). *Language, Thought and Other Biological Categories: New Foundations for Realism* (Cambridge, MA: MIT Press).

Mingers, J. (2001). 'Embodying Information Systems: The Contribution of Phenomenology.' *Information and Organization*, **11**(2): 103–127.

Mingers, J. and L. Wilcocks (2017). 'An Integrative Semiotic Methodology for IS Research.' *Information and Organization*, **27**(1): 17–36.

Morris, C. W. (1946). *Signs, Language and Behavior* (New York: Prentice-Hall).

Noth, W. (1990). *Handbook of Semiotics* (Indiana: Indiana University Press).

Orlikowski, W. J. (2006). 'Material Knowing: The Scaffolding of Human Knowledgeability.' *European Journal of Information Systems*, **15**(5): 460–466.

Preda, A. (1999). 'The Turn to Things: Arguments for a Sociology of Things.' *The Sociological Quarterly*, **40**(2): 347–366.

Ravilious, K. (2010). 'The Writing on the Cave Wall.' *New Scientist*, **2748**: 12–14.

Rekisteripooli (2003). Base Registers in Finland. Helsinki.

Rosch, E. H. (1973). 'Natural Categories.' *Cognitive Psychology*, **4**(3): 328–350.

Rose, J., M. Jones and D. Truex (2005). 'Socio-Theoretic Accounts of IS: The Problem of Agency.' *Scandinavian Journal of Information Systems*, **17**(1): 133–152.

Rosenberg, D. and A. Grafton (2010). *Cartographies of Time* (New York: Princeton Architectural Press).

Rudgley, R. (1999). *The Lost Civilisations of the Stone Age* (New York: Simon and Schuster).

Russell, B. (1959). *Wisdom of the West: a Historical Survey of Western Philosophy in its Social and Political Setting* (Oxford: Bloomsbury).

Schmandt-Besserat, D. (1978). 'The Earliest Precursor of Writing.' *Scientific American*, **238**(6): 50–59.

Schmandt-Besserat, D. (1992). *Before Writing* (Austin, TX: The University of Texas Press).

Schmandt-Besserat, D. (1996). *How Writing Came About* (Austin, TX: The University of Texas Press).

Searle, J. R. (1970). *Speech Acts: An Essay in the Philosophy of Language* (Cambridge, UK: Cambridge University Press).

Searle, J. R. (1983). *Intentionality: An Essay in the Philosophy of Mind* (Cambridge, UK: Cambridge University Press).

Searle, J. R. (1995). *The Construction of Social Reality* (London: Penguin).

Searle, J. R. (2005). 'What is an Institution?' *Journal of Institutional Economics*, **1**(1): 1–22.

Searle, J. R. (2006). 'Social Ontology: Some Basic Principles.' *Anthropological Theory*, **6**(1): 12–29.

Searle, J. R. (2007). Social Ontology: The Problem and Steps Toward a Solution. In *Intentional Acts and Institutional Facts: Essays on John Searle's Social Ontology*. S. Tsohatzidis (ed.) (Dordrecht, Netherlands: Springer Verlag), pp. 11–29.

Searle, J. R. (2010). *Making the Social World: The Structure of Human Civilization* (Oxford: Oxford University Press).

SebaqMontifiore, H. (2004). *Enigma: The Battle for the Code* (London: Phoenix).

Sebeok, T. A. (1972). *Perspectives in Zoosemiotics* (The Hague: Mouton).

Sebeok, T. A. (1976). *Contributions to the Doctrine of Signs* (Bloomington, IN: Indiana University Press).

Simon, H. (1996). *The Sciences of the Artificial*. 3rd edition (Cambridge, MA: MIT Press).

Skyrms, B. (2010). *Signals: Evolution, Learning and Information* (Oxford: Oxford University Press).

Slobodchikoff, C. N., B. S. Perla and J. L. Verdolin (2009). *Prairie Dogs: Communication and Community in Animal Society* (Cambridge, MA: Harvard University Press).

Sobel, D. (1996). *Longitude* (London: Fourth Estate).

Sowa, J. F. (2000). Ontology, Metadata, and Semiotics. In *Conceptual Structures: Logical, Linguistic, and Computational Issues*, ICCS 2000. Ganter, B. and Mineau, G.W. (eds.) ((Berlin: Springer, pp. 55–81).

Spencer-Brown, G. (1969). *Laws of Form* (London: Allen and Unwin).

Spiegelhalter, D. (2019). *The Art of Statistics: Learning from Data* (London: Pelican).

Suchman, L. (1994). 'Do Categories have Politics? The Language/Action Perspective Reconsidered.' *Computer Supported Cooperative Work*, **3**(2): 177–190.

Szabo, N. (1997). 'Formalizing and Securing Relationships on Public Networks.' *First Monday*, **2**(9). doi.org/10.5210/fm.v2i9.548.

Te'eni, D. (2006). 'The Language-Action Perspective as a Basis for Communication Support Systems.' *Communications of the ACM*, **49**(5), 65–70.

Thaler, R. H. and C. S. Sunstein (2009). *Nudge: Improving Decisions About Health, Wealth and Happiness* (Harmondsworth: Penguin).

The Economist (2010). 'All too Much.' **394**, 5.

The Economist (2011). 'Costing the Count.' **399**, 81.

The Economist (2014). 'Getting on the Map.' 20 September, **569**, 70.

The Economist (2017). 'The World's Most Valuable Resource Is No Longer Oil But Data.' 6 May, **739**, 10.

Tsitchizris, D. C. and F. H. Lochovsky (1982). *Data Models* (Englewood-Cliffs, NJ: Prentice Hall).

Uexküll, J. (1957). A Stroll Through the Worlds of Animals and Men: A Picture Book of Invisible Worlds. In *Instinctive Behavior: The Development of a Modern Concept*. C. H. Schiller (ed.) (New York: International Universities Press).

Urton, G. (2002). An Overview of Spanish Colonial Commentary on Andean Knotted-String Records. In *Narrative Threads: Accounting and Recounting in Andean Khipu*. J. Quilter and G. Urton (eds.) (Austin, TX: University of Texas Press), pp. 3–25.

Urton, G. (2003). *Signs of the Inka Khipu: Binary Coding in the Andean Knotted-String Records* (Austin, TX: University of Texas Press).

Urton, G. and C. J. Brezine (2005). 'Khipu Accounting in Ancient Peru.' *Science*, **309**(5737), pp. 1065–1067. DOI: 10.1126/science.1113426.

Usher, S. (2014). *Lists of Note* (Edinburgh: Canongate Books).

Varela, F. J., E. Thompson and E. Rosch (1993). *The Embodied Mind: Cognitive Science and Human Experience* (Cambridge, MA: MIT Press).

Wardle, C. (2020). 'A New World Disorder: Our Willingness to Share Content Without Thinking is Exploited to Spread Disinformation.' *Scientific American Specials*, Fall 2020.

Weber, M. (1946). *Essays in Sociology* (Oxford: Oxford University Press).

Weigand, H. (2003). 'The Language/Action Perspective.' *Data and Knowledge Engineering*, **47**: 299–300.

Wheeler, S. (ed.) (1969a). *On Record: Files and Dossiers in American Life* (New York: Russell Sage Foundation).

Wheeler, S. (1969b). Problems and Issues in Record-Keeping. In *On Record: Files and Dossiers in American Life*. S. Wheeler (ed.) (New York: Russell Sage Foundation), pp. 3–24.

Whitley, E. A., U. Gal and A. Kjaergaard (2014). 'Who Do You Think You Are? A Review of the Complex Interplay Between Information Systems, Identification and Identity.' *European Journal of Information Systems*, **23**(1): 17–35.

Wiener, N. (1948). *Cybernetics* (New York: Wiley).

Winograd, T. and F. Flores (1986). *Understanding Computers and Cognition: A New Foundation for Design* (Norwood, NJ: Ablex Publishing).

Wolmar, C. (2007). *Fire and Steam: A New History of the Railways in Britain* (London: Atlantic Books).

Wood, D., K. Ball, D. Lyon, C. Norris and C. Raab (2006). *A Report on the Surveillance Society* (Wilmslow, UK: Office of the Information Commissioner).

Wyssusek, B. (2006). 'On Ontological Foundations of Conceptual Modelling.' *Scandinavian Journal of Information Systems*, **18**(1): 63–80.

Zimmerman, D. H. (1975). Fact As A Practical Accomplishment. In *Ethnomethodology: Selected Readings*. R. Turner (ed.) (Harmondsworth, UK: Penguin), pp. 128–143.

Zuboff, S. (2015). 'Big Other: Surveillance Capitalism and the Prospects of an Information Civilization.' *Journal of Information Technology*, **30**: 75–89.

Zuboff, S. (2019). *The Age of Surveillance Capitalism* (London: Profile Books).

Index

Printed in the United States
by Baker & Taylor Publisher Services